D0864588

A Hudson Valley
R E A D E R

Other Books by the author

Interculturalism and Performance
Theatrewritings
The Theatre of Images
American Garden Writing
The Theatre of the Ridiculous
American Dreams: The Imagination of Sam Shepard
American Playwrights: A Critical Survey
Animations: A Trilogy for Mabou Mines

A Hudson Valley
READER

Edited by
BONNIE
MARRANCA

THE OVERLOOK PRESS
WOODSTOCK • NEW YORK

First published in 1995 by
The Overlook Press, Peter Mayer Publishers, Inc.
Woodstock & New York

NEW YORK:
141 Wooster Street
New York, NY 10012

WOODSTOCK:
One Overlook Drive
Woodstock, NY 12498
www.overlookpress.com
[for individual orders, bulk and special sales, contact our Woodstock office]

Copyright © 1991 Bonnie Marranca

All rights reserved. No part of this publication may be reproduced or
transmitted in any form or by any means, electronic or mechanical, including
photocopy, recording, or any information storage and retrieval system now
known or to be invented, without permission in writing from the publisher,
except by a reviewer who wishes to quote brief passages in connection
with a review written for inclusion in a magazine, newspaper, or broadcast.

Library of Congress Cataloging-in-Publication Data

Marranca, Bonnie
A Hudson Valley Reader / [edited by] Bonnie Marranca.
p. cm.
Includes bibliographical references. (p.395-397) and index.
1. Legends—Hudson River Valley (N.Y. and N.J.). 2. Hudson RiverValley
(N.Y. and N.J.)—Biography. 3. Hudson River Valley (N.Y. and N.J.)—History.
I. Marranca, Bonnie.
CT251.H53 1991   974.7'3—dc20   91009569

Printed in the United States of America
ISBN 0-87951-598-8
4 6 8 9 7 5 3

Grateful acknowledgment is made for permission to use the following works:

Excerpt from *The Hudson River: A Natural and Unnatural History*, Expanded Edition, by Robert H. Boyle. Copyright © 1979, 1969 by Robert H. Boyle. Used by permission of the author and W. W. Norton & Company, Inc.

Excerpt from *Dutchess County Historical Society Year Book*, Vol. 12 (1927), by Lewis Mumford. Used by permission of the Dutchess County Historical Society, Poughkeepsie, N.Y.

Excerpt from *The Hudson*, by Carl Carmer. Copyright © 1967, 1939 by Carl Carmer. Used by permission of Henry Holt and Company, Inc.

Libertymen's Declaration of Independence. Manuscripts and Special Collections. New York State Library, Albany, N.Y. Used by permission of New York State Library at Albany.

Excerpt from Livingston-Fulton Manuscript Collection, Research Library, Clermont State Historic Site, New York State Office of Parks, Recreation and Historic Preservation, Taconic Region.

Excerpt from *Centennial Illustrated Catalogue and Price List of Shaker Chairs*, by Robert M. Wagan. Albany, N.Y., 1876. Used by permission of the Shaker Museum, Old Chatham, N.Y.

Frederic E. Church. Excerpts from Archives, Olana State Historic Site, New York State Office of Parks, Recreation and Historic Preservation, Taconic Region. (Erastus Dow Palmer) Excerpt from McKinney Library, Albany Institute of History and Art, Albany. (Martin J. Heade) Excerpt from Archives of American Art, New York.

Excerpt from *An American Aristocracy: The Livingstons*, by Clare Brandt. Copyright © 1986 by Clare Brandt. Used by permission of Doubleday, a division of Bantam, Doubleday, Dell Publishing Group, Inc.

Excerpt from *Selected Letters on Politics and Society*, by Alexis de Tocqueville, edited by Roger Boesche. Copyright © 1985 The Regents of the University of California. Used by permission of the University of California Press, Berkeley, CA.

Excerpt from *The Catskill Mountain House*, by Roland Van Zandt. Copyright © 1982, 1966 by Roland Van Zandt. Used by permission of Hope Farm Press, Cornwallville, N.Y.

Excerpt from *The Catskills: From Wilderness to Woodstock*, by Alf Evers. Copyright © 1982 by Alf Evers. Reprinted by permission of The Overlook Press, Woodstock, N.Y.

Excerpt from "Gypsy Moths and Man: A Still Unfolding Story of Mutual Accommodation," by Daniel Smiley. Mohonk Preserve, New Paltz, N.Y., 1987. Used by permission of Mohonk Preserve.

Excerpt from *The Letters and Papers of Cadwallader Colden*. Collections of the New-York Historical Society, Vols. 51, 52, 53. New York: Printed for the New-York Historical Society, 1918, 1919, 1920. Used by permission of the New-York Historical Society, N.Y.

Excerpt from "Storm King Saved!", by Albert Butzel. *Scenic Hudson News* 1, no. 2 (Spring 1981), Poughkeepsie, N.Y. Used by permission of Albert Butzel.

Excerpt from "A Place for Regionalism?", by David C. Pierce and Richard C. Wiles. *Hudson Valley Regional Review* 1, no. 1 (March 1984), Annandale-on-Hudson, N.Y. Copyright © 1984 by the Bard College Center. Used by permission of the authors.

Excerpt from *The Dream of the Earth*, by Thomas Berry. Copyright © 1988 by Thomas Berry. Used by permission of Sierra Club Books.

to Stanley Kauffmann,
    who has known time and the valley

Each century loves a different sorrow

—Maurice Maeterlinck

ACKNOWLEDGMENTS

T HE SPAN OF TIME and place in *A Hudson Valley Reader* led me to consult many individuals, organizations, and archival centers throughout the Hudson Valley for both research materials and friendly advice. This book would not have been possible without the vast resources, human and institutional, available to draw upon in the region. In particular, I would like to thank Richard C. Wiles at Bard College for his generous support and scholarly exchange throughout the evolution of this project; Paul Huth, Mohonk Preserve; Klara Sauer and Sue Rogers, Scenic Hudson; James Ryan, Olana State Historic Site; Joan Chernoff, Newburgh Free Library; Oliver Shipp, Newburgh Town Historian; James Corsaro and Paul Mercer, New York State Library, Albany; Stephen Ridler and Nancy Rucks, Department of State, Division of Coastal Resources and Waterfront Revitalization; David Meschutt, Curator of Art, West Point Museum; Philip Lord, New York State Museum, Albany; Alf Evers; A. J. Williams-Myers, Department of African-American Studies, SUNY—New Paltz; William B. Rhoads, Department of Art, SUNY—New Paltz; Kris Gibbons, Bureau of Historic Sites, Waterford; Jerry Grant, The Shaker Museum, Old Chatham; Bob Grumet, National Parks Service, Philadelphia; Diana Shewchuk, Clermont State Historic Site; Eric Kiviat, Hudsonia; Franklin D. Roosevelt Library archivists; Diana Arecco, New-York Historical Society; Joyce Hu, Albany Institute of History and Art; Hudson River Sloop Clearwater; Historic Hudson Valley; Paul Rooney, Hudson River Valley Greenway Council.

I am grateful for the financial support of my research from the Greene County Arts Council (Catskill) and its director Kay Stamer. The Greene County Historical Society graciously sponsored my application, with the help of Board President Robert Stackman and Trustee Robert D'Agostino. The Hudson River Foundation awarded me a generous grant for this book, and its Science Director, Dennis J. Suszkowski, showed a special openness to this project.

On a more personal note, I would like to express my appreciation to Scott Walters at PAJ Publications for his good-natured and steady help in preparing the typescripts of much of the manuscript; to Tom Funk at The Overlook Press for his easygoing editorial advice; and to my husband, Gautam Dasgupta, with whom I have discovered so much of the Hudson Valley.

EDITOR'S NOTE

Since the selections in this anthology range from the seventeenth century to the present, they naturally include typographical differences, British spellings, and obsolete usage. In the interest of preserving the spirit of these writings, I have kept them in their original format, with only minor changes or corrections here and there for the purposes of clarification or readability. The modern entries and my own notes reflect a more standardized, contemporary approach. The literary source I have used for each selection, some of which have been reprinted over the centuries, or published decades after their completion, follows each piece. The Bibliography at the end of the volume indicates the full source reference and recent reprints of editions.

For the sake of liveliness or brevity, and in cases where none existed, I have created titles for the selections of these authors:

George Washington, Henry James, Franklin D. Roosevelt, Mrs. Anne Grant, Benson Lossing, Robert Fulton, James Thacher, Orson S. Fowler, Robert M. Wagan, Frederic E. Church, Clare Brandt, Alexis de Tocqueville, Frederick Butler, Captain Basil Hall, Anthony Trollope, James Kirke Paulding, Hector St. John de Crèvecoeur, Peter Kalm, and Cadwallader Colden.

CONTENTS

PREFACE

T HE MOST BELOVED writers through the ages and throughout the world reflect in their work one of the basic truths of humankind: the realization that in local knowledge begins self-knowledge. Here is the starting point for what used to be thought of as worldliness, now transformed into global consciousness. Whichever expression one chooses, the essential premise, in large measure, still points to an understanding of what it means to live on this planet, with its galaxies of grief and pleasure. But what exactly is "local knowledge," and how does one attain this state of presumed comfort and wisdom?

For most of the history of human presence on earth experience of this kind was rather the natural rhythm of daily life, because one simply had to know as much as possible about the land and the sky and the sea and folkways, as a matter of sheer survival. Human history has reached a point at which technological transformations have so reordered the perception of space and time and human relations that many people spend much of their lives in a physical and cultural world they do not truly know in their bones, much less in their neighborhoods. It is like learning only parts of the language one speaks, not knowing the names of important objects.

Learning the language of a country is a life's work, enraptured by the many themes of this language that find expression in the manner of speaking and writing that defines a particular place and time and people. Besides, there are many narratives in the life of a country, region, or town, by turn historical, social, ecological, and cultural.

What kind of struggles did a people fight, were their houses made of stone, which bird songs awakened them, did they love honor?

Social history and natural history are bound together in the composition of the world we inhabit, like leaves in a solemn book that reminds us it comes from a sturdy tree. Broadly speaking, if we are to contemplate the true nature of a place, the cultural system cannot justly be separated from the ecosystem in the life of a society. Now we have learned to tell time by the trees.

In the Western heritage Herodotus, the father of history, made geography an aspect of the description of momentous events. But in our era of overspecialization the strands of human affairs have become disengaged, not intertwined, erasing geography from the understanding of history, agriculture from the context of culture, the humanities from science. Through this process of erosion the trans-mission of knowledge becomes more and more restricted by a kind of forced zoning regulation, while the universe of knowledge itself is continually enriched. In the most profound analysis, a society is ultimately judged by the connections its people make between the urgent themes of their world. There is a good deal of truth and subtlety in Emerson's view that "no man can write anything who does not think that what he writes is for the time the history of the world."

Here again is that irreducible leap from the local to the global perspective. For what is the sense of place if not the beginning of a world view of things. Can one rightly think of place, which is history, without thinking of nature, the natural history of habitats? It is not possible, I have found, to write of the Hudson Valley without writing of nature. More than a region it is a topography of the spirit.

Some landscapes are known by foot, others by horseback or boat, many more by automobile. Regions themselves are usually defined by dialect, cuisine, by music or dance, by furniture, costume, and art forms. The more than five million current inhabitants of the Hudson Valley have not been joined over the centuries by any of these cultural inflections, not in the nearly four hundred years of European settlement, nor in the millennia-old tribal ways of vanquished Indians. One cannot construct a continuous "Hudson Valley culture" out of these themes. No, the people of the Hudson Valley are unified by one earthly fact: geography. They are joined, spectacularly, by the shared presence of the Hudson River, which spills a 315-mile watery trail through New York State, from its headquarters at Lake Tear of the Clouds in the Adirondacks, to the end of Manhattan Island, where it moves out toward the Atlantic Ocean. Perhaps as many as 65 million years ago what Henry Hudson called the "great River of the Mountains" began to slice a valley through the Catskill Mountains to the east and the Taconic Mountains to the west.

The stretch of the Hudson most celebrated is the 150-or-so miles from Manhattan to Albany, where towering Palisades, elegant mountain passes of the Highlands, and the soft figuration of the Catskills beyond the west shore create a blue-green haze of reflected grandeur and winding calm. East and west the shores play with images of each other, and again north and south, in continual forced double perspective. The Janus-faced riverbanks, like opposite pages of an open book radiating diverse people's histories and the history of the landscape, remind us that Janus, the god of passageways, is another name for Chaos. This, the name of our contemporary condition— let's call it another version of the persistent American theme, urban versus rural life (corruption versus innocence).

Nowhere in the Hudson Valley is this duality more certain than in the land between the boundary lines of Manhattan and Albany that once was New Netherland and is now New York. The word "New" is significant in every sense. The Hudson Valley was the "New World" whose profundity of natural resources Adriaen Van der Donck, its early historian, proclaimed to would-be Dutch settlers. Here Crèvecoeur was sure he found democracy's "New Man" who would eventually influence his own French compatriots. And the Swede Peter Kalm discovered new species to populate the plant kingdoms of old Europe.

The Hudson River itself was never a passive scenic partner, but an active participant in new currents of thought in the American mind. Along its waters the people made a Revolution to shake off British colonialism, many of its residents—Robert R. Livingston, Robert Morris, John Jay, DeWitt Clinton, Alexander Hamilton, Martin Van Buren, Franklin D. Roosevelt—were statesmen who helped to make a country. The Hudson was the surface on which innovative modes of transportation played, the steamboat and the Erie Canal, and then the railroad that ran along its shores. In small river towns and growing cities the Industrial Revolution moved people and forests and mountains in the surge toward prosperity. The very landscape captured the American imagination in some of the country's earliest travel writing and nature writing set in the Valley, which also became, in the national period, a center for painting, tourism, architecture, and horticulture whose influence radiated throughout the country and across the Atlantic.

Ideas flowed to and from New York City, as surely as the Catskills sent its cool, clear, refreshing waters there, making it a world capital of culture and finance, and a gateway to new possibilities for those who would call it home. From everywhere they came. Multiculturalism defined New York from the very start. When the English took the colony from the Dutch in 1664, at least eighteen languages were already spoken around what is now Manhattan, which at the time had a European-descended population of less than 2,000.

The Hudson Valley region embraces a heritage that has fed every tributary of American enlightenment. That is what it means to be a landscape rather than merely scenery, a world not a setting. But it is past history alone that has cast emblematic shadows over its velvet hillsides. In the twentieth century the Hudson Valley has not been a frequent theme in the American cultural consciousness. More than a century ago the West superseded it as the symbol of wilderness and spirituality. American myth has always looked to the landscape for its sense of poetry and identification, and in times of trouble, for solace. Even today the population swells westward.

There were other cultural changes that would draw attention away from the region, those occurring from the third quarter of the nineteenth century to the decades before World War II, such as the decline of the Hudson River School of painting, whose canvases by Thomas Cole, Asher B. Durand, Frederic E. Church, and others had symbolized national themes for tourists and natives. The lack of a sustained *belles lettres* tradition, originated by the likes of Washington Irving, James Fenimore Cooper, James Kirke Paulding, Nathaniel P. Willis, and William Cullen Bryant, surfacing only sporadically at opposite ends of the century, between the publication of Henry

James's *The American Scene* and T. Coraghessan Boyle's *World's End*, is an overwhelming factor in the loss of the image of Hudson Valley life in the literary imagination. There are, of course, Edith Wharton's *Hudson River Bracketed,* Maxwell Anderson's *High Tor,* John Gardner's *Nickel Mountain,* William Kennedy's more urban novels of Albany, to name a random sampling of twentieth-century works set in the Valley. But no modern novelist, poet, or essayist has made so prominent and permanent a literary home in Hudson Valley country themes that his or her work is identified with the region, as writers have done elsewhere in the country. To this day, a century and a half later, Edgar Allan Poe's picturesque tale "Landor's Cottage" remains unsurpassed in its exquisite portrait of the mid-Hudson landscape.

The overwhelming attraction of the Valley has always been more visual than literary, though a school of painting is now long gone. The untimely death in the 1850s of young Andrew Jackson Downing, whose indigenous architectural style gave its name to the Wharton novel, was a great loss to horticultural and architectural life here. His partner Calvert Vaux remained a few years more at Newburgh to design homes, before bringing his feeling for the region's romantic landscape to the creation of Central Park and Brooklyn's Prospect Park, which he conceived with Frederick Law Olmsted.

Even accounting for the great beauty and variety of nature, the absence of any local nature writer of national reputation since the death of John Burroughs in 1921 is unsettling to discover. Unlike New England, for example, the Hudson Valley has not developed an ongoing tradition of nature writing or travel writing, a puzzling condition, given the proximity of such a magnificent landscape close to New York, with its substantial population of writers. Indeed, a comprehensive cultural history of the Hudson Valley has yet to be written.

Here is a place where history is marked indelibly in the land-scape. Ancient Indian arrowheads jostle with bottle caps in the dirty silence beneath wild meadows, old country barns are mirrored in satellite dishes, the ghosts of dying main streets haunt shopping malls that push profligacy and prophylactics. Everywhere the incongruent images pile up: meat and potatoes and Tex-Mex, dumpsites and country seats, prison farms and golf courses, high tech and migrant workers, and here and there an occasional glimpse of "Hudson River Bracketed" through the urban detritus, ironically framing the alternating scene of wealth and welfare that winds its way through towns up and down the Valley. Endangered species of bald eagle and the short-nose sturgeon glide over and around the magenta nuisance of bountiful loosestrife, and the shad runs through toxic waste. Fireflies light up backyards like stage sets, the gypsy moths pitch their tents in our trees. Welcome to the New World! Scientists are just coming around to tell us there is no balance or order in nature, no original scene to which we can return, as if we hadn't suspected that all along. Americans have always been busy "peopling solitudes," to use Tocqueville's majestic turn of phrase. Isn't it time to rethink the myth of country life? The great estates nostalgia of the Hudson Valley shrouds its stubborn *pentimenti,* and disordered sublime.

Already by the middle of the nineteenth century mid-Hudson life was contrasted with the brutalities of New York City streets. In the 1850s the dandy Willis wrote about declining pastoralism in the face of what we now call "development" that changed the look of the land in the antebellum years. Farms have been going continually out of business, about 93,000 acres worth in the Hudson Valley—more than 13 pecent of the farmland—between 1982 and 1987. Even with all the farmland remaining, 700,000 or so acres, it is sometimes easier to find fresh vegetables in the middle of Manhattan than in a small rural town upstate. Still, many of these towns have all the amenities associated with the contemporary good life: environmental awareness, artists and arts organizations, imported foods, historic restoration, service industries, ethnic restaurants, waste recycling . . . the list goes on and on. Now that IBM is the Valley's largest private employer, it is becoming increasingly difficult to define the borders between urban and rural life.

In a rather strange reversal of history, the twentieth century has brought to the region its own "ruins," the absence of which was much lamented by the romantic travelers of a hundred and fifty years ago. But our ruins do not evoke the passion of Medieval or Renaissance poetry, only the industrial and agricultural attrition of modern life. Kindly neglect, failing economy, disregard for historic buildings, lack of civic responsibility, wanton destruction are often to blame. I believe in what the landscape historian J. B. Jackson calls "the necessity for ruins." Our landscape is littered with these sorrows of architecture, but history is not a theme park.

I rarely take the Thompson Street hill down past the old cemetery to the center of Catskill without looking up at the distant hills where the Catskill Mountain House once grandly presided over the aesthetics of the picturesque, before it was torched into a burning forgetfulness nearly three decades ago by the New York State Conservation Department. The absence of the Mountain House is not merely the loss of a building but the end of its life as a metaphor that would have aged in the pages of our histories of culture, social life, and ecology, an image in which generations would continue to define who they are. When we neglect or destroy the things of our world, we silence chapters of our history, and without history society is bereft of the sense of itself as a people.

The urge for history, or more simply, rootedness and connection, grows more compelling as a source of nourishment in our world of computer menus and sound bites and fast food. Tasting the deep satisfying aromas of one's own small world takes a little time.

What makes a Hudson Valley life different from any other life? It begins with knowing where you live. For me, local knowledge is the smell of a wet woods, the color of autumn, patterns of traffic and deer damage; it's stores opening and closing in town, the revival of Kingston and Athens, the hard work of turning clay into garden soil; it's following the year-to-year population of cicadas and Japanese beetles, measuring the violence of sudden storms, and the sour tears of acid rain. But most important, is to hear the first song of the oriole who nests each year in the silver maple, signaling the start of summertime, and then to follow little by little the buttery glaze of evening light that sweeps across my lawn.

The history of a place is written in the landscape as surely as in its books, and memory acts as a kind of dormant seed. Hudson Valley history, from its earliest entry into literature, has been depicted in a dreamy disremembering, the sleeping and waking theme that Irving introduced in his story of Rip Van Winkle. A century and a half later there was another awakening, this time less a literary than an ecological quake—the Storm King controversy, which threatened to disrupt the sanctity of the Hudson Highlands with a hydroelectric plant Consolidated Edison planned to build there. The legal issues that grew out of the protests by local residents influenced environmental law, and put Hudson Valley conservation ethics at the forefront of a new ecological activism.

Today, there is a third awakening in the New York State Legislature's creation of the Hudson River Valley Greenway Council which has proposed a Hudson River Trail on both sides of the River from the Mohawk to Battery Park. Such a plan, involving twelve counties and eighty-two units of local government would surely generate a new social organization of cities, towns, and countrysides, sound land-use policies, joint public and private responsibilities, long-range planning by regional and local governments. The scope of this vision is unprecedented in a place where community independence has always superseded regional cooperation. Plans for the Catskill Interpretive Center have slowed since Governor Mario Cuomo's support of it a few years ago in his State of the State address. Earlier, Governor Nelson Rockefeller's Hudson Valley Commission (1966–1974) proved ineffectual in the long run, failing to meet the environmental challenge of the region's future. The Greenway Council plan, on the other hand, matches desire with vision and timeliness, complementing the Department of State's recent inventory of ten sites designated by the Coastal Resources Management Division as "scenic areas" of statewide significance, thus acknowledging their need for special protection. More recently, parts of Dutchess and Columbia counties have been declared the Hudson River National Historic Landmark District.

Up and down the Hudson, environmental groups, local residents, and planning commissions are joining together to accept the stewardship of the Hudson Valley's natural resources, and to influence greater public awareness of environmental issues. This is in contrast to the necessarily more local and site-specific battles Scenic Hudson fought in the 1960s and '70s on behalf of Storm King Mountain. Now everyone is getting involved.

More than anything else a new environmental ethos will bring the Hudson Valley into the twenty-first century, as a humanistic model for the people of the region, as a gift to themselves. A large population reflecting diverse interests and pleasures can perhaps come together to create a contemporary Hudson Valley culture in new spatial and cultural configurations of the very landscape in which they live, work, raise their children, and at the end of the day, dream. When all else is done, it is in their plans for the future that societies distinguish themselves.

To be sure, the future is always rooted in a usable past. Knowledge of the world begins where each of us lives—in our body, in our town, in our country. Literature, too, is a home, the repository of memory in which fact, myth, and fantasy cohabit to engender the various histories by which an age measures its presence in time. Like any writer surveying a surrounding world, I looked to old books to describe the place where I live. In nearly four hundred years of this "decayed literature" that Thoreau claimed makes the best soil, I found a gathering of travelers, artists, inventors, writers, statesmen, scientists, and historians. Here is what they wrote of a place, and people who have dwelled there.

—BONNIE MARRANCA
Catskill & New York City
August 1990

I

A PLACE
IN TIME

THE HAND OF MAN

Robert H. Boyle

FOR MORE THAN *two decades Robert H. Boyle
(1928–   ) has been writing about environmental issues and
sports in a wonderfully impassioned style. He is an activist author
and well-known sportsman of the area whose work reflects a
deep sense of commitment to social issues, and a fierce attachment
to the Hudson Valley. No where is this more apparent than in
Boyle's valuable work,* The Hudson River: A Natural and Unnatural
History. *Boyle is outspoken, knowledgeable about scientific research, and far-ranging in his interests. A long time contributor
to* Sports Illustrated, *he is also the author of several books, which
include* The Fly-Tyers Almanac, At the Top of Their Game, Malignant
Neglect, *and* Acid Rain. *Here he is equally at ease writing on hunters, naturalists, marine life, public policy, and pollution. In* Dead
Heat: The Race Against the Greenhouse Effect, *his most recent book,
he takes on the controversial subject of global warming.*

*But Boyle's great love is fishing, and he serves as president of
the Hudson River Fishermen's Association, which he helped found
in the early days of the struggle more than two decades ago against
Consolidated Edison's plan to build a power plant at Storm
King Mountain in the Highlands. In his continuing efforts to conserve the natural resources of the River, he also acts as president of the Hudson Riverkeeper Fund, set up by Con Ed as part of
the Storm King settlement. These are fair rewards for the Cold*

3

*Spring outdoorsman who seems to know all the fishes, birds, and
plants of the region.*

*What makes Boyle's writing so timely and effective is the assured
way he links social themes and natural history in the definition
of place, as inseparable forces of interaction and transformation.
His crusty good will and hands-on style are reinforced by a real
intellectual energy—Boyle is the sort of fisherman who would be
likely to have Nabokov's work on the Karner butterfly jostling
in a vestpocket with the latest study of Hudson River shad.*

AFTER THE RETURN OF the *Half Moon* to Holland, individual Dutch
traders began to visit New Netherland, as the land that Hudson had
discovered came to be known. The States General of Holland gave
control of trade to the United Netherlands Company in 1614 and
then to the newly formed West India Company in 1621. From the
beginning, furs were the major interest of the Dutch, and beaver,
otter, mink, and muskrat skins were soon going to Holland in great
numbers.

The Dutch did not begin serious settlement until 1623, and they
were fortunate that they did not lose the colony to the English, who
regarded the coast as theirs because of voyages dating back to John
Cabot. In point of fact, the Pilgrims planned to settle along Hudson's
River, but a storm at sea drove them to Plymouth in 1620. Dutch
settlement was slow. The company offered each settler a *bouwerie,* a
farm, but few Dutchmen had reason to leave the pleasant life at
home. In 1629, in a misguided effort to spur colonization, the West
India Company drew up a charter of Privileges and Exemptions
under the terms of which the company allowed any member to buy
enormous tracts of land from the Indians along the bank of any
navigable river. These tracts could extend for sixteen miles on one
shore or eight miles on both shores, and they could run as far inland
"as the situation of the occupiers will permit." The only requirement
was that the purchaser, styled a *patroon,* should establish on his land

a colony of at least fifty persons within four years. Manhattan Island and Fort Orange, reserved for the company, were exempt from claim.

A patroon had considerable powers. He was able to "administer civil and criminal justice, in person, or by deputy, within his colonie, to appoint local officers and magistrates; to erect courts...to keep a gallows, if such were required." A patroon had the right of trade in everything but furs, which were reserved for the company. Several patroonships were soon established along the Hudson. In 1630, Michael Pauw bought what is now Jersey City and the whole of Staten Island, calling it Pavonia, a Latinized version of his name. In that same year, Killian Van Rensselaer, an Amsterdam diamond merchant, had an agent start buying land near Fort Orange, and by 1637, Van Rensselaer was in control of a patroonship, Rensselaerswyck, comprising nearly seven hundred square miles on both banks of the Hudson. In 1646, Adriaen Van der Donck purchased a patroonship north of Manhattan. A member of the gentry in Holland, Van der Donck was called by the title of *Jonkheer,* young heir, and from this the name Yonkers derives. Nearby, Jonas Bronck settled on five hundred acres of land that are now part of the Bronx.

Rensselaerswyck was the only successful patroonship, but when the English took over New Netherland in 1664, they allowed manors to be established on similar lines. In 1668, Robert Livingston purchased 160,000 acres in what is now Columbia County; in 1680, Frederick Philipse acquired large holdings in southern Westchester, and in 1697, Colonel Stephanus Van Cortlandt bought northern Westchester. In terms of generating settlement, the patroonships and manors were doomed to failure. At Rensselaerswyck, a tenant had to pay rent of five hundred guilders (two hundred dollars) a year, give three days' annual service with his horse and wagon, keep up roads, split and deliver two fathoms of firewood, and deliver a "quit rent" of two bushels of wheat, two pairs of fowl, and twenty-five pounds of butter. In 1701, the Earl of Bellemont, governor of New York, observed that Livingston "has on his great grant of sixteen miles long and twenty-four broad but four or five cottages, as I am told—men live in vassalage under him, and work for him, and are too poor to be farmers, having not the wherewithal to buy cattle to start a farm."

Peter Kalm, a Swedish botanist and student of Linnaeus, visited the Hudson Valley in 1749 and on his journey upriver noted the scarcity of settlement. The feelings between landlord and tenants were often strong, and they lasted for years. In the early nineteenth century, Martin Van Buren got his start in politics by battling the Van Rensselaers and Livingstons. In essence, the semifeudal system of patroonships and manors remained in force until an armed revolt by farmers in Columbia County in the 1840s. Whatever the injustices of the system, and there were many, the net effect was that the Hudson was lightly settled for more than two centuries, and as a result the river was spared much indiscriminate abuse.

Of course, there was some settlement under Dutch and English rule. Farmers raised potatoes, corn, barley, oats, wheat, and flax, and Kalm reported that the wheat flour from the valley "is reckoned the best in all North America." Timber was cut and exported. Albany shipped vast quantities of white pine downriver. Sawmills and gristmills sprang up on tributary streams, or "kills" as the Dutch called them. For instance, Peekskill was named for the stream explored by Jan Peek, an early trader who mistook it for the main stem of the Hudson. The Dutch called the Catskill Mountains the Katzberg, the mountains where bobcats and lynx abounded. The major stream that flowed east toward the Hudson was called the Katz Kill, now, redundantly, Catskill Creek.

Roads along the Hudson were poor, and the river itself served as the main highway. Both passengers and produce were carried up and down the river by so-called Hudson River sloops. These broad-bottomed ships, obviously patterned after canal craft in Holland, were used on the river for more than three hundred years, until the 1890s, when they were rendered uneconomical by steam-powered tugs pulling barges. A typical river sloop was sixty-five to seventy-five feet long and had a capacity of one hundred tons.

The sloops had one mast placed well forward, a large mainsail to catch the fickle breezes, a small jib, and sometimes a topsail. The use of the centerboard was developed on these sloops. They had high quarterdecks, a relic of the poops of medieval ships, and the vessels were painted in gaudy colors. The sloops were eminently seaworthy; between 1785 and 1787, Captain Stewart Dean of Albany sailed the sloop *Experiment* around Cape Horn to Canton to make the first direct voyage from the United States to China. On the Hudson, passengers could promenade or dance on deck, and a trip from New York to Albany occasioned as much excitement as a voyage to Europe. Sometimes, it seemed to take as long. Alexander Hamilton is said to have written the first paper in *The Federalist* while a passenger on a windless voyage along the Hudson. . . .

When the English seized New Amsterdam in 1664, the name was changed to New York and the North River finally became the Hudson. To the English, the Dutch were known by the nickname of "Jankees," a derisive combination of John and cheese pronounced *Yankees*. Calling Dutchmen Jankees was like calling an Irishman a Harp or a German a Kraut. In *The American Language,* H. L. Mencken asks: "But how did this nickname for Dutchmen ever come to be applied to Englishmen, and particularly to the people of New England, male and female alike? To this day no satisfactory answer has been made. All that may be said with any certainty is that it was already in use by 1765 [in New England] as a term of derision, and that by 1775 the Yankees began to take pride in it." I suspect that there is a satisfactory answer to Mencken's question, and that the answer is this: in 1757, during the French and Indian War, a Dr. Shuckburgh, a British Army surgeon stationed at Fort Cralo in Rensselaer on the Hudson, wrote the song "Yankee Doodle" to ridicule the Colonial Militia. Many of the militia were from New England, and I assume that they carried the song back home, where they started calling one another Yankees.

Under English rule, many of the Dutch persisted in staying among themselves. Dutch was spoken in Albany until the Revolution, and Franklin D. Roosevelt told Carl Carmer that Dutch was still spoken in isolated communities when he was born in 1882. Over the years any number of Dutch words passed into English, among them *stoop, waffle, cookie,* and *coleslaw.*

With the English in charge, New York grew in importance as a trading center. Indeed, the city so thrived on trade that at first pirates actually were welcomed. The pirates were not above carrying on business in local waters; an Albany report of 1696 states "pirates in great numbers invest the Hudson River at its mouth and waylay vessels on their way to Albany, speeding out from behind coves and from behind islands and again returning to the rocky shores, or ascending the mountains along the river to conceal their plunder." Piracy off the coast became so great a scandal that New Yorkers formed a company to buy a ship equipped with thirty-six guns to drive pirates off the seas. One of the shareholders in the company was Robert Livingston, and the man the company picked to captain the ship was a resident of Liberty Street, William Kidd, whose crew was supposedly composed in the main of Hudson River men who came from the vicinity of Livingston Manor. The scandal became even greater when Kidd himself turned pirate. He was eventually captured and executed. According to legends, part of Kidd's treasure from a Moorish ship, *Quedah Merchant,* is sunk in the Hudson off Jones Point, opposite Peekskill, where the crew, returning home, scuttled the prize during a storm. At one point in the nineteenth century, a promoter raised twenty-two thousand dollars to build a coffer dam and pumping station to retrieve the treasure, but nothing was ever found, not even the promoter, who apparently ran off with most of the money.

At the time of the American Revolution, life along the Hudson was bucolic. However, by its very geographical position, the river became the pivot upon which British grand strategy turned. They aimed to seize the Hudson and thus divide the rebelling colonies in two. In this they failed. They occupied Manhattan for the duration of the war, and they made a few forays upriver, burning Kingston in 1777, but they never were able to assume control of the Hudson. From the beginning, Washington appreciated the value of the High-lands, and work was commenced on forts on Constitution Island, at West Point, and elsewhere. The greatest battle of the war, in fact, what is perhaps the most significant battle in American history, took place on the Hudson near Saratoga in 1777. Here General John Burgoyne and his army of ten thousand men were defeated on October 7, when General Benedict Arnold, who later attempted to betray West Point, led three regiments into the center of the British line and broke it. Burgoyne withdrew, but victory was not possible, and on October 14 he sent an aide, Major Kingston, to negotiate a cessation of hostilities. Before discussing terms, the major "expatiated with taste and eloquence on the beautiful scenery of the Hudson's river and the charms of the season."

During the Revolution, the Iroquois supported the British against the Americans, who were called the *Was-to-heh-no,* "people of Boston." (The name was used until the 1900s.) After the war, the Iroquois, who had become the Six Nations in the early 1700s by taking in the Tuscororas, lost most of their lands, and they are now settled on reservations in New York State and Canada. As a result of a savage American campaign against the Senecas during the Revolution, George Washington is still called *Honandaganius,* "destroyer of towns," as are all the presidents who have followed him.

After the Revolution, the population of the Hudson Valley grew rapidly. In 1771, New York City had a population of only 21,862; by 1820, it had grown to 123,705, by far the largest in the nation. Further up the Hudson, Yankees moved in from New England. The city of Hudson was founded in 1783 by Nantucket whaling men seeking protection from the ravages of British ships, and within three years Hudson was the home port of twenty-five vessels and had its own shipbuilding yards. Poughkeepsie, too, became a port for Yankee whalers, and Yankee merchants founded Troy to rival Albany as a center of commerce. A Troy meatpacker, Samuel Wilson, supplied the army during the war of 1812 and stamped government consignments "U. S." One of his workmen said the initials stood for "Uncle Sam." The joke spread, and the symbol of Uncle Sam came into national existence.

One of the earliest industries was iron mining. In 1751, the Sterling mine and furnace opened in Orange County, and it was here that a giant chain, with each link weighing about 150 pounds, was forged to protect the Hudson during the Revolution. The fifteen-hundred-foot chain was stretched from West Point to Constitution Island to stop British ships from moving upriver. In the years that followed other iron deposits were mined.

Limestone was required for the making of iron, and soon it was being used for cement as well. About 1820, the manufacture of natural cement began at Rosendale in Ulster County. The Rosendale cement was of excellent quality, and was used in the construction of the Brooklyn Bridge and the base of the Statue of Liberty, but it lost out to Portland cement, also made in the Hudson Valley, because it took much longer to dry. The deposits of clay gave rise to a thriving brick industry along the Hudson. The hills were also quarried for traprock and sandstone. Although there is some specialized mining— the plains near Albany yield a fine molding sand, and outside Peekskill is one of the few emery mines in the world—the Hudson Valley has traditionally supplied the materials which New York City consumes in its never-ending cycle of rebuilding.

In the early nineteenth century, several developments were of profound importance to the Hudson Valley. The first of these was the practical demonstration of the steamboat by Robert Fulton. On August 7 and 8, 1807, the steamboat *Clermont,* named after the river estate of Robert Livingston, Fulton's backer, steamed from New York to Albany in twenty-eight hours and forty-five minutes. Belching smoke and fire from her stack, the *Clermont* was such a strange sight that a farmer said he said "seen the devil going up the river in a sawmill." Fulton failed in his attempt to have a monopoly on river traffic, and the steamboat competition grew so fierce that the ships evolved into floating palaces and the fare between New York and Albany on occasion dropped from seven or eight dollars to twenty-five cents.

Rival steamboat lines tried to establish supremacy by speed, and racing was common on the river. In 1945, the steamer *Swallow* was racing two other boats downriver near Hudson when she ran head-on into a rocky island, which became known as Swallow Rock. She broke up and caught fire, and at least fifty of her three hundred passengers perished. In 1852, the *Henry Clay* was racing downriver near Yonkers when she caught fire. The captain ran her on shore, but more than sixty persons died, among them Maria Hawthorne, sister of the novelist, who was returning home to Salem, on a roundabout route from Saratoga in order to enjoy the beauties of the river.

The most famous race—inspired by a one-thousand-dollar bet— occurred in 1847 between the *Cornelius Vanderbilt,* owned by Commodore Vanderbilt, a former Staten Island ferryman, and the *Oregon,* belonging to George Law. The race was from the Battery to Sing Sing and back. Vanderbilt was at the wheel of his own boat. The race was close until Vanderbilt miscalculated the turn at Sing Sing. The *Oregon* ran out of fuel downriver, but the Captain ordered the chairs, benches, berths, and any other woodwork that would burn thrown into the furnaces, and the gutted steamer won by twelve hundred feet. The greatest boat on the river was the *Mary Powell*. Three hundred feet long, trim, graceful, and beautifully kept by one family, the Andersons, for almost sixty years, the *Mary Powell* was the acknowledged queen of the river. She began service from Rondout Creek, Kingston, to New York City in 1861, and for many years she was the fastest boat on the Hudson. She never had a serious accident, and she never lost a passenger. To many oldtimers on the Hudson, the sight of this great sidewheeler moving along the river was the most magnificent spectacle they ever saw. Toward the end of her days, the *Mary Powell* was sold to the Day Line, and then she was finally sold to a junk dealer and dismantled. Today the only vestige of the river traffic of olden times is the Day Line's *Alexander Hamilton,* built in 1922, the only sidewheeler still in service in American coastal waters.

A second development was the opening of the Erie and Champlain canals. The idea of a canal linking the Hudson with the Great Lakes dates back to 1785, but it took the push and drive of De Witt Clinton, chairman of a canal commission, to get the Erie and Champlain Canals authorized by the legislature. Work on both started in 1817. The Champlain canal, only sixty-four miles long from Fort Edward on the Hudson to Whitehall, New York, was completed first. The Erie Canal was a far more ambitious undertaking, involving three thousand men with picks and shovels, five hundred horses, and two hundred yoke of oxen. On July 4, 1817, shortly after Clinton had become governor, he dug the first spadeful of dirt at Rome. The first task was to complete the middle section of the canal linking the Mohawk and Seneca rivers. All told, the Erie was 363 miles long, and it had eighty-three regular locks. Near Buffalo, special locks had to be built to raise the water level sixty feet in a two-mile stretch, and a 750-foot aqueduct carried the canal over the Genesee River.

The Erie was completed in late 1825. On October 26 of that year, the canalboat *Seneca Chief* began a triumphant journey from Buffalo pulled by four gray horses. It was followed by another boat, fittingly called *Noah's Ark,* which carried two eagles, a bear, two fawns, a variety of other animals and birds, and several species of fish. At Albany, the steamboat *Chancellor Livingston* took the *Seneca Chief* in tow for the trip downriver. Upon arrival in New York, the boats proceeded toward Sandy Hook, where Governor Clinton, in symbolic ceremony, poured a keg of Lake Erie water into the Atlantic. As an added touch, Clinton's fellow naturalist, Dr. Samuel Latham Mitchill, poured in water from the Mississippi, Thames, Nile, Seine, Danube, Rhine, Amazon, Orinoco, Ganges, Indus, Gambia, Columbia, and La Plata rivers.

The way to the Middle West was open; the Appalachians had been outflanked. Shipping time from Buffalo to Manhattan was cut from twenty to eight days, and the freight rate dropped from one hundred dollars to five dollars a ton. The canal, which had cost more than seventeen million dollars to build, soon collected more than one million dollars a year in tolls. Canal towns, with names proudly bespeaking navigation—Middleport, Gasport, Lockport, Weedsport, and Brockport—sprouted, and New York City prospered.

Then there was the development of the railroads. The first railroad incorporated in the United States was the Mohawk and Hudson, chartered by the state in 1826. It began operation in 1831 and ran from Albany to Schenectady. The line was the genesis of the New York Central. Railroads were slow in coming to eastern New York because of opposition from canal and steamboat interests. The Hudson River route to Albany from New York City was not completed until 1851.

As New York City grew, it outraced its supply of water. Ever since it was first settled, the city had depended on wells, but as early as 1748 water had become so bad that even horses refused to drink it. In 1799, the state legislature granted a charter to the Manhattan Company to supply water for the city, but the Manhattan Company was little more than a device by which Aaron Burr could get into the banking business. In 1828, fires ravaged Manhattan, and in 1832, thirty-five hundred people died from cholera. As a result, the city decided to go thirty miles north to dam and tap the Croton River, a large tributary of the Hudson. In 1842, the Croton dam and aqueduct were finished, and although the supply was supposed to be adequate for a century, more water was needed within twenty years' time. Over the years, New York City has constantly reached upstate for water. The original Croton Reservoir has been much enlarged, and there are numerous other reservoirs in northern Westchester and Putnam counties. In 1907, the city began developing reservoirs in the Catskills, and streams there which formerly flowed to the Hudson or Delaware have been impounded....

The coming of the steamboat and railroad, the development of the canal system, and the building of reservoirs had their effects, subtle and otherwise, on the ecology of the Hudson Valley. The use of steamboats encouraged the cutting of trees for fuel. As early as 1825, the thirteen steamers on the Hudson and the ferries in the harbor used one hundred thousand cords of wood in the eight months of the year that the river was free of ice. Wood was cut on the top of the Palisades and slid down the cliffs to deep water. Thus the name High Gutter Point on the New York–New Jersey state line. In time, the steamers turned to coal, and nowadays coal clinkers are to be found on the bottom of the river. Iron furnaces consumed enormous amounts of charcoal, and the brick kilns relied on cordwood. Neither industry demanded particularly good wood, and the end result was that much of the valley was clear-cut every thirty or forty years. Other timber was cut for telegraph and telephone poles, posts, railroad ties, and building lumber. In the Catskills, mile upon mile of hemlocks were left to die after being stripped of their bark for tanning, and as the hemlocks vanished between 1830 and 1870, the color of the mountains changed from a very dark blue to the soft green of hardwoods. Other lands, of course, were cleared for farms. Much of the forest cover has since returned because of a decline in agriculture, but contrary to popular belief, there are no virgin forests between New York and Albany. In the 1930s, Rogers McVaugh, a plant ecologist, investigated the flora of Columbia County, and he found that what had been taken for virgin forests were in actuality mature second-growth forests that began growing in the early 1700s after the original trees had been cut.

Changing land practices prompted the spread of some native animals. The cottontail rabbit (*Sylvilagus floridanus*) originally was not found north of the New York City area; the Dutch name for rabbit was *coney,* hence Coney Island. But in the early nineteenth century, the cottontail rabbit literally followed the cabbage patches up the Hudson Valley, reaching Albany in 1850. The bobwhite quail (*Colinus virginianus*) did much the same, but now, for various reasons, including the decline in agriculture, it has retreated down the valley and is found in Westchester. The prolific rabbit, however, has not only hung on upriver but has penetrated north into Canada.

The opening of the canal system caused an agricultural upheaval in the valley. Catskill lost its position as a wheat and flour market, while Rochester on Lake Ontario boomed. In 1812, Rochester had a population of fifteen; by 1840, the population was twenty thousand and Rochester was the leading flour-milling center in the country. The Hudson Valley was finished as a wheat producer, and farmers had to turn to other crops. Andrew Jackson Downing and his brother, Charles, pioneered in efforts to replace wheat with specialty crops— apples, pears, plums, melons, and grapes—and this heritage still persists, with apples from the valley shipped abroad to Britain and Sweden. The leading vegetable crop is corn, grown on ten thousand acres of the old floodplains of the tributary Esopus and Walkill. The cool weather allows farmers to produce excellent corn, U. S. Fancy grade, in volume from the middle of July to the beginning of October, and it is shipped as far as Texas, Florida, and Europe. In the old days, the floodplains of the Walkill were celebrated for their abundance of woodcock (*Philohela minor*).

The opening of the Erie and Champlain canals allowed several fishes not native to the Hudson Watershed to gain entrance. De Witt Clinton, keen naturalist that he was, suspected that this would happen, and in 1820, he wrote: "I expect great changes from the junction of the western and eastern water on the subject of fish. Already several have penetrated the canal at Rome into the Mohawk river."

The most notable species to get into the Hudson through the canals were the smallmouth bass (*Micropterus dolomieui*) and largemouth bass (*M. salmoides*). Prior to the completion of the canals, the smallmouth and largemouth had been found in the western part of the state, in waters draining into the Great Lakes. They were probably present also in Lake Champlain, but not elsewhere in New England. The canals offered both fish a way to the Hudson, and they swam in and flourished.

The smallmouth is primarily a creature of streams and large, cold, rocky lakes, while the largemouth is fond of quiet backwaters in rivers, streams, and ponds. In the Hudson watershed both species found sufficient variety, and their presence made an impact. The smallmouth doubtless drove trout from portions of some streams. Moreover, the smallmouth, revered by some anglers as "pound for pound, inch for inch, the gamest fish that swims," was stocked in any number of Adirondack lakes, where the native trout suddenly found themselves under siege. The largemouth probably did less damage; the damage had already been done to brook trout by farmers who dammed up streams for mills or ice ponds. Such ponds, usually shallow and warmed by the sun, were unsuitable for trout, but the tough largemouths are able to endure water temperatures into the nineties. Similarly, many of the trout streams dammed for city reservoirs are now bass lakes.

Once bass were established in the Hudson Valley, their popularity grew, and it is interesting to trace their movements into New England, which Louis Agassiz called a "zoological island" because of its sparse fish fauna. In 1850, Samuel Tisdale of East Wareham, Massachusetts, brought twenty-seven live bass, species not given, from Saratoga Lake and put them into a pond near his home. From there bass were taken and stocked in twenty-five other ponds. In 1867, descendants from Tisdale's plantings were stocked in a lake in New Hampshire. As early as 1852, bass from a pond in Dutchess County were introduced into a lake in Litchfield County, Connecticut, and by 1867, bass were stocked in lakes and ponds throughout that state. In 1869, officials of the state of Maine and the Oquossoc Angling Association procured "a quantity of black bass" from Newburgh on the Hudson, and stocked various waters where the bass soon were reported "to have increased largely in numbers." Nowadays, Maine is celebrated for its excellent smallmouth bass fishing.

New York's position as a port made it a place of entry for many inadvertent pests. One of the first to arrive was the Hessian fly (*Phytophaga destructor*), a scourge of wheat, which came over during the Revolution in the straw bedding of Hessian mercenaries who landed at New York. The so-called German cockroach (*Blattella germanica*) first became obvious in 1842 when Manhattan began receiving water from the Croton Aqueduct. The cockroach was then nicknamed the Croton bug, and it apparently underwent a population explosion, utilizing the new maze of wet pipes throughout the city somewhat like cockroach superhighways.

The Central railroad tracks that skirt the river from New York to Albany have been cursed by many persons for denying access to the river, but they have not been without some small beneficial influence. The blocks of stone used for the roadbed serve as a refuge for small fish and invertebrates, and in some cases the causeways have turned bays into productive coves and marshes. This is the case, for instance, with the extensive river marshes north and south of both Tivoli and Hudson; all four of these bays were open water until the late nineteenth century.

Foreign weeds are numerous on the railroad rights of way along the river and around old docks. The troublesome "Stockport weed" (*Galium mollugo*) is believed to have come by ship, and the "bird-foot trefoil" (*Lotus corniculatus*) probably came in ballast. The bird-foot trefoil has value as forage, and it is now planted and cut as hay. The pesty knapweed (*Centaurea jacea*) may have come by rail, and the same holds true of its relative *Centaurea maculosa*, distinguished by its pinkish-purple flowers along roadsides.

The harmful purple loosestrife (*Lythrum salicaria*), which takes root in marshes and dries them up, came as seeds entangled in wool wastes unloaded at a Newburgh factory. According to Stanley Smith, the erudite curator of botany at the New York State Museum, Japanese lady's thumb (*Persicaria caespitosa*) arrived in Albany in rice straw packed around china, circus wagons from the Middle West brought in tumbleweed (*Cycloloma atriplicifolium*), and botanists at the state museum have discovered a smut (*Ustilago commelinae*), hitherto known only from the Yalu River in Korea, on both banks of the Hudson from Manhattan north to the mouth of the Sacandaga River.

Then again, escapes from gardens have resulted in the establishment of any number of foreign plants and flowers which many persons regard as native, such as the dandelion (*Taraxacum officinale*), the common daisy (*Chrysanthemum leucanthemum*), catnip (*Nepeta cataria*), peppermint (*Mentha piperita*), spearmint (*M. spicata*), multiflora rose (*Rosa multiflora*), Queen Anne's lace (*Daucus carota*), the wineberry (*Rubus phoenicolasius*), the common orange daylily (*Hemerocallis fulva*), the iris that is the *fleur-de-lis* of France (*Iris pseudacorus*), and sweet woodruff (*Asperula odorata*), used to make May wine. According to Morris K. Jacobson and William K. Emerson, authorities on shells, the common cellar snail of Europe (*Oxychilus cellarius*) is well established in the Hudson Valley. They report it in the city as "inhabitating dank spots in old basements where it is not above hiding near barrels of pickles, wine, potatoes, and other stored foods," and fine, large specimens live under loose boulders in the highway cut near Annsville Creek, Peekskill, a favorite collecting ground. Another successful immigrant is the Chinese mystery snail (*Viviparus malleatus*), which probably gained entry with exotic water plants. It has been found in the Hudson near Saratoga and in the tributary Saw Mill River in Westchester. A native freshwater mollusk that was not recognized as a different species until 1934 is the Hudson rams horn (*Promenetus hudsonicus*), first taken from a small swamp near the Poughkeepsie Rural Cemetery.

There were, of course, some purposeful introductions of flora and fauna. The ring-necked pheasant (*Phasianus colchicus*) was brought to New York during colonial times but did not thrive. Before the 1900s, it was re-introduced from China and England, and it has since given joy. Other exotics have caused trouble. The pestiferous English sparrow (*Passer domesticus*) is not native to the United States. Its initial introduction to this continent came in 1852, when fifty birds were let loose in the Narrows from the steamship *Europa*. In 1890, Eugene Schieffelin, a New York drug manufacturer and a misguided Shakespeare enthusiast, introduced starlings (*Sturnus vulgaris*) to North America. Schieffelin wished to see every species of bird mentioned by Shakespeare living in the United States. He released the starlings in Central Park, and they first nested beneath the eaves of the northeast wing of the American Museum of Natural History. From there the pests began spreading up the Hudson Valley, reaching Ossining by 1899, and then moved across the continent, arriving at Juneau, Alaska, in 1952. Both the starling and sparrow are particularly annoying in that they are aggressive birds and harass native species, notably the bluebird (*Sialia sialis*).

But for all the introductions of exotics, the clearing of forests, the damming of tributary streams, the development of manufacturing, the spread of settlement, and the spiralling of pollution, the Hudson River Valley has held up surprisingly well. This is not to say that all is well. Each stretch of the Hudson has its own serious problems, its own character, its own delights.

Robert H. Boyle, *The Hudson River: A Natural and Unnatural History* (New York: W. W. Norton and Company, 1979).

THE VALUE OF
LOCAL HISTORY

Lewis Mumford

L*EWIS MUMFORD (1895-1990) was a cosmopolitan man who equally celebrated the notion of regionalism. For him, a region was "a collective work of art," the locus of human communities unified through geographic, historic, economic, and cultural ties over a long period of time. Mumford was a visionary and social reformer who combined modernism's belief in spiritual transformation through the beneficent use of technology, with a progressive politics that could imagine a new world order. He loved urban life as much as rural culture, creating his great studies,* The Culture of Cities *and* The City in History *out of this interest, in the early years commuting between a farmhouse in Amenia and Manhattan. He was also a founding member of the Regional Planning Association, one of whose projects was the design of Sunnyside, Queens, where Mumford lived in the twenties.*

Mumford decried the overdevelopment and commercialization of urban centers, preferring instead organically designed towns and architecture where human creativity could be at the heart of daily life. In more than thirty books written over sixty years, his sturdy, handsome prose set forth new values for modern civilization. His works are immensely learned commentaries on art, architecture, literature, science, urban planning, conservation, and history. Overall, Mumford's great subject is technics and civilization, also the title of his influential work.

A passionate gardener and nature lover whose writings espoused a profound eco-humanism, Mumford was part of a tradition of early modern thinkers on conservation descending from George Perkins Marsh, author of the pioneering work Man and Nature *(1864), and including Aldo Leopold and Cornell scientist Liberty Hyde Bailey. This tradition enlarged the ecological theme by setting it in the context of a cultural and historical vision that addressed the future of human societies and their goals. Likewise, Mumford did not reject modern life for an imagined ideal past. One of America's formidable twentieth-century minds, he accepted the now regrettably lost role of the independent intellectual in public culture, offering a generalist's views on important national concerns. The long career of this man whom Malcolm Cowley called "the last of the great humanists" extended from the end of World War I to the post-Vietnam era, forcing him to confront spectacular changes in science, history, and society.*

From the local history of Amenia he rooted his life in a continuum that stretched from the classical Greek ideals he revered to the literary spirit of Whitman and Emerson, and on up to the vision of a future in which human beings struggle with technology to create a more livable world. Decades ago Mumford wrote and lectured on many issues that are prominent now in contemporary thought, such as land use, housing for the elderly, world culture and post-historic man, ideologies of power and the construction of public space. Chief among his meticulously analyzed themes is the significance he gave to regionalism. Ironically, positions that once made him seem utopian have now become mainstream. In Mumford's credo local knowledge is a form of self-knowledge, and both unite to make one truly a citizen of the world. Here is a talk on local history that he gave in the twenties at the splendid Leedsville literary gathering place known as Troutbeck.

ALL OF US FEEL at bottom with Walt Whitman, that there is no sweeter meat than that which clings to our own bones. It is this conviction that gives value to local history: we feel that our own lives, the lives of our ancestors and neighbors, the events that have taken place in the particular locality where we have settled, are every bit as important as the lives of people who are more remote from us, no matter how numerous these others may be; or how insignificant we may seem alongside of them.

People who live in great cities are accustomed to identify themselves with the whole nation; for the Londoner, London is the British Empire; and for the New Yorker, New York is the United States. A great deal of our national history is written upon the assumption that nothing interesting or important has taken place in the country which did not, as it were, pass through Washington, by coming under public debate, or by being enacted into a law. If wars, political elections, and laws were all that history consisted of there would be some truth, perhaps, in these habits and beliefs; but ever since Green wrote his history of the English people we have come, slowly, to see that the main subject of history is the drama of a community's life—that is, in what manner and to what purpose people have lived: what did they eat, how did they dress, at what did they work, what kind of houses had they to shelter their heads, what ideas and beliefs had they to fill their heads?

At present, it is almost impossible to write national history along these lines; for people's lives and habits differ from region to region; and we must know a great deal more than we do about each separate region, with all its intimate characteristics and peculiarities, before we can even begin to work this up into a single picture. In providing the materials for this new kind of history the older parts of the country are in a more fortunate position than the newer ones: in New England, for example, the local historian has been busy since the early part of the nineteenth century, and as a result of the great mass of material local historical societies and local archaeologists have dug up, New England can boast such classic regional histories as Weeden's Economic and Social History of New England or S. E. Morrison's Maritime History of Massachusetts, or Messrs. Cousins and Riley's complete description of Salem architecture. The first two of these books are models for regional histories in the grand style; and they have the great merit of showing the immense interest and significance of local life in all its various details—details which the

national historian is compelled to gloss over or neglect entirely
when he is trying to treat as a single unit all the regional communities between the Atlantic and the Pacific oceans.

Dutchess County has a past that is in some ways little poorer than
New England's. In Dutchess County two different streams of civilization, the landholding and trading civilization of the Dutch, and the
more firmly knit and communal civilization of the Puritans, came
together and mingled. Dutchess County is historically what the
geographer would call an area of transition: in a small way it has
been in the position of the Paris Basin, let us say, where two different
traditions, the North and the South, came together. The gain and the
loss that took place in this mingling and exchange show themselves
very plainly in the architecture of the surviving houses, and in the
layout of the villages. The patient Dutchman, used to building in
solid brick in the old country, took every opportunity to build with
stone or brick in his new home: the old Church at Fishkill or the
Winegar House on the road to Amenia Union from Leedsville, are
examples of his sturdy architecture. When the New Englander came
as a separate individual into these new parts of the country, instead of
coming as a member of a municipal corporation, he neglected to
bring along the Common: and the absence of the common, or its
reduction to a mere strip, as at Pawling, was a serious loss to the life
of the Dutchess County villages. One who knows the early history of
this region does not need the frontier marker to tell him that Sharon
is in Connecticut and Amenia is in New York: the layout of the
villages tells the whole story.

To come a little closer home, the mingling of the Dutch, English,
and Huguenot strains is witnessed in almost every stone and every
bit of history connected with Troutbeck. The Delamater Cottage
reminds us of the numerous French Protestant names that were
scattered about the early colony: the Century Lodge is an excellent
example of the Dutch tradition in American country architecture,
while down the Leedsville Road are a pair of houses, one of them
bearing the repainted date 1837, which shows the penetration of the
English influence, with the formality of a Palladian window, looking
down upon the tight little Dutch stoop, built with the Dutchman's
steady eye to comfort and convenience, let fashion be what it may.

Just as the naturalist can reconstruct a whole animal from the few bones he may find in an old gravel pit, so the historian could reconstruct a large part of the history of the whole country, with no more to guide him than the existing names, places, houses, legends, and histories that have to do with so small a part of Dutchess County as the Amenia township. Local history implies the history of larger communities to a much greater extent than national history implies the local community. Every great event sweeps over the country like a wave; but it leaves its deposit behind in the life of the locality; and meanwhile that life goes on, with its own special history, its own special interests.

To follow even the life of a single family, like the Bentons, who worked over the land and the landscape of Troutbeck, is to see in a fresh and more intimate light events which are merely names and dates, not living experiences, when they are focussed at a long distance in an ordinary history book. Local history shows us the Bentons tilling the land around Troutbeck for upward a century; it shows them helping to establish a woolen mill during the years when the Napoleonic Wars and the Embargo Act cut off the English supply of woolens; it shows them helping to project the Sharon to New York Canal, as men throughout the state were projecting imaginary canals when the success of the Erie was demonstrated; the minutes of an Amenia Literary Society show a young Benton suggesting names for the streets of the future metropolis of Amenia; it shows Myron Benton listening to the distant voice of Whitman, and corresponding with Thoreau, whose last letter was addressed to him; it shows another Benton going into the Civil War, and living to write about it in a vivid and veracious book. I am merely using Troutbeck and the Benton family as examples of a hundred other equally interesting histories: to preserve these histories and to understand them is an important and indispensable step to understanding what was going on in the country at large.

Because local history is relatively accessible and immediate; because it deals with the concrete and the commonplace, it is what is necessary to vitalize the teaching of general history to the child at school, to say nothing of more mature students. The things that we can see and touch are those that awaken our imagination. Gibbon suddenly felt the Decline and Fall of Rome as he sat amid the ruined stones of the Forum; and nothing has ever made me, for one, feel the might of the Roman empire more keenly than stumbling across the tiles and foundations of a Roman villa in the midst of a quiet English field. Local history touches off these things that have happened on the spot; and the facts of local history become parts of a person's own life to an extent which is rare with scenes and incidents one has taken solely out of books and secondhand accounts. To learn about the Indians who once lived in America, and not to pick out the Indian place-names on the map or to dig up the arrowheads that still remain here; to learn about the Dutch and the Puritan settlers and not to follow the place-names and the family names creeping up and down the Dutchess County countryside; to learn about the Revolutionary War and not be able to recognize at sight the houses that survive from that period, or to be able to locate the mines and forges which supplied the soldiers with muskets and swords and ammunition; to learn about the commercial growth of the United States after the Civil War and not to know that the first school of business was started upon in Poughkeepsie just before the conflict broke out, and was overrun with pupils by the end of it—in short, to learn the abstractions of history and never to observe the concrete reality is to throw away local bread under the impression that imported stones are more nourishing.

Every old part of the country is filled with the memorials of our past: tombstones and cottages and churches, names and legends, old roads and trails and abandoned mines, as well as the things we built and used yesterday. All these memorials bring us closer to the past, and, so doing, they bring us closer to our own present; for we are living history as well as recording it; and our memories are as necessary as our anticipations. Communities seem to differ from individuals in this respect, that their expectation of life grows the older they become: the more history lies in back of them, the more confident we are that more will lie in front. A good past is a guarantee of a good future; and to preserve the records of what came before us promotes that sense of continuity which gives us the faith to continue our own work, with the expectation that our descendants will find it equally interesting.

Local history is a sort of benchmark which all more generalized and specialized kinds of history must come back to, for verification, as a point of reference. The value of local history for stimulating the imagination and giving the student something concrete and accessible to work upon has been recognized in the best English school; and it is beginning to take root in America, as well. At King's Langley and at Saffron Walden in England one group of children after another has contributed material to a little museum of local history. If nothing of this sort exists in Dutchess County, the local historical society members might well look into the possibilities of using their local material, and it remains for enterprising teachers of history to turn it to their special advantage. The point is that history begins at home, inevitably, but it does not end there. With local history as a starting point the student is drawn into a whole host of relationships that lead him out into the world at large: the whaling ships that used to cast anchor at Poughkeepsie and other river towns will carry him to the South Seas; the discovery of the Hudson will take him back to the Crusades; once one begins to follow the threads of local history, local manners, local industry, local peoples, one finds that they lead in every direction. And that is the proper method. Local history is not a means of exciting false pride in little things or exaggerated pretensions to local virtues that do not exist: on the contrary, it promotes to a decent self-respect: it is that form of self-knowledge which is the beginning of sound knowledge about anyone else. Just as the story of everyone's life would make at least one novel, so the story of any community's life would make at least one history. To know that history and to take pleasure in it is the beginning of that sympathy with remote times and foreign peoples which tends to make one truly a man of the world.

Lewis Mumford, *Dutchess County Historical Society Year Book,* Vol. 12 (Poughkeepsie, N.Y.: Dutchess County Historical Society, 1927).

LETTERS FROM THE AMERICAN REVOLUTION

George Washington

TWO MONTHS AFTER *the shots were fired, in April 1775, at Lexington and Concord, Congress voted George Washington (1732–99) commander-in-chief of the Continental Army. An early priority was the decision to fortify the Highlands, which were only forty miles from New York City, in the hope of obstructing navigation on the Hudson. As the gateway to Canada, and the link between the Northern and Southern colonies, the Hudson Valley region was of prime importance strategically. The British considered it the "Key to America," and indeed it would prove to be so.*

From the start the line was drawn at the lower Hudson. The British Army easily defeated the frightened, untrained Patriots, taking possession of New York City in 1776, and occupying it until the end of the war. New York State had only 6 percent of the population of the colonies, but the area around Manhattan, Long Island, and the lower Hudson Valley—filled with English, Scottish, Irish, Huguenot, and Swedish immigrants—reflected strong Tory sentiments. In fact, up to a third of the population of the states was pro-British, including a number of Indians besides the Iroquois nation who fought alongside the British and their German allies.

The Americans immediately set to work building fortifications in the Highlands, putting in place beacons, redoubts, and chevaux-de-frise *to hold back the British. The most ingenious plan turned out to be the construction of an iron chain across the River at Fort Montgomery (near what is now Bear Mountain Bridge)*

26

in 1776. That chain failed, until it was readjusted, then a second chain and boom, about 750 links and weighing sixty tons, connected West Point to Constitution Island, remaining in place for the rest of the war. In his recent book Chaining the Hudson, *the historian Lincoln Diamant deftly chronicles the complicated struggle for control of the Hudson. Before General Anthony Wayne's victory at Stony Point in 1779 put an end to further significant British activity in the North, and fighting shifted southward, many famous events were to occur along the Hudson—the burning, in 1777, of the then state capital of Kingston, and farther north the Battle of Saratoga, then three years later the treason of Benedict Arnold, who commanded West Point.*

By this time the Continental Army was hungry, angry, and short of supplies and clothing. The situation would only worsen in the next two years, with mounting foreign debt, pitiful military accommodations, scarce gunpowder and fodder, and no money to pay the mutinous army. Not a moment too soon for the distraught Washington the French Army joined the Americans in 1780, helping in the decisive defeat of Cornwallis at Yorktown. There were no more major battles, but 12,000 British troops still held New York City.

Washington went with half of his army, and his wife Martha, to protect the Highlands, setting up headquarters in April 1782, in the Hasbrouck house at Newburgh, for almost a year and a half, while the army camped at nearby New Windsor. In his letters during this long stay, while the country waited for the Treaty of Paris to end the war, Washington continued his distressed account of the desperate situation of the army, especially to his Secretary of War, Benjamin Lincoln, and to the prominent New Yorker and businessman Gouverneur Morris. The crisis was so severe it caused the near disintegration of the Continental Army until Washington's special appeal to the men, now part of the compelling "Newburgh Addresses." At last peace arrived. Washington's last letters include a note of deep gratitude to General Rochambeau, Commander of the French forces in America, a joyful announcement of peace to the heroic General Nathanael Greene (the upstate county was named after him), and a "Circular to the States"

*addressed to all the governors. This document, which came to be
called "Washington's Legacy," expressed a political vision that
was reflected eventually in the Constitution. The Hasbrouck house,
built in the style of Huguenot and Dutch Hudson Valley homes
of the eighteenth century, opened on July 4, 1850, as Washington's
Headquarters, becoming the first public historic site in the country.*

*Proclaiming the cessation of hostilities in one of his last direc-
tives from Newburgh, Washington declared that, "Nothing now
remains but for the actors of this mighty Scene to preserve a perfect, unvarying, consistency of character through the very last
act; to close the Drama with applause; and to retire from the Military Theatre with the same approbation of Angells and men
which have crowned all their former vertuous Actions." It was not
the last time theatrical metaphor would describe American political life.*

To The New York Legislature

Head Quarters, July 14, 1776.

Gentn.: The passage of the Enemy up the North River, is a point
big with many Consequences to the Public Interest; one particularly
occurs to me well deserving your attention, and to prevent which, I
shall gladly give every assistance in my power, consistent with the
Safety of the Army. I am informed, there are several passes on each
side the River, upon which the Communication with Albany depends,
of so commanding a Nature, that an inconsiderable Body of Men may
defend them against the largest Numbers. It may be, that on Board
these Ships there may be Troops for this purpose, who expecting to
be joined by the disaffected in that Quarter, or Confiding in their own
Strength, may endeavour to seize those defiles in which case the
intercourse between the two Armies, both by land and Water, will be
wholly cut off; than which a greater Misfortune could hardly befall
the Service and Army, I must intreat you, to take the measure into
Consideration and if possible provide against an Evil so much to be

apprehended. I should hope the Militia of those Counties, might be used on such an Emergency until further provision was made; I have also thought it very probable, those Ships may have carried up Arms and Ammunition, to be dealt out to those who may favor their Cause and cooperate with them at a prefix'd time. I would, to guard against this submit to your Consideration, the propriety of writing to the leading Men on our Side in these Counties, to be very vigilant in observing any movements of this kind, in order that so dangerous a Scheme may be nipped in the Bud. For that purpose to keep the utmost attention to the Conduct of the principle Tories in those parts; any attempts of intercourse with the Ships and all other Circumstances which may lead to a discovery of their Schemes and the Destruction of their Measures.

To Gouveneur Morris

New Windsor, December 10, 1780.

Dear Sir: . . . It gives me please. at all times to know the Sentiments of others upon points of public utility; those however which you have delivered relative to an enterprize against the enemy in New York, exhibit strong evidence how little the world is acquainted with the circumstances, and strength of our Army. A *Small* second embarkation took place about the middle of last Month; if another is in contemplation to take effect at the reduction of our force (which I think *exceedingly* probable) it is too much in embryo to form more than conjectural opinions of it, at this time; but I will suppose it large, and that not more than 6,000 regular troops will be left behind. Where are the Men; Where are the provisions; Where the Cloaths; the everything necessary to warrant the attempt you propose, in an inclement Season? Our numbers, never equal to those of the enemy in New York. Our State lines, never half compleat in Men, but perfectly so in every species of want, were diminished in the *Field,* so soon as the Weather set in cold; near 2000 Men on account of Cloaths, which I had not to give, nor ought to have given (supposing a surplusage) to the levies, whose dismission was near at hand. And *now,* to save the Man who is a permanent Soldier from

starving I am obliged in place of calling in the aid of Militia for new
enterprizes to dismiss the levies on account of the Provision. Under
this description of our circumstances, (which is not high coloured),
And when to it is added that instd. of getting Lumber from Albany for
building Barracks on York Island in the manner, and for the purposes
you mention that we have neither money nor credit adequate to the
purchase of a few boards for Doors to our Log huts. When every
ounce of Forage that has been used all the latter part of the Campaign, and a good deal of the provision, has been taken at the point
of the Bayonet. When we were from the Month of May to the Month
of Sepr. collecting Militia that ought to have been in the field by the
middle of July, and then obliged to dismiss them for want of
Supplies. When we cannot dispatch an Officer, or common Express
upon the most urgent occasion for want of the means of support; and
when I add but this is a matter of trivial concern because it is of a
personl. nature that I have not been able to obtain a farthing of
public money for the support of my Table for near two Months, you
can be at no loss as I have before observed to discover the
impracticability of executing the measure you suggested even supposing the enemy's numbers were reduced to your Standerd, but
which by the way neither is, nor will be the case, till the reduction of
our Army takes place, the period of which they know as well as we
do, and will, I have little doubt, govern themselves accordingly. An
Earnest desire however of closing the campaign with some degree of
eclat led me to investigate the means most thoroughly of doing it and
my wishes had so far got the better of my judgment that I had
actually made some pretty considerable advances in the prosecution
of a plan for this purpose when alas! I found the means inadequate
to the end and that it was with difficulty I could remove the army to
its places of Cantonment where it would be well for the Troops, if
like Chameleons, they could live upon Air, or like the Bear, suck their
paws for sustenance during the rigour of the approaching season.

To The Secretary at War

Head Quarters, October 2, 1782.
My dear Sir: Painful as the task is to describe the dark side of our

affairs, it some times becomes a matter of indispensable necessity. Without disguize or palliation, I will inform you candidly of the discontents which, at this moment, prevail universally throughout the Army.

The Complaint of Evils which they suppose almost remediless are, the total want of Money, or the means of existing from One day to another, the heavy debts they have already incurred, the loss of Credit, the distress of their Families (i e such as are Maried) at home, and the prospect of Poverty and Misery before them. [It is vain Sir, to suppose that Military Men will acquiesce *contently* with bare rations, when those in the civil walk of life (unacquainted with half the hardships they endure) are regularly paid the emoluments of Office; while the human Mind is influenced by the same passions, and have the same inclinations to endulge it cannot be. A Military Man has the same turn to sociability as a person in Civil life; he conceives himself equally called upon to live up to his rank; and his pridperfect treasure of mild moralities? The highway, the old State road to Albany, bristling now with the cloud-compelling motor, per when they cannot invite a French Officer, a visiting friend, or travelling acquaintance to a better repast than stinking Whiskey (and not always that) and a bit of Beef without Vegitables, will afford them.] . . .

While I premise, that tho' no one that I have seen or heard of, appears opposed to the principle of reducing the Army as circumstances may require; Yet I cannot help fearing the Result of the measure in contemplation, under present circumstances when I see such a Number of Men goaded by a thousand stings of reflexion on the past, and of anticipation on the future, about to be turned into the World, soured by penury and what they call the ingratitude of the Public, involved in debts, without one farthing of Money to carry them home, after having spent the flower of their days [and many of them their patrimonies] in establishing the freedom and Independence of their Country, and suffered every thing human Nature is capable of enduring on this side of death. . . .

I wish not to heighten the shades of the picture, so far as the real life would justify me in doing, or I would give Anecdotes of patriotism and distress which have scarcely ever been paralleled, never surpassed in the history of Mankind; but you may rely upon it, the patience and long sufferance of this Army are almost exhausted, and that there never was so great a spirit of Discontent as at this instant: While in the field, I think it may be kept from breaking out into Acts of Outrage, but when we retire into Winter Quarters (unless the Storm is previously dissipated) I cannot be at ease, respecting the consequences. It is high time for a Peace.

To Comte de Rochambeau

Newburgh, December 14, 1782.

I cannot, My dear Genl., permit you to depart from this Country without repeating to you the high sense I entertain of the Services you have rendered America, by the constant attention which you have paid to the Interests of it.

By the exact order and discipline of the Corps under your Command, and by your readiness, at all times, to give facility to every measure which the force of the Combined Armies was competent to.

To this testimony of your Public character I should be wanting to the feelings of my heart, was I not to add expressions of the happiness I have enjoyed in your private friendship. The remembrance of which, will be one of the most pleasing Circumstances of my life.

My best wishes will accompany you to France, where I have no doubt of your meeting the Smiles and rewards of a generous Prince; and the warmest embraces of Affectionate friends. I have the honor etc.

To Major General Nathanael Greene

Head Quarters, March 31, 1783.

Dear Sir: I have the pleasure to inclose to you a letter from the Marquis de la fayette, which came under cover to me, by the Packet Triumph, dispatched by the Marquis and the Count de Estaing from Cadiz to Phila.

All the Accounts which this Vessel has bro't, of a Conclusion of a General Peace, you will receive before this can reach you.

You will give the highest Credit to my Sincerity, when I beg you to accept my warmest Congratulations on this glorious and happy Event, an Event which crowns all our Labors and will sweeten the Toils which we have experienced in the Course of eight Years distressing War. The Army here, universally participate in the general Joy which this Event has diffused, and, from this Consideration, together with the late Resolutions of Congress, for the Commutation of the Half pay, and for a Liquidation of all their Accounts, their Minds are filled with the highest Satisfaction. I am sure you will join with me in this additional occasion of joy.

It remains only for the States to be Wise, and to establish their Independence on that Basis of inviolable efficacious Union, and firm Confederation, which may prevent their being made the Sport of European Policy; may Heaven give them Wisdom to adopt the Measures still necessary for this important Purpose. I have the honor etc.

Circular to the States

Head Quarters, Newburgh, June 8, 1783.

Sir: The great object for which I had the honor to hold an appointment in the Service of my Country, being accomplished, I am now preparing to resign it into the hands of Congress, and to return to that domestic retirement, which, it is well known, I left with the greatest reluctance, a Retirement, for which I have never ceased to sigh through a long and painful absence, and on which (remote from the noise and trouble of the World) I meditate to pass the remainder of life in a state of undisturbed repose; But before I carry this resolution into effect, I think it a duty incumbent on me, to make this my last official communication, to congratulate you on the glorious events which Heaven has been pleased to produce in our favor, to offer my sentiments respecting some important subjects, which appear to me, to be intimately connected with the tranquility of the United States, to take my leave of your Excellency as a public

Character, and to give my final blessing to that Country, in whose service I have spent the prime of my life, for whose sake I have consumed so many anxious days and watchfull nights, and whose happiness being extremely dear to me, will always constitute no inconsiderable part of my own.

Impressed with the liveliest sensibility on this pleasing occasion, I will claim the indulgence of dilating the more copiously on the subjects of our mutual felicitation. When we consider the magnitude of the prize we contended for, the doubtful nature of the contest, and the favorable manner in which it has terminated, we shall find the greatest possible reason for gratitude and rejoicing; this is a theme that will afford infinite delight to every benevolent and liberal mind, whether the event in contemplation, be considered as the source of present enjoyment or the parent of future happiness; and we shall have equal occasion to felicitate ourselves on the lot which Providence has assigned us, whether we view it in a natural, a political or moral point of light.

The Citizens of America, placed in the most enviable condition, as the sole Lords and Proprietors of a vast Tract of Continent, comprehending all the various soils and climates of the World, and abounding with all the necessaries and conveniences of life, are now by the late satisfactory pacification, acknowledged to be possessed of absolute freedom and Independency; They are, from this period, to be considered as the Actors on a most conspicuous Theatre, which seems to be peculiarly designated by Providence for the display of human greatness and felicity; Here, they are not only surrounded with every thing which can contribute to the completion of private and domestic enjoyment, but Heaven has crowned all its other blessings, by giving a fairer opportunity for political happiness, than any other Nation has ever been favored with. Nothing can illustrate these observations more forcibly, than a recollection of the happy conjuncture of times and circumstances, under which our Republic assumed its rank among the Nations; The foundation of our Empire was not laid in the gloomy age of Ignorance and Superstition, but at an Epocha when the rights of mankind were better understood and more clearly defined, than at any former period, the researches of the human mind, after social happiness, have been carried to a great extent, the Treasures of knowledge, acquired by the labours of Philosophers, Sages and Legislatures, through a long succession of years, are laid open for our use, and their collected wisdom may be happily applied in the Establishment of our forms of Government; the free cultivation of Letters, the unbounded extension of Commerce, the progressive refinement of Manners, the growing liberality of sentiment, and above all, the pure and benign light of Revelation, have had a meliorating influence on mankind and increased the blessings of Society. At this auspicious period, the United States came into existence as a Nation, and if their Citizens should not be completely free and happy, the fault will be entirely their own.

Such is our situation, and such are our prospects: but notwithstanding the cup of blessing is thus reached out to us, notwithstanding happiness is ours, if we have a disposition to seize the occasion and make it our own; yet, it appears to me there is an option still left to the United States of America, that it is in their choice, and depends upon their conduct, whether they will be respectable and prosperous, or contemptible and miserable as a Nation; This is the time of their political probation, this is the moment when the eyes of the whole World are turned upon them, this is the moment to establish or ruin their national Character forever, this is the favorable moment to give such a tone to our Federal Government, as will enable it to answer the ends of its institution, or this may be the ill-fated moment for relaxing the powers of the Union, annihilating the cement of the Confederation, and exposing us to become the sport of European politics, which may play one State against another to prevent their growing importance, and to serve their own interested purposes. For, according to the system of Policy the States shall adopt at this moment, they will stand or fall, and by their confirmation or lapse, it is yet to be decided, whether the Revolution must ultimately be considered as a blessing or a curse: a blessing or a curse, not to the present age alone, for with our fate will the destiny of unborn Millions be involved.

With this conviction of the importance of the present Crisis, silence in me would be a crime; I will therefore speak to your Excellency, the language of freedom and of sincerity, without disguise; I am aware, however, that those who differ from me in political sentiment, may perhaps remark, I am stepping out of the proper line of my duty, and they may possibly ascribe to arrogance or ostentation, what I know is alone the result of the purest intention, but the rectitude of my own heart, which disdains such unworthy motives, the part I have hitherto acted in life, the determination I have formed, of not taking any share in public business hereafter, the ardent desire I feel, and shall continue to manifest, of quietly enjoying in private life, after all the toils of War, the benefits of a wise and liberal Government, will, I flatter myself, sooner or later convince my Countrymen, that I could have no sinister views in delivering with so little reserve, the opinions contained in this Address.

There are four things, which I humbly conceive, are essential to the well being, I may even venture to say, to the existence of the United States as an Independent Power:

1st. An indissoluble Union of the States under one Federal Head.

2dly. A Sacred regard to Public Justice.

3dly. The adoption of a proper Peace Establishment, and

4thly. The prevalence of that pacific and friendly Disposition, among the People of the United States, which will induce them to forget their local prejudices and policies, to make those mutual concessions which are requisite to the general prosperity, and in some instances, to sacrifice their individual advantages to the interest of the Community.

These are the Pillars on which the glorious Fabrick of our Independency and National Character must be supported; Liberty is the Basis, and whoever would dare to sap the foundation, or overturn the Structure, under whatever specious pretexts he may attempt it, will merit the bitterest execration, and the severest punishment which can be inflicted by his injured Country.

The Writings of George Washington, ed. by John C. Fitzpatrick, Vols. 5, 25, 26 (Washington, D.C.: U.S. Government Printing Office, 1938).

THE GENIUS
OF THE SCENE

Henry James

Henry JAMES (1843–1916) was sixty-two years old *when he returned to the United States after two decades abroad. He came to rest, lecture, visit, and write a different kind of work— an American travel book. By this time he had already complet- ed all the novels that brought him international renown in a ca- reer that spanned the period of the Civil War up to World War I. In the few years before his trip back, James wrote his well-known novels* The Wings of a Dove, The Ambassadors, *and* The Gold- en Bowl. *Even earlier than his long sojourn abroad, where he set- tled in England, he published* The Portrait of a Lady, *whose hero- ine was a woman from Albany. James had spent part of his childhood in Albany, and his grandfather died there in 1832. The James family later lived in New York City and Boston, but Henry was to spend all his life traveling back and forth to Europe which was his literary home. There his friends over the decades included Browning, Eliot, Tennyson, Ruskin, Kipling, Trollope, Flaubert, Turgenev, Zola, and Conrad, the great names of nineteenth-century letters.*

On his 1904 trip, which lasted nearly a year, James visited New England, the New Jersey shore, Philadelphia, Washington, D.C., and the Carolinas, also journeying to Chicago, St. Louis, Los Angeles, and Seattle. He dined at the White House with President Theodore Roosevelt whom, as could be expected, he did not like. Up north he visited his famous philosopher brother William, and spent some days at his friend Edith Wharton's home at Lenox, in the

Berkshires. James, who had already written A Little Tour in France, *and would later compose* Italian Hours, *chose for his American subject only the Eastern seaboard. This "restless analyst" who found much to criticize in American society and manners, indeed in modern life in general, had a special fondness for the Hudson Valley. James was one of the few major American authors to write an extended essay on the region in the twentieth century. He recalls childhood imagery with a certain nostalgia, in an altogether romantic portrait of the River, from his seat on a train southbound for New York City. No one has ever spun as exquisite a web of silver light and language over the Hudson as James, in his pictorial reverie one spring afternoon of 1905.*

IT IS STILL VIVID to me that, returning in the spring-time from a few weeks in the Far West, I re-entered New York State with the absurdest sense of meeting again a ripe old civilization and travelling through a country that showed the mark of established manners. It will seem, I fear, one's perpetual refrain, but the moral was yet once more that values of a certain order are, in such conditions, all relative, and that, as some wants of the spirit *must* somehow be met, one knocks together any substitute that will fairly stay the appetite. We had passed great smoky Buffalo in the raw vernal dawn—with a vision, for me, of curiosity, character, charm, whatever it might be, too needfully sacrificed, opportunity perhaps forever missed, yet at the same time a vision in which the lost object failed to mock at me with the last concentration of shape; and history, as we moved Eastward, appeared to meet us, in the look of the land, in its more overwrought surface and thicker detail, quite as if she had ever consciously declined to cross the border and were aware, precisely, of the queer feast we should find in her. The recognition, I profess, was a preposterous ecstasy: one couldn't have felt more if one had passed into the presence of some seated, placid, rich-voiced gentlewoman after leaving that of an honest but boisterous hoyden. It was doubtless a matter only of degrees and shades, but never was such a pointing of the lesson that a sign of any sort may count double if it be but artfully placed. I spent that day, literally, in the company of the rich-voiced gentlewoman, making my profit of it even in spite of a second privation, the doom I was under of having only, all wistfully, all ruefully, to avert my lips from the quaint silver bowl, as I here quite definitely figured it, in which she offered me the entertainment of antique Albany. At antique Albany, to a certainty, the mature matron involved in my metaphor would have put on a particular grace, and as our train crossed the river for further progress I almost seemed to see her stand at some gable-window of Dutch association, one of the two or three impressed there on my infantile imagination, to ask me why then I had come so far at all.

I could have replied but in troubled tones, and I looked at the rest of the scene for some time, no doubt, as through the glaze of all-but filial tears. Thus it was, possibly, that I saw the River shine, from that moment on, as a great romantic stream, such as could throw not a little of its glamour, for the mood of that particular hour, over the city at its mouth. I had not even known, in my untravelled state, that we were to "strike" it on our way from Chicago, so that it represented, all that afternoon, so much beauty thrown in, so much benefit beyond the bargain—the so hard bargain, for the traveller, of the American railway-journey at its best. That ordeal was in any case at its best here, and the perpetually interesting river kept its course, by my right elbow, with such splendid consistency that, as I recall the impression, I repent a little of having just now reflected with acrimony on the cost of the obtrusion of track and stations to the Riverside view. One must of course choose between dispensing with the ugly presence and enjoying the scenery by the aid of the same—which but means, really, that to use the train at all had been to put one's self, for any proper justice to the scenery, in a false position. That, however, takes us too far back, and one can only save one's dignity by laying all such blames on our detestable age. A decent respect for the Hudson would confine us to the use of the boat—all the more that American river-steamers have had, from the earliest time, for the true *raffiné,* their peculiar note of romance. A possible commerce, on the other hand, with one's time—which is always also the time of so many other busy people—has long since

made mincemeat of the rights of contemplation; rights as reduced, in
the United States, to-day, and by quite the same argument, as those of
the noble savage whom we have banished to his narrowing reserva-
tion. Letting that pass, at all events, I still remember that I was able to
put, from the car-window, as many questions to the scene as it could
have answered in the time even had its face been clearer to read.

Its face was veiled, for the most part, in a mist of premature
spring heat, an atmosphere draping it indeed in luminous mystery,
hanging it about with sun-shot silver and minimizing any happy
detail, any element of the definite, from which the romantic effect
might here and there have gained an accent. There was not an accent
in the picture from the beginning of the run to Albany to the
end—for which thank goodness! one is tempted to say on remembering
how often, over the land in general, the accents are wrong. Yet if the
romantic effect as we know it elsewhere mostly depends on them,
why *should* that glamour have so shimmered before me in their
absence?—how should the picture have managed to be a constant
combination of felicities? Was it just *because* the felicities were all
vaguenesses, and the "beauties," even the most celebrated, all blurs?
—was it perchance on that very account that I could meet my
wonder so promptly with the inference that what I had in my eyes on
so magnificent a scale was simply, was famously, "style"? I was landed
by that conclusion in the odd further proposition that style could
then exist without accents—a quandary soon after to be quenched,
however, in the mere blinding radiance of a visit to West Point. I was
to make that memorable pilgrimage a fortnight later—and I was to
find my question, when it in fact took place, shivered by it to mere
silver atoms. The very powers of the air seemed to have taken the
case in hand and positively to have been interested in making it
transcend all argument. Our Sunday of mid-May, wet and windy, let
loose, over the vast stage, the whole procession of storm-effects; the
raw green of wooded heights and hollows was only everywhere
rain-brightened, the weather playing over it all day as with some
great grey water-colour brush. The essential character of West Point
and its native nobleness of position can have been but intensified, I
think, by this artful process; yet what was mainly unmistakable was
the fact again of the suppression of detail as in the positive interest of

the grand style. One had therefore only to take detail as another name for accent, the accent that might prove compromising, in order to see it made good that style *could* do without them, and that the grand style in fact almost always must. How on this occasion the trick was played is more than I shall attempt to say; it is enough to have been conscious of our being, from hour to hour, literally bathed in that high element, with the very face of nature washed, so to speak, the more clearly to express and utter it.

Such accordingly is the strong silver light, all simplifying and ennobling, in which I see West Point; see it as a cluster of high promontories, of the last classic elegance, overhanging vast receding reaches of river, mountain-guarded and dim, which took their place in the geography of the ideal, in the long perspective of the poetry of association, rather than in those of the State of New York. It was as if the genius of the scene had said: "No, you *shan't* have accent, because accent is, at the best, local and special, and might here by some perversity—how do I know after all?—interfere. I want you to have something unforgettable, and therefore you shall have *type*— yes, absolutely have type, and even tone, without accent; an impossibility, you may hitherto have supposed, but which you have only to look about you now really to see expressed. And type and tone of the very finest and rarest; type and tone good enough for Claude or Turner, if they could have walked by these rivers instead of by their thin rivers of France and Italy; type and tone, in short, that gather in shy detail under wings as wide as those with which a motherly hen covers her endangered brood. So there you are—deprived of all 'accent' as a peg for criticism, and reduced thereby, you see, to asking me no more questions." I was able so to take home, I may add, this formula of the matter, that even the interesting facts of the School of the Soldier which have carried the name of the place about the world almost put on the shyness, the air of conscious evasion and escape, noted in the above allocution: they struck me as forsaking the foreground of the picture. It was part of the play again, no doubt, of the grey water-colour brush: there was to be no consent of the elements, that day, to anything but a generalized elegance—in which effect certainly the clustered, the scattered Academy played, on its high green stage, its part. But, of all things in the world, it massed, to

my vision, more mildly than I had somehow expected; and I take that
for a feature, precisely, of the pure poetry of the impression. It
lurked there with grace, it insisted without swagger—and I could
have hailed it just for this reason indeed as a presence of the last
distinction. It is doubtless too much to say, in fine, that the Institution, at West Point, "suffers" comparatively, for vulgar individual
emphasis, from the overwhelming liberality of its setting—and I
perhaps chanced to see it in the very conditions that most invest it
with poetry. The fact remains that, both as to essence and as to
quantity, its prose seemed washed away, and I shall recall it in the
future much less as the sternest, the world over, of all the seats of
Discipline, than as some great Corot-composition of young, vague,
wandering figures in splendidly-classic shades.

I make that point, for what it is worth, only to remind myself of
another occasion on which the romantic note sounded for me with
the last intensity, and yet on which the picture swarmed with
accents—as, absent or present, I must again call them—that contributed alike to its interest and to its dignity. The proof was complete,
on this second Sunday, with the glow of early summer already in
possession, that affirmed detail was not always affirmed infelicity—
since the scene here bristled with detail (and detail of the importance that frankly *constitutes* accent) only to the enhancement of its
charm. It was a matter once more of hanging over the Hudson on the
side opposite West Point, but further down; the situation was founded,
as at West Point, on the presence of the great feature and on the
consequent general lift of foreground and distance alike, and yet
infinitely sweet was it to gather that style, in such conditions and for
the success of such effects, had not really to depend on mere kind
vaguenesses, on any anxious deprecation of distinctness. There was
no vagueness now; a wealth of distinctness, in the splendid light, met
the eyes—but with the very result of showing them how happily it
could play. What it came back to was that the accents, in the
delightful old pillared and porticoed house that crowned the cliff and
commanded the stream, were as right as they were numerous; so
that there immediately followed again on this observation a lively
recognition of the ground of the rightness. To wonder what this was
could be but to see, straightway, that, though many reasons had

worked together for them, mere time had done more than all; that beneficence of time enjoying in general, in the United States, so little even of the chance that so admirably justifies itself, for the most part, when interference happens to have spared it. Cases of this rare mercy yet exist, as I had had occasion to note, and their consequent appeal to the touched sense within us comes, as I have also hinted, with a force out of all proportion, comes with a kind of accepted insolence of authority. The things that have lasted, in short, whatever they may be, "succeed" as no newness, try as it will, succeeds, inasmuch as their success is a created interest.

There we catch the golden truth which so much of the American world strikes us as positively organized to gainsay, the truth that production takes time, and that the production of interest, in particular, takes *most* time. Desperate again and again the ingenuity of the offered, the obtruded substitute, and pathetic in many an instance its confessed failure; this remark being meanwhile relevant to the fact that my charming old historic house of the golden Sunday put me off, among its great trees, its goodly gardens, its acquired signs and gathered memories, with no substitute whatever, even the most specious, but just paid cash down, so to speak, ripe ringing gold, over the counter, for all the attention it invited. It had character, as one might say, and character is scarce less precious on the part of the homes of men in a raw medium than on the part of responsible persons at a difficult crisis. This virtue was there within and without and on every face; but perhaps nowhere so present, I thought, as in the ideal refuge for summer days formed by the wide north porch, if porch that disposition may be called—happiest disposition of the old American country-house—which sets tall columns in a row, under a pediment suitably severe, to present them as the "making" of a high, deep gallery. I know not what dignity of old afternoons suffused with what languor seems to me always, under the murmur of American trees and by the lap of American streams, to abide in these mild shades; there are combinations with depths of congruity beyond the plummet, it would seem, even of the most restless of analysts, and rather than try to say why my whole impression here melted into the general iridescence of a past of Indian summers hanging about mild ghosts half asleep, in hammocks, over still milder novels, I would renounce altogether the art of refining. For the iridescence consists, in this connection, of a shimmer of association that still more refuses to be reduced to terms; some sense of legend, of aboriginal mystery, with a still earlier past for its dim background and the insistent idea of the River as above all romantic for its warrant. Helplessly analyzed, perhaps, this amounts to no more than the very childish experience of a galleried house or two round about which the views and the trees and the peaches and the pony seemed prodigious, and to the remembrance of which the wonder of Rip Van Winkle and that of the "Hudson River School" of landscape art were, a little later on, to contribute their glamour.

If Rip Van Winkle had been really at the bottom of it all, nothing could have furthered the whole case more, on the occasion I speak of, than the happy nearness of the home of Washington Irving, the impression of which I was thus able, in the course of an hour, to work in—with the effect of intensifying more than I can say the old-time charm and general legendary fusion. These are beautiful, delicate, modest matters, and how can one touch them with a light enough hand? How can I give the comparatively coarse reasons for my finding at Sunnyside, which contrives, by some grace of its own, to be at once all ensconced and embowered in relation to the world, and all frank and uplifted in relation to the river, a perfect treasure of mild moralities? The highway, the old State road to Albany, bristling now with the cloud-compelling motor, passes at the head of a deep, long lane, winding, embanked, overarched, such an old-world lane as one scarce ever meets in America; but if you embrace this chance to plunge away to the left you come out for your reward into the quite indefinable air of the little American literary past. The place is inevitably, to-day, but a qualified Sleepy Hollow—the Sleepy Hollow of the author's charming imagination was, as I take it, off somewhere in the hills, or in some dreamland of old autumns, happily unprofanable now; for "modernity," with its terrible power of working its will, of abounding in its sense, of gilding its toy—modernity, with its pockets full of money and its conscience full of virtue, its heart really full of tenderness, has seated itself there under pretext of guarding the shrine. What has happened, in a word, is very much what has happened in the case of other shy retreats of anchorites doomed to celebrity—the primitive cell has seen itself encompassed, in time, by a temple of many chambers, all dedicated to the history of the hermit. The cell is still there at Sunnyside, and there is even yet so much charm that one doesn't attempt to say where the parts of it, all kept together in a rich conciliatory way, begin or end—though indeed, I hasten to add, the identity of the original modest house, the shrine within the gilded shell, has been religiously preserved.

One has, in fact, I think, no quarrel whatever with the amplified state of the place, for it is the manner and the effect of this amplification that enable us to read into the scene its very most interesting message. The "little" American literary past, I just now said—using that word—(whatever the real size of the subject) because the caressing diminutive, at Sunnyside, is what rises of itself to the lips; the small uncommodious study, the limited library, the "dear" old portrait-prints of the first half of the century—very dear to-day when properly signed and properly sallow—these things, with the beauty of the site, with the sense that the man of letters of the unimproved age, the age of processes still comparatively slow, could have wanted no deeper, softer dell for mulling material over, represent the conditions that encounter now on the spot the sharp reflection of our own increase of arrangement and loss of leisure. This is the admirable interest in the exhibition of which Wolfert's Roost had been, a hundred years before the date of Irving's purchase, the rudimentary principle—that it throws the facts of our earlier "intellectual activity" into a vague golden perspective, a haze as of some unbroken spell of the same Indian summer I a moment ago had occasion to help myself out with; a fond appearance than which nothing could minister more to envy. If we envy the spinners of prose and tellers of tales to whom our American air anciently either administered or refused sustenance, this is all, and quite the best thing, it would seem, that we need do for them: it exhausts, or rather it forestalls, the futilities of discrimination. Strictly critical, mooning about Wolfert's Roost of a summer Sunday, I defy even the hungriest of analysts to be: his predecessors, the whole connected company, profit so there, to his rueful vision, by the splendour of their possession of better conditions than his. It has taken *our* ugly era to thrust in the railroad at the foot of the slope, among the masking trees; the railroad that is part, exactly, of the pomp and circumstance, the quickened pace, the heightened fever, the narrowed margin expressed within the very frame of the present picture, as I say, and all in the perfect good faith of collateral piety. I had hoped not to have to name the railroad—it seems so to give away my case. There was no railroad, however, till long after Irving's settlement— he survived the railroad but by a few years, and my case is simply that, disengaging *his* Sunnyside from its beautiful extensions and arriving thus at the sense of his easy elements, easy for everything but rushing about and being rushed at, the sense of his "command" of the admirable river and the admirable country, his command of all the mildness of his life, of his pleasant powers and his ample hours, of his friends and his contemporaries and his fame and his honour and his temper and, above all, of his delightful fund of reminiscence and material, I seemed to hear, in the summer sounds and in the very urbanity of my entertainers, the last faint echo of a felicity forever gone. That is the true voice of such places, and not the imputed challenge to the chronicler or the critic.

Henry James, *The American Scene* (New York: Harper & Brothers Publishers, 1907).

RADIO ADDRESS
ON ELECTION EVE

Franklin D. Roosevelt

F*RANKLIN DELANO ROOSEVELT (1882–1945) had a life-
long interest in the local history of his birthplace, Hyde Park,
and the Dutch ancestry of his family who had roots in New York
since the middle of the seventeenth century. Growing up in the
beautiful countryside of Dutchess county, he developed an attachment to the land from boyhood when he learned the birds and
plants of the area. Later as a young man he took an avid interest
in planting trees on the family property, assiduously recorded
in his farm journal. In 1914 he helped found the Dutchess County
Historical Society, and in the next decade became town historian. He began his political career as New York State Senator for
1911–13, then was elected Governor of New York in 1928 and
1930, always supporting conservation measures. By this time he had
planted thousands of trees at Hyde Park, at first under the guidance of the State Conservation Department at the Syracuse College
of Forestry. In the most recent volume of his long study of FDR,
Geoffrey C. Ward notes that he planted in his lifetime more than
300,000 trees, over 70 percent of them by 1928. Roosevelt, with
a mixture of glee and modesty, liked to call himself a "tree farmer."*

*Nonetheless, he was just as passionate about the architectural
legacy of the area as its natural history, working during the
period of his first presidency in 1934 with the local architectural
historian Helen Wilkinson Reynolds. They set out plans for new
post offices at Poughkeepsie, Rhinebeck, and Wappingers Falls which
were eventually modeled after lost historic buildings. The*

47

Rhinebeck Post Office was rebuilt on the model of the old Kip-Beekman house near the town, and features murals on local historical themes by the artist Olin Dows, who had lived there. Roosevelt also supervised the remodeling of the family home "Springwood," which assumed its present Georgian-Revival style features in the decade after his marriage to Eleanor Roosevelt. He is buried in the rose garden there.

Once he became president Roosevelt considered his home the "Summer White House." He welcomed there many royal guests and celebrities over the years. Churchill came to Hyde Park three times, where in 1942 he and the president signed a momentous agreement that led to the building of the atomic bomb. Roosevelt liked to vote in the Hyde Park Town Hall for presidential elections. He gave a number of his speeches and fireside chats from his home, too.

Election eve of his third campaign for the presidency in 1940, FDR appeared as usual to greet a torchlight parade by the local citizens which started from the village center and proceeded to his house. It was a year after the Hitler-Stalin Pact, a few months since the Battle of Britain was fought, and a year away from the Pearl Harbor bombing. Looking back on this speech from half a century's distance, no longer an age when people sit beside the radio to hear words of reassurance from their president, it is ironic that once more the eyes of the world are turned on the political upheavals in Europe. Roosevelt himself helped to construct the post-war configuration of Europe and the Soviet Union that is just now reshaping itself. His timeless theme of the fragility of democratic process seems all the more compelling in the context of contemporary events.

My Fellow Americans:

Once more I am in the quiet of my home in Hyde Park on the eve of Election Day. I wish to speak to you not of partisan politics but of the Nation, the United States of America, to which we all owe such deep and inborn allegiance.

As I sit here tonight with my own family, I think of all the other American families—millions of families all through the land—sitting in their own homes. They have eaten their supper in peace, they will be able to sleep in their homes tonight in peace. Tomorrow they will be free to go out to live their ordinary lives in peace—free to say and do what they wish, free to worship as they please. Tomorrow, of all days, they will be free to choose their own leaders who, when that choice has been made, become in turn only the instruments to carry out the will of all of the people.

And I cannot help but think of the families in other lands— millions of families—living in homes like ours. On some of these homes, bombs of destruction may be dropping even as I speak to you.

Across the seas life has gone underground. I think I speak the minds of all of you when I say that we thank God that we live in the sunlight, and in the starlight of peace—that we are not in war and that we propose and expect to continue to live our lives in peace— under the peaceful light of Heaven.

In this town, as in every other community in our nation, friends and neighbors will gather together around the polling place.

They will discuss the state of the Nation, the weather, and the prospect for their favorite football team. They will discuss the present political campaign. Some will wear buttons proclaiming their allegiance to one candidate or another. And, I suppose, there will be a few warm arguments.

But when you and I step into the voting booth, we can proudly say: "I am an American, and this vote I am casting is the exercise of my highest privilege and my most solemn duty to my country."

We vote as free men, impelled only by the urgings of our own wisdom and our own conscience.

In our polling places are no storm troopers or secret police to look over our shoulders as we mark our ballots.

My own personal participation in public affairs goes back as far as the year 1910, when I first became a candidate for the State Senate from this district on the Hudson River.

In the thirty years that have followed, I have taken an active part in nearly every political campaign—local, and state, and national. My interest has been that of a candidate for office; a public official; and a private citizen.

And in every political campaign the question on which we all finally pass judgment through the ballot box is simply this: "Whom do I think is the candidate best qualified to act as President, or Governor, or Senator, or Mayor, or Supervisor or County Commissioner during the next term?"

It is that right, the right to determine for themselves who should be their own officers of government, that provides for the people the most powerful safeguard of our democracy. The right to place men in office, at definite, fixed dates of election for a specific term, is the right which will keep a free people always free.

Dictators have forgotten—or perhaps they never knew—the basis upon which democratic government is founded: that the opinion of all the people, freely formed and freely expressed, without fear or coercion, is wiser than the opinion of any one man or any small group of men.

We have more faith in the collective opinion of all Americans than in the individual opinion of any one American.

Your will is a part of the great will of America. Your voice is a part of the great voice of America. And when you and I stand in line tomorrow for our turn at the polls, we are voting equals.

In the past twenty years the number of those who exercise the right to vote in natural elections has been almost doubled. There is every indication that the number of votes cast tomorrow will be by far the greatest in all our history.

That is the proof—if proof be needed—of the vitality of our democracy.

But our obligation to our country does not end with the casting of our votes.

Every one of us has a continuing responsibility for the Government which we choose.

Democracy is not just a word, to be shouted at political rallies and then put back into the dictionary after election day.

The service of democracy must be something much more than mere lip service.

It is a living thing—a human thing—compounded of brains and muscles and heart and soul. The service of democracy is the birthright of every citizen, the white and the colored; the Protestant, the Catholic, the Jew; the sons and daughters of every country in the world, who make up the people of this land. Democracy is every man and woman who loves freedom and serves the cause of freedom.

Last Saturday night, I said that freedom of speech is of no use to the man who has nothing to say—that freedom of worship is of no use to the man who has lost his God. And tonight I should like to add that a free election is of no use to the man who is too indifferent to vote.

The American people and the cause of democracy owe a great deal to the very many people who have worked in an honorable way on each side of this campaign. I know that after tomorrow they will all continue to cooperate in the service of democracy, to think about it, to talk about it, and to work for it.

Tomorrow you will decide for yourselves how the legislative and executive branches of the Government of your country are to be run during their next terms and by whom.

After the ballots are counted, the real rulers of this country will have had their way, as they have had it every two years or every four years during our whole national existence.

After the ballots are counted, the United States of America will still be united.

Discussion among us should and will continue, for we are free citizens of a free nation. But there can be no arguments about the essential fact that in our desire to remain at peace by defending our democracy, we are one nation and one people.

We people of America know that man cannot live by bread alone.

We know that we have a reservoir of religious strength which can withstand attacks from abroad and corruption from within.

We people of America will always cherish and preserve that strength. We will always cling to our religion, our devotion to

God—to the faith which gives us comfort and the strength to face evil.

On this election eve, we all have in our hearts and minds a prayer for the dignity, the integrity and the peace of our beloved country.

Therefore, in this last hour before midnight, I believe that you will find it fitting that I read to you an old prayer which asks the guidance of God for our nation:

> Almighty God, who hast given us this good land for our heritage; We humbly beseech Thee that we may always prove ourselves a people mindful of Thy favor and glad to do Thy will. Bless our land with honourable industry, sound learning, and pure manners. Save us from violence, discord, and confusion; from pride and arrogancy, and from every evil way. Defend our liberties, and fashion into one united people the multitudes brought hither out of many kindreds and tongues. Endue with the spirit of wisdom those to whom in Thy Name we entrust the authority of government, that there may be justice and peace at home, and that, through obedience to Thy law, we may show forth Thy praise among the nations of the earth. In the time of prosperity, fill our hearts with thankfulness, and in the day of trouble, suffer not our trust in Thee to fail; Amen.

Franklin D. Roosevelt, President's Personal File 1820, Franklin D. Roosevelt Library, Hyde Park, N.Y.

II

LIVES OF
THE PEOPLE

ROLLING TO HYORKY
FROM THE CATSKILL SHORE

Carl Carmer

*C*ARL *CARMER (1893–1976) remains the Hudson Valley's most beloved folklorist-historian, confirmed by the fact that his 1939 classic* The Hudson *is still in print for a new generation of readers. He was a tireless essayist, poet, anthologizer, and contributor of supporting prefaces to books on the area. He rallied for causes to save the Valley's historical architecture, and at the time of his death was involved in the long, but eventually successful, struggle to keep Consolidated Edison from building a pumped storage plant at Storm King Mountain.*

Carmer wrote and edited several books that spread beyond the Hudson to include all of New York State, and other states as well. Whether autobiographical or historical, his writing always emphasized the small but important details of character and setting that make each work so intimate and personable. There is a down-to-earth enjoyment and good sense in Carmer's "people's histories," which leave the narratives of power, wealth, and status to other historians. In more than four decades of teaching and writing, he produced several New York books, including Genesee Fever, Dark Trees to the Wind, My Kind of Country, The Tavern Lamps Are Burning, *and many works for children. He also wrote and narrated documentary films for television and movies. He collected albums of regional songs, too. Even before Carmer began to write on the New York themes for which he is known, he worked as an editor—in the twenties and thirties—for* Vanity Fair *and* Theatre Arts, *two of the most cosmopolitan magazines of the period. Carmer's career was surprisingly expansive to include presidencies of both the Authors Guild and the Poetry Society of America, and prominent membership in the New York State Folklore Society.*

By his example he showed how meaningful and engaged a life can be when one writes from a personal sense of place and time. This guiding intellectual and philosophical principle literally erases the borders between work and pleasure. Carmer makes history come alive in his tales of real people and landscapes that reflect the enterprise and energy of the human imagination.

A SNOW-WHITE WHALE curvetting with its brown mate in the swirling waters of the Hudson startled the settlers of Fort Orange in the rainy spring of 1647. A group of Dutch, Irish, Swedes, and Germans lined the banks, fearing the pale beast as an omen of evil. Assurances of those "who had been to Greenland" that the two visitors were natural sea dwellers did not comfort them. Only when the dark one ran aground on an island at the mouth of the Mohawk and died, thereafter permeating the air for six miles in all directions with an intolerable odor, would they accept a realistic explanation of what they had seen. Then, with practical thrift, they descended on the fat corpse and broiled out of it a great quantity of oil, but not so much as escaped them, for the whole surface of the river was covered with grease for three weeks. This was the first profitable whaling venture of the Hudson valley dwellers, but far from the last.

Although a "considerable large whale" made a tour of Manhattan Island in October, 1773, making itself visible in both boundary rivers, nobody seems to have done anything about it. It was not until more than a decade later that the packets and sloops of the Hudson became accustomed to the stinkers of the whale trade as they tacked up the reaches of the river bound for home ports under the Catskills. In the spring of 1783, Seth and Tom Jenkins, brothers native to Nantucket, left Providence, Rhode Island, with $100,000 in their pockets. They wanted a practical place to locate seagoing folk: it was to be as suitable as Nantucket but less vulnerable. The constant threat of attack by the British Navy had caused islanders many a worrisome night during the past few years and the Jenkinses decided they would lie awake in their beds no more. They had a look at a possible site in Connecticut and almost bought the Henry Rutgers farm on the East river above New York. Colonel Rutgers wanted $200 more than their price and the brothers were willing to split the difference but the colonel was not, and so the searchers went up the Hudson. They liked Poughkeepsie and would have settled there had they not, with Yankee thoroughness, gone farther and seen Claverack Landing. Here was water for boats of any draught and here was a kindly Dutch settlement of busy farmers who needed seafaring neighbors to trade with for mutual profit.

In July Tom and Seth bought land at Claverack and went back to Nantucket. Seth brought his family to the new home almost immediately, arriving in early autumn with his wife, four children, and his mother-in-law. The next spring Tom and all the good New England salt-water folk he and his brother could convert sailed up the Hudson in a fleet unlike any the farmers along the shore had ever seen. The Yankees came in a parade of sturdy whalers that were ready, as soon as they had landed the score of families, to come about and set sail for the South Seas. And to make sure that the time would not be long before they did just that, their owners had brought with them, ready built, the frames of tall, new houses, Nantucket style, soon to stand so close to the placid river that high tide sometimes sent the bowsprit of a moored whale ship crashing through a window. Immediately after these Nantucket, New Bedford, Martha's Vineyard people had landed, they flaxed around and did things. Boats were sent downriver to fill their water casks, for it was already known that Esopus waters not only made the best ale but would not "rope" in the distasteful manner of most fresh water carried on long sea voyages. Then the voyagers left for Hyorky—their name for any far-distant shore—and the men who were left muckled right into building houses, a Quaker meetinghouse, a school, and more whalers. They changed the name of Claverack Landing to Hudson and in less than two years it was an incorporated city with a proud fleet of twenty-five sail on the high seas—more than the big city of New York could boast. The Hudson River whaling business was running before the wind.

Now the Jenkinses, the Paddocks and the Macys, the Bunkers and the Folgers and the Coffins, the same families that made Nantucket an island to be loved and respected, were prospering as they had hoped. Captain Robert Folger returned in the *Hudson* with a stinking cargo of sperm oil for the Jenkins candleworks. Captain Judah Paddock came back with another. Captain Pinkham scudded off to the Falklands after seals and returned with hundreds of hides and a tale of turtle eggs the size of a man's head and turtles so large no man could turn them over. Down off the ways just south of the town slid whaler after whaler—*Liberty, Volunteer* and *American Hero, Juno, Diana* and *Helvetia, Harriet, Huron* and *Namina, Martha Beaver* and *Uncle Toby*—while the band played and cannon roared and everybody— school children, farmers, shopkeepers—cheered themselves hoarse between bites of old Mrs. Newberry's gingerbread. "Greasy luck!" they shouted to the proud captains waving from the decks as they started downriver on their search for whales. Captain Solomon Bunker came back in the *American Hero* with the largest sperm cargo ever brought into the United States. Let Nantucket match that!

The Dutch were doing their part too. At first the newcomers had thought them as odd as huckleberry chowder and made fun of their dialect. But as the store houses filled with ready cargoes of beef and pork and staves and leather and country harvest, the Yankees decided that they had better not try any cornstarch airs. These Dutch fellows understood everything that was said in English and then cooked up their shrewd deals among themselves, jabbering crazy language.

So Hudson grew. In 1790 it became an official seaport with customs officers and government seals, and in 1797 it lost to the upriver town of Albany by only one vote the honor of being the capital of New York State. Within five years it had recovered, however, for on the first day of March, 1802, twenty-eight hundred loaded sleighs entered the city and, as soon as the ice broke in the river, vessels began setting out southward at the rate of around fifteen a day. More boats had been added to the fleet—*Alex Mansfield, Eliza Barker, James Monroe,* and *Edward*. Tom Jenkins bought a gold-headed cane so that he could direct launchings better, and redheaded Squire Worth, who had come to the river country with Tom in 1784, had his portrait painted and scolded the artist for making him look "like a one-story house with the chimney afire."

Then when the young city was bowling along with a fair wind and an even keel a smear blew up. The British declared contraband any ships trading with France and her allies, and Napoleon replied that France would seize any ships entering or leaving a British port. Thomas Jefferson mixed up the whole business further with his embargo act forbidding all commerce with foreign countries.

So tar barrels hung over the mastheads of the Hudson whalers and traders to keep the wood from rotting. Business was struck with the dry wilt and the whole city of Hudson was sunk in the mollygrumps. The sea dogs of the Catskill shore might as well stay home and tend the kitchen halyards.

The War of 1812 did not help matters any—except that Hudsonians were glad they lived a hundred and twenty miles inland and not, like their Nantucket cousins, thirty miles out in an ocean infested by the British. Hudson was shrinking. Its nice proudly boasted limits began to fit like a shirt on a handspike. The Bank of Hudson failed and there was no longer any stir along the wharves. Those farmers who had invested in shipping—and there were many—got no returns. For twenty-five years the upstate whaling trade lay becalmed.

But a man with Nantucket blood in him usually lands on his feet. Around 1830 Captain Laban Paddock, his brother Judah, and some of the other salt-water men decided they had been fooling around long enough and they would go back to whaling. They sent out some boats which returned with hundreds of barrels of oil in the holds. They sailed again, and more ships followed them. One came back with a cargo worth $80,000. That was having your gingerbread cut the right way, said the Paddocks. Hastily they and their associates organized the Hudson Whaling Company. There followed a decade of "greasy luck" and Hudson was a rich and busy city once more.

This time the town did not have the river's whaling trade to itself. Both Poughkeepsie and Newburgh had smelled rich cargo passing their wharves. Newburgh had a whaler on the way to the Pacific in 1832 before the Poughkeepsie Whaling Company was organized "for the purpose of engaging in the whale fisheries in the Atlantic and

Pacific oceans and elsewhere and the manufacture of oil and spermacetti candles." Among the directors of the enterprise were the wealthy brewer, Matthew Vassar—who founded a college; euphoniously named Paraclete Potter, and Alexander J. Coffin (no whaling company could be complete without a Nantucketer). A crowd at the dock cheered lustily and a cannon, booming from a high rock overhead, made the echoes fly back and forth between the October-tinged banks of the Hudson, as the 300-ton *Vermont,* first Poughkeepsie whaler, set sail. Less than a month later the company had bought a second boat, the *Siroc,* and enthusiasm for the trade grew so rapidly that in the following spring Poughkeepsie and Troy businessmen incorporated a rival organization—the Dutchess Whaling Company.

The combined fleets of the four Hudson River companies soon numbered about thirty ships and great quantities of oil were returning to enrich the investors of the valley towns. Captain Norton of the *Vermont* was stabbed by a member of his crew and put ashore at Charles Island in the Galápagos Group where he died; the *Siroc* was wrecked at Valparaiso, Chile; Captain Glasby of the whale ship *Meteor* of Hudson got entangled in the line after harpooning a whale and was dragged overboard and drowned. But oil was still a golden flood along the river front.

More men were needed for crews, and many an upriver farm boy signed on for a voyage to the waters off Hyorky. A smart Harvard College boy named Richard Henry Dana, Jr., working his way on the brig *Pilgrim,* wrote in his journal of a two-year voyage that the *Pilgrim*'s crew had sighted the Poughkeepsie whale ship *New England* off Patagonia and had been honored by a visit from her captain—six-foot, garrulous, Job Terry, "known in every port and by every vessel in the Pacific Ocean." While Terry spun a yarn that lasted through his entire visit, supercilious young Dana looked over the crew that had rowed their captain to the *Pilgrim* and reported them "a pretty raw set just out of the bush" who "hadn't got the hayseed out of their hair." One of them "seemed to care very little about the vessel, rigging or anything else, but went around looking at our livestock and leaned over the pig sty and said he wished he was back tending his father's pigs."

Generally the long-sparred Dutch farm boys made good sailors, though. They learned to eat potato scouse, salt horse, fu-fu, and dandy funk, and to sleep on a "donkey's breakfast" mattress. The Yankees could not fool them more than once by admonishing "Cast hot water and ashes to windward!" The new crew got a little nervous the first time a whale was raised, but it was not long before they could take a Nantucket sleigh ride behind a harpooned whale with the nonchalance of the best of them. On the lee days they carved out scrimshaw for their upriver sweethearts, and shouted "Thar she blows! Thar she white-waters! Thar goes flukes!" on the busy ones. When they returned they sneered at the frosted-cake, gilt-trimmed passenger steamers that passed them on the Hudson and laughed loudly when the villa dwellers on the banks lifted perfumed fingers to aristocratic noses as the whale stench came ashore.

The sailors and the captains and their landlubber employers had the time of their lives for ten years. Sails caught the wind on many seas, because now New York was offering the upriver whalers competition with her sturdy boats—*Autumn, Dawn, Hesper, White Oak, Desdemona, Shibboleth*—but there seemed to be enough business for all.

Then suddenly the bottom dropped out of the whale trade. The great panic of 1837 was much to blame, for all prices dropped to a low level and stayed there. Some of the captains said the upriver businessmen would not put enough money into the trade and that they were too stingy with their pay to officers and hands. The businessmen replied that the river towns were too distant from the whale produce markets and complained because their fleets were crippled for three months every winter when the river was frozen over. Modern inventions began to presage the end of the use of whale oil for illumination.

Whaling died out as a Hudson River industry—but the fascination of far shores remained. The dreamland of Hyorky and the vision of big profits marching in quick-time still enchanted the valley sea dogs. The whaling captains turned traders and their boats knew distant rivers—the Amazon, Congo and Manhissa, the Orinoco, the Plate, and the little streams of the Mosquito Shore. To Catskill, Athens, and New Baltimore, to Peekskill, Hudson, and Poughkeepsie, to Newburgh, Kingston, and Marlboro the sloops and schooners of the

Hudson brought rich cargo—ostrich feathers and elephant bone, tortoise shell and ebony, gold dust, rum, and Spanish dollars.

And with almost every voyage came a new tale of adventure in Hyorky. Sometimes the captain wrote down the story for his neighbors to marvel at. The York State seamen apparently were a little more articulate than the New Englanders, for there are a number of printed "narratives," probably more per capita than the Yankees can boast. Newspaper accounts, taken from the lips of survivors, provided other evidences of the tough fiber and unflinching courage of the boys from the river farms and towns. These melodramas of the sea are still told beside the river, in the slatches of bright spring weather before the sun gets too hot, by old men who had them from their fathers and their grandfathers. Not so long ago Hudson folks buried an old-timer who remembered the fine solemn funeral of a young Hudson naval lieutenant, whose body was brought to his home town five years after he was killed fighting pirates of the Windward Passage. And there are many men in the valley today whose grandfathers recalled a taciturn old man, Captain Benjamin Lawrence, who once commanded the whale ship *Huron* out of Hudson. When he was only a boy he had been a boat steerer on the tragic 1819 voyage of the *Essex* out of Nantucket. Captain Lawrence was so silent, they say, because most of the time he couldn't forget the open boat, the starving and the thirsting, the day that Isaac Cole went mad and died, or the next day when they cooked and ate him.

These and many other Hudson River stories speak of strength and endurance. They tell of foreign places but they also have something to say about the kind of people who once lived in the valley.

Carl Carmer, *The Hudson* (New York: Farrar & Rinehart, 1939).

RIVERSIDE SHAKESPEARE

Mrs. Anne Grant

ONE OF THE MOST *treasured books of colonial literature from the Hudson Valley, along with Crèvecoeur's* Letters from an American Farmer, *is Mrs. Anne Grant's (1755–1838)* Memoirs of an American Lady. *Born in Glasgow Anne MacVicar, the daughter of a Highland regiment officer, came to Albany with her father as a child, and lived for several years with Philip Schuyler and his wife as part of their family.* Memoirs *was written when the author was fifty-two, decades after she had returned to Scotland as a young teenager. But her autobiographical work has all the freshness and wide-eyed attention of a visitor's experiences in a foreign land, untempered by received opinion.*

There are descriptions of the thunderous breaking up of the ice on the Hudson in the spring, winter amusements in the city, the customs of the Indians, and daily life of the townspeople. She tells of her years at The Flats, the Schuyler home outside of town, her relationship with the lady of the house, its special occasions and rural economy. In a frequently cited passage, Mrs. Grant gives an account of the "unseemly ornaments" represented by the skeleton heads of horses and cattle attached to the fence posts near the Schuyler's house to serve as birds' nests. Her writing is so generous a recreation of the pre-Revolutionary world of Albany that Hudson Valley author James Kirke Paulding credited it as the source for his own The Dutchman's Fireside, *calling her book "one of the finest sketches of early American manners ever drawn."*

Mrs. Grant was to write much more in her long life. She lived to be eighty-three and had twelve children. A friend of Sir Walter Scott's, she wrote poetry, the popular Letters from the Mountains, *translated from the Gaelic, and specialized in Highland culture, firmly establishing herself in Scottish literary circles. The selection of* Memoirs *included here gives a marvelous sense of its enduring charm and girlish humor, with the added pleasure of having revealed an eighteenth-century child's circumvention of parental strictures on the reading of plays.*

I BROUGHT OUT SOME volumes of Shakespeare with me, and remembering the prohibition of reading plays promulgated the former winter, was much at a loss how to proceed. I thought rightly that it was owing to a temporary fit of spleen. But then I knew my father was, like all military men, tenacious of his authority, and would possibly continue it merely because he had once said so. I recollected that he said he would have no plays brought to the house; and that I read them unchecked at Madame's, who was my model in all things. It so happened that the river had been higher than usual that spring, and, in consequence, exhibited a succession of very amusing scenes. The settlers, whose increase above towards Stillwater had been for three years past incredibly great, set up saw-mills on every stream, for the purpose of turning to account the fine timber which they cleared in great quantities off the new lands. The planks they drew in sledges to the side of the great river; and when the season arrived that swelled the stream to its greatest height, a whole neighborhood assembled, and made their joint stock into a large raft, which was floated down the river with a man or two on it, who with long poles were always ready to steer it clear of those islands or shallows which might impede its course. There is something serenely majestic in the easy progress of those large bodies on the full stream of this copious river. Sometimes one sees a whole family transported on this simple conveyance; the mother calmly spinning, the children sporting about her, and the father fishing on one end, and watching its safety at the same time. These rafts were taken down to Albany, and put on board vessels there, for conveyance to New York; sometimes, however, it happened that, as they proceeded very slowly, dry weather came on by the time they reached the Flats, and it became impossible to carry them further; in that case they were deposited in great triangular piles opposite our door. One of these, which was larger than ordinary, I selected for a reading closet. There I safely lodged my Shakespeare; and there in my play hours I went to read it undisturbed, with the advantage of fresh air, a cool shade, and a full view of the road on one side, and a beautiful river on the other. While I enjoyed undisturbed privacy, I had the prohibition full in my mind, but thought I should keep to the spirit of it by only reading the historical plays, comforting myself that they were true. These I read over and over with pleasure ever new; it was quite in my way, for I was familiarly acquainted with the English history; now, indeed, I began to relish Shakespeare, and to be astonished at my former blindness to his beauties. The contention of the rival roses occupied all my thoughts, and broke my rest. "Wind-changing Warwick" did not change oftener than I, but at length my compassion for holy Henry, and hatred to Richard, fixed me a Lancastrian. I began to wonder how any body could exist without reading Shakespeare, and at length resolved, at all risks, to make my father a sharer in my new found felicity. Of the nature of taste I had not the least idea; so far otherwise, that I was continually revolving benevolent plans to distribute some of the poetry I most delighted in among the Bezalees and Habakkuks, of the twenty mile line. I thought this would make them happy as myself, and that when they once felt the charm of "musical delight," the harsh language of contention would cease, and legal quibbling give way before the spirit of harmony. How often did I repeat Thompson's description of the golden age, concluding,

"For music held the whole in perfect peace."

At home, however, I was in some degree successful. My father did begin to take some interest in the roses, and I was happy, yet kept both my secret and my closet, and made more and more advances in the study of these "wood notes wild." *As You Like It,* and the *Midsummer Night's Dream* enchanted me; and I thought the comfort of my closet so great, that I dreaded nothing so much as a flood, that should occasion its being once more set in motion. I was one day deeply engaged in compassionating Othello, sitting on a plank, added on the outside of the pile for strengthening it, when happening to lift my eyes, I saw a long serpent, on the same board, at my elbow, in a threatening attitude, with its head lifted up. Othello and I ran off together with all imaginable speed; and as that particular kind of snake seldom approaches any person, unless the abode of its young is invaded, I began to fear I had been studying Shakespeare in a nest of serpents. Our faithful servant examined the place at my request. Under the very board on which I sat, when terrified by this unwished associate, was found a nest with seven eggs. After being most thankful for my escape, the next thing was to admire the patience and good humor of the mother of this family, who permitted such a being as myself so long to share her haunt with impunity. Indeed, the rural pleasures of this country were always liable to those drawbacks; and this place was peculiarly infested with the familiar garter-snake, because the ruins of the burnt house afforded shelter and safety to these reptiles.

Mrs. Anne Grant, *Memoirs of an American Lady* (Albany: Joel Munsell, 1876).

SKETCHING THE HUDSON

Benson Lossing

BORN AT BEEKMAN *in Dutchess county, Benson Lossing (1813–91) descended from the earliest Dutch settlers in the Hudson Valley. As a young man he edited the* Poughkeepsie Telegraph, *the leading weekly of the area, and soon learned wood engraving, before embarking on a career in New York City that would combine writing and illustrating books, and articles for magazines such as* Harper's Weekly. *Later he served on the original Board of Trustees at Vassar College, founded in Poughkeepsie by another of its residents, Matthew Vassar.*

The author of more than forty works, Lossing became one of the most respected popular historians in the second half of the nineteenth century, known especially for his pictorial field books on the American Revolution, the Civil War, and the War of 1812. He also wrote biographies of George Washington and James Garfield, a history of fine arts, and a history of the United States.

Lossing didn't neglect his home state, writing not only a history of New York but of New York City, too. His work on the Hudson Valley is chiefly The Hudson, From the Wilderness to the Sea, *a beautifully illustrated "narrative sketchbook" with over three hundred wood engravings by him, originally prepared for a London publication in 1860–61. In 1859 Lossing, his wife and a friend made their journey by rail and steamboat, starting at the head waters of the Hudson in the Adirondacks and traveling all the way to Sandy Hook, New Jersey, where the Hudson meets the Atlantic ocean. Lossing's pen and pencil sketches are linked to a run-*

67

ning commentary on local color and customs, flora and fauna, transportation, sports, industry, people, folklore, and of course, history, offering a fascinating perspective, both literary and visual, on the Hudson at mid-century.

૪૯

ON THE FOLLOWING MORNING, when the sun had climbed high towards meridian, I left Peek's Kill for a day's sketching and observation in the winter air. The bay was alive with people of all ages, sexes, and conditions. It was the first day since a late snow-storm that the river had offered good sport for skaters, and the navigators of ice-boats.* It was a gay scene. Wrapped in furs and shawls, over-coats and cloaks, men and women, boys and girls, were enjoying the rare exercise with the greatest pleasure. Fun, pure fun, ruled the hour. The air was vocal with shouts and laughter; and when the swift ice-boat, with sails set, gay pennon streaming, and freighted with a dozen boys and girls, came sweeping gracefully towards the crowd,—after making a comet-like orbit of four or five miles to the feet of the Doner Berg, Bear Mountain, and Anthony's Nose,—there was a sudden shout, and scattering, and merry laughter, that would have made old Scrooge, even before his conversion, tremulous with delight, and glowing with desires to be a boy again and singing Christmas Carols with a hearty good-will. I played the boy with the rest for awhile, and then, with long strides upon skates, my satchel with portfolio slung over my shoulder, I bore away towards the great lime-kilns on the shores of Tomkins's Cove, on the western side of the river, four or five miles below.

On my way to Tomkins's Cove I encountered other groups of

---

*The ice-boats are of various forms of construction. Usually a strong wooden triangular platform is placed upon three sled-runners, having skate-irons on their bottoms. The rear runner is worked on a pivot or hinge, by a tiller attached to a post that passes up through the platform, and thereby the boat is steered. The sails and rigging are similar to the common large sail-boat. The passengers sit flat upon the platform, and with a good wind are moved rapidly over the ice, oftentimes at the rate of a mile in a minute.

people, who appeared in positive contrast with the merry skaters on Peek's Kill Bay. They were sober, thoughtful, winter fishermen, thickly scattered over the surface, and drawing their long nets from narrow fissures which they had cut in the ice. The tide was "serving," and many a striped bass, and white perch, and infant sturgeon at times, were drawn out of their warmer element to be instantly congealed in the keen wintry air.

These fishermen often find their calling almost as profitable in winter as in April and May, when they draw "schools" of shad from the deep. They generally have a "catch" twice a day when the tide is "slack," their nets being filled when it is ebbing or flowing. They cut fissures in the ice, at right angles with the direction of the tidal currents, eight or ten yards in length, and about two feet in width, into which they drop their nets, sink them with weights, and stretching them to their utmost length, suspend them by sticks that lie across the fissure. Baskets, boxes on hand-sledges, and sometimes sledges drawn by a horse, are used in carrying the "catch" to land. Lower down the river, in the vicinity of the Palisades, when the strength of the ice will allow this kind of fishing, bass weighing from thirty to forty pounds each are frequently caught. These winter fisheries extend from the Donder Berg to Piermont, a distance of about twenty-five miles.

I went on shore at the ruins of an old lime-kiln at the upper edge of Tomkins's Cove, and sketched the fishermen in the distance toward Peek's Kill. It was a tedious task, and, with benumbed fingers, I hastened to the office and store of the Tomkins Lime Company to seek warmth and information. With Mr. Searing, one of the proprietors, I visited the kilns. They are the most extensive works of the kind on the Hudson. They are at the foot of an immense cliff of limestone, nearly 200 feet in height, immediately behind the kilns, and extend more than half a mile along the river.* The kilns were numerous, and

---

*This deposit of limestone occupies a superficial area of nearly 600 acres, extending in the rear of Stony and Grassy Points, where it disappears beneath the red sandstone formation. It is traversed by white veins of carbonate of lime. In 1837 Mr. Tomkins purchased 20 acres of land covering this limestone bed for 100 dollars an acre, then considered a very extravagant price. The stratum where they are now quarrying is at least 500 feet in thickness. It is estimated that an acre of this limestone, worked down to the water level, will yield 600,000 barrels of lime, upon which a mean profit of 25 cents a barrel is the minimum. Some of this limestone is black and variegated, and makes pleasing ornamental marbles. Most of it is blue.

in their management, and the quarrying of the limestone, about 100 men were continually employed. I saw them on the brow of the wooded cliff, loosening huge masses and sending them below, while others were engaged in blasting, and others again in wheeling the lime from the vents of the kilns to heaps in front, where it is slaked before being placed in vessels for transportation to market. This is a necessary precaution against spontaneous combustion. Many vessels are employed in carrying away lime, limestone, and "gravel" (pulverized limestone, not fit for the kiln) from Tomkins's Cove, for whose accommodation several small wharves have been constructed.

One million bushels of lime were produced at the kilns each year. From the quarries, thousands of tons of the stone were sent annually to kilns in New Jersey. From 20,000 to 25,000 tons of the "gravel" were used each year in the construction of macadamised roads. The quarry had been worked almost twenty-five years. From small beginnings the establishment had grown to a very extensive one. The dwelling of the chief proprietor was upon the hill above the kiln at the upper side of the cove; and near the water the houses of the workmen form a pleasant little village. The country behind, for many miles, is very wild, and almost uncultivated.

I followed a narrow road along the bank of the river, to the extreme southern verge of the limestone cliff, near Stony Point, and there sketched that famous, bold, rocky peninsula from the best spot where a view of its entire length may be obtained. The whole Point is a mass of granite rock, with patches of evergreen trees and shrubs, excepting on its northern side where may be seen a black cliff of magnetic iron ore. It is too limited in quantity to tempt labour or capital to quarry it, and the granite is too much broken to be very desirable for building purposes. So that peninsula, clustered with historic associations, will ever remain almost unchanged in form and feature. A lighthouse, a keeper's lodge, and a fog-bell, occupy its summit. These stand upon and within the mounds that mark the site of the old fort which was built there at the beginning of the war for independence.

———
Benson Lossing, *The Hudson, From the Wilderness to the Sea* (New York: Virtue & Yorston, 1866).

LIBERTYMEN'S DECLARATION
OF INDEPENDENCE

T HE HISTORY of the anti-rent wars that brought
turmoil to the great manors in the middle of the nineteenth century
are much less familiar than the "natural" histories of the Hudson
River School, which in those years celebrated the munificence of
the same lands. But the death of Stephen van Rensselaer in 1839
paved the way for the end of the patroonship system, and the
manors were never the same again. Tenant farmers owed to the
van Rensselaers in perpetuity a rent of up to 14 bushels of wheat
for every 100 acres, plus a day's work and several fowl. On the
Livingston Manor the freehold of a tenant lasted two lives, under
the Schuylers three. There had been periodic anti-rent resistance for
decades, dating from before the American Revolution, especially
on the Livingston, Philipsburg, and Cortlandt manors.

Now in the 1840s the anti-renters were more organized, bolder,
and politically astute. The mood of the country also leaned toward
social reform in the years before the Civil War. The anti-rent
movement, aligned with the Whig Party in New York, helped
elect favored candidates at the local and county level, and held
its own conventions. Members published their own newspapers,
which included the Anti-Renter and Guardian of the Soil, and songs,
broadsides, and handbills, such as the one printed here, promoted
their cause. Martin Van Buren and Horace Greeley were on their
side. Anti-rent dramas imported from Britain were performed
on steamboats traveling the Hudson. On the opposing side, there
were the pro-landlord novels Satanstoe, The Chainbearer, and

71

The Redskins *by James Fenimore Cooper, and Anya Seton's* Dragon-wyck.

Between 1845 and the early years of the next decade violence and upheaval spread on both sides of the Hudson, leading to attacks on sheriffs, the tarring and feathering of opponents, with-holding of rents, and the general disruption of leaseholding pay-ments. The Helderberghs and parts of Schoharie and Delaware counties were particularly active in the fighting, and on the other side of the Hudson, Rensselaer and Columbia counties.

By the decade of the Civil War, land reform had come to the Hudson Valley. The landholders grew weary of court battles, violence, and increased taxes, and they started selling off their lands. Even by 1850 Livingston Manor retained only 35,000 acres of its original 160,000. It is generally believed that the early lack of development of Hudson Valley resources was due to this system, which prompted farmers to move to free lands in other parts of the country.

Perhaps the most dramatic events of the period were provided by the anti-renters who dressed as Indians in deference to the ideals of the Boston Tea Party, and those of the country's indigenous peoples. Men dressed up in Calico smocks and wore sheepskin masks, or painted their faces. Their weapons were pitchforks, pistols, scythes, knives. Tin horns sounded the call to arms. Dr. Smith A. Boughton from Alps was the colorful leader "Big Thunder."

Every year on the Fourth of July in the hamlet of Hoag's Cor-ners the residents, led by Philip Lord, an anthropologist at the New York State Museum, stage Big Thunder Day. The re-enactment of events from the anti-rent years joins the many historical pag-eants around the United States that help to preserve local history and a growing regional consciousness. In this one the Rensselaer county sheriff plays himself.

🜋

WHEREAS, Nobility and Lordships cannot constitutionally exist in the United States of America; and that Patroonry, i.e. Aristocracy, is repugnant to Democratic Republican principles; and that it is constitutionally unlawful in the United States to collect PATROON RENT by force, under any patroon authority or pretence whatever: WE therefore publicly, solemnly and unitedly declare ourselves Free and Independent from, and not under the control of, *patroonry*—relying on the JUSTICE OF OUR CAUSE, and the RULER OF WORLDS, and the LAWS OF OUR COUNTRY, for protection.

Resolved, That in all cases when lands are held for a longer term than twenty years, by lease, conditioned for the payment of annual rent, all persons claiming such annual rent shall establish the validity of their titles, before any of the conditions of such lease shall be enforced by law.

Resolved, That this act shall take effect immediately.

County of Rensselaer, State of New-York, }
  June 8, 1844.

       SETH LEONARD,
       MARLOW COON,
       LEONARD KNOWLTON

 Adopted unanimously by the RENSSELAER COUNTY LIBERTYMEN'S ASSOCIATION.

Libertymen's Declaration of Independence, Manuscripts and Special Collections, New York State Library, Albany, N.Y.

AN ACT FOR
REGULATING OF SLAVES

The Duke's Laws

L*ESS THAN TWO decades after Henry Hudson sailed
into the river that now bears his name, and at the beginning
of the patroonships, the Dutch were importing slaves into New
Netherland. Involved in the slave trade since the early seventeenth
century, they preferred "seasoned" slaves from their own colony of
Curaçao rather than those from Africa. Slaves were needed to
make up for the chronic labor shortage in New Netherland, to work
on farms, in building construction, and for domestic service. Among
the slaves there were also skilled craftsmen. The Dutch even gave
arms to their slaves when they needed help in fighting the Indians
in the wars of the 1640s under Governor-General Willem Kieft. By
the next century slaves worked in the mills and foundries of
the wealthy landowners, at Livingston Manor, Rensselaerswyck,
Philipsburg.*

*The Dutch, who at this time had no slavery at home, made no
formal laws concerning the slaves. Under regular Dutch colonial law slaves were sometimes given "half freedom" but had to
pay a yearly sum to the West India Company. Some were released after long service. Freed slaves were allowed to own property, take part in the legal system, and to marry in the Dutch
Reformed Church. White indentured servants and slaves had the same
rights.*

*It was under British rule that treatment of the slaves grew harsher
and more circumscribed, with laws founded on racial distinctions. When the English forced the Dutch out of New Netherland in*

74

1664, slaves constituted about 10 percent of the population, which was also more culturally diverse than any other North American colony. At least eighteen languages were reportedly spoken around New Amsterdam (Manhattan) at that time.

A year after their takeover, the English introduced the first English laws into the colony in the form of the Duke's Laws, named for the Duke of York who was given Long Island and New York by his brother the King, Charles II. Legislation regarding slavery dates from the 1702 act shown here, though other, tougher laws would be enacted later, particularly in response to slave revolts in the decades to follow. The alleged "Negro Plot of 1741" in Manhattan was the most threatening to the British. When the 1702 law was enacted there were about 18,280 whites and 2,385 blacks in the colony. Slavery continued to be legal even after the American Revolution, in which blacks, like the Indians, fought on both sides of the conflict. A recent study by A. J. Williams-Meyers, who heads the African-American Studies Department at SUNY—New Paltz, concludes that in 1790 the city of Albany had 572 slaves in a population of almost 3,500; in Dutchess county slaves made up 4.1 percent, in Ulster county close to 10 percent. There were repeated attempts by the New York Legislature to approve bills that would free the slaves, but it wasn't until 1827 that slavery came to an end in New York State, and only in 1870, under the Fifteenth Amendment to the Constitution, did blacks receive the unrestricted right to vote.

The Duke's Laws, Passed, November 27, 1702

BE IT ENACTED BY his Excell'cy the Governour and Council and Representatives conven'd in General Assembly, and by authority of the same, that no Person or Persons hereafter throughout this Province, do presume to Trade with any slave either in buying or selling, w'th'out leave and Consent of the Master or Mistress, on penalty of forfeiting Treble the value of the thing traded for, and the

sume of five pounds Current money of New York, to the Master or
Mistress of such slave. . . .

And be it further Enacted by the authority aforesaid, That hereafter it shall and may be lawful for any Master or Mistress of slaves to
punish their slaves for their Crimes and offences at Discretion, not
extending to life or Member. And for as much as the Number of
slaves in the City of New York and Albany, and also in other Towns
within this Province, doth daily increase, and that they have been
found oftentimes guilty of Confederating together in running away,
or other ill practices, Be it therefore Enacted by the authority
aforesaid, That it shall not hereafter be lawful for above three Slaves
to meet together at any other time, nor at any other place, than when
it shall happen they meet in some servile Imploym't for their Master's
or Mistress's profit, and by their Master or Mistress consent, upon
penalty of being whipt upon the naked back, at discretion of any
Justice of the peace, not exceeding forty Lashes. And that it shall and
may be lawful hereafter for any City or Town within this Province; to
have and appoint a Comon Whipper for their slaves, And for this
salary, it shall and may be lawful for any City or Town within this
Province, at their Comon Council or Town meeting, to agree upon
such sum to be paid him by the Master or Mistress of slaves per head,
as they shall think fit, not exceeding three shillings Per head, for all
such slaves as shall be whipt, as aforesaid.

And in Case any slave presume to assault or strike any freeman or
Woman professing Christianity, it shall be in the power of any two
Justices of the peace, who by this Act are thereunto authorized, to
Comit such slave to Prison, not exceeding fourteen days for one
fact, and to inflict such other Corporal punishm't (not extending to
life or limb) upon him, her, or them so offending, as to the said
Justices shall seem meet and reasonable.

And be it further Enacted by the authority aforesaid, That no
person or persons whatsoever do hereafter Imploy, harbour, Conceal,
or entertain other mens slaves at their house, out-house or Plantation,
w'thout the Consent of their Master or Mistress either signifyed to
them verbally or by Certificate in writing, under the Said Master or
Mistress hand, upon forfeiture of five pounds for every night or day,
to the Master or Mistress of such slave or slaves, So that the penalty

do not excuse the value of Said slave; and if any person or persons whatsoever shall be found guilty of harbouring, entertaining or Concealing of any slave, or assisting to the Conveying of them away, if such slave shall thereupon be lost, dead, or otherwise destroyed, such person or persons So harbouring, entertaining, concealing, assisting or Conveying of them away, shall be also lyable to pay the value of Such slave to the Master or Mistress, to be recovered by action of debt, in manner aforesaid. And Whereas slaves are the property of Christians, and cannot without great loss or detriment to their Masters or Mistresses, be subjected in all Cases criminal, to the strict Rules of the Laws of England, Be it Enacted by the Authority aforesaid, That hereafter if any slave by Theft or other Trespass shall damnifie any person or persons to the value of five pounds, or under, the Master or Mistress of such slave shall be lyable to make satisfaction for such damage to the party injured, to be recovered by action of Debt in any Court having Jurisdiction and Cognizance of Pleas to that value, and the slave shall receive Corporal Punishment, at Discretion of a Justice of the peace, and immediately thereafter be permitted to attend his or her Master or Mistress service, without further punishment. And it is further Enacted by the authority aforesaid, That hereafter no slave shall be allowed good evidence in any matter, Cause or thing whatsoever, excepting in Cases of Plotting or Confederacy amongst themselves, either to run away, kill or destroy their Master or Mistress, or burning of houses, or barnes or barracks of Corn, or the killing of their Master's or Mistress's Cattle and that against one another, in which Case the Evidence of one slave shall be allowed good against another slave.

Colonial Laws of New York, Vol. 1 (Albany: James B. Lyon, 1894).

THE FEDERALIST, No. 1

Alexander Hamilton

F*ROM THE TIME of young manhood, Alexander Hamilton (1757–1804) exhibited the intellectual passion and daring that would allow him as a founding father to make an enormous contribution to the shaping of American government. Born in the British West Indies, he was sent to study at King's College (now Columbia University), then fought in the Revolutionary War campaigns on Long Island, and at Trenton and Princeton. In his twenties, he became an aide-de-camp to George Washington. Hamilton left the army after the Yorktown siege, and within a year's time became a lawyer. He had already married into one of the prominent New York families with his 1780 wedding to Elizabeth Schuyler at The Pastures, General Philip Schuyler's mansion in Albany.*

Hamilton became active in the political affairs of his day, first as a New York delegate to the Continental Congress, then later at the Philadelphia convention when the new Constitution was proposed, in September 1787. That fall many articles criticizing the Constitution were printed in the New York papers. In response, and taking the pen name "Publius," Hamilton wrote the first essay, included here, of what came to be collected as The Federalist *papers, on the way to New York City in his sloop cabin. Addressed to the people of New York State, it was published in* The Independent Journal *on October 27, 1787.*

In all, eighty-five essays were eventually published, about two-thirds of them written by Hamilton, the others by James Madison

78

*and John Jay. Seventy-seven appeared in the New York papers in
1787–88. One of the great documents in American political
philosophy, these essays urged the adoption of the Constitution in
carefully reasoned analyses of the structure and necessity of
strong centralized government. Some of the issues discussed were
checks and balances provided by a separation of powers, Congress, national security, the scope of the presidency, and states' rights.
Thomas Jefferson called* The Federalist *"the best commentary
on the principles of government which has ever been written."*

*Ten states had already voted for the Constitution before New
York, and Madison's home state of Virginia, did so. The state
convention meetings were held June 17 to July 26, 1788, in
Poughkeepsie, which had been acting as the state capital since
the British burned Kingston in 1777. Governor George Clinton led
the fight against the proposed Constitution, with a group of
anti-Federalists who far outnumbered the Federalists. In this minority camp were the delegates from New York City who included
John Jay, Robert R. Livingston, Isaac Roosevelt, and Hamilton. In a
series of brilliant speeches Hamilton finally persuaded the sixty-
five delegates to ratify the Constitution.*

*When George Washington became president in 1789, he chose
Hamilton, who would later draft Washington's "Farewell Address,"
as the first Secretary of the Treasury. Having already founded The
Bank of New York, Hamilton set about putting the capitalist
system in place and arguing for greater presidential powers, coming into conflict with Secretary of State Jefferson, who was skeptical of an overbearing Federal authority and disliked the political
alliances of bankers and big business as threats to his agrarian philosophy. Nonetheless, Hamilton would help Jefferson defeat
Aaron Burr for the presidency in 1801. Three years later, in a
continuing political feud, Vice President Burr killed the gifted
Hamilton in a duel at Weehawken, New Jersey. He was forty-
eight years old.*

To the People of the State of New York:

After an unequivocal experience of the inefficiency of the subsisting federal government, you are called upon to deliberate on a new Constitution for the United States of America. The subject speaks its own importance; comprehending in its consequences nothing less than the existence of the UNION, the safety and welfare of the parts of which it is composed, the fate of an empire in many respects the most interesting in the world. It has been frequently remarked that it seems to have been reserved to the people of this country, by their conduct and example, to decide the important question, whether societies of men are really capable or not of establishing good government from reflection and choice, or whether they are forever destined to depend for their political constitutions on accident and force. If there be any truth in the remark, the crisis at which we are arrived may with propriety be regarded as the era in which that decision is to be made; and a wrong election of the part we shall act may, in this view, deserve to be considered as the general misfortune of mankind.

This idea will add the inducements of philanthropy to those of patriotism, to heighten the solicitude which all considerate and good men must feel for the event. Happy will it be if our choice should be directed by a judicious estimate of our true interests, unperplexed and unbiassed by considerations not connected with the public good. But this is a thing more ardently to be wished than seriously to be expected. The plan offered to our deliberations affects too many particular interests, innovates upon too many local institutions, not to involve in its discussion a variety of objects foreign to its merits, and of views, passions and prejudices little favorable to the discovery of truth.

Among the most formidable of the obstacles which the new Constitution will have to encounter may readily be distinguished the obvious interest of a certain class of men in every State to resist all changes which may hazard a diminution of the power, emolument, and consequence of the offices they hold under the State establishments; and the perverted ambition of another class of men, who will either hope to aggrandize themselves by the confusions of their country, or will flatter themselves with fairer prospects of elevation from the subdivision of the empire into several partial confederacies than from its union under one government.

It is not, however, my design to dwell upon observations of this nature. I am well aware that it would be disingenuous to resolve indiscriminately the opposition of any set of men (merely because their situations might subject them to suspicion) into interested or ambitious views. Candor will oblige us to admit that even such men may be actuated by upright intentions; and it cannot be doubted that much of the opposition which has made its appearance, or may hereafter make its appearance, will spring from sources, blameless at least, if not respectable—the honest errors of minds led astray by preconceived jealousies and fears. So numerous indeed and so powerful are the causes which serve to give a false bias to the judgment, that we, upon many occasions, see wise and good men on the wrong as well as on the right side of questions of the first magnitude to society. This circumstance, if duly attended to, would furnish a lesson of moderation to those who are ever so much persuaded of their being in the right in any controversy. And a further reason for caution, in this respect, might be drawn from the reflection that we are not always sure that those who advocate the truth are influenced by purer principles than their antagonists. Ambition, avarice, personal animosity, party opposition, and many other motives not more laudable than these, are apt to operate as well upon those who support as those who oppose the right side of a question. Were there not even these inducements to moderation, nothing could be more ill-judged than that intolerant spirit which has, at all times, characterized political parties. For in politics, as in religion, it is equally absurd to aim at making proselytes by fire and sword. Heresies in either can rarely be cured by persecution.

And yet, however just these sentiments will be allowed to be, we have already sufficient indications that it will happen in this as in all former cases of great national discussion. A torrent of angry and malignant passions will be let loose. To judge from the conduct of the opposite parties, we shall be led to conclude that they will mutually hope to evince the justness of their opinions, and to increase the number of their converts by the loudness of their declamations and the bitterness of their invectives. An enlightened zeal for the energy and efficiency of government will be stigmatized as the offspring of a temper fond of despotic power and hostile to the principles of liberty. An over-scrupulous jealousy of danger to the rights of the people, which is more commonly the fault of the head than of the heart, will be represented as mere pretence and artifice, the stale bait for popularity at the expense of the public good. It will be forgotten, on the one hand, that jealousy is the usual concomitant of love, and that the noble enthusiasm of liberty is apt to be infected with a spirit of narrow and illiberal distrust. On the other hand, it will be equally forgotten that the vigor of government is essential to the security of liberty; that, in the contemplation of a sound and well-informed judgment, their interest can never be separated; and that a dangerous ambition more often lurks behind the specious mask of zeal for the rights of the people than under the forbidding appearance of zeal for the firmness and efficiency of government. History will teach us that the former has been found a much more certain road to the introduction of despotism than the latter, and that of those men who have overturned the liberties of republics, the greatest number have begun their career by paying an obsequious court to the people; commencing demagogues, and ending tyrants.

In the course of the preceding observations, I have had an eye, my fellow-citizens, to putting you upon your guard against all attempts, from whatever quarter, to influence your decision in a matter of the utmost moment to your welfare, by any impressions other than those which may result from the evidence of truth. You will, no doubt, at the same time, have collected from the general scope of them, that they proceed from a source not unfriendly to the new Constitution. Yes, my countrymen, I own to you that, after having given it an attentive consideration, I am clearly of opinion it is your interest to adopt it. I am convinced that this is the safest course for your liberty, your dignity, and your happiness. I affect not reserves which I do not feel. I will not amuse you with an appearance of deliberation when I have decided. I frankly acknowledge to you my convictions, and I will freely lay before you the reasons on which they are founded. The consciousness of good intentions disdains ambiguity. I shall not, however, multiply professions on this head. My motives must remain in the depository of my own breast. My arguments will be open to all, and may be judged of by all. They shall at least be offered in a spirit which will not disgrace the cause of truth.

I propose, in a series of papers, to discuss the following interesting particulars:—*The utility of the UNION to your political prosperity*— *The insufficiency of the present Confederation to preserve that Union*— *The necessity of a government at least equally energetic with the one proposed, to the attainment of this object*—*The conformity of the proposed Constitution to the true principles of republican government*— *Its analogy to your own State constitution*—and lastly, *The additional security which its adoption will afford to the preservation of that species of government, to liberty, and to property.*

In the progress of this discussion I shall endeavor to give a satisfactory answer to all the objections which shall have made their appearance, that may seem to have any claim to your attention.

It may perhaps be thought superfluous to offer arguments to prove the utility of the UNION, a point, no doubt, deeply engraved on the hearts of the great body of the people in every State, and one, which it may be imagined, has no adversaries. But the fact is, that we already hear it whispered in the private circles of those who oppose the new Constitution, that the thirteen States are of too great extent for any general system, and that we must of necessity resort to separate confederacies of distinct portions of the whole. This doctrine will, in all probability, be gradually propagated, till it has votaries enough to countenance an open avowal of it. For nothing can be more evident, to those who are able to take an enlarged view of the subject, than the alternative of an adoption of the new Constitution or a dismemberment of the Union. It will therefore be of use to begin by examining the advantages of that Union, the certain evils, and the probable dangers, to which every State will be exposed from its dissolution. This shall accordingly constitute the subject of my next address. Publius

The Federalist, ed. by Henry Cabot Lodge (New York: G.P. Putnam's Sons, 1888).

THE NORTH RIVER STEAM BOAT

Robert Fulton

O*N AUGUST 17, 1807, the first steamboat took a trip up the Hudson from New York City to Albany under a full moon. Traveling about four and a half miles per hour,* The Steamboat, *as it was called (though others referred to it as "Fulton's Folly") stopped at Clermont, the Hudson Valley seat of Robert R. Livingston, who was the partner of Robert Fulton (1765–1815) in this revolutionary enterprise. The 110-mile trip took twenty-four hours. Picking up Livingston and other passengers, it went on to Albany, then shortly returned to New York in thirty hours, at five miles per hour. Sloop captains sensed a real threat to their livelihood. The press barely noticed the event. Before long the newly named* North River Steam Boat *(it was later known as* The Clermont, *though not in Fulton's lifetime) started offering tickets to the public between Manhattan and Albany for $7, round trip. The partners in this business venture secured a monopoly on steam vessel travel that was to last almost twenty years, until it was declared unconstitutional by the courts.*

Robert Fulton and Robert R. Livingston, who was then Minister to France, and a member of one of the powerful, wealthy families of the Hudson Valley, met in Paris at the beginning of the nineteenth century. Livingston, who as Chancellor of New York State administered the oath of office to George Washington, held a seat on the committee that drafted the Declaration of Independence, and later negotiated the Louisiana Purchase. He also had an amateur interest in mechanics and as early as the 1790s had backed

84

*failed experiments with steamboat design. Fulton had gone abroad
to study painting with the successful artist Benjamin West. But
in England and France he also became infatuated with mechanical inventions, and it is for his achievements and ideas in canal navigation, submarine experiments, the construction of bombs
and torpedoes, and, finally, steam power that Fulton found a
place in American history. He married one of the Livingston
women and lived for a time at the Columbia county estate
Teviotdale.* Robert Fulton, *a new biography by Cynthia Owen Philip,
amply chronicles his technological brilliance.*

When The Steam Boat *made its first voyage up the Hudson, the
same trip took a week to ten days by sloop, depending on weather and tide conditions. But by 1807 New York had supplanted Philadelphia as the commercial capital of America, which had doubled in size with the Louisiana Purchase. The successful Lewis and
Clark expedition forged a transcontinental route. Young Fulton
was bursting with the combination of engineering skill and entrepreneurial spirit that the expanding nation under Thomas Jefferson
demanded. It was somewhat of a historical coup that steamboat
travel was inaugurated on the Hudson rather than on the more
commercialized and larger Mississippi River, which was also considered for the experiment. Unavoidably, the steamboat supplanted
the romantic Hudson River sloop, bringing noise, pollution, crowds,
and commerce in ever-greater numbers to the Valley, to the cha-
grin of many, and the profit of even more. But the memory of well-
fitted boats like the* Mary Powell, Washington Irving, *and* Albany
*still evoke a lost world of languid time and elegance not likely to
be seen again.*

Robert Fulton to Robert R. Livingston

Paris, June 13, 1802

Sir

I wrote you on the 5th of June. I have now some further

observations to make. If the communication between New York and Albany is equal to 100 passengers a day I can carry each person at the expense of about 25 cents. That I believe is one quarter of a dollar and run 12 miles, making the voyage which if I recollect right is 140 miles, in about 13 or 14 hours, supposing the tide to be sometimes for and sometimes against the Boat.

If this can be clearly demonstrated by experiment and calculation I think you will agree with me that it is not important at present to make more experiments, but it is important to proceed immediately to securing the patent and executing the work....

I am Sir with much esteem and Respect
Yours Rob't Fulton

Robert R. Livingston to Robert Fulton

Paris, July 20, 1802

Dear Sir

I have examined your calculations with attention & should before now have written to you had I not been in daily expectation of having the pleasure of seeing you here. I have no doubt of the accuracy of your calculations and I conclude from them that if there is no objection in practice the chain is the best application, since it is obvious that half the power is according to the principles I laid down when I first spoke to you on the subject, or that can be obtained unless the motion could be so rapid as to render the water a solid body. But tis not in the application of the power done that the difficulty appears to me to lay but in the accommodating the engine to the boat....

As I have already expended considerable sums on this object I have a kind of claim that the present legislature of New York would admit. The chains could not obtain a patent right by any other means, as I have informed you that the idea is not an original one but the inventor is one of those that I w'd engage in the plans. He is an excellent practical workman and a very able mecanician. All these considerations make the demand you make of half the profits without any risk upon an untried scheme, which requires the joint labours and interest of several, and which if it succeeds must be extremely profitable, and extremely expensive if it fails, much too great a compensation for the labour and time it will cost you. I am also of the opinion that it would be necessary to examine the late improvements in steam engines now in operation and also their price. . . .

I am Dear Sir

with much optimism

Your Most Obedient Humble Servant

Robert Fulton to Robert R. Livingston

Philadelphia, December 20, 1806

Dear Sir

On Sunday last I wrote you from New York but having through mistake directed for you at Albany it is possible the letter may not find You. My wish now is to apply the steam boat to the best advantage and it will require some calculation to decide whether most emoluments will arise from the Hudson or Mississippi. You will be so good as to say when and where we can meet to go into details on this subject. On Monday I go to Washington. And I shall endeavour to persuade Mr. Jefferson to order that the officers or agents of Government on or near the Mississippi measure the velocity of that river from station to station and from month to month during a year: did I know the velocity of the water and the quantity of goods sent from New Orleans to the Junction with the Ohio I could then tell what would be the profits of the steam boats. . . .

Best Respects to the Ladies and believe me with Sincere esteem Yours

Rob't Fulton

Robert Fulton to Robert R. Livingston

New York, August 10, 1807

Dear Sir

Yesterday about 12 o'clock I put the steam boat in motion first with a paddle 8 inches broad 3 foot long, with which I ran about one mile up the East river against a tide of about one mile an hour, it being nearly high water. I then anchored and put in another paddle 8 inches wide 3 foot long, started again and then according to my best observations I went 3 miles an hour, that is two against a tide of one. Another board of 8 inches was wanting which had not been prepared. I therefore turned the boat and ran down with the tide on our boat 3 equal four, and turned her round neatly into the berth from which I parted. She answers the helm equal to any thing that ever was built. . . .

Yesterday I beat all the sloops that were endeavouring to stern tide with the slight breeze which she had; had I hoisted my sails I consequently should have had all their means added to my own. What ever may be the fate of steam boats for the Hudson my thing is completely probed for the Mississippi and the object is immense— please to forward me 1000 or 1500 dollars as soon as possible.

Yours truly

R. Fulton

Best respect to Mrs Livingston

Robert Fulton to Robert R. Livingston

New York, August 21, 1807

Dear Sir,

I arrived here yesterday afternoon at 4 o'clock, thus performing the voyage from Albany in 30 hours; this will do. Funds and spirit are now only wanting to do one of the handsomest and lucrative things which has been performed for some years.

Yours truly,

R. Fulton

[Ed.—letter incorrectly dated, should read Aug. 22]

Livingston-Fulton Manuscript Collection, Clermont State Historic Site, Germantown, N.Y.

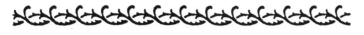

ARTICLES OF THE PEACE

The Dutch and the Esopus Indians

*N*EW NETHERLAND WAS HOME *to the Iroquois, organized as the League of Five Nations in the north around Albany and further west, and in the lower Hudson Valley to the Algonkian Indians, who inhabited the Eastern seaboard all the way to the south. It was the Algonkians that the Dutch fought repeatedly in severe battles throughout the last two decades of their control of the colony, though the significance of the fur trade precluded war with the Iroquois. For the first half of the 1640s, under the leadership of Governor Willem Kieft, who is largely considered responsible for the bloodshed, by unfairly taxing the Indians, there were brutal massacres in the areas around Manhattan Island, Staten Island, and New Jersey. After years of fighting and setting fire to each other's property and crops, the Indians and the settlers found peace in 1645, and Kieft was replaced by Peter Stuyvesant, who would remain as governor until the end of Dutch rule.*

There were to be constant flare-ups in the next decade, brought on by land disputes, drunkenness of the Indians, and Dutch livestock ruining Indian crops. The so-called Peach War started in 1655 in New Amsterdam when an Indian woman was murdered by a Dutchman for supposedly stealing peaches from his land. But due to Stuyvesant's decisive steps to avert more killings by fortifying the city, attacks ceased there well before the decade ended. Not only did the Indians in this period suffer the loss of lives in warfare, but their numbers were decreasing because of their exposure to diseases after the Europeans arrived. One contempo-

rary Dutch author concluded that 90 percent of the Indians in the Hudson Valley died from smallpox in the middle of the century. On their part, the Dutch were frightened of the continual attacks, many moved away or returned home, and emigrants were discouraged from coming abroad to settle in New Netherland.

Upriver the Esopus area was less fortified than New Amsterdam, though eventually the Dutch settlers would move from their scattered farms into a more confined settlement, in order to protect themselves. But renewed conflicts between the Dutch and the Esopus resulted in new killings, a 1600 treaty with the chiefs of Mahican, Hackensack, and other tribes bringing only temporary relief. The treaty restricted Indian travel around Esopus, now called Wiltwyck by the Dutch, and made the Indians give up their lands surrounding the Dutch settlement. But three years later the Second Esopus War erupted when the Indians attacked, and in retaliation the Dutch initiated a relentless campaign that destroyed the Indian camps and food supplies, in effect putting an end to Indian strength in this part of the region. Captain Martyn Kregier, who led the Dutch forces, left behind a detailed journal that chronicles the day-by-day assault throughout the summer and late fall of 1663.

By this time many of the Indians were hoping for an alliance with the British, which didn't materialize, but others wanted an end to the warfare and extermination of their way of life over the years since Kieft. The result of the truce was the "Articles of the Peace" which Peter Stuyvesant, Kregier, and other Dutchmen signed with several of the Esopus sachems in May 1664. This was the last treaty the Dutch were to make with them. By the end of the summer the British had sailed into the Hudson and claimed New Netherland, which they called New York, and Esopus was renamed Kingston. Governor Richard Nicolls, under the Duke's Laws set in force by the new administration, made a treaty with the same Indians the following year, along the same terms. This treaty would be renewed periodically by the Indians, effectively keeping the peace for the most part the rest of the colonial period.

ON THE 15TH OF MAY 1664, Thursday, the following Sachems or chiefs of the savages appeared in the Council Chamber at *Fort Amsterdam*:

> *Seweckenamo, Onagkotin, Powsawagh,* chiefs of the *Esopus,*
> *t'Sees-Sagh-Gauw,* chief of the *Wappinghs,*
> *Meeght Sewakes,* chief of *Kightewangh,*
> *Ses-Segh-Hout,* chief of *Rewechnongh* or *Haverstraw,*
> *Sauwenarocque,* chief of *Wiechquaskeck,*
> *Oratamy,* chief of *Hackingkesacky* and *Tappaen,*
> *Matteno,* chief of the *Staten-Island* and *Nayack* savages,
> *Siejpekenouw,* brother of *Tapusagh,* chief of *Marsepingh* etc.
> with about twenty other savages of that tribe.

Seweckenamo arose and said in behalf of the *Esopus* savages substantially, that he had asked his God (whom he called *Bachtamo* and to whom he appealed several times as a witness to grant), that he might negotiate something good with the *Dutch* in presence of all the chiefs now here and that the treaty made might be as solid as in a stick, which he took hold of, one end was attached and firmly united to the other.

2. He proposes and says, that all the chiefs and tribes in the neighborhood, as far as the *Maquaes,* are well satisfied and pleased, that the peace between the *Esopus* and the *Dutch* is to be concluded and that the *Marsepingh* savages shall be included in it.

3. That the chiefs and savages present have now heard, what he has proposed and said, which is all that he has to say for the present.

As this chief had so far not said in his speech, that the *Esopus* savages asked for peace, but only, that all the savages would be glad, if the peace between us and the *Esopus* was made and concluded, therefore the said chief and the other savages were asked by the interpreter, whether they wanted peace now and came to ask for it.

The chief *Seweckenamo* answered in substance, that he had come to ask for peace in behalf of the *Esopus* and that it should be henceforth so firm and binding as the arms, which he folded; he gave then his right hand to the General and said, that he meant sincerely, what he had said and it was also the intention and desire of all the *Esopus,* in whose name he spoke.

2. The chief was asked, why, if all the *Esopus* desired peace, all the chiefs of the *Esopus* had not come, to wit: *Keercop, Pamyrawech,* and *Niskahewan,* and what proof they could give, that these chiefs and the other savages desired peace also.

He answers, that one of these chiefs is a very old and blind man and the other two are his friends, who have given him their instructions and are satisfied with all, that he shall say and conclude.

After hearing the foregoing answer, it was unanimously resolved, to tell the *Esopus* savages, that they had made peace with us before this and that they had broken it without cause or reason; that nevertheless, as they have now returned all our prisoners and got back from us all theirs and as they now asked us for peace, we would make peace with them, but on conditions, which we shall propose.

The above was stated to them in detail by the interpreter, who gave them also a short account of all what they had done formerly and again now lately; they acknowledged all this to be the truth without any contradiction whatever. They were further reminded, that notwithstanding all this we were inclined to make peace at their request and to keep it, if we could be assured, that they would also keep it on their side.

They answered, that henceforth they would keep the peace inviolate and the following conditions were proposed:

> Terms and Conditions, on which a firm and everlasting peace has been made and concluded between their Noble Honors, *Petrus Stuyvesant,* Director-General and the Council of *New-Netherland* and the Sachems or chiefs of the *Esopus* savages.

1.

All, that has happened formerly, shall be forgiven and forgotten and not be remembered again: the people killed and gone on either side shall and must be forgotten.

2.

All the land, which they have previously given to the *Dutch* in payment of losses, caused by them, and which we have now retaken with the sword shall be and remain ours as far as their two captured forts, they shall not be allowed to plant this land again nor to come into the villages there nor into any of our distant places, neither with nor without arms, except here to the *Manhatans* and to *Fort Orange.*

3.

But that they may not be entirely deprived of their land, they shall have permission to plant around their new fort and during this year also near the old fort, as they inform us, that they have already planted there: but after that the land taken by the sword, as well around the new fort as near the old, shall be and remain ours.

4.

To prevent all troubles in the future, the savages shall do no harm to our people nor our people to them and it is covenanted, that no savage shall be allowed to come either armed or unarmed, as was said in the second section, upon land, where the *Dutch* are ploughing, sowing, mowing, planting or pasturing cattle neither at the *Esopus* nor elsewhere and if they are found there and caught, they shall be sent hither. It is however conceded to them, that they may come to the *Redoubt* to sell their corn, meat etc., but not more than at the highest 2 or 3 canoes, provided that they shall be obliged, to send a savage with a flag of truce ahead, who is to give information of their coming. For their better accommodation a house shall be built for them over the kil, where they can remain.

5.

If it should happen, that a Dutchman killed a savage or a savage a Dutchman, then it is covenanted, that no war shall immediately be begun on that account, but that a meeting shall first be held over it and the murderer shall be punished by death in presence of the *Dutch* and savages.

6.

It is also covenanted, that if an *Esopus* savage should happen to
kill some horses, cattle, pigs etc., the chiefs shall have to pay for it or
if they refuse, one of them shall be arrested and kept in prison, until
the killed animal has been paid for, and the loser satisfied, while the
Director-General on the other side promises, that no Dutchman shall
do any damage to the *Esopus* savages.

7.

The chief of *Marsepingb* and all his savages are included in this
peace.

8.

The aforesaid *Esopus* Sachems engage themselves to have these
articles of peace ratified by the other *Esopus* Sachems and savages, to
inform us thereof within a month and come hither with the other
Sachems.

9.

It is also covenanted, that they or some of their people shall
come down here every year, to renew this compact and that, if they
bring a present, we shall also give them one.

Thus done and concluded at *Fort Amsterdam* in *New-Netherland*
the 16th of May A° 1664 in presence of his Noble Worship the
Director-General *Petrus Stuyvesant,* the Honble Mr. *de Sille,* of both
the Burgomasters of this city, their Honors *Cornelis Steenwyck* and
Paulus Leendertsen van der Grist, of Captain Lieutenant *Martyn
Kregier,* Lieutenant *Couwenhoven, Govert Loockermans,* old Schepen,
and *Thomas Chambers,* Commissary of the village of *Wiltwyck, Jacob
Backer* President of the Schepens, *Abraham Wilmerdonx junior, Sara
J. Kiersteede* as interpreter and the aforesaid chiefs and savages.

The mark	made by	P. STUYVESANT
SEWECKENAMO	himself.	

The mark	made by	NICASIUS DE SILLE
PAWSAWAGH	himself.	C. V. RUYVEN.

As interpreter and witness   As witnesses

SARA KIERSTEEDE	COR. STEENWYCK
GOVERT LOOCKERMANS	P. L. VAN DER GRIST
PIETER COUWENHOVEN	J. BACKER
THOMAS CHAMBERS	ABR. WILMERDONX.
	MARTYN KREGIER

MAERHINNIE TUWEE

Whereas *Oratamy* and *Matteno* have asked first for this peace in behalf of the *Esopus* savages, it is further stipulated and covenanted, that they shall be securities for this peace, that it be kept well and inviolate and if the *Esopus* savages should be the first to break it, that they and their savages shall then assist to make war upon the *Esopus* and to subdue them and should the *Dutch* at any time violate the aforesaid peace, then they shall go to war with all their men against the *Dutch*. Thus done at *Fort Amsterdam* in *New-Netherland,* the 16th of May 1664 in presence of the above-named witnesses, who have signed this in testimony thereof.

PETRUS STUYVESANT	The mark	made by
MARTYN KREGIER	OTATAM	himself
COR. STEENWYCK		
P. L. VAN DER GRIST	The mark	made
	by MATTENO himself.	

The mark   made by
HANS alias PIEWESERENVES himself.

B. Fernow, trans. and ed., *Documents Relating to the Colonial History of the State of New York,* Vol. 13 (Albany: Weed, Parsons and Company, 1881).

THE CAPTURE AND
EXECUTION OF
MAJOR JOHN ANDRÉ

James Thacher

F EW DIARIES WRITTEN *during the Revolutionary War have*
the scope and literary quality of James Thacher's (1754–1844)
military journal, which he kept during the years 1775–83.
He had joined the Continental Army from his home state of
Massachusetts at twenty-one, as a surgeon's mate, and traveled
extensively afterward. During these crucial years he was pres-
ent at many of the key battle sites: Saratoga, Ticonderoga, Morristown,
Penobscot, West Point. In grave, decorous tones, he describes
subjects as disparate as the condition of military hospitals, dinner
at Washington's headquarters, the surrender of Cornwallis, and
the burning of Kingston.

Thacher also witnessed events that unfolded after the most no-
torious act of the Revolutionary War was discovered—the trea-
son of General Benedict Arnold, who commanded West Point. Arnold's
plans had ensnared the highly regarded British officer Major John
André, who was captured at Tarrytown, and executed as a spy in
October 1780. In his moving account Thacher relates the cir-
cumstances surrounding this pivotal scene of the war, and the sym-
pathy Major André inspired through his manliness as a soldier.
Washington, though forced to observe the codes of war, could not
bring himself to watch André's execution, which attracted many.
Alexander Hamilton said of André, whom he visited several times
during his confinement, "... in the midst of his enemies, he died
universally esteemed and universally regretted." In 1821 André's
remains were removed to Westminster Abbey.

The versatile Thacher later wrote the first important medical reference work in America, in addition to books on fruit trees, bees, witchcraft, and medicine. But he is remembered for his journal, which is among the best firsthand memoirs of the American Revolution, covering nearly the entire period of the war.

September 26th.—At three o'clock this morning an alarm was spread throughout our camp. Two regiments from the Pennsylvania line were ordered to march immediately to West Point, and the whole army to be held in readiness to march at a moment's warning. It was soon ascertained that this sudden movement was in consequence of the discovery of one of the most extraordinary events in modern history, and in which the interposition of Divine Providence is remarkably conspicuous. It is the treacherous conspiracy of Major-General Arnold, and the capture of Major John Andre, adjutant-general to the British army. The army being paraded this morning, the following communication in the orders of General Greene was read by the adjutants to their respective regiments:

> Treason, of the blackest dye, was yesterday discovered. General Arnold, who commanded at West Point, lost to every sentiment of honor, of private and public obligation, was about to deliver up that important post into the hands of the enemy. Such an event must have given the American cause a dangerous, if not a fatal wound; happily the treason has been timely discovered, to prevent the fatal misfortune. The providential train of circumstances which led to it, affords the most convincing proofs that the liberties of America are the object of Divine protection. . . .

West Point is situated in the midst of the highlands, on the west side of the Hudson, sixty miles above New York, and seven below Fishkill. It is a strongly-fortified castle, which, with its dependencies, is considered by General Washington as the key which locks the communication between the Eastern and Southern states; and of all the posts in the United States, this is the most important. The position is remarkably well calculated by nature for a defensive post, being on a bend of the river, with rocky ridges rising one above another, and the lofty summit is covered with a range of redoubts and batteries, planned by the most skillful engineers. The most elevated and formidable fortress is erected on a natural platform of rocks, very steep, and almost inaccessible on every side; this is called "Fort Putnam," from the general who had the principal share in its plan and construction. It overlooks the whole plain below, and commands a landscape-view thirty miles in extent, the Hudson having the appearance of a vast canal, cut through huge mountains. As additional security, an iron chain of immense strength is thrown across at the short bend of the river, and fixed to huge blocks on each shore, and under the fire of batteries on both sides the river. The links of this chain are about twelve inches wide, and eighteen long, the bars about two inches square. It is buoyed up by very large logs, of about sixteen feet long, pointed at the ends to lessen their opposition to the force of the current at flood and ebb tide. The logs are placed at short distances from each other, the chain carried over them and made fast to each by staples. There are also a number of anchors dropped at proper distances, with cables made fast to the chain to give it a greater stability. Such is the formidable state and strength of this post, that it has received the appellation of the American Gibraltar, and when properly guarded, may bid defiance to an army of twenty thousand men. General Arnold was well apprised of the great importance of this fortress; no position in America could afford the British greater advantages. It commands the whole extent of country on the Hudson, from New York to Canada, and secures a communication between the Eastern and Southern states.

From the commencement of the American war, General Arnold has been viewed in the light of a brave and heroic officer, having exhibited abundant proof of his military ardor and invincible temper. He has fought in various battles, with an intrepid gallantry which cannot be exceeded, and it is from his bravery in the field, more than any intrinsic merit, that his character and fame have been established. His meritorious services have been amply rewarded by his promotion to the rank of major-general, but his name will now be transmitted to posterity with marks of infamy, and the pages of our history will be tarnished by the record of crimes of the most atrocious character by a native of our land. After the evacuation of Philadelphia by the British, Arnold was appointed to the command in that city, and such was his conduct, as respects both his official station and individual concerns, that his former standing and important services could no longer shield him from public odium and the just censure of the government. Being afterward, by his own solicitation, intrusted with the command of the post at West Point, he engaged in a secret correspondence with Sir Henry Clinton, and actually agreed to put him in possession of this very important garrison. The British general, ever ready to avail himself of treachery to accomplish an object which he could not achieve by the strength of his arms, selected Major John Andre, his adjutant-general and aide-de-camp, to have a personal interview with the traitor, to mature the plan, and make arrangements for the surrender of the post. A British sloop-of-war, called the Vulture, came up the North river, and anchored near King's ferry, about twelve miles below West Point. On board of this vessel were a Colonel Robinson, and Major Andre, under the assumed name of John Anderson. A communication was now maintained between Arnold and the persons on board the Vulture, without exciting the least suspicion of treasonable designs. But a personal interview was found necessary, and the place chosen for this purpose was the beach near the house of Joshua Smith, Esquire, who has long been suspected of a predilection for the British interest. In the night of the 21st instant, Smith, by the desire of Arnold, went with a boat, rowed by some men employed on his farm, and brought Major Andre, *alias* John Anderson, on shore, where he was received by Arnold, and conducted to the house of Smith, within our lines. Andre remained concealed at Smith's house till the following night, when he became extremely anxious to return on board the Vulture; but the boatmen, whom Arnold and Smith had seduced to bring him on shore the preceding night, could not be prevailed on to reconduct him on board, as the Vulture had been driven from her station by a cannon on shore. Finding it impossible to procure a boat and men for the purpose, it was resolved that Andre should return to New York by land, to which he reluctantly submitted, as the only alternative, to escape the danger into which he had been betrayed. For this hazardous attempt Arnold and Smith furnished him with a horse, and with clothes, in exchange for his military uniform; and Arnold gave him a passport under the fictitious name of John Anderson, as being on public business. Thus prepared, and accompanied by Smith part of the way, he proceeded on his journey. The passport served his purpose till he got beyond all our out-posts and guards without suspicion. They lodged together at Crompond that night, and Smith having given him directions about the road, left him the next morning, within about thirty miles of New York. Having arrived at Tarrytown, however, near the lines of the royal army, Andre was arrested by one of three men, who were patrolling between the out-posts of the two armies. He held his horse by the bridle, till his two companions came from their concealment to his assistance. This was the moment which was to decide the fate of the adjutant-general of the royal army. Alarmed and disconcerted, instead of producing his passport, he asked where they belonged? They replied, "To below," alluding to New York. "And so do I," said Andre; "I am a British officer, on urgent business, and must not be detained." He was soon, however, undeceived, and confounded on being obliged to yield himself a prisoner, and finding his passport, though having the authority of Arnold's signature, availed him nothing. His captors, suspecting that they had taken a valuable prize, resolved to hold him in durance, and realize his worth. The unfortunate prisoner now produced his gold watch, and said, "This will convince you that I am a gentleman, and if you will suffer me to pass, I will send to New York, and give you *any amount you shall name,* in cash, or in dry goods"; and, pointing to an adjacent wood, "you may keep me in that wood till it shall be delivered to you." All his offers, however, were rejected with disdain, and they declared that ten thousand guineas, or any other sum, would be no temptation. It is to *their virtue, no less glorious to America,* than Arnold's apostacy is disgraceful, that his detestable crimes are discovered. Their names are John Paulding, David Williams, and Isaac Van Vert. Taking their prisoner into the bushes, to undergo a search and examination, they found, concealed in his boots, the important papers, containing exact returns of the state of the forces, ordnance and defences at West Point and its dependencies, with critical remarks on the works, with a return of the number of troops at West Point, and their distribution; copies of confidential letters from General Washington, &c., &c., all in the hand-writing of General Arnold. Besides which, it is ascertained that the traitor carried with him to the interview a general plan of West Point and its vicinity, and all the works, and also particular plans of each work on a large scale, elegantly drawn by the engineer at that post. But these were not given up to Major Andre; it is supposed they were to be delivered at a future time. The captors now very properly delivered their prisoner, with the papers found on him, into the hands of Lieutenant-Colonel Jameson, the commanding officer on our lines. Andre, with the view, no doubt, of giving Arnold an opportunity to escape, had the address to induce Colonel Jameson to inform the traitor, by letter, that John Anderson was taken on his way to New York. It is probable that Colonel Jameson had not examined the papers in his possession, or it may well be supposed that, having such ample evidence before him, he would have hesitated before complying with this request; but, unsuspicious of treachery, and under the embarrassment of the moment, as though his mind was bewildered, or devoid of reason, he immediately despatched an express to Arnold, at Robinson's house, with the intelligence.

After sufficient time had elapsed for Arnold to receive the information and make his escape, Major Andre declared himself to Colonel Jameson to be the adjutant-general of the British army. Sensible of the *finesse* which had been practised on him, Colonel Jameson now despatched an express to meet General Washington, on his return from Hartford to Arnold's quarters, with an account of the capture of Major Andre, and the papers which were found on him, and this was accompanied by a letter from the prisoner, disclosing to his excellency his real character and condition, and relating the manner of his capture, &c. It unfortunately happened that the express took a different road, and missed of meeting the commander-in-chief, and Arnold first received the information about ten o'clock on the morning of the 15th instant. At this moment Major Shaw and Dr. McHenry, two of his excellency's aides, had arrived, and were at breakfast at Arnold's table. His confusion was visible, but no one could devise the cause. Struck with the pressing danger of his situation, expecting General Washington would soon arrive, the guilty traitor called instantly for a *"horse, any one, even if a wagon horse"*—bid a hasty adieu to his wife, and enjoined a positive order on the messenger not to inform that he was the bearer of a letter from Colonel Jameson, and having repaired to his barge, he ordered the cockswain with eight oarsmen to proceed down the river, and he was soon on board the Vulture, which Andre had left two nights before, and which immediately sailed with her prize for New York. General Washington arrived about twelve o'clock, and was informed that Arnold had absented himself, saying he was going to West Point, and should soon return. His excellency passed over the river to view the works there; but, not finding Arnold at his post, he returned, in the hope of meeting him at his quarters. But here he was again disappointed, for no person could account for his absence. Mrs. Arnold was now in her chamber, in great agitation and distress, deprived of her reason, and Dr. Eustis in attendance. At a lucid interval she inquired of the doctor if General Washington was in the house, desiring to see him. Believing that she intended to say something which would explain the secret of Arnold's unaccountable absence, he hastened below, and conducted the general to her chamber, who remained no longer than to hear her deny that he was General Washington, and to witness the return of her distraction. His excellency sat down to dine, but soon rose from table with apparent agitation, called out Colonel Lamb, the commander of artillery at West Point, and expressed to him his suspicion that Arnold had deserted to the enemy. In less than two hours it was ascertained that the conjecture was too well founded, for the despatches arrived from Colonel Jameson, with an account of the capture of Major Andre, accompanied by his own letter of confession. Major Andre was conducted to West Point, and thence to headquarters at Tappan; and a board, consisting of fourteen general officers, is constituted and directed to sit on the 29th instant, for his trial. It was to be expected that Sir Henry Clinton would make every possible overture and exertion, with the hope of rescuing his friend, and the adjutant-general of his army, from an ignominious death. Accordingly he addressed General Washington, claimed the release of Major Andre, alleging that he ought not to be considered in the character of a spy, as he had a passport from, and was transacting business under the sanction of General Arnold; but arguments so obviously absurd and futile could have no influence, and the prisoner was ordered before the military tribunal for trial, and the following are the particulars of their proceedings.

Major Andre, adjutant-general to the British army, was brought before the board, and the following letter from General Washington to the board, dated "Head-Quarters, Tappan, September 29th, 1780," was laid before them and read:

> GENTLEMEN: Major Andre, adjutant-general to the British army, will be brought before you, for your examination. He came within our lines in the night, on an interview with Major-General Arnold, and in an assumed character; and was taken within our lines, in a disguised habit, with a pass under a feigned name, and with the inclosed papers concealed on him. After a careful examination, you will be pleased as speedily as possible to report a precise state of his case, together with your opinion of the light in which he ought to be considered, and the punishment that ought to be inflicted. The judge-advocate will attend to assist in the examination, who has sundry other papers relative to this matter, which he will lay before the board.
>
> I have the honor to be, gentlemen, your
most obedient and humble servant,
G. WASHINGTON.

The names of the officers composing the board were read to Major Andre, with the following letter of his to General Washington—namely:

> SALEM, 24*th September,* 1780.
> SIR: What I have as yet said, concerning myself, was in the justifiable attempt to be extricated; I am too little accustomed to duplicity to have succeeded.
>
> I beg your excellency will be persuaded, that no alteration in the temper of my mind, or apprehension for my safety, induces me to take the step of addressing you, but that it is to secure myself from an imputation of having assumed a mean character for treacherous purposes or self-interest—a conduct incompatible with the principles that actuated me, as well as with my condition in life.

It is to vindicate my fame, that I speak, and not to solicit security. The person in your possession is Major John Andre, adjutant-general to the British army.

The influence of one commander in the army of his adversary is an advantage taken in war. I agreed to meet, on ground not within the posts of either army, a person who was to give me intelligence; I came up in the Vulture man-of-war, for this effect, and was fetched by a boat from the shore to the beach: being there, I was told that the approach of day would prevent my return, and that I must be concealed till the next night. I was in my regimentals, and had fairly risked my person.

Against my stipulation, my intention, and without my knowledge before hand, I was conducted within one of your posts. Your excellency may conceive my sensation on this occasion, and will imagine how much more I must have been affected by a refusal to reconduct me back the next night, as I had been brought. Thus become a prisoner, I had to concert my escape. *I quitted my uniform,* and was passed another way in the night, without the American posts to neutral ground, and in formed I was beyond all armed parties, and left to press for New York. I was taken at Tarrytown by some volunteers.

Thus, as I have had the honor to relate, was I betrayed into the vile condition of an enemy in disguise within your posts.

Having avowed myself a British officer, I have nothing to reveal but what relates to myself, which is true, on the honor of an officer and a gentleman.

The request I have to make your excellency, and I am conscious I address myself well, is that in any rigor which policy may dictate, a decency of conduct towards me may evince that, though unfortunate, I am branded with nothing dishonorable, as no motive could be mine but the service of my king, and as I was involuntarily an impostor. . . .

It is no less, sir, in a confidence in the generosity of your mind, than on account of your superior station, that I have chosen to importune you with this letter. I have the honor to be, with great respect, sir your excellency's most obedient and most humble servant,

JOHN ANDRE, Adjutant-General.

During the trial of this unfortunate officer, he conducted with unexampled magnanimity and dignity of character. He very freely and candidly confessed all the circumstances relative to himself, and carefully avoided every expression that might have a tendency to implicate any other person. So firm and dignified was he in his manners, and so honorable in all his proceedings on this most trying occasion, that he excited universal interest in his favor. He requested only to die the death of a soldier, and not on a gibbet. The following is a copy of a very pathetic letter from Major Andre to General Washington, dated

TAPPAN, *October* 1*st* 1780.

SIR: Buoyed above the terrors of death by the consciousness of a life devoted to honorable pursuits, and stained with no action that can give me remorse, I trust that the request I make to your excellency at this serious period, and which is to soften my last moments, will not be rejected. Sympathy towards a soldier will surely induce your excellency and a military tribunal to adapt the mode of my death to the feelings of a man of honor. Let me hope, sir, if aught in my character impresses you with esteem towards me—if aught in my misfortunes marks me as the victim of policy, and not of resentment—I shall experience the opera-tion of these feelings in your breast by being informed that I am not to die on a gibbet.

I have the honor to be your excellency's most
obedient and most humble servant,
JOHN ANDRE,
Adjutant-General to the British army.

This moving letter, as may be supposed, affected the mind of General Washington with the tenderest sympathy, and it is reported that he submitted it to a council of general officers, who decided that as Major Andre was condemned as a spy, the circumstances of the case would not admit of the request being granted, and his excellen-cy, from a desire to spare the feelings of the unfortunate man, declined making a reply to the letter.

October 1*st.*—I went this afternoon to witness the execution of Major Andre: a large concourse of people had assembled, the gallows was erected, and the grave and coffin prepared to receive the remains of this celebrated but unfortunate officer; but a flag of truce arrived with a communication from Sir Henry Clinton, making another and further proposals for the release of Major Andre, in consequence of which the execution is postponed till tomorrow, at twelve o'clock.

The flag which came out this morning brought General Robertson, Andrew Eliot, and William Smith, Esquires, for the purpose of pleading for the release of Major Andre, the royal army being in the greatest affliction on the occasion. The two latter gentlemen, not being military officers, were not permitted to land, but General Greene was appointed by his excellency to meet General Robertson at Dobbs' ferry, and to receive his communications. He had nothing material to urge, but that Andre had come on shore under the sanction of a flag, and therefore could not be considered as a spy. But this is not true; he came on shore in the night, and had no flag, on business totally incompatible with the nature of a flag. Besides, Andre himself, candidly confessed on his trial that he did not consider himself under the sanction of a flag. General Robertson, having failed in his point, requested that the opinion of disinterested persons might be taken, and proposed Generals Knyphausen and Rochambeau as proper persons. After this he had recourse to threats of retaliation on some people in New York and Charleston, but he was told that such conversation could neither be heard nor understood. He next urged the release of Andre on motives of humanity, saying, he wished an intercourse of such civilities as might lessen the horrors of war, and cited instances of General Clinton's merciful disposition; adding that Andre possessed a great share of that gentleman's affection and esteem, and that he would be infinitely obliged if he was spared. He offered that, if his earnest wishes were complied with, to engage that any prisoner in their possession, whom General Washington might name, should immediately be set at liberty. But it must be viewed as the height of absurdity that General Robertson should, on this occasion, suffer himself to be the bearer of a letter which the vile traitor had the consummate effrontery to write to General Washington. This insolent letter is filled with threats of retaliation, and the accountability of his excellency for the torrents of blood that might be spilled if he should order the execution of Major Andre. It should seem impossible that General Robertson could suppose that such insolence would receive any other treatment than utter contempt.

October 2d.—Major Andre is no more among the living. I have just witnessed his exit. It was a tragical scene of the deepest interest. During his confinement and trial, he exhibited those proud and elevated sensibilities which designate greatness and dignity of mind. Not a murmur or a sigh ever escaped him, and the civilities and attentions bestowed on him were politely acknowledged. Having left a mother and two sisters in England, he was heard to mention them in terms of the tenderest affection, and in his letter to Sir Henry Clinton, he recommended them to his particular attention.

The principal guard officer, who was constantly in the room with the prisoner, relates that when the hour of his execution was announced to him in the morning, he received it without emotion, and while all present were affected with silent gloom, he retained a firm countenance, with calmness and composure of mind. Observing his servant enter the room in tears, he exclaimed, "Leave me till you can show yourself more manly!" His breakfast being sent to him from the table of General Washington, which had been done every day of his confinement, he partook of it as usual, and having shaved and dressed himself, he placed his hat on the table, and cheerfully said to the guard officers, "I am ready at any moment, gentlemen, to wait on you." The fatal hour having arrived, a large detachment of troops was paraded, and an immense concourse of people assembled; almost all our general and field officers, excepting his excellency and his staff, were present on horseback; melancholy and gloom pervaded all ranks, and the scene was affectingly awful. I was so near during the solemn march to the fatal spot, as to observe every movement, and participate in every emotion which the melancholy scene was calculated to produce. Major Andre walked from the stone house, in which he had been confined, between two of our subaltern officers, arm in arm; the eyes of the immense multitude were fixed on him, who, rising superior to the fears of death, appeared as if conscious of the dignified deportment which he displayed. He betrayed no want of fortitude, but retained a complacent smile on his countenance, and politely bowed to several gentlemen whom he knew, which was respectfully returned. It was his earnest desire to be shot, as being the mode of death most conformable to the feelings of a military man, and he had indulged the hope that his request would be granted. At the moment, therefore, when suddenly he came in view of the gallows, he involuntarily started backward, and made a pause. "Why this emotion, sir?" said an officer by his side. Instantly recovering his composure, he said, "I am reconciled to my death, but I detest the mode." While waiting and standing near the gallows, I observed some degree of trepidation; placing his foot on a stone, and rolling it over and choking in his throat, as if attempting to swallow. So soon, however, as he perceived that things were in readiness, he stepped quickly into the wagon, and at this moment he appeared to shrink, but instantly elevating his head with firmness, he said, "It will be but a momentary pang," and taking from his pocket two white handkerchiefs, the provost-marshal, with one, loosely pinioned his arms, and with the other, the victim, after taking off his hat and stock, bandaged his own eyes with perfect firmness, which melted the hearts and moistened the cheeks, not only of his servant, but of the throng of spectators. The rope being appended to the gallows, he slipped the noose over his head and adjusted it to his neck, without the assistance of the awkward executioner. Colonel Scammel now informed him that he had an opportunity to speak, if he desired it; he raised the handkerchief from his eyes, and said, "I pray you to bear me witness that I meet my fate like a brave man." The wagon being now removed from under him, he was suspended, and instantly expired; it proved indeed "but a momentary pang." He was dressed in his royal regimentals and boots, and his remains, in the same dress, were placed in an ordinary coffin, and interred at the foot of the gallows; and the spot was consecrated by the tears of thousands.

Thus died, in the bloom of life, the accomplished Major Andre, the pride of the royal army, and the valued friend of Sir Henry Clinton. He was about twenty-nine years of age, in his person well proportioned, tall, genteel and graceful. His mien respectable and dignified. His countenance mild, expressive and prepossessing, indicative of an intelligent and amiable mind. His talents are said to have been of a superior cast, and, being cultivated in early life, he had made very considerable proficiency in literary attainments. Colonel Hamilton, aide-de-camp to General Washington, having had an interview with him, entertains an exalted opinion of his character. In the line of his profession, Major Andre, was considered as a skilful, brave and enterprising officer, and he is reported to have been benevolent and humane to our people who have been prisoners in New York. Military glory was the mainspring of his actions, and the sole object of his pursuits, and he was advancing rapidly in the gratification of his ambitious views, till by a misguided zeal he became a devoted victim. He enjoyed the confidence and friendship of Sir Henry Clinton, being consulted in his councils and admitted to the secrets of his cabinet. The heart of sensibility mourns when a life of so much worth is sacrificed on a gibbet. General Washington was called to discharge a duty from which his soul revolted; and it is asserted that his hand could scarcely command his pen, when signing the warrant for the execution of Major Andre. But, however abhorrent in the view of humanity, the laws and usages of war must be obeyed, and in all armies it is decreed that the gallows shall be the fate of spies from the enemy.

James Thacher, *Military Journal During the Revolution, From 1775 to 1783* (Boston: Richardson and Lord, 1823).

RIP VAN WINKLE

Washington Irving

T HERE IS NO *author more identified with the Hudson Valley than Washington Irving (1783–1859), named for the General who had safely brought his country through the war with England. He was born in New York City in the last year of the American Revolution, studied law, and early on began writing about the theatre for a newspaper published by his brother. Soon both brothers were joined by James Kirke Paulding, to create the satirical magazine* Salmagundi. *A few years later, in 1809, Irving published the book that established him as a writer,* The History of New-York, *under the pseudonym Diedrich Knickerbocker. It was only one of the many literary masks he was to wear.*

By this time Irving, an early cosmopolitan writer at a time when there was virtually no literary culture in America to speak of, already had traveled to Europe. In fact, he was living in England when he wrote The Sketch Book of Geoffrey Crayon, Gent.*(1819–20), which contains his beloved Hudson Valley story "Rip Van Winkle," now part of Catskill Mountains legend. But Irving had only ever seen the Catskills as a teenager from a sloop deck, and it wasn't until more than three decades later, long after he was an internationally celebrated author, that he actually explored the area he had up to then only richly imagined. "Rip Van Winkle" and another story in the same volume, "The Legend of Sleepy Hollow," came in time to symbolize the romance of Hudson Valley life in the Dutch period.*

America's first successful man of letters, Irving had a long, illus-

*trious career as a humorist, historian, biographer, and travel
writer. But he also had a sophisticated life abroad for years as a
diplomat in Spain and in England, at the request of President
Andrew Jackson, and nearly two decades later for William Tyler.
From his experiences in Spain came* The Alhambra, A Chronicle of the Conquest of Granada, *and* Spanish Papers, *works that
indicated his keen interest in Hispanic culture.*

*Back home in the 1830s Irving took a rugged tour to the Mid-
West, the Mississippi Valley, and the Far West, his* Astoria *and* A
Tour on the Prairies *growing out of that journey. This time he also
purchased the Tarrytown cottage, which had been originally the
home of a tenant farmer on Philipsburg Manor, and transformed
it into his picturesque retreat, Sunnyside. There, close to the
Hudson, surrounded by beautiful walkways and views, the bache-
lor Irving lived in the gabled home, surrounded by his books
and family members. A long biography of George Washington rounded out his life in letters. Irving is buried at Sleepy Hollow Cemetery, in the glen that he immortalized in "The Legend of Sleepy
Hollow."*

A POSTHUMOUS WRITING OF DIEDRICH KNICKERBOCKER

> By Woden, God of Saxons,
> From whence comes Wensday, that is Wodensday.
> Truth is a thing that ever I will keep
> Unto thylke day in which I creep into
> My sepulchre—
> CARTWRIGHT.

[THE FOLLOWING TALE was found among the papers of the late Diedrich
Knickerbocker, an old gentleman of New-York, who was very curious
in the Dutch history of the province, and the manners of the
descendants from its primitive settlers. His historical researches,
however, did not lie so much among books as among men; for the
former are lamentably scanty on his favorite topics; whereas he

found the old burghers, and still more their wives, rich in that legendary lore, so invaluable to true history. Whenever, therefore, he happened upon a genuine Dutch family, snugly shut up in its low-roofed farmhouse, under a spreading sycamore, he looked upon it as a little clasped volume of black-letter, and studied it with the zeal of a book-worm.

The result of all these researches was a history of the province during the reign of the Dutch governors, which he published some years since. There have been various opinions as to the literary character of his work, and, to tell the truth, it is not a whit better than it should be. Its chief merit is its scrupulous accuracy, which indeed was a little questioned, on its first appearance, but has since been completely established; and it is now admitted into all historical collections, as a book of unquestionable authority.

The old gentleman died shortly after the publication of his work, and now that he is dead and gone, it cannot do much harm to his memory to say, that his time might have been much better employed in weightier labors. He, however, was apt to ride his hobby his own way; and though it did now and then kick up the dust a little in the eyes of his neighbors, and grieve the spirit of some friends, for whom he felt the truest deference and affection; yet his errors and follies are remembered "more in sorrow than in anger," and it begins to be suspected, that he never intended to injure or offend. But however his memory may be appreciated by critics, it is still held dear by many folk, whose good opinion is well worth having; particularly by certain biscuit-bakers, who have gone so far as to imprint his likeness on their new-year cakes; and have thus given him a chance for immortality, almost equal to the being stamped on a Waterloo Medal, or a Queen Anne's farthing.]

Whoever has made a voyage up the Hudson must remember the Kaatskill mountains. They are a dismembered branch of the great Appalachian family, and are seen away to the west of the river, swelling up to a noble height, and lording it over the surrounding country. Every change of season, every change of weather, indeed every hour of the day, produces some change in the magical hues and shapes of these mountains, and they are regarded by all the good wives, far and near, as perfect barometers. When the weather is fair and settled, they are clothed in blue and purple, and print their bold outlines on the clear evening sky; but sometimes, when the rest of the landscape is cloudless, they will gather a hood of gray vapors about their summits, which, in the last rays of the setting sun, will glow and light up like a crown of glory.

At the foot of these fairy mountains, the voyager may have descried the light smoke curling up from a village, whose shingle-roofs gleam among the trees, just where the blue tints of the upland melt away into the fresh green of the nearer landscape. It is a little village, of great antiquity, having been founded by some of the Dutch colonists, in the early times of the province, just about the beginning of the government of the good Peter Stuyvesant, (may he rest in peace!) and there were some of the houses of the original settlers standing within a few years, built of small yellow bricks brought from Holland, having latticed windows and gable fronts, surmounted with weather-cocks.

In that same village, and in one of these very houses (which, to tell the precise truth, was sadly time-worn and weather-beaten) there lived many years since, while the country was yet a province of Great Britain, a simple good-natured fellow, of the name of Rip Van Winkle. He was a descendant of the Van Winkles who figured so gallantly in the chivalrous days of Peter Stuyvesant, and accompanied him to the siege of Fort Christina. He inherited, however, but little of the martial character of his ancestors. I have observed that he was a simple good-natured man; he was, moreover, a kind neighbor, and an obedient hen-pecked husband. Indeed, to the latter circumstance might be owing that meekness of spirit which gained him such universal popularity; for those men are most apt to be obsequious and conciliating abroad, who are under the discipline of shrews at home. Their tempers, doubtless, are rendered pliant and malleable in the fiery furnace of domestic tribulation, and a curtain lecture is worth all the sermons in the world for teaching the virtues of patience and long-suffering. A termagant wife may, therefore, in some respects, be considered a tolerable blessing; and if so, Rip Van Winkle was thrice blessed.

Certain it is, that he was a great favorite among all the good wives of the village, who, as usual with the amiable sex, took his part in all family squabbles; and never failed, whenever they talked those matters over in their evening gossipings, to lay all the blame on Dame Van Winkle. The children of the village, too, would shout with joy whenever he approached. He assisted at their sports, made their playthings, taught them to fly kites and shoot marbles, and told them long stories of ghosts, witches, and Indians. Whenever he went dodging about the village, he was surrounded by a troop of them, hanging on his skirts, clambering on his back, and playing a thousand tricks on him with impunity; and not a dog would bark at him throughout the neighborhood.

The great error in Rip's composition was an insuperable aversion to all kinds of profitable labor. It could not be from the want of assiduity or perseverance; for he would sit on a wet rock, with a rod as long and heavy as a Tartar's lance, and fish all day without a murmur, even though he should not be encouraged by a single nibble. He would carry a fowling-piece on his shoulder for hours together, trudging through woods and swamps, and up hill and down dale, to shoot a few squirrels or wild pigeons. He would never refuse to assist a neighbor even in the roughest toil, and was a foremost man at all country frolics for husking Indian corn, or building stone-fences; the women of the village, too, used to employ him to run their errands, and to do such little odd jobs as their less obliging husbands would not do for them. In a word Rip was ready to attend to any body's business but his own; but as to doing family duty, and keeping his farm in order, he found it impossible.

In fact, he declared it was of no use to work on his farm; it was the most pestilent little piece of ground in the whole country; every thing about it went wrong, and would go wrong, in spite of him. His fences were continually falling to pieces; his cow would either go astray, or get among the cabbages; weeds were sure to grow quicker in his fields than any where else; the rain always made a point of setting in just as he had some out-door work to do; so that though his patrimonial estate had dwindled away under his management, acre by acre, until there was little more left than a mere patch of Indian corn and potatoes, yet it was the worst conditioned farm in the neighborhood.

His children, too, were as ragged and wild as if they belonged to nobody. His son Rip, an urchin begotten in his own likeness, promised to inherit the habits, with the old clothes of his father. He was generally seen trooping like a colt at his mother's heels, equipped in a pair of his father's cast-off galligaskins, which he had much ado to hold up with one hand, as a fine lady does her train in bad weather.

Rip Van Winkle, however, was one of those happy mortals, of foolish, well-oiled dispositions, who take the world easy, eat white bread or brown, whichever can be got with least thought or trouble, and would rather starve on a penny than work for a pound. If left to himself, he would have whistled life away in perfect contentment; but his wife kept continually dinning in his ears about his idleness, his carelessness, and the ruin he was bringing on his family. Morning, noon, and night, her tongue was incessantly going, and every thing he said or did was sure to produce a torrent of household eloquence. Rip had but one way of replying to all lectures of the kind, and that, by frequent use, had grown into a habit. He shrugged his shoulders, shook his head, cast up his eyes, but said nothing. This, however, always provoked a fresh volley from his wife; so that he was fain to draw off his forces, and take to the outside of the house—the only side which, in truth, belongs to a hen-pecked husband.

Rip's sole domestic adherent was his dog Wolf, who was as much hen-pecked as his master; for Dame Van Winkle regarded them as companions in idleness, and even looked upon Wolf with an evil eye, as the cause of his master's going so often astray. True it is, in all points of spirit befitting an honorable dog, he was as courageous an animal as ever scoured the woods—but what courage can withstand the ever-during and all-besetting terrors of a woman's tongue? The moment Wolf entered the house his crest fell, his tail drooped to the ground or curled between his legs, he sneaked about with a gallows air, casting many a sidelong glance at Dame Van Winkle, and at the least flourish of a broomstick or ladle, he would fly to the door with yelping precipitation.

Times grew worse and worse with Rip Van Winkle as years of matrimony rolled on; a tart temper never mellows with age, and a sharp tongue is the only edged tool that grows keener with constant use. For a long while he used to console himself, when driven from home, by frequenting a kind of perpetual club of the sages, philosophers, and other idle personages of the village; which held its sessions on a bench before a small inn, designated by a rubicund portrait of His Majesty George the Third. Here they used to sit in the shade through a long lazy summer's day, talking listlessly over village gossip, or telling endless sleepy stories about nothing. But it would have been worth any statesman's money to have heard the profound discussions that sometimes took place, when by chance an old newspaper fell into their hands from some passing traveler. How solemnly they would listen to the contents, as drawled out by Derrick Van Bummel, the schoolmaster, a dapper learned little man, who was not to be daunted by the most gigantic word in the dictionary; and how sagely they would deliberate upon public events some months after they had taken place.

The opinions of this junto were completely controlled by Nicholas Vedder, a patriarch of the village, and landlord of the inn, at the door of which he took his seat from morning till night, just moving sufficiently to avoid the sun and keep in the shade of a large tree; so that the neighbors could tell the hour by his movements as accurately as by a sun-dial. It is true he was rarely heard to speak, but smoked his pipe incessantly. His adherents, however (for every great man has his adherents), perfectly understood him, and knew how to gather his opinions. When any thing that was read or related displeased him, he was observed to smoke his pipe vehemently, and to send forth short, frequent and angry puffs; but when pleased, he would inhale the smoke slowly and tranquilly, and emit it in light and placid clouds; and sometimes, taking the pipe from his mouth, and letting the fragrant vapor curl about his nose, would gravely nod his head in token of perfect approbation.

From even this strong-hold the unlucky Rip was at length routed by his termagant wife, who would suddenly break in upon the tranquillity of the assemblage and call the members all to naught; nor was that august personage, Nicholas Vedder himself, sacred from the daring tongue of this terrible virago, who charged him outright with encouraging her husband in habits of idleness.

Poor Rip was at last reduced almost to despair; and his only alternative, to escape from the labor of the farm and clamor of his wife, was to take gun in hand and stroll away into the woods. Here he would sometimes seat himself at the foot of a tree, and share the contents of his wallet with Wolf, with whom he sympathized as a fellow-sufferer in persecution. "Poor Wolf," he would say, "thy mistress leads thee a dog's life of it; but never mind, my lad, whilst I live thou shalt never want a friend to stand by thee!" Wolf would wag his tail, look wistfully in his master's face, and if dogs can feel pity, I verily believe he reciprocated the sentiment with all his heart.

In a long ramble of the kind on a fine autumnal day, Rip had unconsciously scrambled to one of the highest parts of the Kaatskill mountains. He was after his favorite sport of squirrel shooting, and the still solitudes had echoed and re-echoed with the reports of his gun. Panting and fatigued, he threw himself, late in the afternoon, on a green knoll, covered with mountain herbage, that crowned the brow of a precipice. From an opening between the trees he could overlook all the lower country for many a mile of rich woodland. He saw at a distance the lordly Hudson, far, far below him, moving on its silent but majestic course, with the reflection of a purple cloud, or the sail of a lagging bark, here and there sleeping on its glassy bosom, and at last losing itself in the blue highlands.

On the other side he looked down into a deep mountain glen, wild, lonely, and shagged, the bottom filled with fragments from the impending cliffs, and scarcely lighted by the reflected rays of the setting sun. For some time Rip lay musing on this scene; evening was gradually advancing; the mountains began to throw their long blue shadows over the valleys; he saw that it would be dark long before he could reach the village, and he heaved a heavy sigh when he thought of encountering the terrors of Dame Van Winkle.

As he was about to descend, he heard a voice from a distance, hallooing, "Rip Van Winkle! Rip Van Winkle!" He looked round, but could see nothing but a crow winging its solitary flight across the mountain. He thought his fancy must have deceived him, and turned again to descend, when he heard the same cry ring through the still evening air; "Rip Van Winkle! Rip Van Winkle!"—at the same time Wolf bristled up his back, and giving a low growl, skulked to his master's side, looking fearfully down into the glen. Rip now felt a vague apprehension stealing over him; he looked anxiously in the same direction, and perceived a strange figure slowly toiling up the rocks, and bending under the weight of something he carried on his back. He was surprised to see any human being in this lonely and unfrequented place, but supposing it to be some one of the neighborhood in need of his assistance, he hastened down to yield it.

On nearer approach he was still more surprised at the singularity of the stranger's appearance. He was a short square-built old fellow, with thick bushy hair, and a grizzled beard. His dress was of the antique Dutch fashion—a cloth jerkin strapped round the waist— several pair of breeches, the outer one of ample volume, decorated with rows of buttons down the sides, and bunches at the knees. He bore on his shoulder a stout keg, that seemed full of liquor, and made signs for Rip to approach and assist him with the load. Though rather shy and distrustful of this new acquaintance, Rip complied with his usual alacrity; and mutually relieving each other, they clambered up a narrow gully, apparently the dry bed of a mountain torrent. As they ascended, Rip every now and then heard long rolling peals, like distant thunder, that seemed to issue out of a deep ravine, or rather cleft, between lofty rocks, toward which their rugged path conducted. He paused for an instant, but supposing it to be the muttering of one of those transient thunder-showers which often take place in mountain heights, he proceeded. Passing through the ravine, they came to a hollow, like a small amphitheatre, surrounded by perpendicular precipices, over the brinks of which impending trees shot their branches, so that you only caught glimpses of the azure sky and the bright evening cloud. During the whole time Rip and his companion had labored on in silence; for though the former marveled greatly what could be the object of carrying a keg of liquor up this wild mountain, yet there was something strange and incomprehensible about the unknown, that inspired awe and checked familiarity.

On entering the amphitheatre, new objects of wonder presented themselves. On a level spot in the centre was a company of odd-looking personages playing at nine-pins. They were dressed in a quaint outlandish fashion; some wore short doublets, others jerkins, with long knives in their belts, and most of them had enormous breeches, of similar style with that of the guide's. Their visages, too, were peculiar: one had a large head, broad face, and small piggish eyes: the face of another seemed to consist entirely of nose, and was surmounted by a white sugar-loaf hat, set off with a little red cock's tail. They all had beards, of various shapes and colors. There was one who seemed to be the commander. He was a stout old gentleman, with a weather-beaten countenance; he wore a laced doublet, broad belt and hanger, high crowned hat and feather, red stockings, and high-heeled shoes, with roses in them. The whole group reminded Rip of the figures in an old Flemish painting, in the parlor of Dominie Van Shaick, the village parson, and which had been brought over from Holland at the time of the settlement.

What seemed particularly odd to Rip was, that though these folks were evidently amusing themselves, yet they maintained the gravest faces, the most mysterious silence, and were, withal, the most melancholy party of pleasure he had ever witnessed. Nothing interrupted the stillness of the scene but the noise of the balls, which, whenever they were rolled, echoed along the mountains like rumbling peals of thunder.

As Rip and his companion approached them, they suddenly desisted from their play, and stared at him with such fixed statue-like gaze, and such strange, uncouth, lack-lustre countenances, that his heart turned within him, and his knees smote together. His companion now emptied the contents of the keg into large flagons, and made signs to him to wait upon the company. He obeyed with fear and trembling; they quaffed the liquor in profound silence, and then returned to their game.

By degrees Rip's awe and apprehension subsided. He even ventured, when no eye was fixed upon him, to taste the beverage, which he found had much of the flavor of excellent Hollands. He was naturally a thirsty soul, and was soon tempted to repeat the draught. One taste provoked another; and he reiterated his visits to the flagon so often that at length his senses were overpowered, his eyes swam in his head, his head gradually declined, and he fell into a deep sleep.

On waking, he found himself on the green knoll whence he had first seen the old man of the glen. He rubbed his eyes—it was a bright sunny morning. The birds were hopping and twittering among the bushes, and the eagle was wheeling aloft, and breasting the pure mountain breeze. "Surely," thought Rip, "I have not slept here all night." He recalled the occurrences before he fell asleep. The strange man with a keg of liquor—the mountain ravine—the wild retreat among the rocks—the wobegone party at nine-pins—the flagon—"Oh! that flagon! that wicked flagon!" thought Rip—"what excuse shall I make to Dame Van Winkle!"

He looked round for his gun, but in place of the clean well-oiled fowling-piece, he found an old firelock lying by him, the barrel incrusted with rust, the lock falling off, and the stock worm-eaten. He now suspected that the grave roysters of the mountain had put a trick upon him, and having dosed him with liquor, had robbed him of his gun. Wolf, too, had disappeared, but he might have strayed away after a squirrel or partridge. He whistled after him and shouted his name, but all in vain; the echoes repeated his whistle and shout, but no dog was to be seen.

He determined to revisit the scene of the last evening's gambol, and if he met with any of the party, to demand his dog and gun. As he rose to walk, he found himself stiff in the joints, and wanting in his usual activity. "These mountain beds do not agree with me," thought Rip, "and if this frolic should lay me up with a fit of the rheumatism, I shall have a blessed time with Dame Van Winkle." With some difficulty he got down into the glen: he found the gully up which he and his companion had ascended the preceding evening; but to his astonishment a mountain stream was now foaming down it, leaping from rock to rock, and filling the glen with babbling murmurs. He, however, made shift to scramble up its sides, working his toilsome way through thickets of birch, sassafras, and witch-hazel, and sometimes tripped up or entangled by the wild gravevines that twisted their coils or tendrils from tree to tree, and spread a kind of network in his path.

At length he reached to where the ravine had opened through the cliffs to the amphitheatre; but no traces of such opening remained. The rocks presented a high impenetrable wall, over which the torrent came tumbling in a sheet of feathery foam, and fell into a broad deep basin, black from the shadows of the surrounding forest. Here, then, poor Rip was brought to a stand. He again called and whistled after his dog; he was only answered by the cawing of a flock of idle crows, sporting high in air about a dry tree that overhung a sunny precipice; and who, secure in their elevation, seemed to look down and scoff at the poor man's perplexities. What was to be done? the morning was passing away, and Rip felt famished for want of his breakfast. He grieved to give up his dog and gun; he dreaded to meet his wife; but it would not do to starve among the mountains. He shook his head, shouldered the rusty firelock, and, with a heart full of trouble and anxiety, turned his steps homeward.

As he approached the village he met a number of people, but none whom he knew, which somewhat surprised him, for he had thought himself acquainted with every one in the country round. Their dress, too, was of a different fashion from that to which he was accustomed. They all stared at him with equal marks of surprise, and whenever they cast their eyes upon him, invariably stroked their chins. The constant recurrence of this gesture induced Rip, involuntarily, to do the same, when, to his astonishment, he found his beard had grown a foot long!

He had now entered the skirts of the village. A troop of strange children ran at his heels, hooting after him, and pointing at his gray beard. The dogs, too, not one of which he recognized for an old acquaintance, barked at him as he passed. The very village was altered; it was larger and more populous. There were rows of houses which he had never seen before, and those which had been his familiar haunts had disappeared. Strange names were over the doors—strange faces at the windows—every thing was strange. His mind now misgave him; he began to doubt whether both he and the world around him were not bewitched. Surely this was his native village, which he had left but the day before. There stood the Kaatskill mountains—there ran the silver Hudson at a distance— there was every hill and dale precisely as it had always been—Rip was sorely perplexed—"That flagon last night," thought he, "has addled my poor head sadly!"

It was with some difficulty that he found the way to his own house, which he approached with silent awe, expecting every moment to hear the shrill voice of Dame Van Winkle. He found the house gone to decay—the roof fallen in, the windows shattered, and the doors off the hinges. A half-starved dog that looked like Wolf was skulking about it. Rip called him by name, but the cur snarled, showed his teeth, and passed on. This was an unkind cut indeed—"My very dog," sighed poor Rip, "has forgotten me!"

He entered the house, which, to tell the truth, Dame Van Winkle had always kept in neat order. It was empty, forlorn, and apparently abandoned. This desolateness overcame all his connubial fears—he called loudly for his wife and children—the lonely chambers rang for a moment with his voice, and then all again was silence.

He now hurried forth, and hastened to his old resort, the village inn—but it too was gone. A large rickety wooden building stood in its place, with great gaping windows, some of them broken and mended with old hats and petticoats, and over the door was painted, "The Union Hotel, by Jonathan Doolittle." Instead of the great tree that used to shelter the quiet little Dutch inn of yore, there now was reared a tall naked pole, with something on the top that looked like a red night-cap, and from it was fluttering a flag, on which was a singular assemblage of stars and stripes—all this was strange and incomprehensible. He recognized on the sign, however, the ruby face of King George, under which he had smoked so many a peaceful pipe; but even this was singularly metamorphosed. The red coat was changed for one of blue and buff, a sword was held in the hand instead of a sceptre, the head was decorated with a cocked hat, and underneath was painted in large characters, GENERAL WASHINGTON.

There was, as usual, a crowd of folk about the door, but none that Rip recollected. The very character of the people seemed changed. There was a busy, bustling, disputatious tone about it, instead of the accustomed phlegm and drowsy tranquillity. He looked in vain for the sage Nicholas Vedder, with his broad face, double chin, and fair long pipe, uttering clouds of tobacco-smoke instead of idle speeches; or Van Bummel, the schoolmaster, doling forth the contents of an ancient newspaper. In place of these, a lean, bilious-looking fellow, with his pockets full of handbills, was haranguing vehemently about rights of citizens—elections—members of congress—liberty—Bunker's Hill—heroes of seventy-six—and other words, which were a perfect Babylonish jargon to the bewildered Van Winkle.

The appearance of Rip, with his long grizzled beard, his rusty fowling-piece, his uncouth dress, and an army of women and children at his heels, soon attracted the attention of the tavern politicians. They crowded round him, eyeing him from head to foot with great curiosity. The orator bustled up to him, and drawing him partly aside, inquired "on which side he voted?" Rip stared in vacant stupidity. Another short but busy little fellow pulled him by the arm, and, rising on tiptoe, inquired in his ear, "Whether he was Federal or Democrat?" Rip was equally at a loss to comprehend the question; when a knowing, self-important old gentleman, in a sharp cocked hat, made his way through the crowd, putting them to the right and left with his elbows as he passed, and planting himself before Van Winkle, with one arm akimbo, the other resting on his cane, his keen eyes and sharp hat penetrating, as it were, into his very soul, demanded in an austere tone, "what brought him to the election with a gun on his shoulder, and a mob at his heels, and whether he meant to breed a riot in the village?"—"Alas! gentlemen," cried Rip, somewhat dismayed, "I am a poor quiet man, a native of the place, and a loyal subject of the king, God bless him!"

Here a general shout burst from the by-standers—"A tory! a tory! a spy! a refugee! hustle him! away with him!" It was with great difficulty that the self-important man in the cocked hat restored order; and, having assumed a tenfold austerity of brow, demanded again of the unknown culprit, what he came there for, and whom he was seeking? The poor man humbly assured him that he meant no harm, but merely came there in search of some of his neighbors, who used to keep about the tavern.

"Well—who are they?—name them."

Rip bethought himself a moment, and inquired, "Where's Nicholas Vedder?"

There was a silence for a little while, then an old man replied, in a thin piping voice, "Nicholas Vedder! why, he is dead and gone these eighteen years! There was a wooden tombstone in the church-yard that used to tell all about him, but that's rotten and gone too."

"Where's Brom Dutcher?"

"Oh, he went off to the army in the beginning of the war; some say he was killed at the storming of Stony Point—others say he was drowned in a squall at the foot of Antony's Nose. I don't know—he never came back again."

"Where's Van Bummel, the schoolmaster?"

"He went off to the wars too, was a great militia general, and is now in congress."

Rip's heart died away at hearing of these sad changes in his home and friends, and finding himself thus alone in the world. Every answer puzzled him too, by treating of such enormous lapses of time, and of matters which he could not understand: war—congress—Stony Point;—he had no courage to ask after any more friends, but cried out in despair, "Does nobody here know Rip Van Winkle?"

"Oh, Rip Van Winkle!" exclaimed two or three, "Oh, to be sure! that's Rip Van Winkle yonder, leaning against the tree."

Rip looked, and beheld a precise counterpart of himself, as he went up the mountain: apparently as lazy, and certainly as ragged. The poor fellow was now completely confounded. He doubted his own identity, and whether he was himself or another man. In the midst of his bewilderment, the man in the cocked hat demanded who he was, and what was his name?

"God knows," exclaimed he, at his wit's end; "I'm not myself—I'm somebody else—that's me yonder—no—that's somebody else got into my shoes—I was myself last night, but I fell asleep on the mountain, and they've changed my gun, and every thing's changed, and I'm changed, and I can't tell what's my name, or who I am!"

The by-standers began now to look at each other, nod, wink significantly, and tap their fingers against their foreheads. There was a whisper, also, about securing the gun, and keeping the old fellow from doing mischief, at the very suggestion of which the self-important man in the cocked hat retired with some precipitation. At this critical moment a fresh comely woman pressed through the throng to get a peep at the gray-bearded man. She had a chubby child in her arms, which, frightened at his looks, began to cry. "Hush, Rip," cried she, "hush, you little fool; the old man won't hurt you." The name of the child, the air of the mother, the tone of her voice, all awakened a train of recollections in his mind. "What is your name, my good woman?" asked he.

"Judith Gardenier."

"And your father's name?"

"Ah, poor man, Rip Van Winkle was his name, but it's twenty years since he went away from home with his gun, and never has been heard of since—his dog came home without him; but whether he shot himself, or was carried away by the Indians, nobody can tell. I was then but a little girl."

Rip had but one question more to ask; but he put it with a faltering voice:

"Where's your mother?"

"Oh, she too had died but a short time since; she broke a blood-vessel in a fit of passion at a New-England peddler."

There was a drop of comfort, at least, in this intelligence. The honest man could contain himself no longer. He caught his daughter and her child in his arms. "I am your father!" cried he—"Young Rip Van Winkle once—old Rip Van Winkle now!—Does nobody know poor Rip Van Winkle?"

All stood amazed, until an old woman, tottering out from among the crowd, put her hand to her brow, and peering under it in his face for a moment, exclaimed, "Sure enough! it is Rip Van Winkle—it is himself! Welcome home again, old neighbor—Why, where have you been these twenty long years?"

Rip's story was soon told, for the whole twenty years had been to him but as one night. The neighbors stared when they heard it; some were seen to wink at each other, and put their tongues in their cheeks: and the self-important man in the cocked hat, who, when the alarm was over, had returned to the field, screwed down the corners of his mouth, and shook his head—upon which there was a general shaking of the head throughout the assemblage.

It was determined, however, to take the opinion of old Peter Vanderdonk, who was seen slowly advancing up the road. He was a descendant of the historian of that name, who wrote one of the earliest accounts of the province. Peter was the most ancient inhabitant of the village, and well versed in all the wonderful events and traditions of the neighborhood. He recollected Rip at once, and corroborated his story in the most satisfactory manner. He assured the company that it was a fact, handed down from his ancestor the historian, that the Kaatskill mountains had always been haunted by strange beings. That it was affirmed that the great Hendrick Hudson, the first discoverer of the river and country, kept a kind of vigil there every twenty years, with his crew of the Half-moon; being permitted in this way to revisit the scenes of his enterprise, and keep a guardian eye upon the river, and the great city called by his name. That his father had once seen them in their old Dutch dresses playing at nine-pins in a hollow of the mountain; and that he himself had heard, one summer afternoon, the sound of their balls, like distant peals of thunder.

To make a long story short, the company broke up, and returned to the more important concerns of the election. Rip's daughter took him home to live with her; she had a snug, well-furnished house, and a stout cheery farmer for a husband, whom Rip recollected for one of the urchins that used to climb upon his back. As to Rip's son and heir, who was the ditto of himself, seen leaning against the tree, he was employed to work on the farm; but evinced an hereditary disposition to attend to any thing else but his business.

Rip now resumed his old walks and habits; he soon found many of his former cronies, though all rather the worse for the wear and tear of time; and preferred making friends among the rising generation, with whom he soon grew into great favor.

Having nothing to do at home, and being arrived at that happy age when a man can be idle with impunity, he took his place once more on the bench at the inn door, and was reverenced as one of the patriarchs of the village, and a chronicle of the old times "before the war." It was some time before he could get into the regular track of gossip, or could be made to comprehend the strange events that had taken place during his torpor. How that there had been a revolutionary war—that the country had thrown off the yoke of old England— and that, instead of being a subject of his Majesty George the Third, he was now a free citizen of the United States. Rip, in fact, was no politician; the changes of states and empires made but little impression on him; but there was one species of despotism under which he had long groaned, and that was—petticoat government. Happily that was at an end; he had got his neck out of the yoke of matrimony, and could go in and out whenever he pleased, without dreading the tyranny of Dame Van Winkle. Whenever her name was mentioned, however, he shook his head, shrugged his shoulders, and cast up his eyes; which might pass either for an expression of resignation to his fate, or joy at his deliverance.

He used to tell his story to every stranger that arrived at Mr.

Doolittle's hotel. He was observed, at first, to vary on some points every time he told it, which was, doubtless, owing to his having so recently awaked. It at last settled down precisely to the tale I have related, and not a man, woman, or child in the neighborhood, but knew it by heart. Some always pretended to doubt the reality of it, and insisted that Rip had been out of his head, and that this was one point on which he always remained flighty. The old Dutch inhabitants, however, almost universally gave it full credit. Even to this day they never hear a thunderstorm of a summer afternoon about the Kaatskill, but they say Hendrick Hudson and his crew are at their game of nine-pins; and it is a common wish of all henpecked husbands in the neighborhood, when life hangs heavy on their hands, that they might have a quieting draught out of Rip Van Winkle's flagon.

NOTE

The foregoing Tale, one would suspect, had been suggested to Mr. Knickerbocker by a little German superstition about the Emperor Frederick der Rothbart, and the Kypphaüser mountain: the subjoined note, however, which he had appended to the tale, shows that it is an absolute fact, narrated with his usual fidelity:

The story of Rip Van Winkle may seem incredible to many, but nevertheless I give it my full belief, for I know the vicinity of our old Dutch settlements to have been very subject to marvelous events and appearances. Indeed, I have heard many stranger stories than this, in the villages along the Hudson; all of which were too well authenticated to admit of a doubt. I have even talked with Rip Van Winkle myself, who, when last I saw him, was a very venerable old man, and so perfectly rational and consistent on every other point, that I think no conscientious person could refuse to take this into the bargain; nay, I have seen a certificate on the subject taken before a country justice, and signed with a cross, in the justice's own handwriting. The story, therefore, is beyond the possibility of doubt.

D.K.

POSTSCRIPT

The following are traveling notes from a memorandum-book of Mr. Knickerbocker:

The Kaatsberg, or Catskill Mountains, have always been a region full of fable. The Indians considered them the abode of spirits, who influenced the weather, spreading sunshine or clouds over the landscape, and sending good or bad hunting seasons. They were ruled by an old squaw spirit, said to be their mother. She dwelt on the highest peak of the Catskills, and had charge of the doors of day and night to open and shut them at the proper hour. She hung up the new moons in the skies, and cut up the old ones into stars. In times of drought, if properly propitiated, she would spin light summer clouds out of cobwebs and morning dew, and send them off from the crest of the mountain, flake after flake, like flakes of carded cotton, to float in the air: until, dissolved by the heat of the sun, they would fall in gentle showers, causing the grass to spring, the fruits to ripen, and the corn to grow an inch an hour. If displeased, however, she would brew up clouds black as ink, sitting in the midst of them like a bottle-bellied spider in the midst of its web; and when these clouds broke, wo betide the valleys!

In old times, say the Indian traditions, there was a kind of Manitou or Spirit, who kept about the wildest recesses of the Catskill Mountains, and took a mischievous pleasure in wreaking all kinds of evils and vexations upon the red men. Sometimes he would assume the form of a bear, a panther, or a deer, lead the bewildered hunter a weary chase through tangled forests and among ragged rocks; and then spring off with a loud ho! ho! leaving him aghast on the brink of a beetling precipice or raging torrent.

The favorite abode of this Manitou is still shown. It is a great rock or cliff on the loneliest part of the mountains, and, from the flowering vines which clamber about it, and the wild flowers which abound in its neighborhood, is known by the name of the Garden Rock. Near the foot of it is a small lake, the haunt of the solitary bittern, with water-snakes basking in the sun on the leaves of the pond-lilies, which lie on the surface. This place was held in great awe by the Indians, insomuch that the boldest hunter would not pursue his game within its precincts. Once upon a time, however, a hunter who had lost his way, penetrated to the garden rock, where he beheld a number of gourds placed in the crotches of trees. One of these he seized and made off with it, but in the hurry of his retreat he let it fall among the rocks, when a great stream gushed forth, which washed him away and swept him down precipices, where he was dashed to pieces, and the stream made its way to the Hudson, and continues to flow to the present day; being the identical stream known by the name of the Kaaters-kill.

Washington Irving, *The Sketch Book of Geoffrey Crayon, Gent.*, rev. ed. (New York: George P. Putnam, 1850).

Franklin Delano Roosevelt made Springwood, his Georgian-Revival home, the "Summer White House." The first of America's presidential libraries, and a museum, were created on the grounds in 1939. FDR and Eleanor Roosevelt are buried in the rose garden. (*Franklin D. Roosevelt Library*)

The stately east facade of Clermont, the Livingston family seat in Germantown, opens onto rolling lawns and the canopies of gnarled old trees. By the end of the nineteenth century there were more than forty Livingston homes along the Hudson River. (*Clermont State Historic Site, New York State Office of Parks, Recreation and Historic Preservation, Taconic Region*)

Frederic Edwin Church started work on Olana, his Persian-style villa which overlooks the Hudson, in the 1870s. With a superb artist's eye he filled his home with exquisite treasures from world travels, and landscaped its winding pathways and grounds, creating one of the most magnificent settings in the Hudson Valley. (*Olana State Historic Site, New York State Office of Parks, Recreation and Historic Preservation, Taconic Region*)

Washington Irving's picturesque Sunnyside was home from the 1830s until his death in 1859. Before the Dutch, Gothic, and Romanesque renovation, it was a simple stone cottage on Philipsburg Manor owned a century earlier by a branch of the Van Tassel family whose name was immortalized in "The Legend of Sleepy Hollow." (*Historic Hudson Valley*)

This north portico view by Alexander Jackson Davis of the great estate Montgomery Place appeared in an 1847 issue of *The Horticulturist*. The Classical-Revival home features almost 200 years of original family possessions, a rare occurrence in historic restorations. (*The New York State Library, Albany*)

George Washington, as Commander-in-Chief of the Continental Army, set up headquarters in the Highlands toward the end of the Revolutionary War. He used this desk when he stayed at New Windsor. Now it is on view at the historic site of Washington's Headquarters, Newburgh. (*Washington's Headquarters State Historic Site, New York Office of Parks, Recreation and Historic Preservation, Palisades Interstate Park Commission*)

Cadwallader Colden (1688-1776) was one of the most gifted men in colonial America. A Lieutenant-Governor of New York State, he was part of an international circle of men who exchanged the latest knowledge in botany, science, philosophy, and medicine. Portrait made after Matthew Pratt (n.d.). *(The New-York Historical Society, New York City)*

Gilbert Stuart painted this portrait of Robert R. Livingston (1746-1813) who was known as "The Chancellor." One of the most powerful men in New York State, he administered the presidential oath of office to George Washington, and later served as Minister to France. (*The New-York Historical Society, New York City*)

Andrew Jackson Downing (1815-1852) was a renowned landscape gardener and author whose books on domestic architecture and the cultivation of rural taste were highly influential in their day. He lost his life in a steamboat fire on the Hudson, cutting short a brilliant career. (*Dumbarton Oaks, Trustees for Harvard University*)

John Burroughs in front of his fireplace at Slabsides. He built this secluded retreat in the woods near his West Park home Riverby in 1895, initiating a stream of visitors there who to this day continue to pay homage to his spirit. Photo by Ernest Harold Baynes. (*Department Library Services, American Museum of Natural History*)

Village of Catskill (1839). This engraving after the drawing by the accomplished Englishman William H. Bartlett appeared in one of the most influential books of scenic views in the nineteenth century: Nathaniel P. Willis's *American Scenery.* It shows the stagecoach route to the Catskill Mountain House, set in the distant mountains. Henry Hudson and his crew docked at Catskill and found there "a very loving people, and a very old man." (*The New York State Library, Albany*)

In 1859 Benson Lossing sketched this scene of winter fishing at Tomkin's Cove for one of the more than 300 engravings that highlight his guidebook *The Hudson, From the Wilderness to the Sea.* The men are taking striped bass, white perch, and young sturgeon from the river. (*The New York State Library, Albany*)

The Rondout (near Kingston), engraved from the painting by Daniel Huntington, offers a view of the Walkill Creek near its entrance to the Hudson. It was included in the popular *Home Book of the Picturesque* (1852) which featured essays by Irving, Cooper, Willis, and Bryant, and landscapes by Cropsey, Durand, Church, Cole, Weir, and Kensett. *(The New York State Library, Albany)*

III

HOUSES AND
GARDENS

A VISIT TO
MONTGOMERY PLACE

Andrew Jackson Downing

O*NE OF THE grandest of Livingston family homes is
the 434-acre Annandale-on-Hudson estate known as Montgomery
Place. The original Federal style house was built in 1804–5 by
Janet Montgomery, widow of the Revolutionary War hero General Richard Montgomery, who was killed at Quebec, and daughter
of Judge Robert R. Livingston. In the 1840s and 1860s the prominent architect Alexander Jackson Davis, who also worked on the
country seat Blithewood nearby, made additions and embellishments that transformed the building into one of the superb examples of Classical Revival domestic architecture in the United
States. He also designed the coach house on the grounds.*

*Andrew Jackson Downing (1815–52), a friend and adviser
to Edward Livingston, secretary of state for President Andrew
Jackson, and heir to the estate, offers a lovely account of the landscape he considered among the finest in the Hudson Valley.
Downing, who wrote this piece for* The Horticulturist, *a sophisticated gardening magazine which he edited at mid-century, was
then one of the country's most articulate voices in the development
of rural taste and domestic architecture. Born in Newburgh, where
he conducted a landscape and nursery business with his brother
Charles, he was an internationally recognized authority on fruit
trees. Downing's* Treatise on landscape gardening *and* The Architecture of Country Houses *were enormously successful in spreading his views on landscape and architectural design, particularly
the villa and cottage, and the "Hudson River Bracketed" style.*

The culmination of his career came when he received a commission to redesign the grounds of the Capitol, White House, and Smithsonian Institution. But America lost its enthusiastic arbiter of taste and refinement when, at thirty-six, Downing was drowned in the notorious steamboat race between the Henry Clay *and the* Armenia *on his beloved Hudson River.*

His reputation and influence have become more apparent in recent years in the increasing interest in the legacy of Hudson Valley homes that reflect the impact of Downing, his mentor Davis, and later his business partner Calvert Vaux, who had come from England to work with the young American. Downing's description of his October 1847 visit to Montgomery Place reflects his appreciation of the relation between landscape and home, which made him so valuable a guide to readers in the 1830s and 1840s. He especially loved the Valley's private views, which followed the English style of John C. Loudon and Humphry Repton, in establishing the picturesque tradition here.

A century and a half later, Montgomery Place enchants modern visitors from the moment they walk under the tall canopy of locust trees that lead to the house. This site, newly opened to the public, is a masterful example of historic restoration being carried out today. One of the fine features of an excursion to Montgomery Place is the opportunity to see almost two hundred years of family furniture and possessions, a rare mark of continuity in historic homes. Also, in keeping with Janet Montgomery's earlier establishment of a commercial nursery, the estate maintains orchards of more than five thousand fruit trees, from which apples, peaches, and pears are sold on Dutchess county's Route 9G. Set back 180 feet above the Hudson, and framed by gardens, shady walks, woods, and bristling cataracts— though minus the original conservatory and a rustic seat or two—the Romantic setting of Montgomery Place offers the ordinary twentieth-century stroller, accustomed to a mere lawn, the chance to experience the rapture of what once were called "pleasure-grounds."

THERE ARE FEW PERSONS, among what may be called the travelling class, who know the beauty of the finest American country-seats. Many are ignorant of the very existence of those rural gems that embroider the landscapes here and there, in the older and wealthier parts of the country. Held in the retirement of private life, they are rarely visited, except by those who enjoy the friendship of their possessors. The annual tourist by the railroad and steamboat, who moves through wood and meadow and river and hill, with the celerity of a rocket, and then fancies he knows the country, is in a state of total ignorance of their many attractions; and those whose taste has not led them to seek this species of pleasure, are equally unconscious of the landscape-gardening beauties that are developing themselves every day, with the advancing prosperity of the country.

It has been our good fortune to know a great number of the finest of these delightful residences, to revel in their beauties, and occasionally to chronicle their charms. If we have not sooner spoken at large of Montgomery Place, second as it is to no seat in America, for its combination of attractions, it has been rather that we were silent—like a devout gazer at the marvellous beauty of the Apollo—from excess of enjoyment, than from not deeply feeling all its varied mysteries of pleasure-grounds and lawns, wood and water.

Montgomery Place is one of the superb old seats belonging to the Livingston family, and situated in that part of Dutchess county bordering on the Hudson. About one hundred miles from New York, the swift river steamers reach this part of the river in six hours; and the guest, who leaves the noisy din of the town in the early morning, finds himself, at a little past noon, plunged amid all the seclusion and quiet of its leafy groves.

And this *accessible* perfect seclusion is, perhaps, one of the most captivating features in the life of the country gentleman, whose lot is cast on this part of the Hudson. For twenty miles here, on the eastern shore, the banks are nearly a continuous succession of fine seats. The landings are by no means towns, or large villages, with the busy air of trade, but quiet stopping places, serving the convenience of the neighboring residents. Surrounded by extensive pleasure-grounds,

fine woods or parks, even the adjoining estates are often concealed
from that part of the grounds around the house, and but for the
broad Hudson, which forms the grand feature in all these varied
landscapes—the Hudson always so full of life in its numberless
bright sails and steamers—one might fancy himself a thousand miles
from all crowded and busy haunts of men.

Around Montgomery Place, indeed, this air of quiet and seclusion
lurks more bewitchingly than in any other seat whose hospitality we
have enjoyed. Whether the charm lies in the deep and mysterious
wood, full of the echo of water-spirits, that forms the Northern
boundary, or whether it grows out of a profound feeling of completeness
and perfection in foregrounds of old trees, and distances of calm
serene mountains, we have not been able to divine; but certain it is
that there is a spell in the very air, which is fatal to the energies of a
great speculation. It is not, we are sure, the spot for a man to plan
campaigns of conquest, and we doubt even whether the scholar,
whose ambition it is

> "To scorn delights,
> And live laborious days,"

would not find something in the air of this demesne, so soothing as
to dampen the fire of his great purposes, and dispose him to believe
that there is more dignity in repose, than merit in action.

There is not wanting something of the charm of historical association here. The estate derives its name from Gen. Montgomery, the
hero and martyr of Quebec (whose portrait, among other fine family
pictures, adorns the walls of the mansion). Mrs. Montgomery, after his
lamented death on the heights of Abraham, resided here during the
remainder of her life. At her death, she bequeathed it to her brother,
the Hon. Edward Livingston, our late Minister to France. Here this
distinguished diplomatist and jurist passed, in elegant retirement, the
leisure intervals of a life largely devoted to the service of the State,
and here still reside his family, whose greatest pleasure seems to be
to add, if possible, every year, some admirable improvement, or elicit
some new charm of its extraordinary natural beauty.

The age of Montgomery Place heightens its interest in no ordinary degree. Its richness of foliage, both in natural wood and planted trees, is one of its marked features. Indeed, so great is the variety and intricacy of scenery, caused by the leafy woods, thickets and bosquets, that one may pass days and even weeks here, and not thoroughly explore all its fine points.

About four hundred acres comprise the estate called Montgomery Place, a very large part of which is devoted to pleasure-grounds and ornamental purposes. The ever-varied surface affords the finest scope for the numerous roads, drives, and walks, with which it abounds. Even its natural boundaries are admirable. On the west is the Hudson, broken by islands into an outline unusually varied and picturesque. On the north, it is separated from Blithewood, the adjoining seat, by a wooded valley, in the depths of which runs a broad stream, rich in waterfalls. On the south is a rich oak wood, in the centre of which is a private drive. On the east it touches the post road. Here is the entrance gate, and from it leads a long and stately avenue of trees, like the approach to an old French chateau. Half-way up its length, the lines of planted trees give place to a tall wood, and this again is succeeded by the lawn, which opens in all its stately dignity, with increased effect after the deeper shadows of this vestibule-like wood. The eye is now caught at once by the fine specimens of hemlock, lime, ash and fir, whose proud heads and large trunks form the finest possible accessories to a large and spacious mansion, which is one of the best specimens of our manor houses. Built many years ago, in the most substantial manner, the edifice has been retouched and somewhat enlarged within a few years, and is at present both commodious, and architectural in character.

Without going into any details of the interior, we may call attention to the unique effect of the *pavilion,* thirty feet wide, which forms the north wing of this house. It opens from the library and drawing-room by low windows. Its ribbed roof is supported by a tasteful series of columns and arches, in the style of an Italian arcade. As it is on the north side of the dwelling, its position is always cool in summer; and this coolness is still further increased by the abundant shade of tall old trees, whose heads cast a pleasant gloom, while their tall trunks allow the eye to feast on the rich landscape spread around it.

To attempt to describe the scenery, which bewitches the eye, as it wanders over the wide expanse to the west from this pavilion, would be but an idle effort to make words express what even the pencil of the painter often fails to copy. As a foreground, imagine a large lawn waving in undulations of soft verdure, varied with fine groups, and margined with rich belts of foliage. Its base is washed by the river, which is here a broad sheet of water, lying like a long lake beneath the eye. Wooded banks stretch along its margin. Its bosom is studded with islands, which are set like emeralds on its pale blue bosom. On the opposite shores, more than a mile distant, is seen a rich mingling of woods and corn-fields. But the crowning glory of the landscape is the background of mountains. The Kaatskills, as seen from this part of the Hudson, are, it seems to us, more beautiful than any mountain scenery in the middle States. It is not merely that their outline is bold, and that the summit of Roundtop, rising three thousand feet above the surrounding country, gives an air of more grandeur than is usually seen, even in the Highlands; but it is the *color* which renders the Kaatskills so captivating a feature in the landscape here. Never harsh or cold, like some of our finest hills, Nature seems to delight in casting a veil of the softest azure over these mountains—immortalized by the historian of Rip Van Winkle. Morning and noon, the shade only varies from softer to deeper blue. But the hour of sunset is the magical time for the fantasies of the color-genii of these mountains. Seen at this period, from the terrace of the pavilion of Montgomery Place, the eye is filled with wonder at the various dyes that bathe the receding hills—the most distant of which are twenty or thirty miles away. Azure, purple, violet, pale grayish-lilac, and the dim hazy hue of the most distant cloud-rift, are all seen distinct, yet blending magically into each other in these receding hills. It is a spectacle of rare beauty, and he who loves tones of color, soft and dreamy as one of the mystical airs of a German maestro, should see the sunset fade into twilight from the seats on this part of the Hudson.

THE MORNING WALK

Leaving the terrace on the western front, the steps of the visitor, exploring Montgomery Place, are naturally directed towards the river bank. A path on the left of the broad lawn leads one to the fanciful rustic-gabled seat, among a growth of locusts at the bottom of the slope. Here commences a long walk, which is the favorite morning ramble of guests. Deeply shaded, winding along the thickly wooded bank, with the refreshing sound of the tide-waves gently dashing against the rocky shores below, or expending themselves on the beach of gravel, it curves along the bank for a great distance. Sometimes overhanging cliffs, crested with pines, frown darkly over it; sometimes thick tufts of fern and mossy-carpeted rocks border it, while at various points, vistas or long reaches of the beautiful river scenery burst upon the eye. Half-way along this morning ramble, a rustic seat, placed on a bold little plateau, at the base of a large tree, eighty feet above the water, and fenced about with a rustic barrier, invites you to linger and gaze at the fascinating river landscape here presented. It embraces the distant mountains, a sylvan foreground, and the broad river stretching away for miles, sprinkled with white sails. The *coup-d'oeil* is heightened by its being seen through a dark framework of thick leaves and branches, which open here just sufficiently to show as much as the eye can enjoy or revel in, without change of position.

A little farther on, we reach a flight of stony steps, leading up to the border of the lawn. At the top of these is a rustic seat with a thatched canopy, curiously built round the trunk of an aged tree.

Passing these steps, the morning walk begins to descend more rapidly toward the river. At the distance of some hundred yards, we found ourselves on the river shore, and on a pretty jutting point of land stands a little *rustic pavilion,* from which a much lower and wider view of the landscape is again enjoyed. Here you find a boat ready for an excursion, if the spirit leads you to reverse the scenery, and behold the leafy banks from the water.

THE WILDERNESS

Leaving the morning walk, we enter at once into "The Wilderness." This is a large and long wooded valley. It is broad, and much varied in surface, swelling into deep ravines, and spreading into wide hollows. In its lowest depths runs a large stream of water, that has, in portions, all the volume and swiftness of a mountain torrent. But the peculiarity of "The Wilderness," is in the depth and massiveness of its foliage. It is covered with the native growth of trees, thick, dark and shadowy, so that once plunged in its recesses, you can easily imagine yourself in the depths of an old forest, far away from the haunts of civilization. Here and there, rich thickets of the kalmia or native laurel clothe the surface of the ground, and form the richest underwood.

But the wilderness is by no means savage in the aspect of its beauty; on the contrary, here as elsewhere in this demesne, are evidences, in every improvement, of a fine appreciation of the natural charms of the locality. The whole of this richly wooded valley is threaded with walks, ingeniously and naturally conducted so as to penetrate to all the most interesting points; while a great variety of rustic seats, formed beneath the trees, in deep secluded thickets, by the side of the swift rushing stream, or on some inviting eminence, enables one fully to enjoy them.

There are a couple of miles of these walks, and from the depth and thickness of the wood, and the varied surface of the ground, their intricacy is such that only the family, or those very familiar with their course, are at all able to follow them all with any thing like positive certainty as to their destination. Though we have threaded them several seasons, yet our late visit to Montgomery Place found us giving ourselves up to the pleasing perplexity of choosing one at random, and trusting to a lucky guess to bring us out of the wood at the desired point.

Not long after leaving the *rustic pavilion,* on descending by one of the paths that diverges to the left, we reach a charming little covered resting-place, in the form of a rustic porch. The roof is prettily thatched with thick green moss. Nestling under a dark canopy of evergreens in the shelter of a rocky fern-covered bank, an hour or two may be whiled away within it, almost unconscious of the passage of time.

THE CATARACT

But the stranger who enters the depths of this dusky wood by this route, is not long inclined to remain here. His imagination is excited by the not very distant sound of waterfalls.

> Above, below, aërial murmurs swell,
> From hanging wood, brown heath and bushy dell;
> A thousand gushing rills that shun the light,
> Stealing like music on the ear of night.

He takes another path, passes by an airy-looking rustic bridge, and plunging for a moment into the thicket, emerges again in full view of the first cataract. Coming from the solemn depths of the wood, he is astonished at the noise and volume of the stream, which here rushes in wild foam and confusion over a rocky fall, forty feet in depth. Ascending a flight of steps made in the precipitous banks of the stream, we have another view, which is scarcely less spirited and picturesque.

This waterfall, beautiful at all seasons, would alone be considered a sufficient attraction to give notoriety to a rural locality in most country neighborhoods. But as if Nature had intended to lavish her gifts here, she has, in the course of this valley, given two other cataracts. These are all striking enough to be worthy of the pencil of the artist, and they make this valley a feast of wonders to the lovers of the picturesque.

There is a secret charm which binds us to these haunts of the water spirits. The spot is filled with the music of the falling water. Its echoes pervade the air, and beget a kind of dreamy revery. The memory of the world's toil gradually becomes fainter and fainter, under the spell of the soothing monotone; until at last one begins to doubt the existence of towns and cities, full of busy fellow-beings, and to fancy the true happiness of life lies in a more simple existence, where man, the dreamy silence of thick forests, the lulling tones of babbling brooks, and the whole heart of nature, make one sensation, full of quiet harmony and joy.

THE LAKE

That shadowy path, that steals away so enticingly from the neighborhood of the cataract, leads to a spot of equal, though a different kind of loveliness. Leaving the border of the stream, and following it past one or two distracting points, where other paths, starting out at various angles, seem provokingly to tempt one away from the neighborhood of the water, we suddenly behold, with a feeling of delight, the lake.

Nothing can have a more charming effect than this natural mirror in the bosom of the valley. It is a fine expansion of the same stream, which farther down forms the large cataract. Here it sleeps, as lazily and glassily as if quite incapable of aught but reflecting the beauty of the blue sky, and the snowy clouds, that float over it. On two sides, it is overhung and deeply shaded by the bowery thickets of the surrounding wilderness; on the third is a peninsula, fringed with the graceful willow, and rendered more attractive by a *rustic temple;* while the fourth side is more sunny and open, and permits a peep at the distant azure mountain tops.

This part of the grounds is seen at the most advantage, either towards evening, or in moonlight. Then the effect of contrast in light and shadow is most striking, and the seclusion and beauty of the spot are more fully enjoyed than at any other hour. Then you will most certainly be tempted to leave the curious rustic seat, with its roof wrapped round with a rude entablature like Plato's crown; and you will take a seat in *Psyche's boat,* on whose prow is poised a giant butterfly, that looks so mysteriously down into the depths below as to impress you with a belief that it is the metempsychosis of the spirit of the place, guarding against all unhallowed violation of its purity and solitude.

The peninsula, on the north of the lake, is carpeted with the dry leaves of the thick cedars that cover it, and form so umbrageous a resting-place that the sky over it seems absolutely dusky at noon-day. On its northern bank is a rude sofa, formed entirely of stone. Here you linger again, to wonder afresh at the novelty and beauty of the *second cascade.* The stream here emerges from a dark thicket, falls about twenty feet, and then rushes away on the side of the peninsula opposite the lake. Although only separated by a short walk and the mass of cedars on the promontory, from the lake itself, yet one cannot be seen from the other; and the lake, so full of the very spirit of repose, is a perfect opposite to this foaming, noisy little waterfall.

Farther up the stream is another cascade, but leaving that for the present, let us now select a path leading, as near as we can judge, in the direction of the open pleasure-grounds near the house. Winding along the sides of the valley, and stretching for a good distance across its broadest part, all the while so deeply immersed, however, in its umbrageous shelter, as scarcely to see the sun, or indeed to feel very certain of our whereabouts, we emerge in the neighborhood of the Conservatory.

This is a large, isolated, glazed structure, designed by Mr. Catherwood, to add to the scenic effect of the pleasure-grounds. On its northern side are, in summer, arranged the more delicate greenhouse plants; and in front are groups of large oranges, lemons, citrons, Cape jasmines, eugenias, etc., in tubs—plants remarkable for their size and beauty. Passing under neat and tasteful archways of wirework, covered with rare climbers, we enter what is properly

THE FLOWER-GARDEN

How different a scene from the deep sequestered shadows of the Wilderness! Here all is gay and smiling. Bright parterres of brilliant flowers bask in the full daylight, and rich masses of color seem to revel in the sunshine. The walks are fancifully laid out, so as to form a tasteful whole; the beds are surrounded by low edgings of turf or box, and the whole looks like some rich oriental pattern or carpet of embroidery. In the centre of the garden stands a large vase of the Warwick pattern; others occupy the centres of parterres in the midst of its two main divisions, and at either end is a fanciful light summer-house, or pavilion, of Moresque character. The whole garden is surrounded and shut out from the lawn, by a belt of shrubbery, and above and behind this, rises, like a noble framework, the background of trees of the lawn and the Wilderness. If there is any prettier flower-garden scene than this *ensemble* in the country, we have not yet had the good fortune to behold it.

It must be an industrious sight-seer who could accomplish more than we have here indicated of the beauties of this residence, in a day. Indeed there is enough of exercise for the body, and enjoyment for the senses in it, for a week. But another morning may be most agreeably passed in a portion of the estate quite apart from that which has met the eye from any point yet examined. This is

THE DRIVE

On the southern boundary is an oak wood of about fifty acres. It is totally different in character from the Wilderness on the north, and is a nearly level or slightly undulating surface, well covered with fine Oak, Chestnut, and other timber trees. Through it is laid out the drive; a sylvan route as agreeable for exercise in the carriage, or on horseback, as the "Wilderness," or the "Morning Walk," is for a ramble on foot. It adds no small additional charm to a country place in the eyes of many persons, this secluded and perfectly private drive, entirely within its own limits.

Though Montgomery Place itself is old, yet a spirit ever new directs the improvements carried on within it. Among those more worthy of note, we gladly mention an *arboretum,* just commenced on a fine site in the pleasure-grounds, set apart and thoroughly prepared for the purpose. Here a scientific arrangement of all the most beautiful hardy trees and shrubs, will interest the student, who looks upon the vegetable kingdom with a more curious eye than the ordinary observer.

The whole extent of the private roads and walks, within the precincts of Montgomery Place, is between *five and six miles.* The remarkably natural beauty which it embraces, has been elicited and heightened every where, in a tasteful and judicious manner. There are numberless lessons here for the landscape gardener; there are an hundred points that will delight the artist; there are meditative walks and a thousand suggestive aspects of nature for the poet; and the man of the world, engaged in a feverish pursuit of its gold and its glitter, may here taste something of the beauty and refinement of rural life in its highest aspect.

Andrew Jackson Downing, *Rural Essays* (George Putnam and Company, 1853).

THE OCTAGON HOUSE

Orson S. Fowler

I
N THE MIDDLE OF *the last century, Orson S. Fowler (1809–87) was a best-selling author whose books were stand-ard reading matter in the average household. The first of these was on the new pseudo-science of phrenology, which James Kirke Paulding later satirized in his* Merry Tales of the Three Wise Men of Gotham. *From his New York City office the former Cohocton farm boy, aided by family members, read the head of anyone who stopped by, and managed his growing nationwide lecture tours and many publications. Fowler's entrepreneurial skills and pro-syletizing spirit catered to the growing demand for self-im-provement and health advice by a substantial American middle class, enthralled by his blend of sentimentality, folk wisdom, and prom-ise of the good life. He wrote wildly popular "how-to" manuals on parenting, marriage, sexuality, and love, one of them called* Amativeness, or Evils and Remedies of Excessive and Perverted Sensuality, *a title only slightly more euphemistic than some of today's self-help psychology guides.*

Fowler also became obsessed with the architecture of the octa-gon house whose spherical shape, he claimed, was superior to all other forms. His 1849 book A Home for All *was a guide to building such a structure, a later edition adding a description of the author's own four-story home, plus cupola, at Fishkill. What is noteworthy about Fowler's architectural fantasy is the atten-tion he gives to ventilation, recreational space, storage, sanitation, and air-quality control, features thought to be important to*

143

the modern homeowner. In the selection featured here, the author rhapsodizes on the spaciousness of his parlor rooms which often served as lecture hall. His Victorian, Italianate dream house also boasted central heating, gaslights, and flush toilets.

Alas, Fowler's famous gravel wall construction proved disastrous when sewage seeped into his well, creating a typhoid scare that signaled eventual doom for the house. But the octagon design was an architectural craze that inspired many a domestic vision throughout the country in the 1850s. Rokeby, one of the homes still owned by the Livingston family, has an octagonal library considered to be one of the most splendid Gothic Revival rooms in the country. Another famous building in this style is The Octagon in Irvington, which Carl Carmer once owned.

ALLUSION HAS ALREADY BEEN made to the residence of the author. For two reasons it seems proper to give its description a place in these pages—first, because those studies which have eventuated in this work were instituted primarily to erect this very house; and, secondly, because an account of it will call up many points about building, uses of rooms, etc., which can be presented in this form better than in any other. It is, moreover, intrinsically worthy of such a place....

While the ground story is exactly adapted by its position for work, storage, etc., the main living story is peculiarly fitted to become the main pleasure story of the house, first, because just far enough from the ground to prevent all dampness, and high enough to catch any summer breeze afloat, and yet not too high to render ascent to it laborious—the lower story being eight and a half feet high. Being *surrounded* by a portico, promenaders, at any hour of the day, can walk in either the shade or sun as suits them, or walk round a covered circle of some 300 feet—the house itself being 256.

Members of the family, and familiar acquaintances, will pass up those stairs alongside of the green or ice houses, and, passing along the portico, enter into that triangular entry, in the angle of which is a place just large enough for a hatstand, and lighted from around and over the door, and pass thence into the sitting, or more properly, drawing-room, or into the parlor, as occasion requires; while strangers will ring the bell at the story below, and pass up the stairs into the great central stairway, and thence into parlor, drawing, dining, or amusement rooms. This arrangement gives us every valuable end attained by an entry, without either taking up much room, or separating those four large rooms, each 22 by 39, less those corners taken off for entry, stairway, and closets. Each of these rooms is larger than one story of an entire house 25 by 28, and contains over 700 square feet, or some 75 yards of carpet. Now unfold two such magnificent rooms into one—and they join each other *lengthwise,* so that, thus thrown together, they are almost square, or 39 by 44—and what a place for a large assembly, a minister's donation party, or any social gathering on a large scale! Now it is submitted whether such free and cosy meetings of neighbors and congenial spirits can not be turned to great practical purposes of mental *profit* as well as pleasure. Should they not be universally adopted in this country? And what a place for such gatherings!

If two rooms are not large enough, throw open the dining and amusement rooms, and you have *four* spacious, magnificent rooms, embracing an area of over 300 square yards, and—please observe this beautiful feature—*having four side rooms adjoining* for dressing or retiring rooms.

Reader, even though you have made the tour of Europe, attended levees in the mansions of the lords of the Old World, did you ever see the equal of this suite of rooms for entertaining large parties?

Large suppers, having, however, much less reference to physical than *mental* repasts—to good eating than *speaking*—at which many toasts, sparkling suggestions, witty effusions, short, pithy, racy, eloquent, convivial speeches will constitute the chief attraction, and at which woman shall contribute as much as man, or improved editions of our public suppers, will yet be abundant; and how infinitely pleasurable and profitable such *mental, and moral, and social* feasts might be rendered! And what rooms these for such purposes! Three rows of tables, nearly forty feet long, or four rows thirty-five feet, would seat one hundred guests, in the dining and amusement rooms, and as many more in the parlor and drawing rooms, with abundance of side room for wardrobes, conversation, and a thousand uses requisite on such occasions....

Please observe that doors at the inner ends of these rooms connect these four rooms—*all by folding doors,* if desired. Access is also rendered easy from each to each and all, through the stairway. Observe, also, that here are *eight* large rooms, all *adjoining* each other, and all perfectly accessible, and securing all the advantages of an entry, without any of its disadvantages, which are great. If an entry divided them, only half as large a company could be entertained as now, for an intervening entry always breaks the spell of a party; yet different rooms, opening directly into each other, *preserve* this spell, or the *unity* of the assembly, whereas an intervening entry would make *two* companies. Those who have not thought or observed on this point, will not duly appreciate it, or realize the evils of entries. Yet these rooms *need* no entries—first, because the entry in the story below serves every requisition of a through entry or hall; and, second, because the location of the stairs renders the entry only an *up-and-down* entry, whereas, in most large houses, the hall runs through the house, both from *side to side,* AND from bottom to top.

The appearance of this stairway is really magnificent—lighted from a glass dome, 70 feet straight up, cupola included, octagonal in form—a far more beautiful figure than a square or hexagon.

Look again at how completely it ventilates every large room in every story. However hot, however little air may be stirring of a hot, sultry day, open a window and the door in any room of any story into this central ventilator, and up rises a strong current of air—a current rendered *necessary* and *certain* by the greater density of the air below than at the height of the cupola. Besides this glass dome at the top of the cupola, each of its eight sides has a window, out of which this air passes.

To practical housekeepers we submit one other point—the greater ease with which work can be done in rooms thus arranged, than in rooms usually arranged. For example: if you wish to go from either of these eight rooms to either story, above or below, a few steps takes you to this central stairway, by which you ascend or descend; whereas, if its entries and stories were as is usual, if you wish to go from the dining or amusement room up stairs, you must first go, say from the center of the room toward the back-entry door to a door into the entry, then turn a sharp angle to the left, and go clear to the foot of the stairway near the front door, and then turn square and come back again, while ascending the stairs, only, perhaps, to turn square round to the left to go right back towards the front of the house to one of the front upper rooms. But by this arrangement, three or four steps bring you from either of these rooms to the foot of the stairs, ascending which, a few more steps take you to whatever door above you may wish to enter. So, also, if you wish to go from either of these rooms on this story to any other you pass straight from where you start, through this stairway, to your place of destination.

It is now submitted whether you can not go from room to room, and story to story, about this house, with less than half the steps requisite to get from room to room, and story to story, in other houses as usually arranged. Observe, here are a great many rooms, and all *handy to each other.* In short, is not this *centrality* of the stairway incomparably superior to ordinary entries?

But, when these four side rooms are not wanted for entertaining very large parties—yet quite large parties can be entertained comfortably in the amusement-room, appropriated expressly to ordinary free and cosy social gatherings, with or without amusements, thus entertaining company well without throwing open the parlor, or exposing its carpet in muddy weather—they can be occupied profitably thus: a library and room for minerals, shells, etc., including some portraits; "a prophet's chamber," or spare bedroom, which, adjoining the library and also amusement-room, is well located for this purpose, and in summer is on the cool side of the house.

On the south, or lower side, are two other rooms, the former beautifully located and perfectly adapted to a winter sitting-room, and the other a winter sleeping-room. Observe, it *has no outside door,* so that cold can enter only through the *windows,* there being two doors between it and the outside doors. This will render its temperature much more uniform than if it had an outside door, and situated almost over the fireroom, it can be rendered as warm as you please. Is not this a luxurious arrangement for cold days in winter, when an outside, or even an entry door, will admit so much chilling blast?

Both these rooms are also over two like rooms below, so that heat ascending through the floor will help to keep the feet warm. I never like to occupy the first floor, either in summer, for it is more or less damp, or in winter, for cold will creep in, and pass up to the floor timbers and along them to crevices in the floor, whereas, by this mode of building, no cold air can come *to* these floor timbers, and the heat ascends from the workmen's sitting and dining rooms below, so as to keep the feet comfortable. Please, reader, reflect on the importance, as a means of health and luxury, especially to cold-blooded persons, of *warm floors and feet* in winter, and the great discomfort and *injury* to health consequent on *cold* floors and feet.

Observe, again, that often, in fall and spring, when the weather changes rapidly from warm to cold, an outside door, often opened, soon renders a room uncomfortable, so that you have to start a fire, whereas, in this case, no outside door admits cold or emits heat, so that it *retains a uniform temperature.* For a like reason it does not become so hot on a hot day in summer, especially as only about one-third of its wall is at one time exposed to the sun's rays, and this only half the day.

This *uniformity* in the temperature of a room is a most important point. None who have not experienced it can realize how important, or how comfortable. It is again submitted whether here is not an admirable winter luxury, to which every family might treat themselves.

The above allusion to "treating ourselves to luxuries," requires a little further elucidation. I once hired a shrewd Irishman, who had no change of linen, and that all rags and dirt, and without coat or vest. Set to work with other Irishmen, they soon began to tease him about his clothes, to which he replied, "If I were able, I would treat myself to clean linen every day in the year, for *nothing I can give myself is too good* for myself."

Apply this to houses. Should they not be furnished with just as many means of comfort, and even luxury, as their builder is well able to pay for? Yet how often are thousands spent on outside appearances and inside ornaments, which afford no solid comfort, only foster pride! whereas, a moiety of this extra expense would add to the real enjoyments and luxuries of its occupants every day, as long as it stands. And it is further submitted whether this octagonal form, these porticoes, these sumptuous center-rooms, and these convenient side rooms, together with this array of contrivances, do not throw far into the shade even the best and most costly styles of modern domestic architecture?

Orson S. Fowler, *A Home for All; or, The Gravel Wall and Octagon Mode of Building*, rev. ed. (New York: Fowler & Wells, 1853).

TAKING UP LAND
IN NEW NETHERLAND

Cornelis van Tienhoven

I N *1624 thirty Walloon families arrived as the first colonial settlers in New Netherland, which was also the name of
their ship. Soon a patroon system was installed in the new Dutch
colony by the West India Company, which sent with the colonists
farm animals, machinery, and tools. But the lucrative fur and beaver trade at first overwhelmed the establishment of an agricultural economy, and the farms didn't succeed under the rigid monopoly conditions, except at Rensselaerswyck in the Albany area.
By 1639 the Dutch merchants at home masterminding the colonization were offering two hundred acres of land for every head
of household willing to go to New Netherland. But in the next decade the Dutch-Indian wars further discouraged new settlers, so
that by 1645 Dutch colonists only numbered around 2,500.*

*By the middle of the seventeenth century, there were a number
of enthusiastic accounts of the colony available to promote life
there, and to rally new immigrants who would build its economy.
Adriaen Van der Donck, David P. de Vries, and Johan de Laet
wrote such works, as English writers did for the Southern and New
England colonies. Cornelis van Tienhoven (active in America
1641–54), a notorious lecher and the secretary of the colony under the directorships of both Willem Kieft and Peter Stuyvesant,
also made his contribution.*

*In its Golden Age the Netherlands was a world colonial power
conducting substantial trade on several continents. At home citizens enjoyed one of the highest standards of living in Europe, and*

150

*in the 1630s they were so secure that tulipomania ruled their
money markets. In his recent book of the same title historian Simon
Schama described such luxurious living as "the embarrassment
of riches." It was not easy to entice people to leave comfortable
homes for a frontier life of adventure and hardship. In addition, the Netherlands was relatively free of the religious prejudices
that would bring Huguenot, Mennonite, Quaker, Puritan, Luth-
eran, Baptist, Jewish, Calvinist, and Catholic believers from Europe
to the New World.*

*And so, while Vermeer painted the exquisite light that glowed
on the wealthy burghers at their tables spread with rich red Oriental carpets, van Tienhoven was describing life in and around
the mud huts inhabited by hard-working colonists. Restless immigrants did continue to come here, but there were never more
than a few thousand Dutch settlers in the forty years of their
rule, and a combined population of 9,000 or so in all of New
Netherland when the English claimed it in 1664.*

BOERS AND OTHERS who are obliged to work at first in Colonies ought
to sail from this country in the fore or latter part of winter, in order
to arrive with God's help in New Netherland early in the Spring, as in
March, or at latest in April, so as to be able to plant during that
summer, garden vegetables, maize and beans, and moreover employ
the whole summer in clearing land and building cottages as I shall
hereafter describe.

All then who arrive in New Netherland must immediately set
about preparing the soil, so as to be able, if possible to plant some
winter grain, and to proceed the next winter to cut and clear the
timber. The trees are usually felled from the stump, cut up and burnt
in the field, unless such as are suitable for building, for palisades,
posts, and rails, which must be prepared during winter, so as to be
set up in the spring on the new made land which is intended to be
sown, in order that the cattle may not in any wise injure the crops. In
most lands is found a certain root, called red Wortel, which must,

before ploughing, be extirpated with a hoe, expressly made for that purpose. This being done in the winter, some plough right around the stumps, should time or circumstances not allow these to be removed; others plant tobacco, maize and beans, at first. The soil even thus becomes very mellow, and they sow winter grain the next fall. From tobacco, can be realized some of the expenses incurred in clearing the land. The maize and beans help to support both men and cattle. The farmer having thus begun, must endeavour, every year, to clear as much new land as he possibly can, and sow it with such seed as he considers most suitable.

It is not necessary that the husbandman should take up much stock in the beginning, since clearing land and other necessary labor do not permit him to save much hay and to build barns for stabling. One pair of draft horses or a yoke of oxen only is necessary, to ride the planks for buildings or palisades or rails from the land to the place where they are to be set.

The farmer can get all sorts of cattle in the course of the second summer when he will have more leisure to cut and bring home hay, also to build barns and houses for men and cattle.

Of the building of houses at first

Before beginning to build, it will above all things be necessary to select a well located spot, either on some river or bay, suitable for the settlement of a village or hamlet. This is previously properly surveyed and divided into lots, with good streets according to the situation of the place. This hamlet can be fenced all round with high palisades or long boards and closed with gates, which is advantageous in case of attack by the natives who heretofore used to exhibit their insolence in new plantations.

Outside the village or hamlet other land must be laid out which can in general be fenced and prepared at the most trifling expense.

Those in New Netherland and especially in New England, who have no means to build farm houses at first according to their wishes, dig a square pit in the ground, cellar fashion, 6 or 7 feet deep, as long and as broad as they think proper, case the earth inside with wood all round the wall, and line the wood with the bark of trees or something else to prevent the caving in of the earth; floor this cellar with plank and wainscot it overhead for a ceiling, rise a roof of spars clear up and cover the spars with bark or green sods, so that they can live dry and warm in these houses with their entire families for two, three and four years, it being understood that partitions are run through those cellars which are adapted to the size of the family. The wealthy and principal men in New England, in the beginning of the Colonies, commenced their first dwelling houses in this fashion for two reasons; firstly, in order not to waste time building and not to want food the next season; secondly, in order not to discourage poorer laboring people whom they brought over in numbers from Fatherland. In the course of 3 to 4 years, when the country became adapted to agriculture, they built themselves handsome houses, spending on them several thousands.

After the houses are built in the above described manner or otherwise according to each person's means and fancy, gardens are made, and planted in season with all sorts of pot herbs, principally parsnips, carrots, and cabbage, which bring great plenty into the husbandman's dwelling. The maize can serve as bread for men, and food for cattle.

The hogs, after having picked up their food for some months in the woods, are crammed with corn in the fall, when fat they are killed and furnish a very hard and clean pork; a good article for the husbandman who gradually and in time begins to purchase horses and cows with the produce of his grain and the increase of his hogs, and instead of a cellar as aforesaid, builds good farm houses and barns.

Of the necessary Cattle

The cattle necessary in a Colonie or private Bouwery in New Netherland, are good mares and sound stallions.

Yoke oxen for the plough, inasmuch as in new lands full of roots, oxen go forward steadily under the plough, and horses stand still, or with a start break the harness in pieces.

Milch cows of kindly disposition and good bulls, sheep, sows, etc. Fowls are well adapted to Bouweries.

These Cattle are abundant in New Netherland and especially in New England and to be had at a reasonable price, except sheep which the English do not sell and are rare in New Netherland....

Necessary supplies for the farmer

If no wheat or rye can be had for bread, maize can be always had in season from the Indians at a reasonable price. The skepel costs ordinarily 10 @ 15 stivers when bought from the Indians.

Meat	Vinegar
Pork	Pease, and
Butter or Oil instead	Beans

Salad oil and vinegar are not easy to be had in that country except at an excessively high price from the Dutch traders.

All this being arranged it must be noted what description of people are best adapted for agriculture in New Netherland and to perform the most service and return the most profit in the beginning.

First, a person is necessary to superintend the working men; he ought to be acquainted with farming.

Industrious country people, conversant with the working and cultivation of land, and possessing a knowledge of cattle.

It would not be unprofitable to add to these some Highland boers, from the Veluwe, Gulick, Cleef, and Berg.

Northerners are a people adapted to cutting down trees and clearing land, inasmuch as they are very laborious and accustomed to work in the woods.

Northerners can do almost anything, some can build much, others a little, and construct small craft which they call yawls.

Carpenters who can lay brick.

Smiths conversant with heavy work, curing cattle and provided with suitable medicines.

One or more surgeons, according to the number of the people, with a chest well supplied with all sorts of drugs.

One or more Coopers.

A Clergyman, Comforter of the sick, or precentor who could also act as Schoolmaster.

A Wheelwright.

All other tradesmen would [be required] in time; the above mentioned mechanics are the most necessary at first. In order to promote population through such and other means, the people must be provided with Freedoms and Privileges so as to induce them to quit their Fatherland, and emigrate with their families beyond the sea to this far distant New Netherland. And as poor people have no means to defray the cost of passage and other expenses, it were desirable that wealthy individuals would expend some capital, to people this country or at their own expense remove themselves like the English of New England, with funds and a large body of working men, and provide those without means, with land, dwelling, cattle, tools and necessary support; and that, until they could derive the necessary maintenance from the soil and the increase of cattle, after which time they would be able to pay yearly a reasonable quit rent to their Lords and Masters from the effects in their possession.

By the population and cultivation of the aforesaid lands those who shall have disbursed funds for the removal of the laboring classes the purchase of cattle and all other expenses, would, in process of some years, after God had blessed the tillage, and the increase of the cattle, derive a considerable revenue in grain, meat, pork, butter, and tobacco, which form at first the earliest returns, in time can be improved by industry, such as the making pot and pearl ashes, clapboards, knees for ship building, staves, all sorts of pine and oak plank, masts for large ships, square timber, and ash and hickory planks in which a staple trade could be established. The English of New England put this in practice, as is to be seen, after the land had been first brought to proper condition; they sell their provisions at the Caribbean Islands, staves at Madeira and the Canaries, Masts and Fish in Spain and Portugal, and bring in return all sorts of commodities, so much of which returns as they do not consume are again distributed by them throughout all the Islands known and inhabited in the Northern part of America. So that through the variety of the returns, which of necessity was received, a profitable trade is already established in New England, which can also be right well set on foot by the Netherlanders, if the population of the country were promoted.

The following is the mode pursued by the West India Company in the first planting of Bouweries

The Company, at their own cost and in their own ships conveyed several boers to New Netherland, and gave these the following terms:—

The farmer, being conveyed with his family over sea to New Netherland, was granted by the Company for the term of six years a Bouwery, which was partly cleared, and a good part of which was fit for the plough.

The Company furnished the farmer a house, barn, farming implements and tools, together with four horses, four cows, sheep and pigs in proportion, the usufruct and enjoyment of which the husbandman should have during the six years, and on the expiration thereof return the number of cattle he received. The entire increase remained with the farmer. The farmer was bound to pay yearly one hundred guilders ($40) and eighty pounds of butter rent for the cleared land and bouwery.

The country people who obtained the above mentioned conditions all prospered during their residence on the Company's lands.

Afterwards the cattle belonging to the Company in New Netherland were distributed for some years among those who had no means to purchase stock.

The risk of the Cattle dying is shared in common and after the expiration of the contract, the Company receives, if the Cattle live, the number the husbandman first received, and the increase which is over, is divided half and half, by which means many people have obtained stock and even to this day, the Company have still considerable cattle among the Colonists, who make use on the above conditions of the horses in cultivating the farm; the cows serve for the increase of the stock and for the support of their families.

The foregoing is what is necessary to be communicated at present respecting the establishment of one or more Colonies and relative to supplies. What regards the government and preservation of such Colonies; and what persons ought to be in authority there and who these ought to be, I leave to the wise and prudent consideration of your noble High Mightinesses. Meanwhile I pray the Creator of Heaven and Earth to endow your High Mightinesses with the Spirit of grace and wisdom, so that all your High Mightinesses' deliberations may tend to the advantage of the Country and its Inhabitants.

E. B. O'Callaghan, ed., *The Documentary History of the State of New York* (Albany: Charles Van Benthuysen, 1851).

ALTERATION OF
AN OLD HOUSE

Calvert Vaux

*C*ALVERT VAUX *(1824–95) was brought over from his native England in 1850 by Andrew Jackson Downing, who invited the young landscape gardener to become his associate at Newburgh. The two maintained an office there,* Downing and Vaux, *specializing in the English picturesque style then in fashion. After Downing's untimely death Vaux continued to work in the Hudson Valley throughout the 1850s, before moving to New York City to create his masterwork with Frederick Law Olmsted, Central Park. The two men also designed Downing Park in Newburgh in honor of their renowned predecessor.*

In the Hudson Valley Vaux found considerable work on the large country estates and in the river towns. He landscaped an extensive park and gardens at Wilderstein, with curving drives, hiking trails, and a Colonial-Revival potting shed. For his brother-in-law, the painter Jervis McEntee, he conceived a studio at Rondout; the Hudson River State Hospital at Poughkeepsie is Vaux's work. At Newburgh he designed many residences, including those of William Findlay, Dr. Culbert, and W. E. Warren. In this selection he describes alterations he made for the home, still standing on Grand Street, of businessman Thomas Powell, whose widow gave her name to the magnificent steamboat the Mary Powell. *Vaux consulted on Olana for Frederic E. Church and the Tilden Estate in Yonkers.*

From the start, Vaux intended to devise an architecture suited to the economic, political, aesthetic, and ecological realities of

158

*American life. In addition to his picturesque villas and
suburban residences in New York, New Jersey, and Rhode
Island, he left his legacy in the development of the American
urban park, not only Manhattan's Central Park and Riverside
Park, but in Brooklyn's sprawling Prospect Park, on which
he collaborated with Olmsted. Many of New York City's
distinctive buildings, including the Metropolitan Museum of Art,
the American Museum of Natural History, and the Jefferson
Market Courthouse, are the work of Vaux and his later partners.
Vaux designed the sculptural memorial to his friend Downing
erected on the Smithsonian Institution grounds in Washington,
D.C.*

THERE ARE TO BE FOUND in different parts of the country many
families who have been settled for several generations on the same
spot, and their old, simple wooden homesteads, mended and patched
every few years, hold their own with commendable pertinacity. They
have no idea of falling to pieces, and are altogether too solid and
substantial to be pulled down. Now this quality of durability is, of
course, in the abstract, an excellent virtue for a house to possess; but
it must be confessed that, in such very awkward and ungainly
structures as often fall to the lot of these well-settled families, its
presence could be cheerfully dispensed with, were it not for the
many interesting associations and family reminiscences that linger
round the old house, which has been, perhaps, the home of the
father's and grandfather's childhood. These associations are so valuable, and so little fostered by the ordinary course of events in
American families, that they deserve to be cherished in every possible way, and it may therefore, now and then, be more wise to do the
best that can be done with an old house, even at some sacrifice of
external completeness of design and internal convenience, than to
demolish it entirely and build anew from the foundations on a better
plan. It does not often occur that a design can be altered so as to be
entirely satisfactory; but much may be done to compromise matters

without an uneconomical expenditure. The error generally fallen into in such cases may be thus described: Alterations are commenced without any very definite idea as to where they will end. One thing is done after another; partitions are pulled down, floors taken up, ceilings heightened, new windows and doors inserted, till the house is a complete labyrinth of mixed-up work, the clew to which is wholly undiscoverable by either proprietor or mechanic, and the natural result is, that, after many mistakes, and a severe trial of the patience of the owner, the workmen get through somehow, and are paid up and dismissed, while the house, although somewhat more convenient, is almost as ugly as before, and the proceeding, from first to last, has cost four or five times as much as the proprietor had an idea of laying out on it. This question should always be asked and answered fairly before commencing operations, viz., Is the house worth altering *at all*? Sometimes it is not. The frame may be decayed, the sills rotten, the floors out of level, the ceilings altogether too low for comfort; and as points like these can not generally be meddled with economically, it seems useless under such circumstances to spend much money on alterations and additions. If, on the contrary, the house is in a sound, substantial condition, and has no radical defect of interior arrangement that must always make it an objection-able residence, it becomes worth while to consider *how much* alteration and addition the house will bear profitably, and the whole plan and intention, from first to last, of the work to be done, needs to be studied and determined on beforehand more exactly and minute-ly than would be required for a new design altogether, for each part must be, as it were, dovetailed into the other, so as to get the advantage aimed at without awkwardness of appearance or undue sacrifice of the work already in existence. The fact is, that altogether *too much* is generally attempted. The best way is to do as little as possible beyond obtaining the leading features of arrangement and appearance that the alteration or addition is designed to procure. I remember once being called upon to pay a professional visit to a gentleman who wished to alter his house, which was a wooden one. I examined it, and found it had many serious defects, and advised him not to spend a cent upon it, but, if he was dissatisfied with the accommodation it afforded, to sell his present house and lot, purchase a fresh piece of ground, and start anew. He wanted to heighten all the ceilings to begin with, a process which would, of course, throw every door, and window, and beam out of position. Then the doors and windows must be made larger, and the frame must be new-sided, and the roof new-shingled, so that it became evident that what was really wanted was the old knife with the simple addition of a new handle and new blades. My advice seemed to be somewhat unsatisfactory to the proprietor, who evidently expected some encouragement, and perhaps an alteration was ultimately made; if so, I am certain that the result must have been even more unsatisfactory than the advice.

In Mr. Powell's house the whole construction was in good preservation. All that was wanted in the way of interior enlargement was a study with bedroom over, which I planned in a square projection at the rear of the house, and an enlargement of the parlor, which was arrived at by a square projection in front of the depth of the veranda, the old wall above the level of parlor ceiling being carried on iron suspension rods. Some of the windows and doors were shifted along a foot or two one way or the other, so as to bring the arrangement of openings into a form that would admit of proper treatment on the exterior. Small alterations, also, were made here and there to improve the internal convenience of the plan; but still nothing was done of sufficient magnitude to render it necessary for the family to leave the premises, even for a day, and the house was more or less occupied during the whole period required for the execution of the improvements. The chief alteration was made by taking a slice off the top of the original stiff old roof, and then bringing up the flat roof of the wing to the new ridge level. The smoky chimney was thus carried out at a proper elevation, and the whole appearance of the exterior of the house was by this means much enlarged; two of the other chimneys, after being taken down as far as was necessary, and tied together with an iron band, were arched over in the garret, and grouped above the ridge into one double stack. The roof was projected all round, and fitted with brackets. The ventilator was placed, hoods were arranged over a few of the windows, the verandas were somewhat improved, and the addition of a plant cabinet to the library completed the work as far as carpenters and masons were concerned. Both new and old parts were then painted and sanded in quiet, neutral tints, so that all appearance of alteration was at once avoided. Thus it will be perceived that, without much tearing to pieces, a new character may be given to a house, if it is only well built at first.

Calvert Vaux, *Villas and Cottages* (New York: Harper & Brothers, 1857).

THE HIGHLAND TERRACE

Nathaniel P. Willis

N*ATHANIEL P. WILLIS (1806–67) was the most fa- mous American man of letters, besides Washington Irving and James Fenimore Cooper, in Europe in the 1830s, and one of the highest paid writers at home. An arbiter of taste in antebellum America, Willis was a prolific journalist, regarded as the author of some of the best travel writing of his day. His influential* Ameri- can Scenery *includes illustrations from the steel-engraved Hudson Valley views of the prominent British artist William H. Bartlett that are now collectors' items.*

At one time Willis edited the New York Mirror *and became one of the country's earliest foreign correspondents, writing on his journeys throughout Europe and the Near East. The dandyish Willis, who wrote gossipy society news, novels, and plays, became a well-known figure in both New York and Boston literary circles. He was a cosmopolitan, urbane gentleman who helped to ac- quaint his readers with European authors but, like his contempo- rary James Kirke Paulding, praised Americans, too. Willis wrote with an entertaining air for popular audiences. One friend, Oliver Wendell Holmes, called him "an anticipation of Oscar Wilde," and another, Edgar Allan Poe, who had good-naturedly caricatured Willis in one of his stories, called him America's first "magazinist." If at one time the Hudson Valley could count a number of writers like Willis who followed the* belles lettres *tradition, this literary interest has sadly not had a long life in the region in more mod- ern times.*

In mid-century Willis settled in a Calvert Vaux–designed "picturesque country house" he called Idlewild, at Cornwall outside of Newburgh. A year earlier Newburgh had lost one of the country's brilliant young men in its local landscape designer Andrew Jackson Downing, who had shared the writer's high hopes for the cultivation of American taste and refinement. Prior to his move Willis joined Irving, Cooper, and William Cullen Bryant to create The Home Book of the Picturesque, *an influential book which praised and interpreted the American landscape in a series of articles, with wonderful engravings based on paintings by Thomas Cole, Frederic E. Church, Asher B. Durand, Jasper F. Cropsey, and others. Willis's own contribution is a rather snobbish celebration of the town and country set which was building estates along the west bank of the Hudson—a class that could afford "to let the trees grow," as he had noted in his chatty book* Outdoors at Idlewild. *Idlewild itself would soon be featured in Hudson Valley tourist guides to famous homes along the river, written by Wallace Bruce and others in the second half of the century.*

Introduction

THERE ARE *three compulsory and unnatural residents in cities*, whom the improvements of the age are about to set at liberty. But for the inconveniences of distance, TASTE, STUDY, AND LUXURY, WOULD HAVE NEVER LIVED WILLINGLY IN STREETS. Silently and insensibly, however, different parts of the country have become as accessible as different parts of the town. It would be safe, perhaps, to say that everything that is within an hour's reach, is sufficiently at hand; and English rail-trains now travel regularly sixty miles an hour. Fifty miles from New-York will soon be near enough to its amusements, society and conveniences—at least, for the greater portion of the year; and, on the day when this fact shall be recognized, New-Yorkers will be ready for a startling and most revolutionizing change, viz:—*homes in the country and lodgings in town, instead of homes in town and lodgings in the country*. Industry, necessity, or vice, could alone prefer a house in a "block," among disturbances and gutters, to a home unencroached upon, amid fresh air and gardens. Taste, Study, and Luxury, we repeat, are about removing to the country.

It will be observed that we anticipate a general preference, only for *such rural life as leaves the pleasures and advantages of a city within reach*. To be too far in the country, is, for many reasons, a dangerous as well as unpleasant removal from liberalizing and generalizing influences. Its effect on the mind is, perhaps, ultimately, the more important consideration—for it must be a very self-sufficing and unassimilating character that does not narrow and grow egotistic with limited associations and intercourse—but its effect on the sensitiveness as to mental liberty and social position, is sooner to be considered; for, there is no tyranny like that which is occasionally found in a small village, and no slavery like the efforts sometimes necessary to preserve the good will of small neighborhoods. Country life, even with the best natural charms and advantages, is a doubtful experiment of happiness, unless your main dependence for reciprocity, society and amusements, is beyond the reach of local jealousies and caprices. The great charm of a city is the freedom between neighbors as to any obligation of acquaintance, and the power to pick friends and make visits without fear of offending those not picked nor visited. With the city not farther off than an hour or two hours of locomotion, this privilege can be reasonably and harmlessly asserted in the country; and, with theatres, concerts, galleries of art, churches and promenades also within reach, the advantages of both town and country life are combined, while the defects of both are modified or avoided. It is with reference to a *new era of outer life*, therefore—*science having so far reduced distance that we may mix town and country life in such proportion as pleases us*—that we propose to describe a locality where residence, with this view, would be most desirable for New-Yorkers.

Description

West Point is Nature's Northern Gate to New-York City. As soon as our rail-trains shall equal those of England, and travel fifty or sixty miles an hour, the Hudson, as far as West Point, will be but a fifty-mile extension of Broadway. The river-banks will have become a suburban avenue—a long street of villas, whose busiest resident will be content that the City Hall is within an hour of his door. From this metropolitan avenue into the agricultural and rural region, the outlet will be at the city's Northern Gate, of West Point—a gate whose threshold divides Sea-board from In-land, and whose mountain pillars were heaved up with the changeless masonry of Creation.

The passage through the Mountain-Gate of West Point is a three-mile Labyrinth, whose clue-thread is the channel of the river—a complex wilderness, of romantic picturesqueness and beauty, which will yet be the teeming Switzerland of our country's Poetry and Pencil—and, at the upper and northern outlet of this labyrinthine portal of the city, there is a formation of hills which has an expression of most apt significance. *It looks like a gesture of welcome from Nature, and an invitation to look around you!* From the shoulder-like bluff upon the river, an outspreading range of Highlands extends back, *like the curve of a waving arm*—the single mountain of SHAWANGUNK, (connected with the range by a valley like the bend of a graceful wrist), *forming the hand at the extremity*. It is of the area within the curve of this bended arm—a HIGHLAND TERRACE of ten or twelve miles square, on the West Bank of the river—that we propose to define the capabilities, and probable destiny.

The HIGHLAND TERRACE we speak of—ten miles square, and lying within the curve of this outstretched arm of mountains—has an average level of about one hundred and twenty feet above the river. It was early settled; and, the rawness of first clearings having long ago disappeared, the well-distributed *second woods* are full grown, and stand, undisfigured by stumps, in park-like roundness and maturity. The entire area of the Terrace contains several villages, and is divided up into cultivated farms, the walls and fences in good condition, the roads lined with trees, the orchards full, the houses and barns sufficiently hidden with foliage to be picturesque—the whole neighborhood, in fact, within any driving distance, quite rid of the angularity and well-known ungracefulness of a newly-settled country.

Though the Terrace is a ten-mile plain, however, its roads are remarkably varied and beautiful, from the *curious multiplicity of deep glens*. These are formed by the many streams which descend from the half-bowl of mountains enclosing the plain, and—their descent being rapid and sudden, and the river into which they empty being one or two hundred feet below the level of the country around—they have gradually worn beds much deeper than ordinary streams, and are, from this and the character of the soil, unusually picturesque. At every mile or so, in driving which way you will, you come to a sudden descent into a richly wooded vale—a bright, winding brook at bottom, and romantic recesses constantly tempting to loiter. In a long summer, and with perpetual driving over these ten-mile interlacings of wooded roads and glens, the writer daily found new scenery, and heard of beautiful spots, within reach and still unseen. From every little rise of the road, it must be remembered, the broad bosom of the Hudson is visible, with foreground variously combined and broken; and the lofty mountains, (encircling just about as much scenery as the eye can compass for enjoyment), form an *ascending background and a new horizon* which are hardly surpassed in the world for boldness and beauty. To what degree sunsets and sunrises, clouds, moonlight, and storms, are aggrandized and embellished by this peculiar formation of country, any student and lover of nature will at once understand. Life may be, outwardly, as much more beautiful, amid such scenery, as action amid the scenery of a stage is more dramatic than in an unfurnished room.

Local Advantages

The *accessibilities* from Highland Terrace are very desirable. West Point is perhaps a couple of miles below, by the river bank; and, though mountain-bluffs and precipices now cut off the following of this line by land, a road has been surveyed and commenced along the base of Cro'nest, which, when completed, will be one of the most picturesque drives in the world. A part of it is to be blown out from the face of the rock; and, as the lofty eminences will almost completely overhang it, nearly the whole road will be in shade in the afternoon.

To pass along this romantic way for an excursion to the superb military grounds of West Point, and to have the parades and music within an easy drive, will be certainly an unusual luxury for a country neighborhood. The communication is already open for vehicles, by means of a steam ferry, which runs between Cornwall Landing (at the foot of the Terrace), and Cold Spring and the Military Wharf—bringing these three beautiful spots within a few minutes' reach of each other—Morris the song-writer's triple-view site of "Undercliff," by the way, overlooking the central of these Highland-Ferry Landings.

It may be a greater or less attraction to the locality of the Terrace, but it is no disadvantage, at least, that three of the best frequented summer resorts are within an afternoon drive of any part of it—the WEST POINT HOTEL, COZZENS'S, which is a mile below, and POWELTON HOUSE, which is five or six miles above the Point, at Newburgh. For accessibility to these fashionable haunts of strangers and travellers, and the gayeties and hospitalities for which they give opportunity— for enjoyment of military shows and music—for all manner of pleasure excursions by land and water, to glens and mountain-tops, fishing, hunting, and studying of the picturesque—Highland Terrace will probably be a centre of attraction quite unequalled.

The river-side length of the Terrace is about five miles—CORNWALL at one end and NEWBURGH at the other. At both these places there are landings for the steamers, and from both these are steam-ferries to the opposite side of the river, bringing the fine neighborhoods of FISHKILL and COLD SPRING within easy reach. NEWBURGH is the metrop- olis of the Terrace—with its city-like markets, hotels, stores, trades and mechanic arts—an epitome of New-York convenience within the distance of an errand. Downing, one of our most eminent horticul- turists, resides here, and Powell, one of the most enterprising of our men of wealth; and, along one of the high acclivities of the Terrace, are the beautiful country seats of Durand, our first landscape painter; Miller, who has presented the neighborhood with a costly and beautiful church of stone, Verplanck, Sands, and many others whose taste in grounds and improvements adds beauty to the river drive.

To the class of seekers for sites of rural residence, for whom we are drawing this picture, the fact that the Terrace is *beyond suburban distance from New-York*, will be one of its chief recommendations.

What may be understood as "Cockney annoyances" will not reach it. But it will still be sufficiently and variously accessible from the city. On its own side of the river there is a rail-route from Newburgh to Jersey City, whose first station is in the centre of the Terrace, at "Vail's Gate," and by which New-York will eventually be brought within two hours or less. By the two ferries to the opposite side of the river, the stations of the Hudson Railroad are also accessible, bringing the city within equal time on another route. The many boats upon the river, touching at the two landings at all hours of day and night, enable you to vary the journey to and fro, with sleeping, reading, or tranquil enjoyment of the scenery. Friends may come to you with positive luxury of locomotion, and without fatigue; and the monotony of access to a place of residence by any one conveyance—an evil very commonly complained of—is delightfully removed.

There is a very important advantage of the Highland Terrace, which we have not yet named. It is *the spot on the Hudson where the two greatest thoroughfares of the North are to cross each other*. The intended route from Boston to Lake Erie, here intersects the rail-and-river routes between New-York and Albany. Coming by Plainfield and Hartford to Fishkill, it here takes ferry to Newburgh, and traverses the Terrace by the connecting link already completed to the Erie Railroad—thus *bringing Boston within six or eight hours* of this portion of the river. Western and Eastern travel will then be direct from this spot, like Southern and Northern; and Albany and New-York, Boston and Buffalo, will be four points, all within reach of an easy excursion.

To many, the most essential charm of Highland Terrace, however, (as a rural residence in connection with life in New-York), will be the fact that it is the *nearest accessible point of complete inland climate*. Medical science tells us that nothing is more salutary than change from the seaboard to the interior, or from the interior to the seaboard; and, between these two climates, the ridge of mountains at West Point is the first effectual separation.

The raw east winds of the coast, so unfavorable to some constitutions, are stopped by this wall of cloud-touching peaks, and, with the rapid facilities of communication between salt and fresh air, the balance can be adjusted without trouble or inconvenience, and as much taken of either as is found healthful or pleasant. The trial of climate which the writer has made, for a long summer, in the neighborhood of these mountainous hiding-places of electricity, the improvement of health in his own family, and the testimony of many friends who have made the same experiment, warrant him in commending it as a peculiarly salutary and invigorating air.

We take pains to specify, once more, that it is to a certain class, in view of a certain new phase of the philosophy of life, that these remarks are addressed. For those who must be in the city late and early on any and every day, the distance will be inconvenient, unless with unforeseen advances in the rate of locomotion. For those who require the night and day dissipations of New-York, and who have no resources of their own, a nearer residence might also be more desirable. For mere seekers of seclusion and economy, it is too near the city, and the neighborhood would be too luxurious. But, for those who have their time in some degree at their own disposal— who have competent means or luxurious independence—who have rural tastes and metropolitan refinements rationally blended—who have families which they wish to surround with the healthful and elegant belongings of a home, while, at the same time, they wish to keep pace with the world, and enjoy what is properly and only enjoyable in the stir of cities—for this class—the class, as we said before, made up of Leisure, Refinement and Luxury—modern and recent changes are preparing a new theory of what is enjoyable in life. It is a mixture of city and country, *with the home in the country*. And the spot with the most advantages for the first American trial of this new combination, is, we venture confidently to record, the Highland Terrace encircled in the extended arm of the mountains above West Point.

The Home Book of the Picturesque (New York: G. P. Putnam, 1851).

SHAKER CHAIRS

Robert M. Wagan

I N 1774, *Mother Ann led a handful of Shakers, officially called The United Society of Believers, fleeing religious persecution in England to settle at Niskeyuna (Watervliet), near Albany.
The Shakers were a celibate, communal, and vegetarian sect
who believed in God as both Father and Mother. In the decades that
followed their arrival in this country Shaker communities,
supported by self-sufficient agrarian and cottage industries, spread
throughout rural New York, several New England states, Ohio,
Kentucky, and Indiana. For nineteenth-century travelers, a trip to
the utopian community at Niskeyuna was an obligatory stop
on any Hudson Valley tour. Numerous accounts—by Capt. Basil
Hall, Charles Dickens, James Silk Buckingham, Alexis de Tocqueville, and others—remain as a record of Shaker life, particularly the spirited dances that gave the sect its nickname and seemed
to enthrall, or frighten, visitors from "the world." In 1857* Harper's
*published a long article by Benson Lossing, with several illus-
trations, on the Shakers.*

*If on Sundays the Shakers gave up themselves to dance, on week-
days they brought just as much spiritual fervor to their work.
In addition to becoming among the first in the country to offer
seeds and medicinal herbs for sale in paper packets, the Shakers also developed a chair industry. By the last quarter of the nineteenth century, it was firmly centered at New Lebanon, New
York, under the guidance of Robert M. Wagan (1833–83). He standardized the setup of new factories and equipment to meet the*

171

*demands for sales in the next several decades. Chairs could now
be dipped in special dyes for a wide range of colors, and there
were several sizes and styles to choose from. Catalogues were made
available for customers, too. Though the Shakers made exquisite tables, cabinets, and desks, only their chairs and footstools were
sold to the public. All of their designs were characterized by a
lack of ornamentation, and sturdy, utilitarian interest. Ironically,
in one of the twists in the sociology of taste, today Shaker furniture is a valuable and costly collectors' item, while a century or
more ago, the elaborate French and English styles were more prized
in the great houses of the Hudson Valley than the homespun simplicity of local Shaker craftsmanship.*

*The Shakers exhibited their chairs at the famous Philadelphia Cen-
tennial Exposition in 1876, even winning a medal for "Strength,
Sprightliness, and Modest Beauty." Wagan provided the public with
a catalogue, excerpted here, that featured illustrations of the
chairs, and several hymns. In a sense, the furniture itself was an
act of worship, for between the pure unadorned lines of their
chairs, the spirituality of a gentle, humble people was deeply ingrained.*

WE INVITE THE ATTENTION OF our customers and the public to the
contents of this little pamphlet, which will give them, "in a concise
form," a description and a representation of the different sizes of
chairs, foot benches and floor rugs, which we manufacture and sell.
We would also call the attention of the public to the fact that there is
no other chair manufactory which is owned and operated by the
Shakers except the one which is now in operation and owned and
operated by the Society of Shakers at Mount Lebanon, Columbia
county, N.Y. We deem it a duty we owe to the public to enlighten
them in this matter, owing to the fact that there are now several
manufacturers of chairs who have made and introduced in the
market an imitation of our own styles of chairs, which they sell for
Shakers' chairs, and which are unquestionably bought by the public
generally under the impression that they are the real genuine article

made by the Shakers at their establishment in Mount Lebanon, N.Y. Of all the imitations of our chairs which have come under our observation, there is none which we would be willing to accept as a specimen of our workmanship, nor would we be willing to stake our reputation upon their merits. The increasing demand for our chairs has prompted us to increase the facilities for producing and improving them.

We have spared no expense or labor in our endeavors to produce an article that cannot be surpassed in any respect, and which combines all of the advantages of durability, simplicity and lightness. Our largest chairs do not weigh over ten pounds, and the smallest weigh less than five pounds, and yet the largest person can feel safe in sitting down in them without fear of going through them. This is owing to the care we take in our thorough selection of materials which are put into the chairs, and the excellent workmanship which is applied to their construction. Since the establishment of our new factory we have been using a very expensive and durable material in the seating of our chairs, with a great variety of the prettiest colors which can be produced.

Many of our friends who see the Shakers' chairs for the first time may be led to suppose that the chair business is a new thing for the Shakers to engage in. This is not the fact, however, and it may surprise even some of the oldest manufacturers to learn that the Shakers were pioneers in the business, and perhaps the very first to engage in the business after the establishment of the independence of the country.

We have in our possession specimens of chairs made by our people, which, judging from their appearance, would indicate that they were made in revolutionary times, and would adorn any cabinet of antiquities. The contrast between those and our present production is quite amusing.

The material with which we cushion our chairs is a specialty peculiarly our own. It is made of the best stock, and woven in hand looms with much labor, and forms a heavy and durable article, much more so than any thing which we are acquainted with. We have all of the most desirable and pretty colors represented in our cushions, and they can be all one color, or have a different colored border, or with different colored stripes running across the cushion.

We cushion the foot benches to match the cushioned chairs. They are twelve inches square on the top, with an incline to favor one's feet while sitting in the chairs, and they are nicely adapted for the purpose of kneeling stools.

When any of our friends wish some of our chairs they can order them of us by mail, addressed to R. M. WAGAN, Mt. Lebanon, Columbia county, N.Y. Our chairs are all nicely wrapped in papers before shipping, and the cushioned chairs are sacked with a cloth wrapper, for which an additional charge of fifty cents will be made. It is advisable to ship the chairs by express when there are only a few of them; the expense will be more, but the risk will be less than by freight. We do not ship any goods at our own risk, but deliver them at the nearest or most accessible place of shipment, and there take a receipt for them, showing that they were received in good order, when our obligations end.

The year 1876 is the centennial year of the first Shaker settlement in this country, and the commencement of our chair business is recorded back to this date, as the manufacture of home-made articles were then a necessity, and chair-making has always remained with us an occupation to the present time.

Robert M. Wagan, *Centennial Illustrated Catalogue and Price List of Shaker Chairs* (Albany: Weed, Parsons & Co., 1876).

⤸⤸⤸⤸⤸⤸⤸⤸⤸⤸⤸⤸⤸⤸

MAY 1870

Frederic E. Church

"ALMOST AN HOUR *this side of Albany is the Center of the World—I own it," wrote Frederic Edwin Church (1826–1900) to his friend the sculptor Erastus Dow Palmer. South of Hudson, Church had purchased a 126-acre farm and lived with his family on the property in Cozy Cottage, which the architect Richard Morris Hunt designed. By this time the former pupil of Thomas Cole, who said Church 'had the finest eye for drawing in the world," was already internationally known for his powerful* Niagara, *and* Heart of the Andes, *an enormous popular and critical success when it was exhibited in New York City in 1859. The elderly Washington Irving traveled down from Sunnyside to experience the art event of its day. Church was at the height of his fame in the 1850s and early 1860s—expanding his audience, traveling to South America, Europe, and the Middle East, exploring new subject matter, and creating some of the most exquisite Hudson Valley sunsets ever painted. He was about to embark on the great masterwork of his career, the conception and design of his home Olana, dramatically placed 600 feet about the Hudson River, with a breathtaking panorama of the Valley and Catskill Mountains. "Persian, adapted to the Occident," he would describe his earthen-colored refuge.*

Indeed, Church's travels to the Middle East, a few years before he started on plans for the home, in 1870, were the greatest influence on Olana. He became both architect and landscape designer, purchasing more land on the hill north of his farm, eventually planning the roadways, pond, and woodlands of the surroundings. Tens of thousands of trees were planted there, in an undulating landscape Church shaped in harmony with his home, then painted. At the center of what would become a substantial working farm, with wheat crops, orchards, livestock, and vegetable gardens, was Church's Oriental mansion, every detail of which he oversaw. Records show, too, that Calvert Vaux consulted on the foundation and frame. Church studied books on Persian architecture, made numerous sketches and color renderings of the house façade, windows, cornices, staircases. With an impeccable eye, he chose the stencils for the doors, archways, and baseboards inside, and the tiles and stonework outdoors. The statues, art objects, furniture, rugs, and drapes in Olana's richly fashioned rooms came from several corners of the globe, in celebration of Church's cosmopolitanism and appreciation of world cultures. A few donkeys for the family to ride around the grounds were even imported from Syria. Today this state historic site has an ongoing restoration program that is progressively returning the buildings and grounds of Olana to their nineteenth-century appearance, to the delight of its many visitors. Indoors the furnishings are wondrously intact.

In his letters from the spring of 1870—to artists Palmer and Martin J. Heade, and to William H. Osborn, director of the Illinois Central Railroad—a middle-aged Church is just beginning to oversee the construction of Olana. In a humorous mood, he is preoccupied with the glorious apple blossoms in his orchard, and the birth of his son Louis. For the next two decades, and as the Hudson River School itself was slowly eclipsed by a changing taste in painting, Church devoted himself to perfecting Olana, one of the great art treasures of the Hudson Valley. Though many painters besides Church and Cole lived and painted in the region— among them, Asher B. Durand, Jasper F. Cropsey, Jervis McEntee, Robert W. Weir, Albert Bierstadt, Sanford R. Gifford, George Inness— none of them is now more acclaimed as representative of the Hudson River School than Church. His sense of beauty and emotional grandeur brought to light a landscape with a color of passion and purpose the Hudson Valley has not been granted again in art.

Olana is Church's marvelous study in imagination and burnished dreams, reflecting in its worldly stones and other-worldly perspectives the timelessness of an artwork, preserved in the eternity of nature.

To Erastus D. Palmer

Hudson May 13th

My dear Palmer

I intend to run up to Albany for a couple of hours on Monday—that is, if you are likely to be there. I can't leave my wife, at least I don't want to for more than a few hours. I want to show you my plans and have your critical judgment. I also want to purchase a few niceties for my wife. She is getting on rather slowly but I hope securely. The baby is a fine fellow. The other two are splendid. I am in high health and in never better spirits.

I shall begin a stable on the hill next week. I put that up at once so as to have a shelter for the men, work shop, etc., and there will probably be a cookery in it. I will tell you all about this and everything else when I see you. . . .

Kind regards to all

Your friend,
F. E. Church

P.S. May 21

I found that I could not get to Albany the day I fixed, as I expected Vaux the architect, so I suppressed my letter. I now propose to drop in upon you next week—Tuesday—if agreeable to you. In case you should not expect to be in town please telegraph to me *Catskill Station*.

I am puzzled to know where to find a competent and honest builder—do you know of such? . . . The farm is magnificent—such a show of bloom on the fruit trees the world never saw. The season is marked by the extraordinary display.

To William H. Osborn

Farm, May 18th

My dear Mr. Osborn:

We are progressing—Mrs. Church rather slowly—all others famously. Mrs. Church has had a protracted ear ache which has disturbed her so much nights as to retard her recovery. She now sits under the apple trees in luxurious contemplation of the beautiful scenes which encircle our little cottage. I shall not make my trip to New York until she is a little stronger. Domestic arrangements work well. You ought to run up and see the apple trees. These old patriarchs look like mountains of bridal bouquets. I really think you would consider it worth the trip. The weather is delicious. Strawberries within two weeks—some already nearly half grown. Mr. Cole was much exercised about your fruit trees—they were promised in season. I believe, however, that he did not consider them too much advanced for successful planting.

Dr. Sabine has planted a large number of fruit trees. My farmer has just been to New York and brought up two or three hands. He got them at Castle Garden—one a German-Swiss—wears spectacles like a German student and understands grape and fruit culture in general. They don't speak English and get the same wages as ordinary hands.

I expect to begin a stable on the hill in a week. I shall use it for the accommodation of the mechanics at work at the new house. I have ordered the purchase of 100,000 bricks suitable for partition and inside work—offered for $150 the lot. I may get them for $100—or at the rate of $1 per thousand.

I am anxious to see your new arrangements and shall do so on the first opportunity. I imagine you feel that after all a roomy house is preferable to too economical quarters. I never did believe in small houses....

Yours sincerely,
Frederic E. Church.

To Martin J. Heade

Hudson May 26th

My dear Heade

I have been so occupied with our new baby that I haven't had time to write to you or anyone else unless the business was pressing. We are getting on nicely—I had more apple blossoms on my farm this season than you ever painted. It has been a marvelous spring for bloom.

If it hadn't been for that new baby I should have written to you—urging you to come up and apple blossomate for a few days. When the petals began to fall, the ground was white like snow and gave a curious effect.

I believe that A. T. Stewart considers himself the purchaser of the "Niagara." I had a telegraph to the effect that he wanted it. So you may soon expect to be relieved of that miniature—I haven't done a stroke of studio work since we arrived, all giving to the new baby. I am as busy as a hive of bees and ought to be able to fill your Hymettus can.

Talking of bees—so Bierstadt won't speak to you hey—Why don't you draw him out? Ask him if he doesn't want to buy some butterflies. Are you painting a Jamaica picture? Do you use the contents of that demi-John as a vehicle?

I expect to be in New York in a few days.

Yours sincerely
F. E. Church

To Erastus D. Palmer

Hudson May 26th

My dear Palmer,

I enjoyed my flying visit to Albany probably more than you did.

But the greatest pleasure I had was the discovery of your nice little studio (not so very little either). It will be complete when you have changed the light as you suggested. That bas relief is great. You have got twenty years for big things yet—as much time as you have already given to the great work of Art.

Now come down here for summer at least—dig, build and chisel. Begin another era in your art. I will paint you an awful fresco. . . . I feel pretty confident that McEntee will get fixed here. In a few days we shall want to see you at Cosy Cottage.

Mrs. Church is getting on nicely. She enjoyed the chickens I brought from Albany much. But the dozen pigeons were rotten, not one good one among them. They were spoiled before the vender gave them to me. Scented up the car on my way down—all were thrown away half a mile from the house—I expect to hear of typhoid fevers in that direction. As the other articles were good, I am inclined to think that the storekeeper entrusted the putting up the birds to some underling who thought I was a country feller who had no nose. . . .

Enough of that—If your son-in-law will please send me the bill for the lumber I will remit instanter. If it is not inconvenient for him to hold the stuff a little longer I shall be obliged—of course I will pay storage. For I presume I shall have occasion to ship lumber from Albany and would find it convenient to do the storing in a lump, perhaps for a thousand or two feet, though the steamer would do as well?

I am much inclined to think favorably of employing your carpenter as I suppose you will soon be done with him. Please ask him what arrangements he could make with me, so as to relieve me from much care. He would of course furnish his men. I should have a good work shop and sufficient other accommodations. The job would keep him busy probably all winter. I suppose that there would be as many working hours in winter as in summer.

You air a awfully sensible chap in the buildin' business whether its a buildin' buildins or whether its a buildin' busts.

My wrist is lame and hurts me to write. As it will feel better (and so will you) when I stop— I stop—

With kind regards to you all
　　your friend
　　　Frederic E. Church

Do think of buying down here

————

Frederic E. Church, Archives, Olana State Historic Site, Hudson, New York;
McKinney Library, Albany Institute of History and Art, Albany; Archives of
American Art, New York.

LIVINGSTON HOUSES

Clare Brandt

N O *FAMILY HAS HAD a more long-lasting presence in the history of the Hudson Valley than the Livingstons, who have resided there more than three hundred years. The head of this American aristocracy, as Clare Brandt (1934–) calls them in her study of the clan, was the Scotsman Robert Livingston, who arrived in New York in 1674, and within a few years married one of the Schuyler women of Albany, uniting two prominent landholding families. Livingston was to preside over one of the five manors—others were held by the Schuyler, Van Cortlandt, Morris, and Philipse heads—created in New York. A dozen years after he settled in the Valley the ambitious Livingston won for himself the title Lord of the Manor, his patents now totaling more than 160,000 acres of Indian lands. They extended east and west from the Hudson River to the Massachusetts border, and north and south almost twenty miles along the shoreline, including in this territory the Columbia and Dutchess county towns of what are now Clermont, Taghkanic, Linlithgow, Gallatin, Ancram, Germantown, and Copake. Through his holdings in the Hardenbergh Patent Livingston also oversaw hundreds of thousands of acres on the other side of the Hudson, much of it now part of the Catskill Forest Preserve.*

In time the Livingstons amassed a great family fortune, their power and position reaching into every level of state government, commerce, agriculture, and industry. As the country grew and gained independence, they served it as statesmen and entrepre-

182

*neurs, drawing to themselves all the privilege that follows position,
if sometimes unfairly. Now, in a turn of historical irony, the
very manorial system that left so much land between Westchester
and Albany in the hands of a few powerful families, discouraging settlement in more than two centuries of the system, fortuitously
isolated the landscape from the wanton destruction that accompanies development.*

*It was difficult to attract settlers to the manor lands under the
near feudal conditions for tenant farmers, but thousands of
Palatines fleeing war in Europe came to live there in the early part
of the eighteenth century, and some of their sturdy gray stone
houses still exist in the area. There was much to be done at the
manor, organizing crops and livestock, shipbuilding activities,
fur trade, mills, and the ironworks at Ancram, which would supply
cannonballs and shot, and the first chain barrier across the
Hudson, during the Revolution. The first manor home and center
of Livingston life was Clermont, which the British burned on
their rampage up the Hudson in October of 1777, after torching
the Poughkeepsie shipyards and the city of Kingston. Clermont
would be built anew, today reflecting in its long, rolling perspectives the green haze of a lost world.*

*For over two hundred years, a century before the war of independ-
ence, Livingstons had been building homes every few years, until the
east bank of the Hudson had more than forty houses by the end of
the nineteenth century. At least three quarters of them still stand, pre-
siding over unimaginably grand views of the Hudson and the distant
Catskills, especially at Montgomery Place, Edgewater, Staatsburgh, Rokeby,
and Wilderstein, the interiors of which exhibit the range of taste and
wealth, restoration and kindly neglect frequently characteristic of old
country seats. Brandt brings to her commentary which follows the
resigned and playful familiarity with Livingston manners of a Hudson
Valley resident who has walked with Livingstons through their houses
and around their gardens.*

AFTER WORLD WAR II the siege of "Livingston Valley" entered a grim phase. The besiegers without—forces of time and change, strengthened by new postwar social and financial realities—increased the pressure on the Livingston defenders within, who reacted in a variety of ways: some dug in, others cut and ran; many averted their eyes; and a few, sinking into hysterics, crumbled with the castle walls. A notable number, however, remained calm and managed to salvage something of the old way of life, including their own dignity.

Alice Clarkson Livingston, having moved out of the mansion at Clermont and into a gardener's cottage at the beginning of the war, never moved back. In a postwar world where good servants were unavailable or unaffordable, she preferred, in her seventy-third year, to remain in her little cottage and conserve her energy and resources for the Clermont gardens, which she never ceased to enlarge, modify and refine.

Everywhere around her, Livingston family estates were being sold, many to institutions which razed the old mansions and replaced them with modern, functional chapter houses, nursing facilities or school buildings. Sometimes the destruction was subtler: right next door to Alice at Ridgely, the Order of Carmelite Sisters preserved the charming white stucco house, with its graceful wrought-iron balconies and delicate tracery windows, but tacked on an awkward, outsized red brick extension and wavy green plastic sunshading. The Sisters manicured the woods and blacktopped the drive. Elegant, ethereal Ridgely was depersonalized, sterilized, institutionalized.

Private ownership was no guarantee of protection. At Teviotdale during the 1950s the owner (who was not a family member) sheltered his goats and pigs in Walter Livingston's classic eighteenth-century drawing room. Next door, Lady Mary's magnificent The Hill stood empty and abandoned, its tall white columns still dominating the valley below, its balustrades and doorframes, windows and fittings victimized by incessant scavenging. One group of vandals finally set the place afire, finishing the job that Lady Mary's rebellious tenants had started a hundred and fifty years before.

Saddest of all was the fate of The Hermitage, built just before the outbreak of the Revolutionary War by Robert Livingston, the third manor proprietor, for his son Peter R. Livingston. When the estate was purchased in the early 1980s by a wealthy outsider as a horse farm, the house had been derelict for years and was virtually uninhabitable. The new owner tried to sell the old mansion with a few acres attached; but after a short time, with no prospective purchaser forthcoming, she simply hired a bulldozer and knocked The Hermitage down.

A number of the old Livingston houses have endured roller-coaster existences in recent years. Grasmere, near Rhinebeck, originally built in 1774 by Janet and Richard Montgomery and subsequently owned by various Livingston sisters and cousins, eventually passed out of the family and survived the Depression by becoming a boarding school for girls. Twenty years later, in the 1950s, Grasmere became the setting for another family comeback, when Robert Clermont Livingston Timpson, grandson of John Henry Livingston of Clermont, purchased the estate and moved into river society with his wife, the former Duchess of Argyll. Ten years later Grasmere was put on the market again by Mrs. Timpson's son. By this time it was not so easy to find purchasers for large, drafty houses with whopping tax assessments, and Grasmere remained empty for a number of years. The caretaker's daughter camped out in the mansion with her children, husband and cats. The husband ran his motorcycle into the drawing room for an overhaul, leaving as his legacy a large black oil stain in the center of the parquet floor; and the cats deposited generations of droppings throughout Grasmere's elegant parlors, libraries, vestibules, boudoirs and stair landings.

Then, in 1972, Grasmere was purchased by an informal consortium of six New York City couples who began, slowly but surely, to bring the house back to life. Relying almost solely on their own man and woman power, they have restored the elegant marble porch, the graceful colonnaded foyer and the high-ceilinged drawing room (except for the oil stain, which will never disappear). More than ten years later they are still at it; and with luck and perseverance, Grasmere and they will prosper.

Teviotdale also has been redeemed by the cash, labor and devotion of newcomers from the city, as have Wildercliff, Edgewater and a number of other Livingston mansions. Fifteen of the original forty family houses are now the property of non-Livingston private owners. Nine belong to institutions. Seven are still in the family, occupied by descendants of their original builders—most of whom have to work extremely hard at various professions in order to earn the money to maintain their estates. One Livingston runs her late brother's mansion as a bed-and-breakfast establishment. Daisy Suckley's Wilderstein has not had a fresh coat of paint since 1910. (A recently formed nonprofit preservation group hopes to remedy that soon.) At Montgomery Place, raw two-by-fours brace the pillars on the front portico, and in the drawing room gold museum ropes are stretched across sofas and chairs, lest anyone should sit in them.

One contemporary Livingston proprietor puts it bluntly: "These monsters just aren't feasible for living. If you have one, you do nothing else. . . . You're always living poor, worried about things that nobody should worry about." Why, then, do they do it? Because, when all else fails, the land endures. Proprietorship has always furnished the Livingstons with their best demonstration of authenticity as aristocrats. Longevity in place—their continued suzerainty in "Livingston Valley"—defines the Livingston essence and tells them who they are.

It is not surprising, therefore, that the interest in "Livingston Valley" recently evidenced among conservationists, preservationists and architectural historians has prompted members of the family to react in a variety of ways that range from ecstasy to outrage. For every Livingston proprietor who looks to public concern as the salvation of his property, another sees it as rank invasion of privacy. The family simply cannot get together to either encourage or fight the trend. When, in 1979, most of the Livingston river frontage was placed on the National Register of Historic Places, virtually all the Livingston owners attended the ceremony at Clermont, except the owner of Montgomery Place, who deliberately boycotted it. Perhaps he was trying to avoid having to listen to quips like the one made by a valley newcomer who, after receiving his National Register plaque, laughingly dubbed his brand-new, modest summer cabin on the river an "instant landmark."

Given their history, Livingston heirs who choose to sell their estates face a unique set of problems, and letting go becomes an art form. Developers are anathema, of course, although the type of development that would be permitted has been somewhat restricted by the National Register designation. Nobody likes to see the estates go to charitable or religious institutions, neither the landed neighbors along the river nor the local villagers with their eyes on the tax rolls. Selling to a private individual or family is the most desirable course, especially if the buyers look like congenial prospects for the Edgewood Club. But even this can be painful, particularly if the sellers remain in the neighborhood. One former owner bemoans the "desecration" of the family seat by the new owners (or rather, by their decorator); and there are dispossessed Livingstons who consistently refuse invitations from the proprietors of their childhood homes.

In 1962, Alice Clarkson Livingston at the age of eighty-nine sold Clermont to the state of New York as a public historic site. Five years later, after a potentially disastrous false start, the state, in a rare display of bureaucratic competence, began gathering a group of talented, sensitive and knowledgeable conservators to supervise and carry out the restoration and preservation of the house and grounds. The dining-room ceiling beams were at long last laid bare, raised gingerly upward an inch at a time, reinforced and replastered. Clermont's roof was restored, tile by tile; its plumbing and heating systems modernized to museum standards; and the house and grounds opened to the public on a regular basis. Clermont, "disposed of to a Stranger," was saved for posterity.

Since the 1970s, Clermont State Historic Site has celebrated Independence Day with a fireworks display. Thousands of people come to the park for the whole day, to picnic and play Frisbee on the lawn, to listen to patriotic airs played by a local band and witness a hot-air balloon ascension on the east lawn. After dark skyrockets and Roman candles shoot up from the dock where the *North River Steam Boat* stopped on its maiden voyage in 1807. They may also serve as reminders, to the romantics in the crowd, of General Vaughn's cannon balls and bombs fired from the warship *Friendship* off that same point of land in 1777, the day that Clermont burned.

Nobody has a better time at Clermont on the Fourth than Alice and John Henry Livingston's surviving daughter, Honoria, whose husband once said, with a twinkle in his eye, that after Clermont was open to the public "everybody [could] enjoy the privilege of a Hudson River estate without having to pay the taxes."

Clare Brandt, *An American Aristocracy: The Livingstons* (New York: Doubleday and Company, 1986).

IV

SEASONS OF
THE TRAVELER

LETTER ON THE AMERICAN PEOPLE

Alexis de Tocqueville

O*N MAY 12, 1831, William Cullen Bryant's* New York Evening Post *announced the arrival of two magistrates who had come from France to examine the American prison system. The young aristocrats, Alexis de Tocqueville (1805–59) and his good friend Gustave de Beaumont, were fleeing from the 1830 Revolution, and what they really wanted to observe was the nature of the American republic. The first month of their trip they visited Sing Sing, which like Auburn farther upstate New York, and the Eastern Penitentiary in Pennsylvania, were heralded in Europe for skillful management, humane treatment of prisoners, and good health standards. Many visitors from abroad included a stop-over at Sing Sing, which had nine hundred inmates when they visited soon after their arrival here, and La Rochefoucauld had already published his work on American prisons by the time Tocqueville and Beaumont wrote their own book,* On the Penitentiary System in the U.S.

But there was to be another book from this visit which took Tocqueville all over the country for nine months, one that would be celebrated on both sides of the Atlantic, his unsurpassed Democracy in America. *Here was a two-volume study of the American people, their government, laws, customs, arts, and religion, organized with great insight and originality, and not a little hope that France might become a republic. In his own masterful work on the Frenchmen's travels, written on the eve of World War*

191

II, George Wilson Pierson, in a Rooseveltian turn of phrase, declared, "They would make 'democratie' safe for the world."

Pierson offers the best account available of their hilarious journey up the Hudson in his Tocqueville and Beaumont in America. *They started by sloop from Manhattan, intending to visit Edward Livingston, former Minister to France, near Yonkers. In the letter selected here, one of his earliest observations on America, Tocqueville writes home to his friend Louis de Kergorlay, already outlining some of the major themes of the book that will follow a few years later—it is entirely based on experiences in New York City and upstate. He also shoots some birds, Beaumont sketches Hudson views, the two go for a nighttime swim. The next day the real adventure unfolds when they board a steamboat to Peekskill, explore the area, admire the Highlands scenery, and get back on another boat, the* North America. *They plan to stop at West Point and Catskill. At Newburgh, they are surprised by fireworks and skyrockets going off on their boat, with people from town firing back rockets. They discover that the steamboat they are on is winning a race against another steamboat on the way to Albany— and they aren't allowed to get off. Later in a letter to his mother Tocqueville laments, "Not only did we not get to West-point, but we sailed all the way up the north river, the most picturesque spot in the world, in the middle of the night, and we arrived* fraîchement *at five in the morning in the city of Albany." Nearby they visited the Shakers at Niskeyuna, but were unimpressed with their dancing.*

Tocqueville and Beaumont find themselves in Albany for the Fourth of July. The Lieutenant-Governor of the state and city officials coax them into a parade through the city, where they all march with the fire department, various members of industries and associations waving colorful banners, veterans of the American Revolution, and alas, accompanying floats on historical themes!

Tocqueville would return home in the winter and soon prepare to write Democracy in America. *Two of the texts he had with him in France were to prove immensely helpful in his exhaustive research. One was* The Federalist, *the other was James Kent's* Commentaries on the Constitution. *Ironically, when the Marquis de*

Lafayette, the great French champion of America, sailed up the Hudson for his triumphant tour of 1824, he was on the steamboat James Kent.

To Louis de Kergorlay

Yonkers, June 29, 1831,

20 miles from New York

I AM BEGINNING my letter here, my dear friend, but I do not know when or where I will finish it. I have not written you earlier because I have not had anything in particular to tell you; I dislike talking of France from so far away. You would have nearly forgotten the events to which my letter referred by the time it reached you; the things I would be discussing would have changed ten times in the interim. On the other hand, before talking to you about this country, I wanted to know it a little better than I did when I had first arrived. I see that I have not gained much by waiting. The people of every foreign country have a certain external appearance that one perceives at first glance and retains very readily. When one wants to penetrate a little further, one finds real difficulties that were not expected, one proceeds with a discouraging slowness, and doubts seem to grow the more one progresses. I feel at this moment that my head is a chaos into which a throng of contradicting notions are pell-mell making their way. I am wearing myself out looking for some perfectly clear and conclusive points, and not finding any. In this state of mind, it is both agreeable and useful for me to be writing you. Maybe my ideas will untangle themselves a little under the obligation of explaining them.

You ask me in your last letter if there are *beliefs* here. I do not know what precise sense you attach to that word; what strikes me is that the immense majority of people are united in regard to certain *common opinions*. So far, that is what I have envied most about America. To begin with, I have not yet been able to overhear in a conversation with anyone, no matter to what rank in society they belong, the idea that a republic is not the best possible government, and that a people does not have the right to give itself whatever government it pleases. The great majority understands republican principles in the most democratic sense, although among some one can see a certain aristocratic tendency piercing through that I will try to explain to you below. But that a republic is a good government, that it is natural for human societies, no one seems to doubt— priests, magistrates, businessmen, artisans. That is an opinion that is so general and so little discussed, even in a country where freedom of speech is unlimited, that one could almost call it a belief. There is a second idea that seems to me to be of the same character; the immense majority has *faith* in human wisdom and good sense, faith in the doctrine of human perfectibility. That is another point that finds little or no contradiction. That the majority can be fooled once, no one denies, but people think that necessarily in the long run the majority is right, that it is not only the sole legal judge of its interest but also the surest and most infallible judge. The result of this idea is that enlightenment must be diffused widely among the people, that one cannot enlighten the people too much. You know how many times in France we have been anxious (we and a thousand others) to know if it is to be desirable or fearful for education to penetrate through all the ranks of society. This question, which is so difficult for France to resolve, does not even seem to present itself here. I have already posed this question a hundred times to the most reflective men; I have seen, by the way they have answered it, that it has never given them pause, and to them even stating the question had something shocking and absurd about it. Enlightenment, they say, is the sole guarantee we have against the mistakes of the multitude.

There you have, my dear friend, what I will call the *beliefs* of this country. They believe, in good faith, in the excellence of the government that rules them, they believe in the wisdom of the masses, provided that they are enlightened, and they do not seem to suspect that there is some education that can never be shared by the masses and that nonetheless can be necessary for governing a state.

As for what we generally understand by *beliefs*, ancient mores, ancient traditions, the power of memories, I have not seen any trace of these up to now. I even doubt that religious opinions have as great a power as one thinks at first sight. The state of religion among this people is perhaps the most curious thing to examine here. I will try to tell you what I know about this when I again pick up my letter, which I now have to interrupt, perhaps for several days.

Calwell, 45 miles from New York

My mind has been so stirred up since this morning by the beginning of my letter that I feel I have to take it up again without knowing just what I am going to say to you. I was speaking to you above about religion: one is struck on arriving here by the practical exactitude that accompanies the practice of religion. Sunday is observed Judaically, and I have seen streets blocked off in front of churches during the holy services. The law commands these things imperiously, and opinion, much stronger than the law, compels everyone to appear at church and to abstain from all amusements. Nevertheless, either I am badly mistaken or there is a great store of doubt and indifference hidden underneath these external forms. Political passion is not mixed, as it is in our country, with irreligion, but even so religion does not have any more power. It is a very strong impulse that was given in days gone by and which now is expiring day by day. Faith is evidently inert; enter the churches (I mean the Protestant ones) and you hear them speak of morality; of dogma not a word, nothing that could in any way shock a neighbor, nothing that could reveal the hint of dissidence. The human spirit loves to plunge itself into abstractions of dogma, discussions which are especially appropriate to a religious doctrine, whenever a belief has seized it strongly; the Americans themselves were formerly like that. This so-called tolerance, which, in my opinion, is nothing but a huge indifference, is pushed so far that in public establishments like prisons, the homes for juvenile delinquents . . . seven or eight ministers of different sects come to preach successively to the same inmates. But, I was saying, how those men and those children who belong to one sect find themselves listening to the ministry of another. The infallible response is this: the different preachers, because they occupy themselves only with treating the platitudes of morality, cannot do harm to one another. Besides, it is evident that here, generally speaking, religion does not move people deeply; in France those who believe demonstrate their belief by sacrifices of time, effort, and wealth. One senses that they are acting under the sway of a passion that dominates them and for which they have become agents. It is true that alongside these people one finds the kinds of brutes who hold in horror the very name of religion and who do not very easily even distinguish good from evil. Neither of these groups seems to exist here among the bulk of Protestants. People follow a religion the way our fathers took a medicine in the month of May—if it does not do any good, people seem to say, at least it cannot do any harm, and, besides, it is proper to conform to the general rule. How could it be otherwise? . . .

Do you know what is striking me most vividly about political matters in this country? It is the effect of the laws on estates. At the time of the American Revolution, political equality existed among the colonials, but not equality of wealth. The English had brought here their primogeniture laws, according to the terms of which the oldest took three-quarters of the father's wealth all to himself. As a result, the country had been filled with vast territorial domains passing from father to son, perpetuating riches within families. So, and here I am only following the accounts of the Americans themselves, there was no class of nobles, but a class of great landowners, living a simple but intellectual enough life, having a certain tone, certain elevated manners, attached to the spirit of family to the point of honor. . . . A certain number of these families took England's side and consequently were the cause of the revolution. Now, that was all less than sixty years ago. The laws concerning estates were changed; equal division succeeded the right of primogeniture. A change which has something magical about it has resulted from that. Estates were broken up and passed into other hands, the family spirit was lost, the aristocratic tendency, which had marked the first period of the republic, was replaced by a democratic tendency which is irresistible and which no one can have the least hope of fighting. Now the division of properties is immense, the rapidity with which they change hands surpasses anything I could have imagined. I saw several members of these old families I have been telling you about. It is easy to perceive in the depths of their hearts great discontent

against the new order of things. They regret the passage of patronage, the family spirit, the elevated mores, in a word—aristocracy. But
they submit themselves to a fact that henceforth is irreparable. They
acknowledge that they are no longer anything but a single unit in the
state. But they submit to this necessity in good enough grace,
because if they are no longer favored more than others, at least their
old position has not become a mark of exclusion. Their family having
taken part in the revolution, they themselves never having done
more than struggle indirectly against the extension of democracy,
public opinion has never systematically declared itself against them. I
have heard it said in Europe that there was an aristocratic tendency
in America. Those who say that are mistaken; this is one of the things
that I would affirm most readily. Democracy is, on the contrary, either
in full march in certain states or in its fullest imaginable extension in
others. It is in the mores, in the laws, in the opinion of the majority.
Those who are opposed to it hide themselves and are reduced to
taking its very colors in order to advance. In New York, only vagrants
are deprived of electoral rights. The effects of a democratic government are visible elsewhere; that is, in a perpetual instability in men
and in laws, an external equality pushed to its farthest point, a tone
of manners and a uniformly common turn of ideas. One cannot
doubt that the law concerning estates is one of the principal causes
of this complete triumph of democratic principles. The Americans
recognize this themselves, either because they complain about it or
because they rejoice in it; it is the law of succession that makes us
what we are, it is the foundation of our republic—this is what we
hear every day. . . . In a word, from now on democracy seems to me a
fact that a government can have the pretension of *regulating*, but of
stopping, no. It is not without difficulty, I assure you, that I have
surrendered to this idea; what I see in this country does not prove to
me that, even in the most favorable circumstances, and they have
existed here, the government of the multitude is an excellent thing.
It is generally agreed that in the first days of the republic, the men of
state, the members of the chambers, were much more distinguished
than they are today. They almost all belonged to the class of
proprietors, of which I spoke to you above. Now the people no
longer have *so fortunate a hand*. Their choices in general fall on

those who flatter its passions and put themselves within its reach. This effect of democracy, together with the extreme instability in all things, with the absolute lack that one notices here of any spirit of continuation and duration, convinces me more every day that the most rational government is not that in which *all* the interested parties take part, but that which the most enlightened and most moral classes of the society direct. It cannot be concealed, however, that as a whole this country presents an admirable spectacle. It impresses me, I tell you frankly, with the superiority of free governments over all others. I feel more convinced than ever that all peoples are not made to enjoy such government to the same extent, but I am also more than ever disposed to think that it is regrettable that this is so. A universal satisfaction with the existing government prevails here, to an extent you cannot imagine. These people incontestably are situated higher on the moral scale than among us; each man has a sense of his independent position and his individual dignity that does not always make his bearing very agreeable, but which definitely leads him to respect himself and to respect others. I especially admire two things here: the first is the extreme respect people have for the law; alone and without public force, it commands in an irresistible way. I believe, in truth, that the principal cause of this is that they make it themselves and can change it. One is always seeing thieves who have violated all the laws of their countries scrupulously obeying those they make themselves. I believe that something similar is happening in the spirit of the people everywhere. The second thing that I envy in the people here is the ease with which it does without government. Every man here considers himself interested in public security and in the exercise of laws. Instead of counting on the police, he counts only on himself. It follows, in short, that without its ever appearing, public force is everywhere. It is a truly incredible thing to see, I assure you, how this people keeps itself in order by the sole sentiment that it has no safeguard against itself except within itself.

You see that I am giving you the most thorough account I can of all the impressions I am receiving. In short, they are more favorable to America than they were during the first days after my arrival. There is in the picture a throng of defective details, but the ensemble seizes the imagination. I understand especially that it acts in an irresistible way on logical and superficial minds, a combination that is not rare. The principles of government are so simple, the consequences are deduced from them with so perfect a regularity, that the mind is subjugated and carried away if it does not take care. It is necessary to take stock of oneself, to struggle against the current in order to perceive that these institutions which are so simple and so logical would not suit a great nation that needs a strong internal government and fixed foreign policy; that it is not durable by its nature; that it requires, within the people that confers it on itself, a long habit of liberty and of a body of *true* enlightenment which can be acquired only rarely and in the long run. And after all that is said, one comes back again to thinking that it is nonetheless a good thing and that it is regrettable that the moral and physical constitution of man prohibits him from obtaining it everywhere and forever. . . .

Farewell, my dear friend; I embrace you from the bottom of my heart. Keep this letter. It will be interesting for me later on.

Alexis de Tocqueville, *Selected Letters on Politics and Society* (Berkeley: University of California Press, 1985).

THE THIRD VOYAGE OF
MASTER HENRY HUDSON

Robert Juet

O*N APRIL 6, 1609, Henry Hudson set sail from
Amsterdam with his English and Dutch crew in the eighty-ton*
Half Moon *to search for a northeast passage to India. One of the
men onboard was the officer Robert Juet (d. 1611), whose journal is the fullest surviving account of the voyage. The Dutch East
India Company, which had just introduced tea from China into
Europe, sent the English navigator on his historic voyage. That year
the colonial powers Holland and Spain signed a truce that ended
decades of conflict. In England Shakespeare was completing*
Cymbeline, *and Rembrandt, who was to paint so extraordinary
a portrait of seventeenth-century Dutch life, had recently been born.*

*For the accomplished explorer Hudson, it was his third attempt
to discover a new route to Asia. Instead, five thousand miles
off course, he came to the North American continent. The* Half Moon
*made its way along the coastline past Newfoundland, Cape Cod,
as far south as the Carolinas, on the way exploring the waters of
the Delaware and the Chesapeake. The ship entered the Hudson
(known then as the North, Nassau, or Great) River at Sandy Hook
on the Jersey shore. By September the crew was in the Hudson
Valley, sailing as far as the Albany area. In one of the surviving
fragments of Hudson's now lost ship's log he wrote in mid-
September, "The land is the finest for cultivation that I ever in my
life set foot upon, and it also abounds in trees of every description." The* Half Moon *eventually headed out to sea farther south at
the Virginia coast, where Captain John Smith had established*

200

*the first permanent English settlement in the New World at Jamestown,
before arriving home at Devonshire in November.*

*Hudson was not the first European to sail into the waters that
would bear his name. In 1524 Giovanni Verrazano claimed
that distinction. The Portuguese explorer Estevan Gomez, who called
the river Rio San Antonio, was there a year later. But it was
Hudson who was to give his name to the magnificent River and its
Valley, after the English took New Netherland from the Dutch
(who called the river Mauritius) more than half a century later. A
few years after Hudson's discovery Dutch traders came to New
Netherland, and in the decade after that the first colonists followed.
Hudson himself came to a sad end when in 1611 he, his son,
and a few sailors were put out in the open sea by a mutinous
crew that included, alas, Robert Juet of Lime-house, who kept
this record of the 1609 voyage. It begins in September.*

THE ELEVENTH was faire and very hot weather. At one of the clocke in
the after-noone, wee weighed and went into the River, the wind at
South South-west, little winde. Our soundings were seven, sixe, five,
sixe, seven, eight, nine, ten, twelve, thirteene, and fourteene fathomes.
Then it shoalded againe, and came to five fathomes. Then wee
Anchored, and saw that it was a very good Harbour for all windes,
and rode all night. The people of the Countrey came aboord of us,
making shew of love, and gave us Tabacco and Indian Wheat, and
departed for that night; but we durst not trust them.

The twelfth, very faire and hot. In the after-noone at two of the
clocke wee weighed, the winde being variable, betweene the North
and the North-west. So we turned into the River[1] two leagues and
Anchored. This morning at our first rode in the River, there came
eight and twentie Canoes full of men, women and children to betray
us: but we saw their intent, and suffered none of them to come

---

[1]The North or Hudson River.

aboord of us. At twelve of the clocke they departed. They brought with them Oysters and Beanes, whereof wee bought some. They have great Tabacco pipes of yellow Copper, and Pots of Earth to dresse their meate in. It floweth South-east by South within.

The thirteenth, faire weather, the wind Northerly. At seven of the clocke in the morning, as the floud came we weighed, and turned foure miles into the River. The tide being done wee anchored. Then there came foure Canoes aboord: but we suffered none of them to come into our ship. They brought great store of very good Oysters aboord, which we bought for trifles. In the night I set the variation of the Compasse, and found it to be 13 degrees. In the after-noone we weighed, and turned in with the floud, two leagues and a halfe further, and anchored all night, and had five fathoms soft Ozie ground; and had an high point of Land, which shewed out to us, bearing North by East five leagues off us.

The fourteenth, in the morning being very faire weather, the wind South-east, we sayled up the River twelve leagues, and had five fathoms, and five fathoms and a quarter lesse; and came to a Streight betweene two Points,[2] and had eight, nine, and ten fathoms: and it trended North-east by North, one league: and wee had twelve, thirteene, and fourteene fathomes. The River is a mile broad: there is very high Land on both sides. Then wee went up North-west, a league and an halfe deepe water. Then North-east by North five miles; then North-west by North two leagues, and anchored. The Land grew very high and Mountainous. The River is full of fish.

The fifteenth, in the morning was misty, untill the Sunne arose: then it cleered. So wee weighed with the wind at South, and ran up into the River twentie leagues, passing by high Mountaines.[3] Wee had a very good depth, as sixe, seven, eight, nine, ten, twelve, and thirteene fathoms, and great store of Salmons in the River. This morning out two Savages got out of a Port and swam away. After we were under sayle, they called to us in scorne. At night we came to other Mountaines, which lie from the Rivers side.[4] There wee found

[2]Stony Point and Verplanck's Point. Apparently Hudson anchored this night near West Point.
[3]The upper Highlands
[4]The Catskills.

very loving peeple, and very old men: where wee were well used. Our Boat went to fish, and caught great store of very good fish.

The sixteenth, faire and very hot weather. In the morning our Boat went againe to fishing, but could catch but few, by reason their Canoes had beene there all night. This morning the people came aboord, and brought us eares of Indian Corne, and Pompions, and Tabacco: which wee bought for trifles. Wee rode still all day, and filled fresh water; at night wee weighed and went two leagues higher, and had shoald water:[5] so wee anchored till day.

The seventeenth, faire Sun-shining weather, and very hot. In the morning, as soone as the Sun was up, we set sayle, and ran up sixe leagues higher, and fould shoalds in the middle of the channell, and small Ilands, but seven fathoms water on both sides. Toward night we borrowed so neere the shoare, that we grounded: so we layed out our small anchor, and heaved off againe. Then we borrowed on the banke in the channell, and came aground againe; while the floud ran we heaved off againe, and anchored all night.[6]

The eighteenth, in the morning was faire weather, and we rode still. In the after-noone our Masters Mate went on land with an old Savage, a Governour of the Countrey; who carried him to his house, and made him good cheere. The nineteenth, was faire and hot weather: at the floud, being neere eleven of the clocke, wee weighed, and ran higher up two leagues above the shoalds, and had no lesse water then five fathoms; wee anchored, and rode in eight fathomes. The people of the Countrie came flocking aboord, and brought us Grapes and Pompions, which wee bought for trifles. And many brought us Bevers skinnes, and Otters skinnes, which wee bought for Beades, Knives, and Hatchets. So we rode there all night.[6]

The twentieth, in the morning was faire weather. Our Masters Mate with foure men more went up with our Boat to sound the River, and found two leagues above us but two fathomes water, and the channell very narrow; and above that place, seven or eight fathomes. Toward night they returned: and we rode still all night. The one and twentieth, was faire weather, and the wind all Southerly: we determined yet once more to goe farther up into the River, to trie what

[5]Probably near Hudson and Athens.
[6]Near the present site of Albany.

depth and breadth it did beare; but much people resorted aboord, so wee went not this day. Our Carpenter went on land, and made a fore-yard. And our Master and his Mate determined to trie some of the chiefe men of the Countrey, whether they had any treacherie in them. So they tooke them downe into the Cabbin, and gave them so much Wine and *Aqua vitae*, that they were all merrie: and one of them had his wife with him, which sate so modestly, as any of our countrey women would doe in a strange place. In the end one of them was drunke, which had beene aboord of our ship all the time that we had beene there: and that was strange to them; for they could not tell how to take it. The Canoes and folke went all on shoare: but some of them came againe, and brought stropes of Beades: some had sixe, seven, eight, nine, ten; and gave him. So he slept all night quietly.

The two and twentieth, was faire weather: In the morning our Masters Mate and foure more of the companie went up with our Boat to sound the River higher up. The people of the Countrey came not aboord till noone: but when they came, and saw the Savages well, they were glad. So at three of the clocke in the after-noone they came aboord, and brought Tabacco, and more Beades, and gave them to our Master, and made an Oration, and shewed him all the Countrey round about. Then they sent one of their companie on land, who presently returned, and brought a great Platter full of Venison dressed by themselves; and they caused him to eate with them: then they made him reverence, and departed all save the old man that lay aboord. This night at ten of the clocke, our Boat returned in a showre of raine from sounding of the River; and found it to bee at an end for shipping to goe in. For they had beene up eight or nine leagues,[7] and found but seven foot water, and unconstant soundings.

The three and twentieth, faire weather. At twelve of the clocke wee weighed, and went downe two leagues to a shoald that had two channels, one on the one side, and another on the other, and had little wind, whereby the tide layed us upon it. So, there wee sate on ground the space of an houre till the floud came. Then we had a little

[7]Perhaps above the mouth of the Mohawk.

gale of wind at the West. So wee got our ship into deepe water, and rode all night very well.

The foure and twentieth was faire weather: the winde at the North-west, wee weighed, and went downe the River seven or eight leagues; and at halfe ebbe wee came on ground on a banke of Oze in the middle of the river, and sate there till the floud. Then wee went on Land, and gathered good store of Chest-nuts. At ten of the clocke we came off into deepe water, and anchored.

The five and twentieth was faire weather, and the wind at South a stiff gale. We rode still, and went on Land[8] to walke on the West side of the River, and found good ground for Corne and other Garden herbes, with great store of goodly Oakes, and Wal-nut trees, and Chest-nut trees, Ewe trees, and trees of sweet wood in great abundance, and great store of Slate for houses, and other good stones.

The sixe and twentieth was faire weather, and the wind at South a stiffe gale, wee rode still. In the morning our Carpenter went on Land, with our Masters Mate, and foure more of our companie, to cut wood. This morning, two Canoes came up the River from the place where we first found loving people, and in one of them was the old man that had lyen aboord of us at the other place. He brought another old man with him, which brought more stropes of Beades, and gave them to our Master, and shewed him all the Countrey there about, as though it were at his command. So he made the two old men dine with him, and the old mans wife: for they brought two old women, and two young maidens of the age of sixteene or seventeene yeeres with them, who behaved themselves very modestly. Our Master gave one of the old men a Knife, and they gave him and us Tabbaco. And at one of the clocke they departed downe the River, making signes that we should come down to them; for wee were within two leagues of the place where they dwelt.

The seven and twentieth, in the morning was faire weather, but much wind at the north, we weighed and set our fore top-sayle, and our ship would not flat, but ran on the Ozie banke at halfe ebbe. Wee

---

[8]Near Athens, apparently.

layed out anchor to heave her off, but could not. So wee sate from halfe ebbe to halfe floud: then wee set our fore-sayle and mayne top-sayl, and got downe sixe leagues. The old man came aboord, and would have had us anchor, and goe on Land, to eate with him: but the wind being faire, we would not yeeld to his request; So hee left us, being very sorrowfull for our departure. At five of the clocke in the after-noone, the wind came to the South South-west. So wee made a boord or two, and anchored in fourteene fathomes water. Then our Boat went on shoare to fish right against the ship. Our Masters Mate and Boat-swaine, and three more of the companie went on land to fish, but could not finde a good place. They tooke foure or five and twentie Mullets, Breames, Bases, and Barbils; and returned in an houre. We rode still all night.

The eight and twentieth, being faire weather, as soone as the day was light, wee weighed at halfe ebbe, and turned downe two leagues belowe water; for, the streame doth runne the last quarter ebbe: then we anchored till high water. At three of the clocke in the after-noon we weighed, and turned downe three leagues, untill it was darke: then wee anchored.

The nine and twentieth was drie close weather: the wind at South, and South and by West, we weighed early in the morning, and turned downe three leagues by a lowe water, and anchored at the lower end of the long Reach;[9] for it is sixe leagues long. Then there came certaine Indians in a Canoe to us, but would not come aboord. After dinner there came the Canoe with other men, whereof three came aboord us. They brought Indian Wheat, which wee bought for trifles. At three of the clocke in the after-noone wee weighed, as soone as the ebbe came, and turned downe to the edge of the Mountaines, or the Northermost of the Mountains, and anchored: because the high Land hath many Points, and a narrow channell, and hath many eddie winds. So we rode quietly all night in seven fathoms water.

The thirtieth was faire weather, and the wind at Southeast a stiffe gale betwene the Mountaynes. We rode still the after-noone.[10] The people of the Countrey came aboord us, and brought some small skinnes with them, which we bought for Knives and Trifles. This a

[9]Below Poughkeepsie.
[10]Near Newburgh.

very pleasant place to build a towne on. The Road is very neere, and very good for all winds, save an East North-east wind. The Mountaynes looke as if some Metall or Minerall were in them. For the Trees that grow on them were all blasted, and some of them barren with few or no Trees on them. The people brought a stone aboord like to Emery (a stone used by Glasiers to cut Glasse) it would cut Iron or Steele: yet being bruised small, and water put to it, it made a colour like blacke Lead glistering; It is also good for Painters Colours. At three of the clocke they departed, and we rode still all night.

The first of October, faire weather, the wind variable betweene the West and the North. In the morning we weighed at seven of the clocke with the ebbe, and got downe below the Mountaynes, which was seven leagues. Then it fell calme and the floud was come, and wee anchored at twelve of the clocke.[11] The people of the Mountaynes came aboord us, wondering at our ship and weapons. We bought some small skinnes of them for Trifles. This after-noone, one Canoe kept hanging under our sterne with one man in it, which we could not keepe from thence, who got up by our Rudder to the Cabin window, and stole out my Pillow, and two Shirts, and two Bandeleeres. Our Masters Mate shot at him, and strooke him on the brest, and killed him. Whereupon all the rest fled away, some in their Canoes, and so leapt out of them into the water. We manned our Boat, and got our things againe. Then one of them that swamme got hold of our Boat, thinking to overthrow it. But our Cooke tooke a Sword, and cut off one of his hands, and he was drowned. By this time the ebbe was come, and we weighed and got downe two leagues, by that time it was darke. So we anchored in foure fathomes water, and rode well.

The second, faire weather. At breake of day wee weighed, the wind being at North-west, and got downe seven leagues; then the floud was come strong, so we anchored. Then came one of the Savages that swamme away from us at our going up the River with many other, thinking to betray us. But wee perceived their intent, and suffered none of them to enter our ship. Whereupon two Canoes full of men, with their Bowes and Arrowes shot at us after our sterne: in recompence whereof we discharged sixe Muskets, and killed two or

---

[11]Near Stony Point.

three of them. Then above an hundred of them came to a point of Land to shoot at us. There I shot a Falcon at them, and killed two of them: whereupon the rest fled into the Woods. Yet they manned off another Canoe with nine or ten men, which came to meet us. So I shot at it also a Falcon, and shot it through, and killed one of them. Then our men with their Muskets killed three or foure more of them. So they went their way, within a while after, wee got downe two leagues beyond that place, and anchored in a Bay, cleere from all danger of them on the other side of the River, where we saw a very good piece of ground: and hard by it there was a Cliffe, that looked of the colour of a white greene, as though it were either Copper, or Silver myne: and I thinke it to be one of them, by the Trees that grow upon it. For they be all burned, and the other places are greene as grasse, it is on that side of the River that is called *Manna-hata*. There we saw no people to trouble us: and rode quietly all night; but had much wind and raine.

J. Franklin Jameson, ed., *Original Narratives of Early American History: Narratives of New Netherland 1609–1664* (New York: Charles Scribner's Sons, 1909).

꒱꒱꒱꒱꒱꒱꒱꒱꒱꒱꒱꒱꒱꒱꒱

PINE ORCHARD HOUSE

Harriet Martineau

A *PROMINENT VICTORIAN woman of letters, Harriet Martineau (1802–76) spent the years 1834–36 in America, and like many a traveler before and after her, she wrote extensively of her trip. Her subjects ranged from politics, slavery, and education to prisons, weather, and cemeteries, drawn from observations in New England, the mid-Atlantic states, and the South. In the Hudson Valley she met Washington Irving, David Hosack (Alexander Hamilton's second at his fateful duel, and a physician and botanist known for his gardens at Hyde Park), and Edward Livingston. By the time she came to America, there was a list of sights, well established as necessary for a cultured traveler here as the Grand Tour on the European continent.*

No visit was as special to Martineau as her weekend at the Catskill Mountain House, which was clearly a religious experience. And what better time to arrive than a stormy Saturday night, the sky trembling with red lightning. This particular kind of sky was on its way to being made famous in the works of the Hudson River School of painters. Martineau visited the Catskill Mountain House a decade after it opened, at a time when it was the only large mountain resort hotel in the country, and renowned for its awesome surroundings. Her long, lyrical description of the view from her hotel window echoes the sentiments of many nineteenth-century tourists, who told of rejoicing in what was then regarded as the "sublime" in nature. Likewise, she writes of being as it were a witness to creation, and the coming of light out of dark-

209

ness. There is a true feeling of spiritual joy in Martineau's words,
a kind of worship that travelers often sensed nearly 2,300 feet up
in the mist. From the escarpment on which the hotel was perched
it was possible to see Connecticut, Vermont, the Berkshires of Massa-
chusetts, and the Hudson Valley from Poughkeepsie to Albany.
Heaven, too, if one wished.

Martineau conveys the full sensuality of her impressions, yet she
was deaf and had no sense of taste or smell. What she had in
abundance was a passionate mind, strong will, and controversial
views on everything from history, economics, and social thought
to farming, religion, mesmerism, and women's rights. Her ideas were
linked to major figures of her day, such as Thomas Malthus,
John Stuart Mill, Auguste Comte, and Adam Smith. Among her lit-
erary friends were Charlotte Brontë, William Wordsworth, and
George Eliot, who wrote that Martineau was "the only English wom-
an that possesses thoroughly the art of writing."

HOWEVER WIDELY European travellers have differed about other things
in America, all seem to agree in their love of the Hudson. The pens
of all tourists dwell on its scenery, and their affections linger about it
like the magic lights which seem to have this river in their peculiar
charge. Yet very few travellers have seen its noblest wonder. I may be
singular; but I own that I was more moved by what I saw from the
Mountain House than by Niagara itself.

What is this Mountain House? this Pine Orchard House? many will
ask; for its name is not to be found in most books of American
travels. "What is that white speck?" I myself asked, when staying at
Tivoli, on the east bank of the Hudson, opposite to the Catskills, whose
shadowy surface was perpetually tempting the eye. That white speck,
visible to most eyes only when bright sunshine was upon it, was the
Mountain House; a hotel built for the accommodation of hardy
travellers who may desire to obtain that complete view of the valley
of the Hudson which can be had nowhere else. I made up my mind
to go; and the next year I went, on leaving Dr. Hosack's. I think I had

rather have missed the Hawk's Nest, the Prairies, the Mississippi, and even Niagara, than this.

The steamboat in which we left Hyde Park landed us at Catskill (thirty-one miles) at a little after three in the afternoon. Stages were waiting to convey passengers to the Mountain House, and we were off in a few minutes, expecting to perform the ascending journey of twelve miles in a little more than four hours. We had the same horses all the way, and therefore set off at a moderate pace, though the road was for some time level, intersecting rich bottoms, and passing flourishing farmhouses, where the men were milking, and the women looked up from their work in the piazzas as we passed. Haymaking was going on in the fields, which appeared to hang above us at first, but on which we afterward looked down from such a height that the haycocks were scarcely distinguishable. It was the 25th of July, and a very hot day for the season. The roads were parched up, and every exposed thing that one handled on board the steamboat or in the stage made one flinch from the burning sensation. The panting horses, one of them bleeding at the mouth, stopped to drink at a house at the foot of the ascent; and we wondered how, exhausted as they seemed, they would drag us up the mountain. We did not calculate on the change of temperature which we were soon to experience.

The mountain laurel conveyed by association the first impression of coolness. Sheep were browsing among the shrubs, apparently enjoying the shelter of the covert. We scrambled through deep shade for three or four miles, heavy showers passing over us, and gusts of wind bowing the treetops, and sending a shiver through us, partly from the sudden chillness, and partly from expectation and awe of the breezy solitude. On turning a sharp angle of the steep road, at a great elevation, we stopped in a damp green nook, where there was an arrangement of hollow trees to serve for water-troughs. While the horses were drinking, the gusts parted the trees to the left, and exposed to me a vast extent of country lying below, checkered with light and shadow. This was the moment in which a lady in the stage said, with a yawn, "I hope we shall find something at the top to pay us for all this." Truly the philosophy of recompense seems to be little understood. In moral affairs people seem to expect recompense for privileges, as when children, grown and ungrown, are told that they will be rewarded for doing their duty; and here was a lady hoping for recompense for being carried up a glorious mountainside, in ease, coolness, leisure, and society, all at once. If it was recompense for the evil of inborn *ennui* that she wanted, she was not likely to find it where she was going to look for it.

After another level reach of road and another scrambling ascent I saw something on the rocky platform above our heads like (to compare great things with small) an illumined fairy palace perched among the clouds in opera scenery; a large building, whose numerous window-lights marked out its figure from amid the thunder-clouds and black twilight which overshadowed it. It was now half past eight o'clock and a stormy evening. Everything was chill, and we were glad of lights and tea in the first place.

After tea I went out upon the platform in front of the house, having been warned not to go too near the edge, so as to fall an unmeasured depth into the forest below. I sat upon the edge as a security against stepping over unawares. The stars were bright overhead, and had conquered half the sky, giving promise of what we ardently desired, a fine morrow. Over the other half the mass of thunder-clouds was, I supposed, heaped together, for I could at first discern nothing of the champaign which I knew must be stretched below. Suddenly, and from that moment incessantly, gushes of red lightning poured out from the cloudy canopy, revealing not merely the horizon, but the course of the river, in all its windings through the valley. This thread of river, thus illuminated, looked like a flash of lightning caught by some strong hand and laid along in the valley. All the principal features of the landscape might, no doubt, have been discerned by this sulphurous light; but my whole attention was absorbed by the river, which seemed to come out of the darkness like an apparition at the summons of my impatient will. It could be borne only for a short time; this dazzling, bewildering alternation of glare and blackness, of vast reality and nothingness. I was soon glad to draw back from the precipice and seek the candlelight within.

The next day was Sunday. I shall never forget, if I live to a hundred, how the world lay at my feet one Sunday morning. I rose very early, and looked abroad from my window, two stories above the platform. A dense fog, exactly level with my eyes, as it appeared, roofed in the whole plain of the earth; a dusky firmament in which the stars had hidden themselves for the day. Such is the account which an antediluvian spectator would probably have given of it. This solid firmament had spaces in it, however, through which gushes of sunlight were poured, lighting up the spires of white churches, and clusters of farm buildings too small to be otherwise distinguished; and especially the river, with its sloops floating like motes in the sunbeam. The firmament rose and melted, or parted off into the likeness of snowy sky-mountains, and left the cool Sabbath to brood brightly over the land. What human interest sanctifies a bird's-eye view! I suppose this is its peculiar charm, for its charm is found to deepen in proportion to the growth of mind. To an infant, a champaign of a hundred miles is not so much as a yard square of gay carpet. To the rustic it is less bewitching than a paddock with two cows. To the philosopher, what is it not? As he casts his eye over its glittering towns, its scattered hamlets, its secluded homes, its mountain ranges, church spires, and untrodden forests, it is a picture of life; an epitome of the human universe; the complete volume of moral philosophy, for which he had sought in vain in all libraries. On the left horizon are the Green Mountains of Vermont, and at the right extremity sparkles the Atlantic. Beneath lies the forest where the deer are hiding and the birds rejoicing in song. Beyond the river he sees spread the rich plains of Connecticut; there, where a blue expanse lies beyond the triple range of hills, are the churches of religious Massachusetts sending up their Sabbath psalms; praise which he is too high to hear, while God is not. The fields and waters seem to him to-day no more truly property than the skies which shine down upon them; and to think how some below are busying their thoughts this Sabbath-day about how they shall hedge in another field, or multiply their flocks on yonder meadows, gives him a taste of the same pity which Jesus felt in his solitude when his followers were contending about which should be greatest. It seems strange to him now that man should call anything *his* but the power which is in him, and which can create somewhat more vast and beautiful than all that this horizon encloses. Here he gains the conviction, to be never again shaken, that all that is real is ideal; that the joys and sorrows of men do not spring up out of the ground, or fly abroad on the wings of the wind, or come showered down from the sky; that good cannot be hedged in, nor evil barred out; even that light does not reach the spirit through the eye alone, nor wisdom through the medium of sound or silence only. He becomes of one mind with the spiritual Berkeley, that the face of nature itself, the very picture of woods, and streams, and meadows, is a hieroglyphic writing in the spirit itself, of which the retina is no interpreter. The proof is just below him (at least it came under my eye), in the lady (not American) who, after glancing over the landscape, brings her chair into the piazza, and, turning her back to the champaign, and her face to the wooden walls of the hotel, begins the study, this Sunday morning, of her lapful of newspapers. What a sermon is thus preached to him at this moment from a very hackneyed text! To him that hath much; that hath the eye, and ear, and wealth of the spirit, shall more be given; even a replenishing of this spiritual life from that which to others is formless and dumb; while from him that hath little, who trusts in that which lies about him rather than in that which lives within him, shall be taken away, by natural decline, the power of perceiving and enjoying what is within his own domain. To him who is already enriched with large divine and human revelations this scene is, for all its stillness, musical with divine and human speech; while one who has been deafened by the din of worldly affairs can hear nothing in this mountain solitude.

The march of the day over the valley was glorious, and I was grieved to have to leave my window for an expedition to the Falls a few miles off. The Falls are really very fine, or, rather, their environment; but I could see plenty of waterfalls elsewhere, but nowhere else such a mountain platform. However, the expedition was a good preparation for the return to my window. The little nooks of the road, crowded with bilberries, cherries, and alpine plants, and the quiet tarn, studded with golden water-lilies, were a wholesome contrast to the grandeur of what we had left behind us.

On returning, we found dinner awaiting us, and also a party of friends out of Massachusetts, with whom we passed the afternoon, climbing higher and higher among the pines, ferns, and blue-berries of the mountain, to get wider and wider views. They told me that I saw Albany, but I was by no means sure of it. This large city lay in the landscape like an anthill in a meadow. Long before sunset I was at my window again, watching the gradual lengthening of the shadows and purpling of the landscape. It was more beautiful than the sunrise of this morning, and less so than that of the morrow. Of this last I shall give no description, for I would not weary others with what is most sacred to me. Suffice it that it gave me a vivid idea of the process of creation, from the moment when all was without form and void, to that when light was commanded, and there was light.

Harriet Martineau, *Retrospect of Western Travel*, Vol. 1 (New York: Harper & Brothers, 1838).

GENERAL LAFAYETTE RETURNS TO AMERICA

Frederick Butler

O*N THE EVE OF his departure for a trip up the Hudson to Albany, the Marquis de Lafayette attended a ball in his honor at New York City's Castle Garden at the Battery. Six thousand guests came to the glamorous entertainment hall to honor Lafayette, who at sixty-seven was the most celebrated man from the Revolutionary period, out-side of Thomas Jefferson, still alive in 1824. This was only the begin-ning of the most spectacular political pageantry of its kind in American history. Before he left Manhattan the Marquis attended numerous ban-quets and receptions, visited arts and educational institutions, and attended evenings at the theater in which he saw himself represented on stage. But in what must surely have been an early linkage of kitsch and commerce, in a year long fete given to excessive sentiment for the return of the hero, mass-produced fans, gold and silver medallions, gloves, sashes, and handkerchiefs were created as souvenirs for the event. There was even such a fashion known as "Lafayette vesting" advertised in the papers—vests with the Marquis's bust and name attached.*

Lafayette spent four glorious September days in the Hudson Valley, accompanied by his son George Washington Lafayette and a host of dignitaries. The historian Frederick Butler (1766–1843) gives a charm-ing account of the outpouring of civic pride that was to greet Lafayette, not only here but everywhere he went. He made it to all of the twenty-four states. Processions, balls, floats, parades, transparencies, triumphal arches, engravings, paintings, fireworks, air balloon demonstrations—every scenic effect and new technology was used to entrance the last surviv-ing general of the Continental Army.

The young Lafayette, whom George Washington loved above all men, served as an aide-de-camp to him, arriving in this country in 1777. He fought at Gloucester, Monmouth, and Yorktown, and as Major General commanding forces for a time at Virginia and Albany. In 1780 the French forces, under the leadership of Comte de Rochambeau, arrived to fight with the Patriots against their own archrival, the British. Seventeen years earlier the French had forfeited all claims to North America under the Treaty of Paris. Lafayette became a tireless promoter of the American cause at the court of Louis XVI, returning to France to help secure loans and supplies. He took part in peace negotiations, and when the American Revolution was finally over, in 1783, he promoted trade agreements between the French and Americans.

Like his older contemporary Crèvecoeur, Lafayette straddled the ancien régime and New World democracy, comfortable equally in the role of aristocrat or republican. After his military service in the American Revolution, he took part in the French Revolution at the fall of the Bastille, in 1789, becoming commander of the National Guard. He was a member of the National Assembly, and drafted a text which became the basis of the great French document the Declaration of the Rights of Man and the Citizen, shaped by the Declaration of Independence.

So, when the Marquis de Lafayette made his triumphant visit to America, he could justly be considered a "hero of two worlds." His love of glory was as great as his love of America, and he was well rewarded by the extravagant patriotism that was so singular an event in American history. President John Quincy Adams hosted a state dinner at the White House for the aging military hero before he sailed home. Adams and Jefferson would be dead the next year, and the Marquis in the following decade.

It was the end of a daunting political era.

GENERAL LAFAYETTE, his son, and suite, together with a select party of ladies and gentlemen, repaired on board of the steamboat James

Kent, directly on retiring from the Grand Fete of Tuesday evening, and proceeded up the Hudson river, to visit Albany, and the intermediate towns upon the river. The party embarked a few minutes after 2 o'clock, Wednesday morning; among the guests were the members of the Cincinnati, with their President, Colonel Varick; His Honour the Recorder and several of the Corporation; Governor Johnson, of Louisiana; Mrs. Lewis of Virginia; Colonel Alexander Hamilton, and his mother, (widow of the late General Hamilton;) General Morton, Colonel Platt, and a number of others.

The boat made very good progress until she arrived off Tarry-Town, where a very dense fog came on; but such was the anxiety of General Lafayette to reach West Point at the appointed time, (10 o'clock), that Commodore Wiswall determined to push slowly on. It was impossible for the pilot to see five rods ahead. The result was, that at about 7 o'clock the boat ran aground upon what is called the Oyster Bank. Here she was obliged to remain for several hours—to the great disappointment of those on board, and also of the thousands who had collected at West Point, to witness his reception, and the tens of thousands at the villages above, which he was expected to pass before dark. As soon as it cleared away, so that the shores were discernible, it was found that every height and cliff were covered with people, anxious to do their utmost in honouring the Guest of the nation. At Stony Point, in particular, there was a large collection of people, a flag was hoisted, and a salute fired from a field piece stationed there for that purpose. One man, more eager than the rest, clambered down the rocks with the agility of a mountain goat, armed with a large musket, which a loud explosion gave us to understand was heavily charged. The boat was near in shore, and as the smoke cleared away, he waved his hand and exclaimed, "There, General, I give you the best I can!"

The population at West Point, including the officers, professors, cadets, the artisans, and their families, &c. &c. ordinarily amount to about one thousand persons. But from day-light yesterday morning, until ten o'clock, the ladies and gentlemen from the country adjacent, continued to flock in sloops and other craft, in great numbers. The suspense from the hours of 9 till 12 was very anxious; but at about fifteen minutes after 12, the welcome signal of his approach was given; and there was instantly more bustle and confusion than there has been before witnessed on the Point since the army of the revolution; the clangour of arms, the thrilling notes of the bugle, and the spirit-stirring drum, imparted life and animation to this wild and magnificent region.—The lofty bank of the Hudson was lined with spectators; and the Cadets were in line, as if they had been summoned from their barracks by the wand of a magician.

The James Kent, gorgeously decorated with flags, came proudly on, cutting away the foaming current, as though she dared Neptune and all his host to strife; and came majestically along side of the dock at half past 12. The General was here received by Colonel Thayer, the commander of the post, accompanied by Major-Generals Brown and Scott, with their respective suites, together with the officers and professors upon the station, under a salute of twenty-one guns from a detachment of artillery, posted upon the bluff, directly north of the old barracks. A landeau was in readiness to receive the General as he stepped ashore, in which he ascended the hill to the plain, followed by a long procession, consisting of the Cincinnati, the officers of the station, gentlemen from New-York, and from the river towns above, delegates from the towns of Newburgh, Poughkeepsie, Clermont, Hudson, and Albany, &c. &c. He was received on the plain by the corps of Cadets, whom he reviewed; and afterwards received the marching salute in front of the marquee erected for him, and witnessed several evolutions, which evinced the perfection of discipline. From the parade ground the General repaired for a few moments to the quarters of Generals Brown and Scott, at Mr. Cozzen's, where the ladies assembled in a spacious room adjoining the library, and partook of refreshments prepared for the occasion. At half past two, the General was conducted by Colonel Thayer to the splendid library of the institution, where the corps of Cadets were individually presented to him by Major Worth; the gentlemen upon the Point who had not previously been introduced, were then presented; after which the ladies were severally introduced.

From the library, the General repaired to the Mess-room of the Cadets, elegantly fitted up for the occasion, and sat down to a dinner, which, whether we regard the quantity, quality, the variety, or the style in which it was served up, we may at once pronounce a sumptuous one.—Including the Officers, Cadets, the Cincinnati, Corporation from New-York, and guests, more than four hundred persons sat down at the table. Colonel Thayer presided, assisted by Major Worth. General Lafayette and General Scott were seated on the right of the President, and General Brown and Colonel Varick on his left. At a cross table at the head, were seated the members of the Cincinnati, and at another similar table, at the other end of the hall, were the members of the Corporation of New-York with Mr. George Washington Lafayette, on the right of the Vice-President. The room was tastefully and elegantly decorated. Festoons of ever-green were suspended from pillar to pillar, in every direction through the spacious hall. Back of the President's chair hung the star-spangled banner. Over the chair was a large spread, an elegantly wrought eagle, with the words "September, 1757," issuing from the streamer in his beak, and "York-Town" grasped in his claws. A crown of laurel, interwoven with roses, was suspended over the General's head. Over the window on his right, was the name of Washington, wrought in leaves of ever-green, and on the left that of Lafayette. At the other end of the hall hung a full-length portrait of "the Father of his Country;" and upon the right wall, in the centre, that of Jefferson, and on the left, President Adams.

At 6 o'clock, the company rose from the table, and the General and his friends re-embarked on board of the James Kent, and proceeded to Newburgh.

Through the whole distance of the Highlands, the hardy mountaineers who inhabit many of the glens manifested their respect by showing themselves ever and anon, and discharging their muskets from the crags and cliffs which in some places seem to frown over the heads of the passing traveller, as the steam-boat ploughs her way close at the base of the mountains. In passing Cold-Spring, a salute was fired from a piece of artillery stationed near the shore for that purpose. A salute was also fired from New-Windsor, (near the old Encampment of the Revolutionary Army.) Unfortunately, however, the delay occasioned by the morning accident, had detained the party so long that the shades of night began now to close in, and on the arrival of the steam-boat at Newburgh the twilight had so far advanced as to render objects indistinct at a very short distance. A corps of infantry were drawn up in handsome array upon the wharf, to receive the General, by whom he was escorted to the Orange Hotel, where he was received by the corporation of the village, by the President of which he was addressed.

The General made a brief and pertinent reply to this address; after which he entered an open carriage and was escorted through the principal streets of the village, which were thronged with people, who were delighted with a glimpse of the General's face, caught even by the aid of a flickering lamp; over the streets at short distances, arches had been erected which were tastefully festooned with ever-greens and flowers, and on several of them were suspended appropriate inscriptions. On one of these arches was the following inscription:—"Thrice welcome Lafayette Columbia's bright Occidental Star." Another arch was formed by the planting of two well grown forest trees, and bending their tops together. The inscription suspended from this lofty arch was too high for the rays of our feeble lamp. The inscription upon another arch was, "Lafayette and Liberty—Welcome Illustrious Chief." But the arch which was far the most beautiful, was erected by the ladies; it extended from the houses on each side of the street, and formed one grand and two smaller arches; these were so richly and beautifully ornamented with festoons and flowers, that they would have answered well for decorations to the portals of the temple of Flora herself; the inscription here was "Welcome our hero, Lafayette." Having returned to the Orange Hotel, an address was presented to the General by Johannis Miller, Esq. President of the Orange county Agricultural Society, in behalf of said Society. . . .

At 12 o'clock, the steam-boat Chancellor Livingston which had also been detained on her passage up by the fog, made her appearance from Albany, when the most of the guests from New-York, both ladies and gentlemen, returned to the city. Among the former were the two Miss Wrights, who have lately arrived from France, and whose "View of the American Society and Manners," has acquired some considerable notoriety. The General and his suite came on board of the Kent at about the same hour, and retired to rest, when the boat made sail, and before day-light anchored off Poughkeepsie.

Our National Guest has no where received a more flattering

reception, than at the beautiful, ancient, and patriotic village of Poughkeepsie; nor has more promptitude, vigour, and taste, been displayed in the arrangements at any other place. At sun-rise all hands were "piped" on deck, and a more imposing spectacle has rarely been presented. The high bluffs below the landing place, were covered with troops, and thousands of citizens were crowding the wharves, showing themselves in large groups from the neighbouring heights, and windows of the houses standing within view of the river. All ages and sexes seemed to press anxiously forward to show their gratitude to their welcome visitor. At half past 6 o'clock, the boat got under way, and took a turn upon the river, while the salute was fired by a corps of artillery stationed upon one of the heights. When the General appeared upon deck, the welkin rang with the cheers from the crowds upon the shore, which were returned from the boat. The boat was then drawn up to the wharf, where a company of horse, many of the officers of General Brush's division on horseback, all mounted on elegant horses, and in complete uniform, together with several uniform companies, were drawn up in great order under the direction of Major-General Brush, assisted by Colonel Cunningham. General Lafayette was then conducted by Thomas T. Oakley, General James Tallmadge, Judge Emott, and Philo Ruggles, Esq. to a barouche, with four beautiful white horses, in which the General took his seat, attended by Colonel Huger, of South Carolina, General Van Courtland, General Fish, and General Lewis. A barouche, also drawn by four white horses, was then drawn up, which was occupied by the son of General Lafayette, and gentlemen attending them. After being conducted to the pleasant and extensive piazza in front of Mr. Forbus' house, and after being introduced to the clergy and gentlemen attending, he was cordially addressed by Colonel Henry A. Livingston.

To this address, the General returned a neat and feeling reply.

A procession was then formed under the direction of the committee, to the Poughkeepsie hotel, at about 8 o'clock, where the General sat down to a sumptuous breakfast, handsomely served up by Mr. Myer. At the head of the table hung the well-known and venerated portrait of Washington, and at the opposite end, the Grand Banner of St. Tammany. On each side of the hall, at suitable distances, were suspended banners, with the arms, name, and motto, of each state in the union. Over the centre of the table, hung a canopy formed of festoons of flowers and ever-greens, of various kinds, belted by a riband, on which was inscribed the names of the thirteen original States. Over the folding doors, were the well-known words of "Welcome Lafayette" made with great accuracy, wholly of pink-coloured blossoms of china-astor, and on one of the walls, were inscribed the names of Washington and Lafayette, wrought in laurel leaves, and encircled in garlands of flowers. Directly in front of the General's seat, stood a representation of the temple of Fame; and the whole suite of apartments were decorated in a style to correspond with the above.

Immediately after breakfast, and with a praise-worthy promptness, the escort was formed, and the General was attended to the boat with every possible mark of respect; the troops again repaired to the heights; and on hauling into the stream, another salute was fired from the artillery, and afterwards several vollies of musketry were fired, with a precision which the General was pleased to say resembled very much the firing of regular troops. The shores were again lined with people, who cheered in all directions.

Passing rapidly up the river, preparations were made for landing with Governor Lewis, at the dock, near his elegant country seat. The boat arrived at about 12 o'clock, and on coming along side, carriages were found in readiness to convey the party to the mansion which stood at some distance from the road, which wound through a beautiful copse to the house. On alighting, the General and suite were introduced to the family, and were shortly after introduced into an apartment, where an elegant collation was provided: peaches, grapes, and melons, were mingled with more substantial fare, and every variety of wine sparkled on the table. After remaining an hour and a half, the General took leave to this hospitable family, and embarked, in order to continue his voyage to Albany.

Soon afterwards, in passing the seat of James Thompson, Esq. a boat came off with a large basket of peaches, of enormous size, and excellent flavour, and with several elegant bouquets of flowers.

In passing the landing at Kingston, (four miles from the village,) a large collection were found to have assembled; a salute was fired from the shore, and hearty cheers given and returned. At this place, Colonel Henry Livingston, who commanded a regiment under Lafayette in Rhode Island, and at Valley Forge, came on board. The General had just been inquiring of Colonel Fish, what had become of his old friend Henry Livingston, and received him most affectionately.

The steam-boat arrived at Clermont at about 4 o'clock in the afternoon, and came to anchor off the elegant mansion of Robert L. Livingston, Esq. formerly the seat of the late Chancellor Livingston. Before the boat arrived at the dock, it was discovered that the groves were literally alive with people, of all ages and sexes, equally anxious with the hospitable proprietor, to manifest their respect for their expected guest, and greet his landing. But while the rocks and glens, and even trees to their top-most branches, presented this animated spectacle, the General, his suite, and friends, were still more surprised by the appearance upon the lawn of this romantic and secluded place, of a regiment of well-disciplined troops, drawn up to receive him.—There were several vessels at anchor in the stream, one of which (a large sloop) was decorated with flags, and a streamer floated from her mast, with the motto of "Welcome Lafayette," in large letters. On landing, a salute was fired from this vessel, which was unexpectedly returned from a field piece planted in a thick copse of trees upon the shore. The General then ascended the shore, and was conducted by Generals Lewis and Fish, to the mansion of Mr. Livingston, where he was received by that gentleman with the utmost courtesy and cordiality.—After the friends of Mr. Livingston, assembled on the occasion, had been presented, the General reviewed the troops upon the lawn, by whom he was honoured with a *feu de joie*. At this moment, a long procession of the ancient and honourable fraternity of Freemasons, consisting of a Chapter of Royal Arch Masons, and the members of "Widow's Son Lodge," of Redhook, emerged from a grove, and on being presented to the General, an appropriate address was delivered by Palmer Cook, Esq. W. M. of the aforementioned lodge.

After a brief and pertinent reply, the General accepted of an invitation to visit the seat of Edward P. Livingston, Esq. which is situated but a short distance to the north, upon the same elevated and beautiful plain. An excellent cold collation, together with refreshments of every suitable kind, were served up. And while the company was partaking of these, the steamboat Richmond, Captain

William Wiswall, came gayly down, and anchored along side of the James Kent, having on board Major-General Jacob Rutsen Van Rensselaer, and suite, Brigadier-General Fleming, and suite, the Mayor of Hudson (Rufus Reed, Esq.), Dr. Tallman, late Mayor, and Colonel Strong, as delegates from the city of Hudson, together with the Hudson Band, and two elegant uniform companies, under the command of Colonel Edwards. This addition to the company already on the ground, repaired immediately to the seat of Mr. E. P. Livingston, from whence, after refreshments were served out to them by Mr. L. and Commodore Wiswall in person, General Lafayette was escorted back to the seat of his liberal entertainer. As night came on, the troops and crowd from the country dispersed, and the Hudson troops were taken on board of the steam-boat James Kent, where refreshments were ordered, and the forward deck and cabin assigned to them for the night. In the evening the whole of Mr. L's. splendid suite of apartments were brilliantly lighted up, and an elegant ball was given in honour of the General's company. The assemblage was very numerous, and a brilliant circle of ladies, arrayed in all the charm of health, beauty, and rich and elegant dresses, were contributing to the festivity and joy of the occasion, by "tripping the light fantastic toe," or by conversation sparkled with wit, or adorned by the graces of polished manners and education. Among the guests this evening, in addition to those already named, were the Honourable Edward Livingston, of New-Orleans, the Honourable Walter Patterson, Captain Ridgeley, of the Navy, the Honorable Peter R. Livingston, A. Vanderpool, Esq. of Kinderhook, Mrs. Montgomery, (widow of the gallant General who fell at Quebec,) and many others whose names are not recollected. During the evening a sumptuous supper was served up in a style of magnificence rarely, if ever equalled in this country. The room selected for this part of the *fete*, was an extensive Greenhouse, or Orangery, and the effect was indescribably fine. The tables had been made and fitted for this occasion, and were spread beneath a large grove of Orange and Lemon trees, with bending branches of fruit, and many other species of exotic shrubs and plants. Flora also, had profusely scattered her blossoms; and the whole scene seemed to partake of enchantment. The beholder stood gazing, as if bound by the wizard spell of the Magician. The night was dark and rainy; but this contributed to the general effect of the *fete*, inasmuch as the darkness heightened the effect of the thousand lamps by which the surrounding groves were illuminated. There was also a fine exhibition of fireworks, which had been prepared and brought from New-York for the occasion. It having been found inconvenient to provide suppers for so many on board of the boat, the whole detachment of troops were invited by Mr. L. to supper in the Green house, which invitation was accepted. At 10 o'clock, General Lafayette retired from this scene of gayety and beauty, and at two the hall was closed, and the company separated, not only highly gratified with the entertainment, but with the manner in which it was got up and imparted to his guests, by Mr. L. whose style of living closely approximates that of the real English gentleman, and whose wealth is equalled by his kindness and liberality.

At 9 o'clock on Friday, the General again embarked, and proceeded on his way, and before 10 o'clock, was in sight of Catskill. The long wharf which projects half a mile into the river, was occupied by two battalions of troops.—The highlands which nearly exclude the whole village from a view of the river, were covered with people, and on the arrival of the James Kent at the dock, a salute of 13 guns was fired from the artillery on one of the heights. The arrangements of General Lafayette rendered it absolutely necessary that he should be at Albany on that day to dinner, and hence it was utterly impossible for him to make any stay at Catskill, although he was earnestly pressed to dine by a very respectable delegation. The General, to gratify the feelings of thousands who were assembled at the landing to hail his arrival and bid him welcome, consented to land and pass through the principal streets, in an elegant carriage, accompanied by the Committee of Arrangements, and escorted by the military, and a large assemblage of citizens in procession. In front of Crowell's Hotel the procession halted, and the General was received by the acclamations of a large concourse of people, eager to see, and embrace the Nation's Guest. Amongst the company was a body of the heroes of the revolution, whose furrowed features, silver locks, and tottering steps, bespoke age and hard service. But at the sight of their old General, they rushed forward to meet the quick-extended grasp of their old Commander. Among the number, was an old servant who was with Lafayette when he was wounded at the battle of Brandywine. This was a touching scene, few eyes were dry, either among the actors or spectators; but the General's time was so short, that he was constrained to leave the further honours that awaited him in this place, bid adieu to the citizens, and embark for Hudson.

The boat arrived at Hudson a few minutes before 2 o'clock, but the same reason that prevented a longer stay at Catskill, also rendered it impossible, consistent with his arrangements, to make any considerable stay here. On landing, the crowd was so great that it was almost impossible to proceed, notwithstanding the active exertions of Colonel Darling, the Marshal of the day, assisted by the military. The General was conducted to an elegant barouche, drawn by four beautiful black horses, attended by four grooms in a special livery. After the General, followed a number of other carriages, with his retinue, and the different delegates from the river towns. The procession passed up Ferry to Warren-street, where an arch was erected, which for its size and elegance of construction, exceeded any that had been previously seen on the tour. The whole street, which is more than a mile in length, was choked with the crowd. And the windows, as at Catskill, were filled with ladies, whose snow-white hands and handkerchiefs, were gracefully waved in the air, while the crowd in the streets were cheering, and the General, with his usual condescension, was bowing, or endeavouring to bow, to every individual in the multitude. After half-way up the street, stood another arch, elegantly adorned; and at the head of the town was a third, superior to all, on the top of which stood a colossal figure of the Genius of Liberty, well proportioned and painted, holding in her hand the American standard, which being of unusual size, floated in the air with an imposing effect. To each of the arches of which we have spoken, were suspended appropriate inscriptions. On arriving at the square, at the head of Warren-street, the procession wheeled and returned to the Court-house, when the troops and citizens opened to the right and left, and all that could, passed through, and up to the Court-room. All the seats without the bar were filled with the "Daughters of Columbia," forming a large and interesting group of well-dressed and beautiful females. The Court-room was superbly decorated—displaying more labour, taste, and skill, than any decorations of the kind that were seen on the route. At the entrance of the bar, on either side, stood a beautiful Corinthian pillar, with caps and cornices of the composite order of architecture, elegantly wrought and ornamented with leaves and gold. On the top of each of these pillars was placed a globe, and the whole were united at the top by a chain of flowers of every hue, festooned with laurel and roses. The General was conducted to this rich and beautiful portal, where His Honour the Mayor delivered an interesting address.

General Lafayette briefly replied to the address, after which the members of the Common Council were severally presented to him. A most interesting and affecting spectacle was then presented; sixty-eight veterans of the revolution, who had collected from the different parts of the country, formed a part of the procession, and were next presented; and it so happened that several of them were officers, and many of them soldiers who had served with Lafayette. Notwithstanding that they were admonished that the greatest haste was necessary, yet every one had something to say; and when they grasped his friendly hand, each seemed reluctant to release it. One of them came up with a sword in his hand, which, as he passed, he remarked was "given to him by the Marquis," at such a place, "in Rhode Island." Another, with a tear glistening in his eye, as he shook the hand of the General, observed—"You, Sir, gave me the first guinea I ever had in my life—I shall never forget that."

The officers of the militia were next presented, and after them, the ladies. But time would not allow of delay; and many thousands who were eagerly pressing forward, were disappointed in not being introduced to the man whom they had assembled to honour. In passing down the street, however, on arriving opposite Allen's hotel, where arrangements had been made for the dinner, the solicitations were so warm and earnest, that the General was constrained to alight and take a glass of wine in the long room. And here, again, was presented a specimen of Hudson taste, which deserves every commendation. The hall was decorated in a style of elegance, that would compare only with the Court-house. The General stopped but for a moment, when he re-entered his carriage, and returned to the boat, followed by the shouts and blessings of thousands. On leaving the dock, three cheers were given by the multitude and returned from the boat—after which a salute was fired from the hill near the Observatory. In passing up the river, the docks at the villages of Coxsackie, New-Baltimore, and Coeymans, were crowded with people, who cheered the General repeatedly, and with as much enthusiasm as though they had had a nearer view. At Castleton, a large collection of people had assembled, and a salute was fired from a six pounder.

In consequence of the unavoidable delays on the way, a freshet in the river, the contrary winds and tide, the James Kent did not arrive at her moorings at the Overslaugh, until five o'clock (on Friday) —three hours later than was originally contemplated. The consequence was, that the arrangements of the committee for the city of Albany were deranged; the committee themselves, consisting of Alderman Townsend and Humphrey, Colonel Bacon, and others, (in addition to the New-York delegation, which had accompanied the General from New-York,) who had been waiting to receive their guest, were much fatigued; and the troops, who had been on duty since 7 o'clock in the morning, without refreshment, were nearly exhausted. On landing, the General was conducted to a superb landeau, drawn by four white horses, and carriages were in readiness for the gentlemen accompanying him. The procession was quickly formed, and moved rapidly on to Greenbush, escorted by a detachment of horse, commanded by Major General Solomon Van Rensselaer, Marshal of the day, assisted by Colonel Cooper. On arriving at the centre of the village, the General was conducted to a large marquee, erected beneath an arch similar to those heretofore described, and bearing appropriate inscriptions, where he was received by the members of the Corporation, who welcomed him with an appropriate address; after which, refreshments were served, and the procession moved on. Night was now rapidly setting in, and the delay at the Ferry, for the want of a sufficient number of boats, rendered it quite dark when the General landed in Albany.

Frederick Butler, *Memoirs of the Marquis de Lafayette, Together with His Tour Through the United States* (Wethersfield, Ct.: Deming & Francis, 1825).

THE ALBANY LEGISLATURE

Captain Basil Hall

NO TRAVEL BOOK *of its day caused as much of an
uproar as* Travels in North America *by the Scottish naval officer Captain Basil Hall (1788–1844). Since its publication in 1829,
the three-volume description of American life was read and talked
about all over the country, offending just about everybody with its
Tory haughtiness. Hall wrote disparagingly about social customs,
schools, industry, slavery, and transportation, though not without
praising many accomplishments of American society, such as
the prison system and the Erie Canal. To its credit, Hall's work is
not a superficial guidebook, but a reflective, analytical social
commentary filled with blunt observations. However, what enraged
Americans in this period of Jacksonian egalitarianism were his
stinging attacks on the practice of democracy. In his characteristic
self-important tone Hall proclaimed, "With the Americans, there
is always a solemn sort of enigmatical assumption of the intricacy
and transcendent grandeur of their whole system, not to be
comprehended by weak European minds." His wife wrote her own
critical book on their trip abroad,* The Aristocratic Journey.

*Mrs. Frances Trollope, who in 1832 produced perhaps the most
vicious book ever written on American life,* Domestic Manners
of the Americans, *defended Hall in one of its chapters. Describing
the "moral earthquake" his book caused, she then further exac-
erbated the whole affair by claiming that one of the remarkable
national character traits of the Americans is "their exquisite
sensitiveness and soreness respecting everything said or written con-*

*cerning them." One American editor even concluded that Hall
had written her book! Though Mrs. Trollope deplored the lack of
refined taste, along with virtually everything else here, she did
take pleasure in "such sights as the Hudson presents." Here nature
overwhelmed her pen.*

*As for Captain Basil Hall, prior to publication of his notorious
book he had already sailed to the East Indies, to China, and
to South America, and wrote many volumes on his travels, before
and after his fifteen months in America. Darwin mentions Hall's
observations on the Chilean coastline in the journal he kept aboard
the* Beagle.

I WAS GLAD to find the legislature in session, as I had a great curiosity
to see how the public affairs were managed. The object of the
present meeting, it is true, was not to transact the ordinary business
of the State, but to revise the laws—a favourite employment all over
the Union. But I had ample means, during a fortnight's stay at Albany,
of seeing how things were conducted, as innumerable incidental
discussions arose out of the matter in hand, to show the current
modes of proceeding.

Each of the Twenty-four States of the American Union has a
separate government, by which its own affairs are regulated. By the
Constitution established after their separation from the Mother Country, a republican form of government is not only made a condition of
the compact, but is guaranteed to the different States by the united
voice of the whole; each one, however, being left entirely free to
modify its own particular constitution, and to make and unmake, or
alter laws, at their good-will and pleasure—in short, to do all that
sovereign states may perform, provided only they do not interfere
with certain matters, specifically appropriated as the duty of the
general, or federative government of the Union.

I shall have frequent occasion, in the course of the Journey, to
refer to these distinctions—at present I mean to speak only of New
York, which is the most populous, wealthy, and, in many respects, the

most important of the whole. This State had recently adopted a new Constitution—remodelled from that adopted in 1777,—and it came into operation on the 1st of January, 1823. By this instrument, the Legislative power is vested in a Senate and House of Assembly; the Senate, consisting of 32 members, who must be freeholders, chosen for four years; and the House of Assembly, consisting of 128 members, who are elected annually by the whole people of the State, the right of suffrage being universal.

I was extremely curious to see how a Legislature formed on such principles would proceed, and I visited the Capitol with the truest wish to be well pleased with all I saw and heard. The hall of the House of Assembly was not unlike the interior of a church; with a gallery for strangers, looking down upon a series of seats and writing-desks, ranged on the floor in concentric semicircles, the Speaker's chair being at the centre, and over his head, of course, the large well-known picture of General Washington, with his hand stretched out, in the same unvaried attitude in which we had already seen him represented in many hundreds, I might say thousands, of places, from the Capitol at Albany to the embellishments on the coarsest blue china plate in the country. Each member of the House was placed in a seat numbered and assigned to him by lot on the first day of the Session.

After prayers had been said, and a certain portion of the ordinary formal business gone through, the regular proceedings were commenced by a consideration of chapter IV. of the Revised Laws. It appeared that a joint committee of the two Houses had been appointed to attend to this subject, and to report the result of their deliberations. The gentlemen nominated had no trifling task to perform, as I became sensible upon a farther acquaintance with the subject. All the existing Laws of the State, which were very voluminous, were to be compared and adjusted so as to be consistent with one another; after which, the result was printed and laid before the Legislature;—so that each chapter, section, and clause, might be discussed separately, when, of course, the members of the Committee of Revision had to explain their proceedings.

Some of the chapters were so completely matters of form, and related to topics upon which no particular interest was felt, that they passed without any opposition. Others, again, which it was supposed would cause no discussion, proved sources of long debate. On the first day I attended, I was sorry to hear from an experienced friend, that in all probability there would be no discussion, as the chapter, No. IV., which related to "the rights of the citizens and inhabitants of the State," was one so perfectly familiar to every native, that it must pass without delay. When the 3d section, however, came to be read by the clerk, as follows, a subject was started which led the assembled Legislators a fine round. "A well-regulated militia," said this clause, "being necessary to the security of a free State, the right of the people to keep and bear arms cannot be infringed." Upon this being read, a member rose, and objected to the article as illogical in itself; and even granting it were altered in this respect, it was totally needless, as the same clause was distinctly given, not only in the Constitution of the United States, but in that of the State of New York; and, finally, it was quite out of place in the Statute Book. This appeared simple enough; but another member got up, and vehemently defended the Revisers of the Laws for having brought forward this chapter, and this particular section; adding, that if ever the Americans relaxed in their exertions and reiterated declarations of what were their rights, their liberties would be in danger. A third gentleman followed, and declared himself so much of the opinion of the first speaker, that he should move, and accordingly he did move, that the whole chapter relating to the rights of the citizens, be rejected, as out of place. This led to a warm discussion by four or five members, none of whom spoke above a few minutes, excepting one gentleman, who addressed the House, now in "Committee of the whole," as it is called, no less than five times, and always in so diffuse and inconsequential a style, that I could with difficulty comprehend how he had earned the reputation of a close reasoner, which I found him in possession of. He not only objected to the article alluded to, but, without the least pretence of adhering to the subject under discussion, or to any thing analogous to it, read over, one by one, every article in the chapter, accompanying each with a long commentary in the most prosy and ill-digested style imaginable. During this excursion among the clouds, he referred frequently to the History of England, gave us an account of the manner in which Magna Charta was wrested from "that monster King John," and detailed the whole history of the Bill of Rights. In process of time, he brought his history down to the commencement of the American Revolution, then to the period of the Declaration of Independence—the Articles of Confederation—and so on, till my patience, if not that of the House, was pretty well worn out by the difficulty of following these threadbare commonplaces.

The next member who spoke declared his ignorance of Latin, and his consequent inability to study Magna Charta—which, I presume, was a good joke—but thought that, if these occasional opportunities were lost, of impressing upon the minds of the people a sense of their rights, their immediate descendants, who were not so familiar, of course, as they themselves were, with the history of their country, to say nothing of posterity, would gradually forget their own privileges; "and then," said he, "the Americans will cease to be the great, the happy, and the high-minded people they are at the present day!"

At length a man of sense, and habits of business, got up, and instantly commanded the closest attention of the House. He had been one of the committee, he said, appointed to revise the laws, and as such, had voted for the insertion of the particular clause, not from any great or immediate good which it was likely to produce, but simply because it was consistent with other parts of the American Government, and because it was suitable to the present genius of the people, to make these frequent references to their rights. "Here," he observed, "is a fair opportunity to enumerate some of these rights, and I trust the committee will see the propriety of embodying these few but important precepts in the Revised Code of Laws which is to become the standard authority of the State."

I imagined this clear explanation would put an end to the debate; but the same invincible speaker who had so frequently addressed them before, rose again, and I don't know when the discussion would have ended, had not the hand of the clock approached the hour of two, the time for dinner. A motion to rise and report progress was then cheerfully agreed to, and the House adjourned.

I do not pretend to have done justice to this debate; in truth the arguments seemed to me so shallow, and were all so ambitiously, or rather wordily, expressed, that I was frequently at a loss for some minutes to think what the orators really meant, or if they meant any thing. The whole discussion, indeed, struck me as being rather juvenile. The matter was in the highest degree commonplace, and the manner of treating it still more so. The speeches, accordingly, were full of set phrases and rhetorical flourishes about their "ancestors having come out of the contest full of glory, and covered with scars—and their ears ringing with the din of battle." This false taste, waste of time—conclusions in which nothing was concluded—splitting of straws, and ingeniously elaborated objections, all about any thing or nothing in the world, appeared to me to arise from the entire absence of those habits of public business, which can be acquired only by long-continued and exclusive practice.

These gentlemen were described to me as being chiefly farmers, shopkeepers, and country lawyers, and other persons quite unaccustomed to abstract reasoning, and therefore apt to be led away by the sound of their own voices, farther than their heads could follow. It is probable too, that part of this wasteful, rambling kind of argumentation may be ascribed to the circumstance of most of the speakers being men, who, from not having made public business a regular profession or study, were ignorant of what had been done before—and had come to the legislature, straight from the plough—or from behind the counter—from chopping down trees—or from the bar, under the impression that they were at once to be converted into statesmen.

Such were my opinions at this early stage of the journey, and I never afterwards saw much occasion to alter them; indeed, the more I become acquainted with the practical operation of the democratical system, the more I became satisfied that the ends which it proposed to accomplish, could not be obtained by such means. By bringing into these popular assemblies men who—disguise it as they may—cannot but feel themselves ignorant of public business, an ascendency is given to a few abler and more intriguing heads, which enables them to manage matters to suit their own purposes. And just as the members begin to get a slight degree of useful familiarity with the routine of affairs, a fresh election comes on, and out they all go; or at least a great majority go out, and thus, in each fresh legislature, there must be found a preponderance of unqualified, or, at all events, of ill-informed men, however patriotic or well-intentioned they may chance to be.

On the same distrustful principle, all men in office are jealously kept out of Congress, and the State legislatures; which seems altogether the most ingenious device ever hit upon for excluding from the national councils, all those persons best fitted by their education, habits of business, knowledge, and advantageous situation of whatever sort, for performing, efficiently, the duties of statesmen: while, by the same device, the very best, because the most immediate and the most responsible sources of information are removed to a distance; and the men who possess the knowledge required for the purposes of deliberation, are placed out of sight, and on their guard, instead of being always at hand, and liable to sudden scrutiny, face to face, with the representatives of the nation.

These ideas arose in my mind—I may say, were forced on my mind—upon seeing the workings of the legislature of New York; but I still trusted I might be wrong in my first views, and looked forward with increased interest to the time when I should be able to examine the whole question on a wider scale, and with greater means of information, at the fountain head—Washington.

Captain Basil Hall, *Travels in North America*, Vol. 2 (Edinburgh: Cadell and Co., 1829).

WEST POINT

Anthony Trollope

ANTHONY TROLLOPE (1815–82) *was already a cele-*
brated novelist by the time he made his second trip to North
America in 1861. By then he had written Barchester Towers *and*
Framley Parsonage, *in addition to a travel book on the West*
Indies. In a long career, during which he kept up his duties as a
postal official, the prolific Trollope wrote novels, arts criticism,
biographies of Caesar, Cicero, and Thackeray, and social commentary.

Admittedly, his North America *was to be an antidote to the harsh*
feelings aroused by his mother, Mrs. Frances Trollope's, sarcastic
Domestic Manners of the Americans. *It was, as he said, "a some-*
what unjust book about our cousins over the water. She had
seen what was distasteful in the manners of a young people, but
had hardly recognized their energy." Trollope's own book came
three decades after hers, a sufficient distance from the American
Revolution and the War of 1812, and also mindful of Tocque-
ville's great work Democracy in America, *which had appeared in*
1835. Nevertheless, Trollope was in America during the period
of the Civil War, when there was sufficient enmity between the Ameri-
cans and the British who, conservative and liberal leaders alike,
tended to favor the South. By this time most of the well-known Eng-
lish travel books had been written, and it was now time to re-
flect on other issues, such as the state of the Union, women's rights,
the literary scene. Besides, the young country had grown and
changed in every way, especially culturally and industrially, by the
second half of the nineteenth century.

237

North America has a more even-handed, contemplative tone than many of the earlier travel books, in part because of Trollope's sensitivities as a novelist and acute observer of human detail. This account of the obligatory trip to West Point, which opened as a military academy in 1802, differs from those of other visitors in its departure from mere sightseeing. Trollope pauses to wonder if the Highlands isn't too beautiful a setting for the study of war.

OF WEST POINT there is something to be said independently of its scenery. It is the Sandhurst of the States. Here is their military school, from which officers are drafted to their regiments, and the tuition for military purposes is, I imagine, of a high order. It must, of course, be borne in mind that West Point, even as at present arranged, is fitted to the wants of the old army, and not to that of the army now required. It can go but a little way to supply officers for 500,000 men; but would do much towards supplying them for 40,000. At the time of my visit to West Point the regular army of the northern States had not even then swelled itself to the latter number.

I found that there were 220 students at West Point, that about forty graduate every year, each of whom receives a commission in the army; that about 120 pupils are admitted every year; and that in the course of every year about eighty either resign, or are called upon to leave on account of some deficiency, or fail in their final examination. The result is simply this, that one third of those who enter succeeds, and that two thirds fail. The number of failures seemed to me to be terribly large,—so large as to give great ground of hesitation to a parent in accepting a nomination for the college. I especially inquired into the particulars of these dismissals and resignations, and was assured that the majority of them take place in the first year of the pupillage. It is soon seen whether or no a lad has the mental and physical capacities necessary for the education and future life required of him, and care is taken that those shall be removed early as to whom it may be determined that the necessary capacity is clearly wanting. If this is done,—and I do not doubt it,—the evil is much mitigated. The effect otherwise would be very injurious. The lads remain till they are perhaps one and twenty, and have then acquired aptitudes for military life, but no other aptitudes. At that age the education cannot be commenced anew, and, moreover, at that age the disgrace of failure is very injurious. The period of education used to be five years, but has now been reduced to four. This was done in order that a double class might be graduated in 1861 to supply the wants of the war. I believe it is considered that but for such necessity as that, the fifth year of education can be ill spared.

The discipline, to our English ideas, is very strict. In the first place no kind of beer, wine, or spirits is allowed at West Point. The law upon this point may be said to be very vehement, for it debars even the visitors at the hotel from the solace of the glass of beer. The hotel is within the bounds of the College, and as the lads might become purchasers at the bar, there is no bar allowed. Any breach of this law leads to instant expulsion; or, I should say rather, any detection of such breach. The officer who showed us over the College assured me that the presence of a glass of wine in a young man's room would secure his exclusion, even though there should be no evidence that he had tasted it. He was very firm as to this; but a little bird of West Point, whose information, thought not official or probably accurate in words, seemed to me to be worthy of reliance in general, told me that eyes were wont to wink when such glasses of wine made themselves unnecessarily visible. Let us fancy an English mess of young men from seventeen to twenty-one, at which a mug of beer would be felony, and a glass of wine high treason! But the whole management of the young with the Americans differs much from that in vogue with us. We do not require so much at so early an age, either in knowledge, in morals, or even in manliness. In America, if a lad be under control, as at West Point, he is called upon for an amount of labour, and a degree of conduct, which would be considered quiet transcendental and out of the question in England. But if he be not under control, if at the age of eighteen he be living at home, or be from his circumstances exempt from professorial power, he is a full-fledged man with his pipe apparatus and his bar acquaintances.

And then I was told at West Point how needful and yet how painful it was that all should be removed who were in any way deficient in credit to the establishment. "Our rules are very exact," my informant told me; "but the carrying out of our rules is a task not always very easy." As to this also I had already heard something from that little bird of West Point, but of course I wisely assented to my informant, remarking that discipline in such an establishment was essentially necessary. The little bird had told me that discipline at West Point had been rendered terribly difficult by political interference. "A young man will be dismissed by the unanimous voice of the Board, and will be sent away. And then, after a week or two, he will be sent back, with an order from Washington, that another trial shall be given him. The lad will march back into the college with all the honours of a victory, and will be conscious of a triumph over the superintendent and his officers." "And is that common?" I asked. "Not at the present moment," I was told. "But it was common before the war. While Mr. Buchanan, and Mr. Pierce, and Mr. Polk were Presidents, no officer or board of officers then at West Point was able to dismiss a lad whose father was a Southerner, and who had friends among the Government."

Not only was this true of West Point, but the same allegation is true as to all matters of patronage throughout the United States. During the three or four last Presidencies, and I believe back to the time of Jackson, there has been an organized system of dishonesty in the management of all beneficial places under the control of the Government. I doubt whether any despotic court of Europe has been so corrupt in the distribution of places,—that is in the selection of public officers,—as has been the assemblage of statesmen at Washington. And this is the evil which the country is now expiating with its blood and treasure. It has allowed its knaves to stand in the high places; and now it finds that knavish works have brought about evil results. . . .

We were taken to the chapel, and there saw, displayed as trophies, two of our own dear old English flags. I have seen many a banner hung up in token of past victory, and many a flag taken on the field of battle mouldering by degrees of dust on some chapel's wall,—but they have not been the flags of England. Till this day I had never seen our own colours in any position but one of self-assertion and independent power. From the tone used by the gentleman who showed them to me, I could gather that he would have passed them

by had he not foreseen that he could not do so without my notice. "I
don't know that we are right to put them there," he said. "Quite
right," was my reply, "as long as the world does such things." In
private life it is vulgar to triumph over one's friends, and malicious to
triumph over one's enemies. We have not got so far yet in public life,
but I hope we are advancing toward it. In the meantime I did not
begrudge the Americans our two flags. If we keep flags and cannons
taken from our enemies, and show them about as signs of our own
prowess after those enemies have become friends, why should not
others do so as regards us? It clearly would not be well for the world
that we should always beat other nations and never be beaten. I did
not begrudge that chapel our two flags. But nevertheless the sight of
them made me sick in the stomach and uncomfortable. As an
Englishman I do not want to be ascendant over any one. But it makes
me very ill when any one tries to be ascendant over me. I wish we
could send back with our compliments all the trophies that we hold,
carriage paid, and get back in return those two flags and any other
flag or two of our own that may be doing similar duty about the
world. I take it that the parcel sent away would be somewhat more
bulky than that which would reach us in return.

The discipline at West Point seemed as I have said, to be very
severe; but it seemed also that that severity could not in all cases be
maintained. The hours of study also were long, being nearly continuous throughout the day. "English lads of that age could not do it," I
said; thus confessing that English lads must have in them less power
of sustained work than those of America. "They must do it here," said
my informant, "or else leave us." And then he took us off to one of
the young gentleman's quarters, in order that we might see the
nature of their rooms. We found the young gentleman fast asleep on
his bed, and felt uncommonly grieved that we should have thus
intruded on him. As the hour was one of those allocated by my
informant in the distribution of the day to private study, I could not
but take the present occupation of the embryo warrior as an indication that the amount of labour required might be occasionally too
much even for an American youth. "The heat makes one so uncommonly drowsy," said the young man. I was not the least surprised at
the exclamation. The air of the apartment had been warmed up to

such a pitch by the hot-pipe apparatus of the building that prolonged life to me would, I should have thought, be out of the question in such an atmosphere. "Do you always have it as hot as this?" I asked. The young man swore that it was so, and with considerable energy expressed his opinion that all his health and spirits and vitality were being baked out of him. He seemed to have a strong opinion on the matter, for which I respected him; but it had never occurred to him, and did not then occur to him, that anything could be done to moderate that deathly flow of hot air which came up to him from the neighbouring infernal regions. He was pale in the face, and all the lads there were pale. American lads and lasses are all pale. Men at thirty and women at twenty-five have had all semblances of youth baked out of them. Infants even are not rosy, and the only shades known on the cheeks of children are those composed of brown, yellow, and white. All this comes of those damnable hot-air pipes with which every tenement in America is infested. "We cannot do without them," they say. "Our cold is so intense that we must heat our houses throughout. Open fire-places in a few rooms would not keep our toes and fingers from the frost." There is much in this. The assertion is no doubt true, and thereby a great difficulty is created. It is no doubt quite within the power of American ingenuity to moderate the heat of these stoves, and to produce such an atmo-sphere as may be most conducive to health. In hospitals no doubt this will be done; perhaps is done at present,—though even in hospitals I have thought the air hotter than it should be. But hot-air-drinking is like dram-drinking. There is the machine within the house capable of supplying any quantity, and those who consume it unconsciously in-crease their draughts, and take their drams stronger and stronger, till a breath of fresh air is felt to be a blast direct from Boreas.

West Point is at all points a military colony, and as such belongs exclusively to the Federal Government as separate from the Govern-ment of any individual State. It is the purchased property of the United States as a whole, and is devoted to the necessities of a military college. No man could take a house there, or succeed in getting even permanent lodgings, unless he belonged to or were employed by the establishment. There is no intercourse by road between West Point and other towns or villages on the river side, and any such intercourse even by water is looked upon with jealousy by the authorities. The wish is that West Point should be isolated and kept apart for military instruction to the exclusion of all other purposes whatever,—especially love-making purposes. The coming over from the other side of the water of young ladies by the ferry is regarded as a great hindrance. They will come, and then the military students will talk to them. We all know to what such talking leads! A lad when I was there had been tempted to get out of barracks in plain clothes, in order that he might call on a young lady at the hotel;—and was in consequence obliged to abandon his commission and retire from the Academy. Will that young lady ever again sleep quietly in her bed? I should hope not. An opinion was expressed to me that there should be no hotel in such a place;—that there should be no ferry, no roads, no means by which the attention of the students should be distracted;—that these military Rasselases should live in a happy military valley from which might be excluded both strong drinks and female charms,—those two poisons from which youthful military ardour is supposed to suffer so much.

It always seems to me that such training begins at the wrong end. I will not say that nothing should be done to keep lads of eighteen from strong drinks. I will not even say that there should not be some line of moderation with reference to feminine allurements. But as a rule the restraint should come from the sense, good feeling, and education of him who is restrained. There is no embargo on the beer-shops either at Harrow or at Oxford,—and certainly none upon the young ladies. Occasional damage may accrue from habits early depraved, or a heart too early and too easily susceptible; but the injury so done is not, I think, equal to that inflicted by a Draconian code of morals, which will probably be evaded, and will certainly create a desire for its evasion.

Nevertheless, I feel assured that West Point, taken as a whole, is an excellent military academy, and that young men have gone forth from it, and will go forth from it, fit for officers as far as training can make men fit. The fault, if fault there be, is that which is to be found in so many of the institutions of the United States; and is one so allied to a virtue that no foreigner has a right to wonder that it is regarded in the light of a virtue by all Americans. There has been an attempt to make the place too perfect. In the desire to have the establishment self-sufficient at all points, more has been attempted than human nature can achieve. The lad is taken to West Point, and it is presumed that from the moment of his reception, he shall expend every energy of his mind and body in making himself a soldier. At fifteen he is not to be a boy, at twenty he is not to be a young man. He is to be a gentleman, a soldier, and an officer. I believe that those who leave the College for the army are gentlemen, soldiers, and officers, and therefore the result is good. But they are also young men; and it seems that they have become so, not in accordance with their training, but in spite of it.

But I have another complaint to make against the authorities of West Point, which they will not be able to answer so easily as that already preferred. What right can they have to take the very prettiest spot on the Hudson—the prettiest spot on the continent—one of the prettiest spots which Nature, with all her vagaries, ever formed—and shut it up from all the world for purposes of war? Would not any plain, however ugly, do for military exercises? Cannot broadsword, goose-step, and double quick time be instilled into young hands and legs in any field of thirty, forty, or fifty acres? I wonder whether these lads appreciate the fact that they are studying fourteen hours a day amidst the sweetest river, rock, and mountain scenery that the imagination can conceive. Of course it will be said that the world at large is not excluded from West Point, that the ferry to the place is open, and that there is even a hotel there, closed against no man or woman who will consent to become a teetotaller for the period of his visit. I must admit that this is so; but still one feels that one is only admitted as a guest. I want to go and live at West Point, and why should I be prevented? The Government had a right to buy it of course, but Government should not buy up the prettiest spots on a country's surface. If I were an American I should make a grievance of this; but Americans will suffer things from their Government which no Englishmen would endure.

Anthony Trollope, *North America* (New York: Harper & Brothers, 1863).

TRAVEL BOOKS
James Kirke Paulding

J
AMES KIRKE PAULDING (1778–1860) took great pride
in his Dutch ancestry, but was even prouder of his father, who
was a colonel in the New York militia during the Revolutionary
War. To a great extent his ancestral and cultural background
accounts for the anger he felt at British attacks, in books and periodicals, on literary and political life in America in the early
decades of the nineteenth century. Besides, America was at war with
the British who had burned down the new White House in 1814.
In England, writers such as Sydney Smith, Henry Fearon, William
Cobbett, and others wrote condescendingly of the young country which was no longer under British rule. Understandably, they
were as unsympathetic as the French travel accounts were full
of enthusiasm for the democratic experiment. Paulding countered
with his New Mirror for Travellers, which lambasted the "Great
Northern Tour" of British tourists, with a special chapter on their
frequently misguided travel writings. And this work predated
the infamous books by Captain Basil Hall, Mrs. Frances Trollope,
and Charles Dickens! Paulding later caricatured Hall in one
of his novels, and did the same to Mrs. Trollope in a newspaper
article and play. His Anglophobia was a great source of inspiration.

Needless to say, he became a tireless champion of an American
national literature. A decade later in "The American Scholar"
Emerson would call for a break from the literary ties of Old Europe.

245

A highly respected literary figure of his day, Paulding wrote novels, satires, verse, plays, and journalism. His stylish wit displayed itself in the satiric journal Salmagundi, *along with that of his brother-in-law Washington Irving who, of course, made his own great contribution, as did their mutual friend James Fenimore Cooper, to the creation of an American literature.*

Some time after the literary tirades between American and British writers had subsided, with his reputation firmly established, Paulding settled down in 1845 at a home he called Placentia, on the banks of the Hudson near Hyde Park. He continued to write stories, essays, and novels, and kept up a correspondence with his good friend, former President Martin Van Buren, whom he had earlier served as Secretary of the Navy. Van Buren, comfortable at Lindenwald, his beautiful country seat up the river in Kinderhook, wrote to him of apples and pears and potatoes rather than politics. Paulding wrote back about his dandelions, grubs, muck, and marl beds.

THERE IS ONE CLASS of travellers deserving a whole book by themselves, could we afford to write one for their especial benefit. We mean the gentlemen who, as the African negro said, "walk big way—write big book;"—tourists by profession, who explore this country for the pleasure of their readers, and their own profit, and travel at the expense of the reputation of one country, and the pockets of another; who pay for a dinner by libelling their entertainer, and their passage in a steam boat, by retailing the information of the steward or coxswain; to whom the sight of a porpoise at sea affords matter for profitable speculation; who make more out of a flying fish than a market woman does out of a sheep's head; and dispose of a tolerable storm at the price of a week's board. These are the travellers for our money, being the only ones on record, except the pedlars, who unite the profits of business with the pleasures of travelling—a consummation which authors have laboured at in vain, until the present happy age of improvements, when sentimental young ladies wear spatter-dashes, and stout young gentlemen white kid gloves; when an opera singer receives a higher salary than an archbishop, and travels about with letters of introduction from kings!

Of all countries in the world, Old England, our kind, gentle, considerate old mamma, sends forth the largest portion of this species of literary *"riders,"* who sweep up the materials for a book by the road side. They are held of so much consequence as to be patronized by the government, which expends large sums in sending them to the North Pole, only to tell us in a "big book," how cold it is there; or to Africa, to distribute glass beads, and repeat over and over the same things, through a score of huge quartos. With these we do not concern ourselves; but inasmuch as it hath been alleged, however unjustly, that those who have from time to time honoured this country with their notice, have been guilty of divers sins of ignorance, prejudice, and malignity, we here offer them a compendium of regulations, by the due observance of which, they may in future avoid these offences, and construct a "big book," which shall give universal satisfaction.

Rules for gentlemen who "walk big way—make big book."

Never fail to seize every opportunity to lament, with tears in your eyes, the deplorable state of religion among "these republicans." People will take it for granted you are a very pious man.

Never lose an opportunity of canting about the sad state of morals among these republicans. People will give you credit for being very moral yourself.

Whenever you have occasion to mention the fourth of July, the birth date of Washington, or any other great national anniversary, don't forget to adduce it as proof of the bitter hostility felt by these republicans towards the English, and to lament these practices, as tending to keep up the memory of the revolution, as well as to foster national antipathies.

Be very particular in noticing stage drivers, waiters, tavern keepers, and persons of importance, who, as it were, represent the character of the people. Whenever you want any deep and profound information, always apply to them:—they are the best authority you can have.

If you happen to fall in company with a public man in the stage or steam boat, take the first opportunity of *pumping* the driver or waiter. These fellows know every thing, and can tell you all the lies that have ever been uttered against him.

If you dine with a hospitable gentleman, don't fail to repay him by dishing up himself, his wife, daughters, and dinner in your book. If the little boys don't behave respectfully towards you, and sneak into a corner with their fingers in their mouths, cut them up handsomely— father, mother, and all. Be sure you give their names at full length; be particular in noting every dish on the table, and don't forget pumping the waiter.

Tell all the old stories which the Yankees repeat of their southern and western neighbours, and which the latter have retorted upon them. Be sure not to forget the gouging of the judge, the roasting of the negro, the wooden nutmegs, the indigo coal; and above all, the excellent story of the wooden bowls. Never inquire whether they are true or not; they will make John Bull twice as happy as he is at present.

Never write a line without having the fear of the reviewers before your eyes, and remember how poor Miss Wright got abused for praising these republicans and sinners.

Never be deterred from telling a story to the discredit of any people, especially republicans, on the score of its improbability. John Bull, for whom you write, will swallow any thing, from a pot of beer to a melo-drama. He is even a believer in his own freedom.

Never be deterred from telling a story on account of its having been told over and over again, by every traveller since the discovery of America by the literati of Europe. If the reader has seen it before, it is only meeting an old friend; if he has not, it is making a new acquaintance. But be sure you don't forget to say that you saw every thing you describe. To quote from another is to give him all the credit, and is almost as bad as robbing your own house. There is nothing makes a lie look so much like truth as frequent repetition. If you know it to be false, don't let that deter you; for as you did not invent it yourself, you cannot be blamed.

Abuse all the women in mass, out of compliment to your own country women. The days of chivalry are past, and more honour comes from attacking, than defending ladies in the present age of public improvements. Besides all the world loves scandal, and a book filled with the praises of one nation is an insult to the rest of the world.

If the stage breaks down with you, give the roads no quarter.

If you get an indifferent breakfast at an inn, cut up the whole town where the enormity was committed, pretty handsomely. If a bad dinner, deprive the whole nation of its morals. If a sorry supper, take away the reputation of the landlady, the cook, and the landlady's daughters incontinently. And if they put you to sleep in a two bedded room, although the other bed be empty, it is sufficient provocation to set them all down for infidels, thereby proving yourself a zealous Christian.

Never read any book written by natives of the country you mean to describe. They are always partial; and besides, a knowledge of the truth always fetters the imagination, and circumscribes invention. It is fatal to the composition of a romance.

Never suffer the hospitalities and kindness of these republicans to conciliate you, except just while you are enjoying them. You may eat their dinners and receive their attentions; but never forget that if you praise the Yankees, John Bull will condemn your book; and that charity begins at home. The first duty of a literary traveller is to make a book that will sell; the rest is between him and his conscience, and is nobody's business.

Never mind what these republicans say of you or your book. You never mean to come among them again; or if you do, you can come *incog.* under a different name. Let them abuse you as much as they please. "Who reads an American book?" No Englishman certainly, except with a view of borrowing its contents without giving the author credit for them. Besides, every true born Englishman knows, that the shortest way of elevating his own country, is to depress all others as much as possible.

Never fail to find fault with every thing, and grumble without ceasing. People won't know you for an Englishman else.

Never mind your geography, as you are addressing yourself to people who don't know a wild turkey from Turkey in Europe. Your book will sell just as well if you place New York on the Mississippi, and New Orleans on the Hudson. You will be kept in countenance by a certain British secretary of foreign affairs, who is said to have declared the right to navigate the St. Lawrence inadmissible to the United States, because it would give them a direct route to the Pacific.

You need not make any special inquiries into the state of morals, because every body knows that republicans have no morality. Nor of religion, because every body knows they tolerate all religions, and of course can have none. Nor of their manners, because as there is no distinction of ranks recognized in their constitution, every body knows they must be all blackguards. The person most completely qualified of any we ever met with for a traveller, was a worthy Englishman, who being very near sighted, and hard of hearing, was not led astray by the villainy of his five senses; and what was very remarkable his book contained quite as much truth as those of his more fortunate contemporaries who were embarrassed by eyes and ears.

James Kirke Paulding, *The New Mirror for Travellers; and Guide to the Springs* (New York: G. & C. Carvill, 1828).

THE SETTING

Roland Van Zandt

THERE WAS NO *real tourist industry to speak of in America until after the War of 1812, but by the end of the next decade the Catskill Mountain House, Niagara Falls, and the Springs at Saratoga were stops on the American equivalent of Europe's "Grand Tour." More significantly, the Catskill Mountain House at Hunter was linked to the development of Hudson Valley tourism, and the cultivation of taste for wilderness landscape. Taking as his point of departure the 1824 opening of the famous resort hotel, Roland Van Zandt (1918–91) creates a fascinating narrative by intercutting themes of tourism, transportation, aesthetics, and social life in the Hudson Valley. These local aspects are set against the larger background of economic and social changes in the U.S. for over a century, demonstrating that regional history broadens in scope when it reflects larger currents in the history of a nation.*

In the two decades after its start, the Catskill Mountain House was the subject of numerous articles, engravings, travel memoirs, and paintings of area views (especially Kaaterskill Falls), by Thomas Cole, William H. Bartlett, William Guy Wall, and others, that filled books, periodicals, and newspapers here and in England. A visit to the grand hotel began with a four-to-six hour stagecoach ride from the village of Catskill to the site, perched 2,250 feet from the level of the Hudson, which commanded a sweeping view of the Valley. To its back were North Lake and South Lake. Under the powerful ownership of Charles L. Beach, several mod-

*ifications and additions made the Catskill Mountain House one of
the finest American examples of Neo-Classical architecture. In
its final form the hotel featured a 140-foot-long piazza, fronted by
thirteen Corinthian columns that stretched to a height of three
stories. There were more than three hundred rooms for guests, with
a dining hall that could seat up to five hundred people. Besides
the celebrated painters and writers who lived in the area, other hotel guests over the decades included Capt. Basil Hall, Ulysses S.
Grant, General William Sherman, Oscar Wilde, and Alexander Gra-
ham Bell.*

*The greatest period of the hotel was the boom years after the
Civil War. But by 1918 vast transformations in travel and vacation habits, brought on by the car and increased railway connections, hastened the decline of the hotel. For decades, too, Western
scenery was competing with the mountains of the East. The wealthy
were moving on to other places—New Jersey, Long Island, New
England. Fortunes of the resort progressively declined after the depression, with the last season opening in 1942. Years of neglect
and physical ruin brought the great hotel to its eventual pitiable
end two decades later. Unfortunately, the Catskill Mountain House
could not wait for the changes in civic attitudes that would lead
communities in more recent years to preserve and restore their
architectural treasures. There are only the names and dates carved
into the escarpment boulders that survive as reminders of the
lives spent in splendor gazing out across the Hudson Valley, once
upon a century.*

THE FINAL SCENE was played to its end during the early hours of the
morning. The exact time was 6:00 A.M., January 25, 1963. The scene
was a dark, massive ruin silhouetted against the dawn on a high
windswept ridge of the Catskill Mountains. The temperature stood
close to zero, the snow was deep, the valley far below lay dark and
quiet. At that time, and in that lonely setting, one of the monuments
of nineteenth-century American culture was being put to the torch.

History was coming full cycle for what had once been known as "the noblest wonder of the Hudson Valley," the world-famous Catskill Mountain House.

Only necessity could justify such destructiveness, and the necessity seemed to lie close at hand. After two decades of neglect and decay the venerable edifice commanding the eastern escarpment of the Catskill Mountains had become a hulking ruin, a threat to the lives and limbs of every curious visitor or trespasser. And its appeal was magnetic: no hiker or camper, no tourist or sightseer, no student of architecture or history, could resist the temptation of its labyrinthine corridors. Signs against trespassing had proved unavailing; a huge fence around the ruins only offered further challenge. Finally, bowing to necessity, officials of the New York State Conservation Department ordered the great structure burned to the ground.

The New York Times noticed the event; every newspaper of the Hudson Valley carried articles and editorial comments, and the Conservation Department received a smattering of irate letters. Among the older residents who had been raised within sight of this "fairy palace" clinging to the edge of the mountain, and among those farther away who had once visited it or known its ancient history, the sense of sudden loss was acutely personal and deeply, disturbingly, national. A few years previous when a midwestern scholar and artist first saw the abandoned ruins, he had lamented an American indifference to cultural heritage and said, "it would be criminal not to maintain this landmark, which has not lost one iota of its inspirational value." A sense of guilt pervaded the high villages of the Catskills. The great white mansion, a delight to successive thousands of Americans as they traveled up the Hudson through 140 years of unbroken history, had disappeared from the earth. "What is that white speck?" a famous English traveler had asked a century and a quarter earlier as her delighted eye first glimpsed its presence on the distant mountaintop, more than twenty miles away. "What is this place?" strangers still ask as they stumble upon the remnants of the gigantic foundations along the mountain's edge.

The keys to history are as diverse as the affairs of men, but in the early stages of history before civilization has conquered the land, none is likely to be more important than geography, one of the oldest of human sciences. Such was the case in America during the first quarter of the nineteenth century when the Mountain House first appeared on a high rim of the Catskill Mountains and the Hudson Valley provided a natural highway from the developing cities of the Atlantic seaboard to the nation's first mountain resort. The rise of the Mountain House to the stature of an American classic within that setting presupposes a deep commitment to time and place, and in early nineteenth century America that meant a nation still dominated by the geographical necessities of the East. Many factors contributed to the rise of the Mountain House, cultural and social as well as economic; but all were dependent upon the *sine qua non* of this basic geographical harmony.

In the decade of 1820–30 during which the Mountain House was established, the Hudson Valley was the focal population center of the nation. In the early nineteenth century, America was a regional rather than continental power, and within that narrow region the Hudson Valley was the main artery of trade and traffic, the fastest-growing commercial and social center of the whole nation.

In 1830 the population of the United States was overwhelmingly confined to the area between the Mississippi and the Atlantic, and at least 65 per cent of the population was still concentrated on the Atlantic slope between the Alleghenies and the sea. The only sizable area with ninety or more inhabitants per square mile was the region extending from New York City across New Jersey to Philadelphia.

In 1820, the three leading cities of the Northeast, Boston, New York, and Philadelphia, had more than twice the population of the four leading Southern cities, Baltimore, Charleston, Mobile, and New Orleans. By 1830 the margin was even greater. In the Northeast there was a further regional differentiation of special significance to this story. In the decade of 1810–1820 New York State took the lead in population over its nearest competitor, Virginia, and retained that lead throughout the 140-year history of the Mountain House. Finally, by 1830 the City of New York had become the largest and wealthiest city in all America. In short, the distribution of population gave the Catskills a geographical importance that could not be duplicated in any other mountains of the Atlantic seaboard.

They were preëminently accessible to the thriving centers of American population, and in the early nineteenth century this advantage had a special significance for the rise of such a social phenomenon as the Catskill Mountain House. Visitors to the hotel were attracted from the start not only by the dramatic location, but by the surprising elegance and luxury of its facilities, for the great hotel stood in the midst of hundreds of square miles of raw wilderness, and it could be reached only after a four-hour stage ride up a precipitous mountain. This ideal combination of wilderness and luxury—so beguiling to the romantic imagination of the early nineteenth century—was a key to the immediate success of the Mountain House, but it was possible only in the Hudson Valley, less than a day's journey from the markets and resources of the greatest city in the nation.

Luxury and the amenities of life receded in 1830 as one traveled away from the centers of population. Travel was slow and uncomfortable relative to today; it required a week to reach Cincinnati from New York City and two weeks to reach the Mississippi frontier; and the farther a man traveled, the more completely he found himself in a world of stark necessities. The frontier was not—as used to be assumed—a boundary between civilization and savagery, but between an inferior state of civilization and its total absence. In 1830, therefore, such amenities as fine hotels and resorts were virtually unknown west of the Alleghenies.

And they were also virtually unknown, though for different reasons, south of the Mason-Dixon Line. Resorts and large hotels and the tourists and vacationers who patronize them have only arisen in modern history as an urban-industrial civilization has come into being. Throughout the antebellum period the rise of such a civilization was retarded, if not frustrated altogether, by the agrarian economy of the southern plantation. The North therefore received a disproportionate share of the rising benefits of a highly complex civilization: just as southern trade and capital flowed north, so the southerner often sent his sons to northern colleges and his family to northern spas and hostelries. The dearth of inns and hotels in the South was notorious throughout the antebellum period. Such social amenities kept pace in the North with the rising wealth and complexity of its population. . . .

The convenient location and exceptional beauty of the Hudson soon encouraged wealthy New Yorkers to build summer homes along its commanding heights, and the lower valley became the scene of America's first vacationland. Even in the early years of the nineteenth century the area south of the Highlands acquired a suburban aspect unknown to the rest of America until long after the advent of the railroad age. While making a trip up the Hudson to visit the Mountain House in 1860, Bayard Taylor discovered that "the elegant summer residences of New Yorkers . . . now extend more than half-way to Albany." Yet as early as 1838 while viewing the Hudson from the steps of the Mountain House, Nathaniel P. Willis found that "there is a suburban look and character about all the villages on the Hudson," and that the steamboat had "destroyed the distance between them and the city" and converted the Catskills themselves into a "resort."

The scenic beauty of the Hudson Valley was a prime factor in the development of America's first vacationland. Even in the post-Civil War period, after people had become aware of the wonders of the West, the Hudson River remained a "must" of American travel. Before the war, when travel was largely confined to the Atlantic seaboard and most American scenery was considered far inferior to Europe's, the Hudson Valley gained special praise.

Occupying about three thousand square miles of the west bank of the river, the Catskills, as William Cullen Bryant once said, "are among the most remarkable objects seen in the voyage up the Hudson." Travel literature of the nineteenth century abounds in descriptions of these mountains as they are first seen from the river, for other than the narrow passage through the Highlands the Catskills provide some of the most beautiful scenery of the whole voyage upriver. To many travelers such as the youthful Thomas Cole in 1825, they were the climax of that voyage. Of all accounts that convey the impact of these mountains upon the romantic sensibility of the early nineteenth century, none has surpassed the description by Washington Irving:

To me they have ever been the fairy region of the Hudson. I speak, however, from early impressions, made in the happy days of childhood, when all the world had a tinge of fairyland. I shall never forget my first view of these mountains. It was in the course of a voyage up the Hudson, in the good old times, before steam-boats and railroads had driven all poetry and romance out of travel. A voyage up the Hudson in those days was equal to a voyage to Europe at present, and cost almost as much time; but we enjoyed the river then; we relished it as we did our wine, sip by sip; not as at present, gulping it down at a draught, without tasting it. My whole voyage up the Hudson was full of wonder and romance. I was a lively boy, somewhat imaginative, of easy faith, and prone to relish everything that partook of the marvellous. Among the passengers on board the sloop was a veteran Indian trader, on his way to the Lakes, to traffic with the natives. He had discovered my propensity, and amused himself throughout the voyage by telling me Indian legends and grotesque stories about every noted place on the river, such as Spuyten Devil Creek, the Tappan Zee, the Devil's Dans Kammer, and other hobgoblin places. The Catskill Mountains, especially, called forth a host of fanciful traditions. We were all day slowly tiding along in sight of them, so that he had full time to.weave his whimsical narratives....All these were doled out to me as I lay on deck, throughout a long summer's day, gazing upon these mountains, the everchanging shapes and hues of which appeared to realize the magical influences in question. Sometimes they seemed to approach, at others to recede; during the heat of the day they almost melted into a sultry haze; as the day declined they deepened in tone; their summits were brightened by the last rays of the sun, and later in the evening their whole outline was printed in deep purple against an amber sky. As I beheld them, thus shifting continually before my eye, and listened to the marvellous legends of the trader, a host of fanciful notions concerning them was conjured into my brain, which have haunted it ever since.

The particular favor with which Americans of the early nineteenth century looked upon the Catskills may be seen in an 1830 statement of William Cullen Bryant that the Catskills are "the highest in the state of New-York." Bryant did not know, and Americans as a whole did not know until after the Civil War, that the highest mountains in New York are the Adirondacks, another hundred miles north. As late as 1850 when hundreds of visitors were frequenting the area of the Mountain House during the summer months, the Adirondacks were known only to a few lumbermen, hunters or trappers. The Green Mountains of Vermont and the White Mountains of New Hampshire— not to mention the Smokies or mountains west of the Mississippi— were also generally unknown when the Catskills had already become a popular American resort.

The various handbooks of travel and picture books of American scenes that began to appear in the pre-Civil War period attest the singular popularity of the Hudson Valley and the Catskills. *Appleton's Illustrated Hand-Book of American Travel* asserted in 1857 that "We can commend to the traveller no pleasanter or more profitable summer excursion for a day, or a month, or even a season, than a visit to the Catskills—one of the grandest and most picturesque of the mountain ranges of the United States." Such a statement can be understood only in terms of the restricted boundaries of the American nation in the 1850s, the relative obscurity of the upper and lower reaches of the Appalachians, the unknown domains of the Rockies and High Sierras. Even as late as 1872–1874 Bryant's *Picturesque America* could still substantiate the singular importance of the Catskills by declaring "there are few places in the whole range of American scenery so attractive and refreshing as the Catskill Mountains."

The heart, though not the full extent, of the Catskills today is bounded by the Catskill State Park and embraces about 900 square miles of Greene, Ulster, Delaware, and Sullivan counties. Measured by the foothills and the outer perimeter of today's resort area, the Catskills include almost thrice that amount of land and extend from the eastern escarpment along the Hudson west to the upper reaches of the Susquehanna, and as far south as the vicinity of Liberty and Monticello. The remarkable fact about this geographical extent of the Catskills is that until the coming of the railroads in the 1880s only one very small part of it formed the famous resort area. This was a sixteen- to twenty-square-mile area of the eastern escarpment just opposite the city of Catskill and close by the precipitous cliffs of Kaaterskill Clove. The geographical center of this small area was called "Pine Orchard," a high plateau-like area between two peaks that included two lakes and large rock "platforms" that protruded

beyond the edge of the mountain and provided the foundations of
the Catskill Mountain House. . . .

Until the opening of the Mountain House there was not a single
hotel in the area. The erection of the Mountain House, one of the
first "mountain hotels" in America, signalized the advent of the resort
history of the Catskills, and led to the development of the whole
historic region.

From the very start, the geographical location and scenic beauty
of Pine Orchard contained the key to all subsequent history. The
combination of topographical features found within a four-mile
radius—of precipitous cloves, high mountain peaks, lakes and waterfalls, secluded dales and panoramic views—are characteristic of the
Catskills as a whole; but nowhere else can they be found in such
concentrated grandeur and so conveniently located to the town of
Catskill.

Descriptions of the area abound in nineteenth-century American
letters. One of the earliest was also one of the most famous—a
three-page encomium in James Fenimore Cooper's *The Pioneers*, the
first of the Leather-Stocking novels. Written in 1823 coincident with
the construction of the Mountain House, Cooper's description was
the progenitor of literally hundreds of such descriptions; and as one
of the few passages in the Leather-Stocking tales that localized the
topographical setting of the stories, it is a revelation of the scenery of
Pine Orchard under the telling guise of nineteenth-century romanticism. The speaker is Leather-Stocking himself:

> "I have travelled the woods for fifty-three years, and have made
> them my home for more than forty; and I can say that I have met but
> one place that was more to my liking; and that was only to eye-sight, and
> not for hunting or fishing."
>
> "And where was that?" asked Edwards.
>
> "Where! why up on the Cattskills. I used often to go up into the
> mountains after wolves' skins and bears; once they paid me to get them
> a stuffed panther, and so I often went. There's a place in them hills that I
> used to climb to when I wanted to see the carryings on of the world,
> that would well pay any man for a barked shin or a torn moccasin. You
> know the Cattskills, lad; for you must have seen them on your left, as
> you followed the river up from York, looking as blue as a piece of clear

sky, and holding the clouds on their tops, as the smoke curls over the head of an Indian chief at the council fire. Well, there's the High-peak, and the Round-top which lay back like a father and mother among their children, seeing they are far above all the other hills. But the place I mean is next to the river, where one of the ridges juts out a little from the rest, and where the rocks fall, for the best part of a thousand feet, so much up and down, that a man standing on their edges is fool enough to think he can jump from top to bottom."

"What see you when you get there?" asked Edwards.

"Creation," said Natty, dropping the end of his rod into the water, and sweeping one hand around him in a circle: "all creation, lad. . . .

"Why, there's a fall in the hills where the water of two little ponds, that lie near each other, breaks out of their bounds and runs over the rocks into the valley. The stream is, maybe, such a one as would turn a mill, if so useless a thing was wanted in the wilderness. But the hand that made that 'Leap' never made a mill. There the water comes crooking and winding among the rocks; first so slow that a trout could swim in it, and then starting and running like a creatur' that wanted to make a far spring, till it gets to where the mountain divides, like the cleft hoof of a deer, leaving a deep hollow for the brook to tumble into. The first pitch is nigh two hundred feet, and the water looks like flakes of driven snow afore it touches the bottom; and there the stream gathers itself together again for a new start, and maybe flutters over fifty feet of flat rock before it falls another hundred, when it jumps about from shelf to shelf, first turning thisaway and then turning thataway, striving to get out of the hollow, till it finally comes to the plain."

"I have never heard of this spot before; it is not mentioned in the books."

"I never read a book in my life," said Leather-Stocking.

Leather-Stocking's description of the mountains became a common quotation of the nineteenth-century literature of the Catskills. Even in the second half of the twentieth century Leather-Stocking's description of "all creation" is still quoted by those who attempt to describe the view from the crest of the mountains. In some cases Cooper's description is ascribed to the region of the Overlook House considerably south of Pine Orchard in the vicinity of Woodstock. There is, indeed, no part of the Catskills which would not like to claim the famous description as its own. A careful reading of the full passage, however, makes it unmistakable that Cooper was referring to Pine Orchard and the view from the Catskill Mountain House. Indeed, so accurate and graphic is Cooper's description of this particular region that it seems obvious he drew it from first-hand acquaintance. It is quite possible that Cooper visited the area some time before the erection of the hotel. Many people did, as several dates that are engraved in the protruding "platform" attest. Since Cooper lived just to the west of the mountains at the foot of Otsego Lake and traveled to and from that place by way of the Hudson and Mohawk rivers, we may safely conclude that on one or more of those trips he made a slight detour to visit the dramatic heights of Pine Orchard.

It was this dramatic region that became the setting of the Catskill Mountain House and a glowing page in the history of American Romanticism. Though, as Leather-Stocking suggested, it extended from High Peak and Round Top on the south, to Kaaterskill Falls on the west, and from there north to the two lakes and North Mountain, it was the eastern boundary of the region along the high escarpment of the mountains that became the focal center of the whole select region. Here midway between Sleepy Hollow and Kaaterskill Clove at the head of an old abandoned road, "a large and singular plain" called Pine Orchard terminated in a remarkable "rock platform." The subject of some of the oldest Indian legends of the Hudson Valley, commemorated in the lore of the American Revolution, known and sought out by early travelers of the nineteenth century as one of the most beautiful sights of the Atlantic seaboard, the high stone "platform" of Pine Orchard became in 1823 the foundation of the Catskill Mountain House and the geographical center of the first great resort area in American history. As this development spread throughout the Catskills, bringing artists and writers, people of wealth and fashion, new towns and villages, extravagant hotels and art colonies, the Mountain House maintained its command of the eastern approaches to the mountains and became the hub and center of the whole movement, the acknowledged monarch of the mountains, one of the great hotels in American history.

The setting, the geography of mountain and seacoast, wilderness and city, was everything. The Mountain House and its growing domain occupied an ideal location on a high but accessible ledge of the American wilderness, just off the center of American population, one hundred and ten miles north of the fastest-growing city in the western hemisphere. This "juxtaposition of civilized and savage life," as one famous commentator called this abiding pattern of American life, was repeated in the nineteenth-century history of the Catskills at a time when the Romantic Movement was making it a universal principle of art and culture. It became almost a metaphysical experience to realize, as William Cullen Bryant expressed it,

> that on that little point, scarce visible on the breast of the mountain, the beautiful and the gay are met, and the sounds of mirth and music arise, while for leagues around the mountain torrents are dashing, and the eagle is uttering his shriek, unheard by human ear.

The Catskills were all the American past, the deep primitivism of the American environment; the Mountain House was a symbol of a young nation's wealth, leisure and cultural attainments. The triumph of one would eventually destroy the other, but in the second quarter of the nineteenth century both were still equal manifestations of the American environment, and under the aegis of Romanticism Americans believed for one glowing moment in their history that they could have both.

Roland Van Zandt, *The Catskill Mountain House* (Cornwallville, N.Y.: Hope Farm Press, 1982).

The Corner of State and North Pearl Streets, Albany (as it appeared in 1814). The watercolor by James Eights was executed in 1849. This street scene, not far from the site of the State Capitol, shows the Dutch architecture of old Albany, and the shapeliness of its cobblestone paths. *(Collection of the Albany Institute of History & Art. Bequest of Ledyard Cogswell, Jr.)*

In 1962 Consolidated Edison announced plans to carve a pumped storage hydroelectric plant out of the 1463-foot Storm King Mountain. This proposal ignited a seven-year struggle by Hudson Valley residents who rallied to preserve the fjord-like splendor of this Highlands setting. *(Scenic Hudson)*

View of West Point (1848) from Fort Putnam by Robert Havell. This aquatint made from the painting shows a view of Newburgh in the distance, the railroad on the west bank, Pollepel Island, and several buildings on the grounds of the Military Academy. (*West Point Museum, United States Military Academy*)

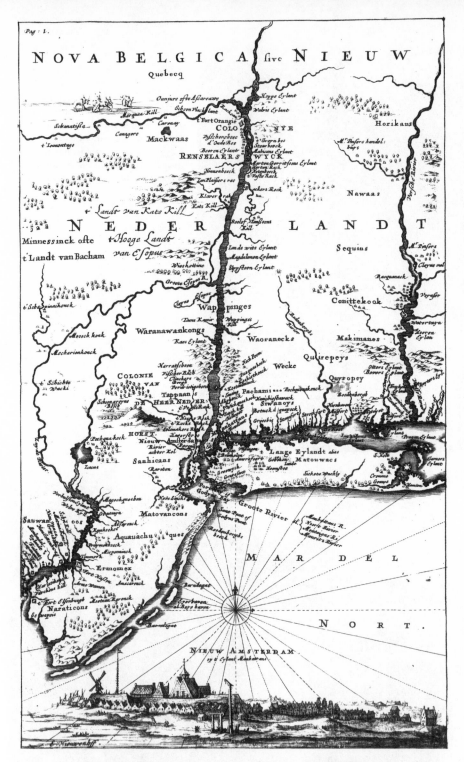

The work of Adriaen Van der Donck, who arrived in the Dutch colony in 1641, this is one of the earliest maps of New York State. It was published in his book *Beschryvinge Van Nieuw-Nederlant (A Description of the New Netherlands)* in 1856. The settlement at New Amsterdam (now Manhattan) is pictured in the inset at the lower portion of the map. (*The New-York Historical Society, New York City*)

Featured here is Plate number 13, "Hudson," a colored aquatint of the town and river view engraved by John Hill after a William Guy Wall watercolor. It was part of the *Hudson River Portfolio* (1821-25), a widely admired collection of landscapes published serially at the time. The prints immediately became collector's items, and remain so. (*The New-York Historical Society, New York City*)

Thomas Cole, *A View of Two Lakes and Mountain House, Catskill Mountains, Morning* (1844). This majestic panorama shows North and South Lakes and the famous hotel resort on the escarpment between them. Cole's many paintings of the wild mountain scenery attracted travelers from here and abroad to the Catskills. (*The Brooklyn Museum, Dick S. Ramsay Fund*)

No visit to the mountains was complete without a hike to one of its most breathtaking wonders, the Kaaterskill Falls. Natty Bumpo described it in James Fenimore Cooper's *The Pioneers.* Widely reproduced in guidebooks in the nineteenth century, The Falls are shown here in a drawing made by the British illustrator Harry Fenn for the immensely popular *Picturesque America,* edited by William Cullen Bryant in the 1870s. *(The New York State Library, Albany)*

Asher B. Durand painted his *Kindred Spirits* (1849) as homage to the friendship of Thomas Cole, who died the year before, and to William Cullen Bryant who delivered his funeral oration. The two men are pictured in the magisterial setting of Kaaterskill Clove, a favorite place of landscape painters in mid-century. (*Collection of the New York Public Library, Astor, Lenox and Tilden Foundations*)

In the 1870s the steamship *Mary Powell*, known as the "Queen of the Hudson," left Vestry Street in Manhattan every afternoon except Sundays, stopping at Cozzens' Hotel, West Point, Gov't Dock, Cornwall, Newburgh, New Hamburgh, Milton, Poughkeepsie, Rondout, and Kingston. An average trip took about 3½ hours, at 22 miles per hour. In this engraving from Beers's *Ulster County Atlas* (1875) the vessel is making a colorful passage through the gate of the Hudson Highlands. (*The New York State Library, Albany*)

V

NATURAL HISTORIES

A BIRD MEDLEY

John Burroughs

JOHN BURROUGHS (1837–1921) first began to write about
birds in his twenties, and after that his life was led, more or
less, in pursuit of the songs of nature. Born in Roxbury, he first
taught in rural schools before moving to Washington, D.C., where
he worked as a clerk in the Department of Treasury. But by 1874
Burroughs was back in New York State, now as a bank exam-
iner for the next decade, and building a home which he called
Riverby at West Park. From here he set out on the excursions
about the woods and fields and streams that would be detailed in
more than thirty books, among them, Locusts and Wild Honey,
Signs and Seasons, Riverby, and Ways of Nature. In a review of his
Winter Sunshine, Henry James wrote that Burroughs "sees sermons in stones and good in everything."

But nature was not the only subject of his work which ranged
widely on literature, philosophy, science, and religion. Burroughs
positioned himself in a humanistic literary tradition that embraced
ecological imperatives, featuring among his mentors its chief
exponents, Emerson, Thoreau, and Whitman. It was a literary legacy that would extend from transcendentalism to romanticism
to conservationism. Burroughs became an enormously popular figure in his lifetime. There were many who made a pilgrimage
to his homey, secluded retreat Slabsides, deep in the woods away
from Riverby. Even today the guest book is astonishing in its
geographical variety. Another house, Woodchuck Lodge in Roxbury,

was a summer home in later years where Burroughs entertained the likes of Thomas Edison and Henry Ford, whom he joined on camping trips to the Adirondacks and Great Smoky Mountains. He camped with John Muir in Yosemite, and tramped with Teddy Roosevelt in Yellowstone. Burroughs enjoyed traveling not only in the United States, but abroad, too: he was not content to worship nature from a tiny corner of his world. Significantly, in his journals he expressed the desire for a point of view that was not provincial, but "metropolitan." But the Sage of Slabsides would also admit, "I love a small house, plain clothes, simple living." In the Catskills he found both intellectual stimulation and what Emerson called "the independence of solitude."

Today a new generation is discovering Burroughs thanks to the growth of environmental awareness, and a renewed interest in nature writing, which he helped to establish as a literary genre. Burroughs is the most celebrated nature writer the Hudson Valley has ever produced, the only one with a national reputation. That this region, so close to the intellectual center of New York City, did not develop an ongoing nature essay tradition in the twentieth century, as New England continued to, is somewhat of a cultural disappointment. The Valley has always been more famous for its painters than its writers. But changing demographics and increased attention to the region suggest that this condition may change in the coming decades. For now, Burroughs remains the quintessential Hudson Valley nature writer. In works that have brought joy to readers for more than a century, he has shown so well in his passionate, wise prose that the best nature writing is always attached to the life of a society beyond the trees.

PEOPLE WHO HAVE not made friends with the birds do not know how much they miss. Especially to one living in the country, of strong local attachments and an observing turn of mind, does an acquaintance with the birds form a close and invaluable tie. The only time I saw Thomas Carlyle, I remember his relating, apropos of this subject, that in his earlier days he was sent on a journey to a distant town on some business that gave him much bother and vexation, and that on his way back home, forlorn and dejected, he suddenly heard the larks singing all about him,—soaring and singing, just as they did about his father's fields, and it had the effect to comfort him and cheer him up amazingly.

Most lovers of the birds can doubtless recall similar experiences from their own lives. Nothing wonts me to a new place more than the birds. I go, for instance, to take up my abode in the country,—to plant myself upon unfamiliar ground. I know nobody, and nobody knows me. The roads, the fields, the hills, the streams, the woods, are all strange. I look wistfully upon them, but they know me not. They give back nothing to my yearning gaze. But there, on every hand, are the long-familiar birds,—the same ones I left behind me, the same ones I knew in my youth,—robins, sparrows, swallows, bobolinks, crows, hawks, high-holes, meadowlarks, etc., all there before me, and ready to renew and perpetuate the old associations. Before my house is begun, theirs is completed; before I have taken root at all, they are thoroughly established. I do not yet know what kind of apples my apple-trees bear, but there, in the cavity of a decayed limb, the bluebirds are building a nest, and yonder, on that branch, the social sparrow is busy with hairs and straws. The robins have tasted the quality of my cherries, and the cedar-birds have known every red cedar on the place these many years. While my house is yet surrounded by its scaffoldings, the phoebe-bird has built her exquisite mossy nest on the projecting stone beneath the eaves, a robin has filled a niche in the wall with mud and dry grass, the chimney swallows are going out and in the chimney, and a pair of house wrens are at home in a snug cavity over the door, and, during an April snowstorm, a number of hermit thrushes have taken shelter in my unfinished chambers. Indeed, I am in the midst of friends before I fairly know it. The place is not so new as I had thought. It is already old; the birds have supplied the memories of many decades of years.

There is something almost pathetic in the fact that the birds remain forever the same. You grow old, your friends die or move to distant lands, events sweep on, and all things are changed. Yet there in your garden or orchard are the birds of your boyhood, the same notes, the same calls, and, to all intents and purposes, the identical birds endowed with perennial youth. The swallows, that built so far out of your reach beneath the eaves of your father's barn, the same ones now squeak and chatter beneath the eaves of your barn. The warblers and shy wood-birds you pursued with such glee ever so many summers ago, and whose names you taught to some beloved youth who now, perchance, sleeps amid his native hills, no marks of time or change cling to them; and when you walk out to the strange woods, there they are, mocking you with their ever-renewed and joyous youth. The call of the high-holes, the whistle of the quail, the strong piercing note of the meadowlark, the drumming of the grouse,—how these sounds ignore the years, and strike on the ear with the melody of that springtime when the world was young, and life was all holiday and romance!

During any unusual tension of the feelings or emotions, how the note or song of a single bird will sink into the memory, and become inseparably associated with your grief or joy! Shall I ever again be able to hear the song of the oriole without being pierced through and through? Can it ever be other than a dirge for the dead to me? Day after day, and week after week, this bird whistled and warbled in a mulberry by the door, while sorrow, like a pall, darkened my day. So loud and persistent was the singer that his note teased and worried my excited ear.

> Hearken to yon pine warbler,
>   Singing aloft in the tree!
> Hearest thou, O traveler!
>   What he singeth to me?
>
> Not unless God made sharp thine ear
>   With sorrow such as mine,
> Out of that delicate lay couldst thou
>   Its heavy tale divine.

It is the opinion of some naturalists that birds never die what is called a natural death, but come to their end by some murderous or accidental means; yet I have found sparrows and vireos in the fields and woods dead or dying, that bore no marks of violence; and I remember that once in my childhood a red-bird fell down in the yard exhausted, and was brought in by the girl; its bright scarlet image is indelibly stamped upon my recollection. It is not known that birds have any distempers like the domestic fowls, but I saw a social sparrow one day quite disabled by some curious malady that suggested a disease that sometimes attacks poultry; one eye was nearly put out by a scrofulous-looking sore, and on the last joint of one wing there was a large tumorous or fungous growth that crippled the bird completely. On another occasion I picked up one that appeared well, but could not keep its centre of gravity when in flight, and so fell to the ground.

One reason why dead birds and animals are so rarely found is, that on the approach of death their instinct prompts them to creep away into some hole or under some cover, where they will be least liable to fall a prey to their natural enemies. It is doubtful if any of the game-birds, like the pigeon and grouse, ever die of old age, or the semi-game birds, like the bobolink, or the "century living" crow; but in what other form can death overtake the hummingbird, or even the swift and the barn swallow? Such are true birds of the air; they may be occasionally lost at sea during their migrations, but, so far as I know, they are not preyed upon by any other species.

The valley of the Hudson, I find, forms a great natural highway for the birds, as do doubtless the Connecticut, the Susquehanna, the Delaware, and all other large watercourses running north and south. The birds love an easy way, and in the valley of the rivers they find a road already graded for them; and they abound more in such places throughout the season than they do farther inland. The swarms of robins that come to us in early spring are a delight to behold. In one of his poems Emerson speaks of

> April's bird,
> Blue-coated, flying before from tree to tree;

but April's bird with me is the robin, brisk, vociferous, musical, dotting every field, and larking it in every grove; he is as easily atop at this season as the bobolink is a month or two later. The tints of

April are ruddy and brown,—the new furrow and the leafless trees,
—and these are the tints of its dominant bird.

From my dining-room window I look, or did look, out upon a
long stretch of smooth meadow, and as pretty a spring sight as I ever
wish to behold was this field, sprinkled all over with robins, their red
breasts turned toward the morning sun, or their pert forms sharply
outlined against lingering patches of snow. Every morning for weeks
I had those robins for breakfast; but what *they* had I never could find
out.

After the leaves are out, and gayer colors come into fashion, the
robin takes a back seat. He goes to housekeeping in the old
apple-tree, or, what he likes better, the cherry-tree. A pair reared
their domestic altar (of mud and dry grass) in one of the latter trees,
where I saw much of them. The cock took it upon himself to keep
the tree free of all other robins during cherry time, and its branches
were the scene of some lively tussles every hour in the day. The
innocent visitor would scarcely alight before the jealous cock was
upon him; but while he was thrusting the intruder out at one side, a
second would be coming in on the other. He managed, however, to
protect his cherries very well, but had so little time to eat the fruit
himself that we got fully our share.

I have frequently seen the robin courting, and have always been
astonished and amused at the utter coldness and indifference of the
female. The females of every species of birds, however, I believe,
have this in common,—they are absolutely free from coquetry, or any
airs and wiles whatever. In most cases, Nature has given the song and
the plumage to the other sex, and all the embellishing and acting is
done by the male bird.

I am always at home when I see the passenger pigeon. Few
spectacles please me more than to see clouds of these birds sweeping across the sky, and few sounds are more agreeable to my ear than
their lively piping and calling in the spring woods. They come in
such multitudes, they people the whole air; they cover townships,
and make the solitary places gay as with a festival. The naked woods
are suddenly blue as with fluttering ribbons and scarfs, and vocal as
with the voices of children. Their arrival is always unexpected. We
know April will bring the robins and May the bobolinks, but we do

not know that either they or any other month will bring the passenger pigeon. Sometimes years elapse and scarcely a flock is seen. Then, of a sudden, some March or April they come pouring over the horizon from the south or southwest, and for a few days the land is alive with them.

The whole race seems to be collected in a few vast swarms or assemblages. Indeed, I have sometimes thought there was only one such in the United States, and that it moved in squads, and regiments, and brigades, and divisions, like a giant army. The scouting and foraging squads are not unusual, and every few years we see larger bodies of them, but rarely indeed do we witness the spectacle of the whole vast tribe in motion. Sometimes we hear of them in Virginia, or Kentucky and Tennessee; then in Ohio or Pennsylvania; then in New York; then in Canada or Michigan or Missouri. They are followed from point to point, and from State to State, by human sharks, who catch and shoot them for market.

A year ago last April, the pigeons flew for two or three days up and down the Hudson. In long bowing lines, or else in dense masses, they moved across the sky. It was not the whole army, but I should think at least one corps of it; I had not seen such a flight of pigeons since my boyhood. I went up to the top of the house, the better to behold the winged procession. The day seemed memorable and poetic in which such sights occurred.

While I was looking at the pigeons, a flock of wild geese went by, harrowing the sky northward. The geese strike a deeper chord than the pigeons. Level and straight they go as fate to its mark. I cannot tell what emotions these migrating birds awaken in me,—the geese especially. One seldom sees more than a flock or two in a season, and what a spring token it is! The great bodies are in motion. It is like the passage of a victorious army. No longer inch by inch does spring come, but these geese advance the standard across zones at one pull. How my desire goes with them; how something in me, wild and migratory, plumes itself and follows fast!

> Steering north, with raucous cry,
> Through tracts and provinces of sky,

Every night alighting down
In new landscapes of romance,
Where darkling feed the clamorous clans
By lonely lakes to men unknown.

Dwelling upon these sights, I am reminded that the seeing of spring come, not only upon the great wings of the geese and the lesser wings of the pigeons and birds, but in the many more subtle and indirect signs and mediums, is also a part of the compensation of living in the country. I enjoy not less what may be called the negative side of spring,—those dark, dank, dissolving days, yellow sposh and mud and water everywhere,—yet who can stay long indoors? The humidity is soft and satisfying to the smell, and to the face and hands, and, for the first time in months, there is the fresh odor of the earth. The air is full of the notes and calls of the first birds. The domestic fowls refuse their accustomed food and wander far from the barn. Is it something winter has left, or spring has dropped, that they pick up? And what is it that holds me so long standing in the yard or in the fields? Something besides the ice and snow melts and runs away with the spring floods.

The little sparrows and purple finches are so punctual in announcing spring, that some seasons one wonders how they know without looking in the almanac, for surely there are no signs of spring out of doors. Yet they will strike up as cheerily amid the driving snow as if they had just been told that to-morrow is the first day of March. About the same time I notice the potatoes in the cellar show signs of sprouting. They, too, find out so quickly when spring is near. Spring comes by two routes,—in the air and underground, and often gets here by the latter course first. She undermines Winter when outwardly his front is nearly as bold as ever. I have known the trees to bud long before, by outward appearances, one would expect them to. The frost was gone from the ground before the snow was gone from the surface.

But Winter hath his birds also; some of them such tiny bodies that one wonders how they withstand the giant cold,—but they do. Birds live on highly concentrated food,—the fine seeds of weeds and grasses, and the eggs and larvae of insects. Such food must be very stimulating and heating. A gizzard full of ants, for instance, what spiced and seasoned extract is equal to that? Think what virtue there must be in an ounce of gnats or mosquitoes, or in the fine mysterious food the chickadee and brown creeper gather in the winter woods! It is doubtful if these birds ever freeze when fuel enough can be had to keep their little furnaces going. And, as they get their food entirely from the limbs and trunks of trees, like the woodpeckers, their supply is seldom interfered with by the snow. The worst annoyance must be the enameling of ice our winter woods sometimes get.

Indeed, the food question seems to be the only serious one with the birds. Give them plenty to eat, and no doubt the majority of them would face our winters. I believe all the woodpeckers are winter birds, except the high-hole or yellow-hammer, and he obtains the greater part of his subsistence from the ground, and is not a *woodpecker* at all in his habits of feeding. Were it not that it has recourse to budding, the ruffed grouse would be obliged to migrate. The quail—a bird, no doubt, equally hardy, but whose food is at the mercy of the snow—is frequently cut off by our severe winters when it ventures to brave them, which is not often. Where plenty of the berries of the red cedar can be had, the cedar-bird will pass the winter in New York. The old ornithologists say the bluebird migrates to Bermuda; but in the winter of 1874–75, severe as it was, a pair of them wintered with me eighty miles north of New York City. They seem to have been decided in their choice by the attractions of my rustic porch and the fruit of a sugar-berry tree (celtis—a kind of tree-lotus) that stood in front of it. They lodged in the porch and took their meals in the tree. Indeed, they became regular lotus-eaters. Punctually at dusk they were in their places on a large laurel root in the top of the porch, whence, however, they were frequently routed by a indignant broom that was jealous of the neatness of the porch floor. But the pair would not take any hints of this kind, and did not give up their quarters in the porch or their lotus berries till spring.

Many times during the winter the sugar-berry tree was visited by a flock of cedar-birds that also wintered in the vicinity. At such times it was amusing to witness the pretty wrath of the bluebirds, scolding and threatening the intruders, and begrudging them every berry they ate. The bluebird cannot utter a hard or unpleasing note. Indeed, he seems to have but one language, one speech, for both love and war, and the expression of his indignation is nearly as musical as his song. The male frequently made hostile demonstrations toward the cedar-birds, but did not openly attack them, and, with his mate, appeared to experience great relief when the poachers had gone.

I had other company in my solitude also, among the rest a distinguished arrival from the far north, the pine grosbeak, a bird rarely seen in these parts, except now and then a single specimen. But in the winter of 1875, heralding the extreme cold weather, and no doubt in consequence of it, there was a large incursion of them into this State and New England. They attracted the notice of the country people everywhere. I first saw them early in December about the head of the Delaware. I was walking along a cleared ridge with my gun, just at sundown, when I beheld two strange birds sitting in a small maple. On bringing one of them down, I found it was a bird I had never before seen; in color and shape like the purple finch, but quite as large again in size. From its heavy beak, I at once recognized it as belonging to the family of grosbeaks. A few days later I saw large numbers of them in the woods, on the ground, and in the trees. And still later, and on till February, they were very numerous on the Hudson, coming all about my house,—more familiar even than the little snowbird, hopping beneath the windows, and looking up at me apparently with as much curiosity as I looked down upon them. They fed on the buds of the sugar maples and upon frozen apples in the orchard. They were mostly young birds and females, colored very much like the common sparrow, with now and then visible the dull carmine-colored head and neck of an old male.

Other northern visitors that tarried with me the same winter were the tree or Canada sparrow and the redpoll, the former a bird larger than the social sparrow or hair-bird, but otherwise much resembling it, and distinguishable by a dark spot in the middle of its breast; the latter a bird the size and shape of the common goldfinch, with the same manner of flight and nearly the same note or cry, but darker than the winter plumage of the goldfinch, and with a red crown and a tinge of red on the breast. Little bands of these two species lurked about the barnyard all winter, picking up the hayseed, the sparrow sometimes venturing in on the haymow when the supply outside was short. I felt grateful to them for their company. They gave a sort of ornithological air to every errand I had to the barn.

Though a number of birds face our winters, and by various shifts worry through till spring, some of them permanent residents, and some of them visitors from the far north, yet there is but one genuine snow bird, nursling of the snow, and that is the snow bunting, a bird that seems proper to this season, heralding the coming storm, sweeping by on bold and rapid wing, and calling and chirping as cheerily as the songsters of May. In its plumage it reflects the winter landscape,—an expanse of white surmounted or streaked with gray and brown; a field of snow with a line of woods or a tinge of stubble. It fits into the scene, and does not appear to lead a beggarly and disconsolate life, like most of our winter residents. During the ice-harvesting on the river, I see them flitting about among the gangs of men, or floating on the cakes of ice, picking and scratching amid the droppings of the horses. They love the stack and hay-barn in the distant field, where the farmer fodders his cattle upon the snow, and every red-root, ragweed, or pigweed left standing in the fall adds to their winter stores.

Though this bird, and one or two others, like the chickadee and nuthatch, are more or less complacent and cheerful during the winter, yet no bird can look our winters in the face and sing, as do so many of the English birds. Several species in Great Britain, their biographers tell us, sing the winter through, except during the severest frosts; but with us, as far south as Virginia, and, for aught I know, much farther, the birds are tuneless at this season. The owls, even, do not hoot, nor the hawks scream.

Among the birds that tarry briefly with us in the spring on their way to Canada and beyond, there is none I behold with so much pleasure as the white-crowned sparrow. I have an eye out for him all through April and the first week in May. He is the rarest and most beautiful of the sparrow kind. He is crowned, as some hero or victor in the games. He is usually in company with his congener, the white-throated sparrow, but seldom more than in the proportion of one to twenty of the latter. Contrasted with this bird, he looks like its more fortunate brother, upon whom some special distinction has been conferred, and who is, from the egg, of finer make and quality. His sparrow color of ashen gray and brown is very clear and bright, and his form graceful. His whole expression, however, culminates in a singular manner in his crown. The various tints of the bird are brought to a focus here and intensified, the lighter ones becoming white, and the deeper ones nearly black. There is the suggestion of a crest, also, from a habit the bird had of slightly elevating this part of its plumage, as if to make more conspicuous its pretty markings. They are great scratchers, and will often remain several minutes scratching in one place, like a hen. Yet, unlike the hen and like all hoppers, they scratch with both feet at once, which is by no means the best way to scratch.

The white-throats often sing during their sojourning in both fall and spring; but only on one occasion have I ever heard any part of the song of the white-crowned, and that proceeded from what I took to be a young male, one October morning, just as the sun was rising. It was pitched very low, like a half-forgotten air, but it was very sweet. It was the song of the vesper sparrow and the white-throat in one. In his breeding haunts he must be a superior songster, but he is very chary of his music while on his travels.

The sparrows are all meek and lowly birds. They are of the grass, the fences, the low bushes, the weedy wayside places. Nature has denied them all brilliant tints, but she had given them sweet and musical voices. Theirs are the quaint and simple lullaby songs of childhood. The white-throat has a timid, tremulous strain, that issues from the low bushes or from behind the fence, where its cradle is hid. The song sparrow modulates its simple ditty as softly as the lining of its own nest. The vesper sparrow has only peace and gentleness in its strain.

What pretty nests, too, the sparrows build! Can anything be more exquisite than a sparrow's nest under a grassy or mossy bank? What care the bird has taken not to disturb one straw or spear of grass, or thread of moss! You cannot approach it and put your hand into it without violating the place more or less, and yet the little architect has wrought day after day and left no marks. There has been an excavation, and yet no grain of earth appears to have been moved. If the nest had slowly and silently grown like the grass and the moss, it could not have been more nicely adjusted to its place and surroundings. There is absolutely nothing to tell the eye it is there. Generally a few spears of dry grass fall down from the turf above and form a slight screen before it. How commonly and coarsely it begins, blending with the debris that lies about, and how it refines and comes into form as it approaches the centre, which is modeled so perfectly and lined so softly! Then, when the full complement of eggs is laid, and incubation has fairly begun, what a sweet, pleasing little mystery the silent old bank holds!

The song sparrow, whose nest I have been describing, displays a more marked individuality in its song than any bird with which I am acquainted. Birds of the same species generally all sing alike, but I have observed numerous song sparrows with songs peculiarly their own. Last season, the whole summer through, one sang about my grounds like this: *swee-e-t, swee-e-t, swee-e-t, bitter*. Day after day, from May to September, I heard this strain, which I thought a simple but very profound summing-up of life, and wondered how the little bird had learned it so quickly. The present season, I heard another with a song equally original, but not so easily worded. Among a large troop of them in April, my attention was attracted to one that was a master songster,—some Shelley or Tennyson among his kind. The strain was remarkably prolonged, intricate, and animated, and far surpassed anything I ever before heard from that source.

But the most noticeable instance of departure from the standard song of a species I ever knew of was in the case of a wood thrush. The bird sang, as did the sparrow, the whole season through, at the foot of my lot near the river. The song began correctly and ended correctly; but interjected into it about midway was a loud, piercing, artificial note, at utter variance with the rest of the strain. When my ear first caught this singular note, I started out, not a little puzzled, to make, as I supposed, a new acquaintance, but had not gone far when I discovered whence it proceeded. Brass amid gold, or pebbles amid pearls, are not more out of place than was this discordant scream or cry in the melodious strain of the wood thrush. It pained and startled the ear. It seemed as if the instrument of the bird was not under control, or else that one note was sadly out of tune, and, when its turn came, instead of giving forth one of those sounds that are indeed like pearls, it shocked the ear with a piercing discord. Yet the singer appeared entirely unconscious of the defect; or had he grown used to it, or had his friends persuaded him that it was a variation to be coveted? Sometimes, after the brood had hatched and the bird's pride was at its full, he would make a little triumphal tour of the locality, coming from under the hill quite up to the house, and flaunting his cracked instrument in the face of whoever would listen. He did not return again the next season; or, if he did, the malformation of his song was gone.

I have noticed that the bobolink does not sing the same in different localities. In New Jersey it has one song; on the Hudson, a slight variation of the same; and on the high grass-lands of the interior of the State, quite a different strain,—clearer, more distinctly articulated, and running off with more sparkle and liltingness. It reminds one of the clearer mountain air and the translucent spring-water of those localities. I never could make out what the bobolink says in New Jersey, but in certain districts in this State his enunciation is quite distinct. Sometimes he begins with the word *gegue, gegue.* Then again, more fully, *be true to me, Clarsy, be true to me, Clarsy, Clarsy*, thence full tilt into his inimitable song, interspersed in which the words *kick your slipper, kick your slipper*, and *temperance, temperance* (the last with a peculiar nasal resonance), are plainly heard. At its best, it is a remarkable performance, a unique performance, as it contains not the slightest hint or suggestion, either in tone or manner or effect, of any other birdsong to be heard. The bobolink has no mate or parallel in any part of the world. He stands alone. There is no closely allied species. He is not a lark, nor a finch, nor a warbler, nor a thrush, nor a starling (though classed with the starlings by late naturalists). He is an exception to many well-known rules. He is the only ground-bird known to me of marked and conspicuous plumage. He is the only black and white field-bird we have east of the Mississippi, and, what is still more odd, he is black beneath and white above,—the reverse of the fact in all other cases. Preeminently a bird of the meadow during the breeding season, and associated with clover and daisies and buttercups as no other bird is, he yet has the look of an interloper or a newcomer, and not of one to the manner born.

The bobolink has an unusually full throat, which may help account for his great power of song. No bird has yet been found that could imitate him, or even repeat or suggest a single note, as if his song were the product of a new set of organs. There is a vibration about it, and a rapid running over the keys, that the mockingbird is dumb in the presence of the bobolink. My neighbor has an English skylark that was hatched and reared in captivity. The bird is a most persistent and vociferous songster, and fully as successful a mimic as the mockingbird. It pours out a strain that is a regular mosaic of nearly all the bird-notes to be heard, its own proper lark song forming a kind of bordering for the whole. The notes of the phoebe-bird, the purple finch, the swallow, the yellowbird, the kingbird, the robin, and others, are rendered with perfect distinctness and accuracy, but not a word of the bobolink's, though the lark must have heard its song every day for four successive summers. It was the one conspicuous note in the fields around that the lark made no attempt to plagiarize. He could not steal the bobolink's thunder.

The lark is only a more marvelous songster than the bobolink on account of his soaring flight and the sustained copiousness of his song. His note is rasping and harsh, in point of melody, when compared with the bobolink's. When caged and near at hand, the lark's song is positively disagreeable; it is so loud and full of sharp, aspirated sounds. But high in air above the broad downs, poured out without interruption for many minutes together, it is very agreeable.

The bird among us that is usually called a lark, namely, the meadowlark, but which our later classifiers say is no lark at all, has nearly the same quality of voice as the English skylark,—loud, piercing, z-z-ing; and during the mating season it frequently indulges while on the wing in a brief song that is quite lark-like. It is also a bird of the stubble, and one of the last to retreat on the approach of winter.

The habits of many of our birds are slowly undergoing a change. Their migrations are less marked. With the settlement and cultivation of the country, the means of subsistence of nearly every species are vastly increased. Insects are more numerous, and seeds of weeds and grasses more abundant. They become more and more domestic, like the English birds. The swallows have nearly all left their original abodes—hollow trees, and cliffs, and rocks—for human habitations and their environments. Where did the barn swallow nest before the country was settled? The chimney swallow nested in hollow trees, and, perhaps, occasionally resorts thither yet. But the chimney, notwithstanding the smoke, seems to suit his taste best. In the spring, before they have paired, I think these swallows sometimes pass the night in the woods, but not if an old, disused chimney is handy.

One evening in early May, my attention was arrested by a band of them containing several hundreds, perhaps a thousand, circling about near a large, tall, disused chimney in a secluded place in the country. They were very lively, and chippering, and diving in a most extraordinary manner. They formed a broad continuous circle many rods in diameter. Gradually the circle contracted and neared the chimney. Presently some of the birds as they came round began to dive toward it, and the chippering was more animated than ever. Then a few ventured in; in a moment more, the air at the mouth of the chimney was black with the stream of descending swallows. When the passage began to get crowded, the circle lifted and the rest of the birds continued their flight, giving those inside time to dispose of themselves. Then the influx began again, and was kept up till the crowd became too great, when it cleared as before. Thus by install-ments, or in layers, the swallows were packed into the chimney until the last one was stowed away. Passing by the place a few days afterward, I saw a board reaching from the roof of the building to the top of the chimney, and imagined some curious person or some predaceous boy had been up to take a peep inside, and see how so many swallows could dispose of themselves in such a space. It would have been an interesting spectacle to see them emerge from the chimney in the morning.

John Burroughs, *Birds and Poets, With Other Papers* (Boston and New York: Houghton and Mifflin Company, 1877).

APPLES

Hector St. John de Crèvecoeur

T*HE FRENCHMAN Hector St. John de Crèvecoeur (1735–1813) served as mapmaker and engineer under General Montcalm in the French and Indian War. He later married an American woman from Yonkers in 1769 and settled on a farm in Orange county, called Pine Hill. Based on his experiences in eighteenth-century rural America, his* Letters from an American Farmer *was to become a classic of colonial literature, and one of the earliest French books on the country. Crèvecoeur was drawn to life in the New World as an expression of the liberal agrarian philosophy that was to characterize the democratic experiment. He exemplified the Enlightenment attraction to social systems that would invent the "new man." His writing is full of praise for the ways of his adopted country, and the independent life of a farmer possible there, far from the political and hereditary constraints of the European continent. He was also a naturalist who wrote lovingly of humming-birds, bees, and animals in the wild.*

But Crèvecoeur's idyllic years didn't last, and he had to flee his home under pressure from the Patriots for his equivocal allegiance during the war. He sailed to France, where he was courted in literary circles that included Diderot, Buffon, d'Alembert, and La Rochefoucauld. Later he returned to New York as French consul, and helped to set up early trade agreements between France and America, at Thomas Jefferson's insistence. Two other famous Frenchmen also spent some time in America before the eighteenth century was over, and both later took up American themes in their work, Tocqueville's cousin in Chateaubriand, and the statesman Talleyrand.

281

Crèvecoeur's Letters *was celebrated in France and in England, followed by treatises on potato culture, the common locust tree, and another book on his American travels. The selection that follows, written before the end of the American Revolution, was gathered with the author's papers and lay unpublished for 150 years, before appearing in* Sketches of Eighteenth-Century America. *Crèvecoeur depicts a tranquil view of family life around the pleasures of the apple. Elsewhere in his* Sketches *he provides a catalogue of "enemies of the farmer"—worms infesting cabbage, blackbirds spoiling corn, summer frosts, drought, grasshoppers in the hemp, mice in the turnips. "I should have never done, were I to recount to you all the inconveniences and accidents which the grain of our fields, the trees of our orchards, as well as those of the wood are exposed to," he admits.*

Crèvecoeur's writings offer an encyclopedia of information about the natural history, society, economy, and climate of his day. No wonder the reflective, self-reliant Frenchman has been called an eighteenth-century Thoreau; but he was just as much a Rousseauist. A fascinating man who led a life on two continents, amidst the upheavals of the American Revolution and the French Revolution, Crèvecoeur experienced the personal turmoil of the eighteenth-century sensibility coming into the modern era. He was both frontiersman and philosophe, *equally at home glorifying wild nature or conversing with high-heeled Encyclopedists in Parisian salons. D. H. Lawrence called him, with a certain degree of truth, "an intellectual savage."*

EACH SEASON BRINGS along with it its pains, pleasures, toils, and unavoidable losses. Often Nature herself opposes us. What then can we do? She is irresistible; I mean the uncertainty of the snows in the winter and the dryness of our summers. It is astonishing how variable the former grows, much more so indeed than formerly, and I make no doubt but that in a few hundred years they will be very different from what they are at present. That mildness, when interrupted by transitory frosts and thaws, will become very detrimental to our husbandry. For though the quantity of snow may diminish, yet it cannot be entirely so with the frost. Our proximity to the horrid mountainous waste which overspreads our north will always expose us to the severe blasts which often nip all our hopes, and destroy the fairest and most promising expectations of the farmer, like a merchant losing his vessel in sight of the harbour. Last spring all my apples dropped in consequence of such an accident, although they were grown to the size of nutmegs. Nor could it be prevented though it was foreseen.

Had my father been as wise as Mr. —— this would not have been the case. This gentleman was very knowing and attentive for a first settler. He planted his orchard on the north side of a hill. This exposure commonly causes the difference of a fortnight in the opening of the blossoms, and this artificial delay always saves his apples. I could wish that [my orchard] had been thus situated, though it is so great an ornament to a farm that most people plant it either on one side of their house or on the other. How naked my settlement would look [were mine] removed! I am surprised, however, that this simple idea has not been more generally extended. The hint, I am sure, was not new, for most people plant their peach orchards in the most northern situation they have, in order to avoid the same inconveniences. You must remember my situation. My loss in apples last year was the greater because of its being the bearing year; for you must know that all our trees (both in the forest and elsewhere) bear but every other year. In a little time I am in hopes to remedy this inconvenience, having planted in the fall a new apple orchard of five acres consisting of three hundred and fifty-eight trees. That of my father was planted in the spring, and by their not bearing at the same time I shall have a yearly supply of apples.

Perhaps you may want to know what it is we want to do with so many apples. It is not for cider. God knows! Situated as we are it would not quit cost to transport it even twenty miles. Many a barrel have I sold at the press for a half dollar. As soon as our hogs have done with the peaches, we turn them into our orchards. The [apples], as well as the preceding fruit, greatly improve them. It is astonishing to see their dexterity in rubbing themselves against the younger trees in order to shake them. They will often stand erect and take hold of the limbs of the trees, in order to procure their food in greater abundance.

In the fall of the year we dry great quantities, and this is one of those rural occupations which most amply reward us. Our method is this: we gather the best kind. The neighbouring women are invited to spend the evening at our house. A basket of apples is given to each of them, which they peel, quarter, and core. These peelings and cores are put into another basket and when the intended quantity is thus done, tea, a good supper, and the best things we have are served up. Convivial merriment, cheerfulness, and song never fail to enliven these evenings, and though our bowls contain neither the delicate punch of the West Indies, nor the rich wines of Europe, nevertheless our cider affords us that simpler degree of exhilaration with which we are satisfied. The quantity I have thus peeled is commonly twenty bushels, which gives me about three of dried ones.

Next day a great stage is erected either in our grass plots or anywhere else where cattle can't come. Strong crotches are planted in the ground. Poles are horizontally fixed on these, and boards laid close together. For there are no provident farmers who have not always great stores of these. When the scaffold is thus erected, the apples are thinly spread over it. They are soon covered with all the bees and wasps and sucking flies of the neighbourhood. This accelerates the operation of drying. Now and then they are turned. At night they are covered with blankets. If it is likely to rain, they are gathered and brought into the house. This is repeated until they are perfectly dried. It is astonishing to what small size they will shrink. Those who have but a small quantity thread them and hang them in the front of their houses. In the same manner we dry peaches and plums without peeling them, and I know not a delicacy equal to them in the various preparations we make of them. By this means we are enabled to have apple-pies and apple-dumplings almost all the year round.

The method of using them is this: we put a small handful in warm water over night; next morning they are swelled to their former size; and when cooked either in pies or dumplings it is difficult to discover by the taste whether they are fresh or not. I think that our farms produce nothing more palatable. My wife's and my supper half of the year consists of apple pie and milk. The dried peaches and plums, as being more delicate, are kept for holidays, frolics, and such other civil festivals as are common among us. With equal care we dry the skins and cores. They are of excellent use in brewing that species of beer with which every family is constantly supplied, not only for the sake of drinking it, but for that of the bawm without which our wives could not raise their bread.

The philosopher's stone of an American farmer is to do everything within his own family; to trouble his neighbours by borrowing as little as possible; and to abstain from buying European commodities. He that follows that golden rule and has a good wife is almost sure of succeeding.

Besides apples we dry pumpkins which are excellent in winter. They are cut into thin slices, peeled, and threaded. Their skins serve also for beer, and admirable pumpkin-pies are made with them. When thus dried they will keep the whole year. Many people have carried the former manufacture of drying apples to a great degree of perfection in the province of New Jersey. They make use of long ovens built on purpose, and when [the apples are] dried, export them to the West Indies. I have heard many planters say that they received nothing from the continent that was more delicate or better adapted to their climates. For it was transplanting the fruits of our orchards in that state in which they could endure the heat without injury.

In the most plentiful years we have a method of reducing the quantity of our cider and of making it a liquor far superior. I think it greatly preferable to many sorts of wines which I have drunk at ——. We boil the quantities of two barrels into one, in a fair copper kettle, just as it comes from the press, and, therefore, perfectly sweet. Sometimes I have reduced one barrel and a half into one. This is preserved till the summer, and then affords a liquor which, when mixed with a due proportion of water, affords us an excellent beverage. Strangers have often been deceived and have taken it for some kind of Spanish wine. Other people prefer hauling their hogsheads out of their cellars, when it freezes hard. In one night or two the frost will congeal the watery parts. They then draw from whatever remains behind, but this is neither so sweet, nor so palatable as the other; it is too potent.

We often make apple-butter, and this is in the winter a most excellent food particularly where there are many children. For that purpose the best, the richest of our apples are peeled and boiled; a considerable quantity of sweet cider is mixed with it; and the whole is greatly reduced by evaporation. A due proportion of quinces and orange peels is added. This is afterwards preserved in earthern jars, and in our long winters is a very great delicacy and highly esteemed by some people. It saves sugar, and answers in the hands of an economical wife more purposes than I can well describe. Thus our industry has taught us to convert what Nature has given us into such food as is fit for people in our station. Many farmers make excellent cherry and currant wines, but many families object to them on account of the enormous quantity of sugar they require. In some parts of this country they begin to distil peaches and cider, from which two species of brandy are extracted, fiery and rough at first, but with age very pleasant. The former is the common drink of the people in the southern provinces.

However careful and prudent we are, the use of tea necessarily implies a great consumption of sugar. A northern farmer should never pronounce these two words without trembling, for these two articles must be replaced by something equivalent in order to pay for them, and not many of us have anything to spare.

Hector St. John de Crèvecoeur, *Sketches of Eighteenth-Century America* (New Haven: Yale University Press, 1925).

FLY-FISHING NEAR NEW YORK

Theodore Gordon

A*BOUT ONE HUNDRED years ago, Theodore Gordon (1854–1915), the legendary Catskill fisherman, was about to invent the first dry fly patterns by an American. Gordon was an enthusiastic sportsman whose favorite fishing places were the Esopus, Big Indian, Neversink, Beaverkill, and Willowemoc. He was an early champion of the German brown trout, which began to be stocked in the Catskills in the 1880s, after the brook trout population had largely been eliminated by voracious fishermen. Fortunately for the generations of fishermen who came after him, he was a generous chronicler of his days and nights on the Catskill rivers, publishing numerous pieces in* Fishing Gazette *and* Forest and Stream *(later titled* Field & Stream*). He called himself "a journalist of the stream," and his own stream of consciousness wound gracefully toward the lyrical.*

Gordon's writing is unmistakable for its modest, boyish charm, and passion for fly-fishing, brimming with information on weather conditions, insects, types of flies, and favorite fishing spots. Because he wrote so long ago, cultural and environmental changes of the area can be measured by the distance from contemporary conditions. One of the most significant topographical transformations was the construction of the Ashokan Reservoir, which he notes in a 1905 article with a certain sadness: "This is probably the last season for fly-fishing in the lower Esopus . . . millions of inhabitants in New York City must be supplied with pure water." By that time, too, fishing clubs had proliferated in the once quiet backwoods, unsettling the peace of the streams Gordon called home.

Besides his impressionistic writings, this gentleman angler left his signature piece in the Quill Gordon fly. According to fisherman and writer Robert H. Boyle, it is now the name used for a few two-tailed species that usually emerge in the first week of May, thought to be Iron fraudator *or* Epeorus pleuralis. *For the non-specialist, there are Gordon's own words, such as "Letters from a Recluse," in which he wrote, alone on a cold spring night, "if we cannot talk we can write, and it is just possible that some dear brother angler will read what we say upon paper." No wonder he called fly-fishing the most "literary" of sports.*

FIFTY YEARS AGO sport of any description had small place in the thoughts and lives of the American people; in fact, the word was seldom used except to express something "fast," and not to be encouraged. Now we are becoming a nation of sportsmen and sportswomen, and are all alive to outdoor amusements and recreations. The benefit resulting from this change in public sentiment is perhaps more marked in the women than in the men, as very possibly it was more needed. No one of mature years can fail to have marked the increased stature and healthfulness of our women. The ideal heroine nowadays is far removed from the wasp-waisted, die-away creature of the early portion of the last century. The girl of the twentieth century is a fine upstanding woman, with a flat back, large frame, and the limbs of a Juno. This article, however, has to do not with angels but with sport. The taste for this once acquired becomes inherent in the blood, and must be gratified or serious loss to health and happiness will result. We have much to be thankful for in this country, but it behooves us to look to the future, as well as to enjoy the present. We must be provident or the outlook for the "coming race" will be poor indeed.

Since the time of Walton, great numbers of the best and wisest men have evinced a love of fly-fishing amounting to a passion, and the increase in the votaries of the sport in recent years has been in the nature of a geometrical progression. There are one hundred fly-fishers now where one was found fifty years ago. When the breath of spring is in the air a kind of *heimweh* or homesickness seizes them; they must be off, if only for a few hours, to the fresh, clean, chill country, where as yet not a leaf is to be seen upon the trees. The real season for sport comes a little later, but this first rush into troutland is a fine thing after a long cold winter like the one we have just experienced. It starts the blood in all one's veins, shakes up the liver, and is an antidote against spring fever. Only a minority of the great army of anglers can hie away to the lakes of Maine or the salmon rivers of the Dominion; the preserves of Long Island and the mountain streams of New York must receive the great majority. The demand upon these waters has thus become very great, and they would long ere this have proved inadequate if the genius of modern fishculture had not stopped in to fill the breach.

We have good spring trout fishing within a short distance of New York City, but the facilities for sport, and the size and number of fish can be largely increased if all the natural advantages of the country are fully developed. We may even have a season for fly-fishing in the autumn, such as we hear of as being enjoyed elsewhere. There are many good streams in the East. They are easily reached by two lines of rail, and the region through which they flow is visited annually by thousands of health and pleasure seekers. We refer to five well known historic streams, having almost a common source, but flowing on widely diverging courses, three being tributary to the Delaware and two to the Hudson River. These are the Esopus and Big Indian, the Neversink, Willowemock, and Beaverkill. The first two are practically one, the Esopus being formed by the junction of the Big Indian with a small brook called Birch Creek, a short distance from Big Indian station. The big Indian has its source away up in the mountain of the same name, the highest peak in the Catskills, and within a few yards is a small trickle of ice cold water which is the beginning of the West Branch of the Neversink. The East Branch rises a little east and south, and the Willowemock north and west, as we remember the points of the compass, and the sources of the Beaverkill are not far away. All these are ideal trout streams, and will well repay the lover of nature as well as the angler. All are clear, cold, and pure, the water of the Neversink being as limpid as air, the smallest object can be seen distinctly at a depth of many feet.

Ten or twelve years ago the native brook trout—*Salvelinus fontinalis*—was master of all the brooks in this fastidious fancy, but now—chiefly owing to the wisdom and liberality of the State of New York—we have several varieties, all beautiful and sport-giving fish. Even at an earlier date (i.e. more than ten years since), the rainbow trout of the West *(Salmo irideus)* had found a congenial home in the Esopus and thriven amazingly, thus affording good fly-fishing where formerly there was little or none. I am referring now to the lower part of the river. It is claimed by some fishculturists that the rainbow trout can live and grow in water of too high a temperature for many other members of the salmon family. The brown trout *(Salmo fario)* has usurped first place in the Big Indian. This is the common European, the trout of the British Isles. It is hardy and prolific, and within the last three years has greatly increased in the lower Esopus. The rainbow is still most abundant in this portion of the river, at least until the second falls is reached. Below these the black bass has, I am informed, taken possession. The Beaverkill holds brook, brown, and rainbow trout, but only a few fry of the last named have been released in it. The same may be said of the Neversink, and the stock of the Willowemock consists, or consisted very recently, almost entirely of native brook trout above Livingston Manor. Clubs and individuals have released many fry and yearlings in these waters, and the Ontario and Western Railroad has carried millions of fry, besides giving transportation to parties engaged in carrying young trout from the State hatcheries.

Modern fishculture can satisfy all demands made upon it by fair fishing, and the development of the brown trout, principally from fry, has been very remarkable. A few years ago a pound trout was considered to be quite a large fish, and in an experience of many years the largest native trout we took from any of these streams was 16 inches in length and less than two pounds in weight. Since the introduction of the brown trout, two to three pounds is not uncommon, and many much larger fish have been taken. All pure tributaries of the Delaware and Hudson should swarm with trout. Brooks that have been barren for years may be made productive. The lower portions of the Beaverkill and Neversink are noble and beautiful rivers, and should afford more sport than they do now. We believe that the rainbow trout would do well there, and possibly the European grayling. Our own Michigan grayling seems to be a delicate fish, and is reported to be almost extinct. The foreign fish of this species must be hardier, as it flourishes in England and on the Continent in streams inhabited by large trout and even pike. It is said to seek the lower portions of trout streams and the same is reported of the rainbow trout. The latter has certainly done this in the Esopus, as it is found where there is plenty of water for a 30-pound salmon, and where the temperature rises high in summer. Both these fish are spring spawners (although the rainbow seems to be somewhat irregular as to time), and if they flourished together delightful sport could be enjoyed in the autumn, when weather conditions would be most favorable.

July and August were formerly good months for fly-fishing in the streams mentioned, as they flow at considerable altitudes, but until the season of 1903 our mountain summers, though very pleasant, have been warmer than of yore. Climatic changes are going on all over the country, the rainfall is less evenly distributed, and the streams get lower and warmer. The last season was all that we could desire in the matter of rainfall after the first of June, but we have had a number of very serious droughts in recent years. In fact, we have been experiencing some of the inconveniences felt in the United Kingdom from modern drainage, forest destruction, and the like. Thirty or forty years ago much of this region was a sea of hemlock, more snow fell and it remained longer, having more protection from the sun. Now deciduous trees have replaced the evergreen forest, and the appearance of the country is greatly changed. It must have looked a wild and savage region one hundred years ago.

The fishing has had many ups and downs. In the days of the first settlers the trout were only too abundant, but we believe that sport is better now than it was thirty years since. Tanneries were located on nearly all trout waters, and log driving and lumbering were constantly going on. There were but few trout below the tanneries, and though they fairly swarmed in the small brooks they were trifling in size and

could have afforded but little sport. We have had sufficient experience of this kind of fishing, and have a poor opinion of it.

We wish that all Eastern anglers could have good fishing for the
rainbow trout, as there appears to be a slight prejudice against this
fish. We know of no better game fish. It leaps again and again when
hooked, and rushes madly down stream. Lying usually in heavy, swift
water, it takes every advantage of the situation, and requires all the
angler's skill to land. Mr. Fred Mather had a high opinion of the rainbow for sport, and also as a table fish, and Herr Jaffé, the well-known
German fishculturist, has expressed himself strongly in its favor. We
think it resembles the Atlantic salmon more closely than any other
trout. The head is small, body round and plump and very silvery
when in good condition, as it almost always is. We never saw any
traces of spawning in the month of May except in fish of 15 inches
and over. A few of the large fish were thin and the vent a trifle
pronounced, but the great majority were in good shape. We have
taken them in August as hard and solid as blocks of marble. With this
fish and the European grayling in the lower portions of our trout
streams and native and brown trout in the upper and middle
reaches, sport would be vastly increased.

On first consideration some objections will appear to a fly-fishing
season in the autumn months, but these will be found to be more
sentimental than real. The brown and brook trout will be working up
into the small brooks and on to the spawning beds, and the few
taken would be promptly returned. They could not be exposed, and
but few persons would care to retain them for food, as being out of
condition, they would soon after death become slimy and unpleasant
objects. The rainbows and the grayling would be in the highest
possible condition and afford the very best of sport. We should
consider all proposals or suggestions bearing upon an increased
supply of game fish, and there are miles of the Beaverkill and
Neversink that might be greatly improved. The European grayling
and the trout do well together, or in the same river, and there is no
good reason why our season for fly-fishing should be so short. With
scientific fishculture and good management there is no need to fear
that our streams will be depleted by any amount of fair fishing. Dry
summers, ice jams, and great floods in winter and fall are the

dangerous features in the situation. All good members of the brotherhood of anglers who love to be quiet and go a-fishing do all that they can to increase the stock of game fish in our streams and lakes—particularly those species which will rise to the artificial fly. There are many other streams besides those mentioned which are easily accessible from New York City, and we know of no pleasanter way of spending the summer vacation than rambling from one to another, casting one's flies as the spirit moveth. It is easy to travel cheaply all over the region referred to. You can go in by way of the Ulster and Delaware and return by the Ontario and Western Railroad. If not in a great hurry, one can travel by the mail hacks which run from Big Indian to Claryville, and thence to Liberty. In fact, these mail hacks will be found making their daily pilgrimages in every valley, and up and down nearly all these rivers. Claryville is on the Neversink, at the junction of the East and West Branches; over the next divide is the Willowemock, and in the valley beyond flows the beautiful Beaverkill, which many people consider one of the most perfect trout rivers in this country. A large portion of the water is posted, but by staying at various farmhouses and summer resorts, enough fishing can be had to satisfy a reasonable person. In the early season good sport is had in the lower reaches in free water. In July and August the angler must seek cooler water far up the stream. Good luck.

Theodore Gordon, *Forest and Stream* 62, vol. 12 (March 19, 1904).

JUNE 1749

Peter Kalm

S ENT BY THE Swedish Academy of Sciences to search
for plants that could be economically valuable and adaptable
at home, Peter Kalm (1716–79) arrived in America in 1748. For
three years he traveled here, chiefly in New York, Pennsylvania,
New Jersey, and southern Canada, eventually bringing back countless specimens of plants and seeds. A pupil of the great eighteenth-
century scientist Carolus Linnaeus who developed the binomial
system of classification, Kalm was part of an international circle of men who traded knowledge and specimens, in an effort to
name and classify the flora and fauna of the New World. He
was one of the earliest plant hunters in the young country, which
was to attract many more, from England, France, and Germany
especially, in the next one hundred years.

In his enduring Travels in North America, Kalm gives a straight-
forward, highly informative commentary on apparently everything he could document: trees, minerals, weather, and fences, not
to mention the colonists' early loss of teeth, marriage customs,
disease, and Indian life. He also wrote a great deal about the community of New Sweden, on the Delaware River. In Pennsylvania
Kalm visited the most famous American botanist of his day, John
Bartram, and discussed many of the curiosities of the continent
with another of its exceptional residents, Benjamin Franklin. In the
Hudson Valley he met with the immensely learned Cadwallader
Colden, who gave him information on subjects as varied as cock-
roaches, skunk cabbage, cedar swamps, and Arbor vitae. Kalm's

description of his voyage to Albany on the way to Canada indicates that even in 1749 inhabitants there were driven to extremes by the proliferation of insects in June. And now, 250 years later, people still smear grease on their faces, as they did in colonial Albany, to keep the pests away. On a happier note, the mountain laurel which brings a glorious bloom to Hudson Valley woods in springtime was named by Linnaeus for his diligent pupil, Kalmia latifolia.

June the 13th

THE WIND FAVORED our voyage during the whole night, so that I had no opportunity of observing the nature of the country. This morning at five o'clock we were but nine English miles from Albany. The country on both sides of the river was low and covered with woods, only here and there were a few little scattered settlements. On the banks of the river were met meadows, covered with sword grass *(Carex)*, and they formed several little islands. We saw no mountains and hastened towards Albany. The land on both sides of the river was chiefly low, and more carefully cultivated as we came nearer to Albany. Here we could see everywhere the type of haystacks with movable roofs. As to the houses which we saw, some were of wood, others of stone. The river was seldom above a musketshot broad, and in several parts of it were sandbars which required great skill in navigating the boats. At eight o'clock in the morning we arrived at Albany.

Arriving at Albany. All the boats which ply between Albany and New York belong to Albany. They go up and down the Hudson River as long as it is open and free from ice. They bring from Albany boards or planks, and all sorts of timber, flour, peas, and furs, which they get from the Indians, or which are smuggled from the French. They come home almost empty, and only bring a few kinds of merchandise with them, the chief of which is rum. This is absolutely necessary to the inhabitants of Albany. They cheat the Indians in the fur trade with it; for when the Indians are drunk they are practically blind and will leave it to the Albany whites to fix the price of the furs. The boats are quite large, and have a good cabin, in which the passengers can be very commodiously lodged. They are usually built of red cedar or of white oak. Frequently the bottom consists of white oak, and the sides of red cedar, because the latter withstands decay much longer than the former. The red cedar is likewise apt to split when it hits against anything, and the Hudson is in many places full of sand and rocks, against which the keel of the boat sometimes strikes. Therefore people choose white oak for the bottom, as being the softer wood, and not splitting so easily. The bottom, being continually under water, is not so much exposed to weathering and holds out longer.

Canoes. The canoes which the boats always have along with them are made of a single piece of wood, hollowed out: they are sharp on both ends, frequently three or four fathoms long, and as broad as the thickness of the wood will allow. The people in it do not row sitting, but usually a fellow stands at each end, with a short oar in his hand, with which he controls and propels the canoe. Those which are made here at Albany are commonly of white pine. They can do service for eight or twelve years, especially if they be tarred and painted. At Albany they are made of pine since there is not other wood fit for them; at New York they are made of the tulip tree, and, in other parts of the country of red or white cedars: but both these trees are so small in the neighborhood of Albany that they are unfit for canoes. There are no seats in them, for if they had any, they would be more liable to be upset, as one could not keep one's equilibrium so well. One has to sit in the bottom of these canoes.

Battoes are another kind of boats which are much in use in Albany: they are made of boards of white pine; the bottom is flat, that they may row the better in shallow water. They are sharp at both ends, and somewhat higher towards the end than in the middle. They have seats in them, and are rowed as common boats. They are long, yet not all alike. Usually they are three and sometimes four fathoms long. The height from the bottom to the top of the board (for the sides stand almost perpendicular) is from twenty inches to two feet, and the breadth in the middle about a yard and six inches.

They are chiefly made use of for carrying goods along the river to the Indians, that is, when those rivers are open enough for the battoes to pass through, and when they need not be carried by land a great way. The boats made of the bark of trees break easily by knocking against a stone, and the canoes cannot carry a great cargo, and are easily upset; the battoes are therefore preferable to them both. I saw no boats here like those in Sweden or other parts of Europe.

Temperature at Albany. Frequently the cold does a great deal of damage at Albany. There is hardly a month in summer during which a frost does not occur. Spring comes very late, and in April and May are numerous cold nights which frequently kill the flowers of trees and kitchen herbs. It was feared last May that the blossoms of the apple trees had been so severely damaged by the frost that next autumn there would be but very few apples. Even the oak blossoms in the woods are very often killed by the cold. The autumn here is of long continuance, with warm days and nights. However, the cold nights commonly commence towards the end of September, and are frequent in October. The people are forced to keep their cattle in stables from the middle of November till March or April, and must find them hay during that time.

During summer, the wind blows mostly from the south and brings a great drought along with it. Sometimes it rains a little, and as soon as it has rained the wind veers to northwest, blowing for several days from that point and then returning to the south. I have had frequent opportunities of seeing this condition of wind happen precisely, both this year and the following.

June the 15th

The fences were made of pine boards, of which there is an abundance in the extensive woods; and there are many saw mills to cut it into boards.

Fruit Trees. The several sorts of apple trees were said to grow very well here, and bear as fine fruit as in any other part of North America. Each farm has a large orchard. They have some apples here which are very large, and very palatable; they are sent to New York and other places as a rarity. People make excellent cider in the autumn in the country round Albany. From the seed which I gathered of these large apples and planted in Abo, Finland, a number of trees have come up which seem to thrive well and have not been injured in the least by our winters; but since they have not yet blossomed I cannot say whether the fruit which they bear will resemble that grown in Albany. Pear trees do not succeed here. This was complained of in many other parts of North America. But I fear that they do not take sufficient care in the management and planting of them, for I have seen fine pears in several parts of Pennsylvania. Peach trees have often been planted here, and never succeed well. This was attributed to a worm which lives in the ground and eats through the root, so that the tree dies. Perhaps the severity of the winter contributes much to it. They plant no other fruit trees at Albany besides these I have mentioned.

Grains. They sow as much hemp and flax here as they want for home consumption. They sow corn in great abundance; a loose soil is reckoned the best for this purpose, for it will not thrive in clay. From half a bushel they reap a hundred bushels. They reckon corn a very suitable kind of crop, because the young plant recovers after being hurt by the frost. They have had instances here of the plants freezing off twice in the spring, close to the ground, and yet surviving and yielding an excellent crop. Corn has likewise the advantage of standing much longer against a drought than wheat. The larger sort of corn which is commonly sown here ripens in September.

Wheat is sown in the neighborhood of Albany to great advantage. From one bushel they get twelve sometimes; if the soil is good, they get twenty bushels. If their crop amounts only to a ten-fold yield, they think it a very mediocre one. The inhabitants of the country round Albany are Dutch and Germans. The Germans live in several great villages, and sow great quantities of wheat which is brought to Albany, whence they send many boats laden with flour to New York. The wheat flour from Albany is reckoned the best in all North America, except that from Sopus (Esopus) or King's Town (Kingston), a place between Albany and New York. All the bread in Albany is made of wheat. At New York they pay for the Albany flour with a few shillings more per hundred weight than for that from other places.

Rye is likewise sown here, but not so generally as wheat. They do not sow much barley, because they do not reckon the profits very great. Wheat is so plentiful that they make malt of that. In the neighborhood of New York, I saw great fields sown with barley. They do not sow more oats than are necessary for their horses.

Peas. The Dutch and Germans who live hereabouts sow peas in great abundance; they grow very well, and are annually carried to New York in great quantities. They were free from insects for a considerable time. But of late years the same pest which destroys the peas in Pennsylvania, New Jersey, and the lower parts of the province of New York, has likewise appeared destructive among the peas here. It is a real loss to this town, and to the other parts of North America, which used to get so many peas from here for their own consumption and that of their sailors. It had been found that if they procured good peas from Albany and sowed them near King's Town, or the lower part of the province of New York, they succeeded very well the first year, but were so full of worms the second and following years that nobody could or would eat them.—Some people put ashes into the pot, among the peas, when they will not boil or soften well; but whether this is wholesome and agreeable to the palate, I do not know.

Potatoes are planted by almost everyone. Some people preferred ashes to sand for keeping them in during winter. Some people in Ireland are said to have the custom in autumn of placing the potatoes in an oven and drying them a bit, when they are said to keep better over winter; but these potatoes cannot later be planted, only eaten. The Bermuda potatoes have likewise been planted here, and succeed pretty well. The greatest difficulty is to keep them during winter, for they generally rot in that season.

The humming bird comes to this place sometimes, but is rather a scarce bird.

The *shingles* with which the houses are covered are made of the white pine, which is reckoned as good and as durable and sometimes better than the white cedar. It is claimed that such a roof will last forty years. The white pine is found abundant here, in such places where common pines grow in Sweden. I have never seen them in the lower parts of the province of New York, nor in New

Jersey or Pennsylvania. A vast quantity of lumber from the white pine is prepared annually on this side of Albany, which is brought down to New York and exported.

Grapevines. The woods abound with grapevines, which likewise grow on the steep banks of the river in surprising quantities. They climb to the tops of trees on the bank and bend them by their weight. But where they find not trees they hang down along the steep shores and cover them entirely. The grapes are eaten after the frost has touched them, for they are too sour before. They are not much used in any other way.

Gnats. The vast woods and uninhabited grounds between Albany and Canada contain immense swarms of gnats which annoy the travellers. To be in some measure secured against these insects some besmear their face with butter or grease, for the gnats do not like to settle on greasy places. The great heat makes boots very uncomfortable; but to prevent the gnats from stinging the legs they wrap some paper round them, under the stockings. Some travellers wear caps which cover the whole face, and some have gauze over the eyes. At night they lie in tents, if they can carry any with them, and make a great fire at the entrance so that the smoke will drive the pests away.

June the 16th

The porpoises seldom go higher up the Hudson River than the salt water goes; after that, the sturgeons fill their place. It has however sometimes happened that porpoises have gone clear up to Albany.

There is a report that a whale once came up the river to this town.

The fireflies *(Lampyris)*, which are the same as those that we find in Pennsylvania during summer, are seen here in abundance every night. They fly up and down in the streets of the town. They come into the houses if the doors and windows are open.

June the 19th

Several of the Pennsylvania trees are not to be seen in these woods: *viz.*

Magnolia glauca, the beaver tree;

Nyssa aquatica, the tupelo tree;

Liquidambar styraciflua, the sweet-gum tree;

Diospyros Virginiana, the persimmon;

Liriodendron tulipifera, the tulip tree;

Juglans nigra, the black walnut tree;

Quercus ——, the swamp oak; [Quercus aquatica?]

Cercis Canadensis, the sallad tree;

Robinia pseudacacia, the locust tree;

Gleditsia triacanthos, the honey-locust tree;

Annona muricata, the papaw tree;

Celtis occidentalis, the nettle tree;

and a number of shrubs, which are never found here. The more northerly location of the place, the height of the Blue Mountains, and the course of the rivers, which flow here southward into the sea, and accordingly carry the seeds of plants from north to south and not the contrary way, are chiefly the causes that several plants which grow in Pennsylvania cannot be found here.

An Island near Albany. This afternoon I went to see an island which lies in the middle of the river about a mile below the town. This island is an English mile long, and not above a quarter of a mile broad. It is almost entirely turned into plowed fields, and is inhabited by a single planter, who besides possessing this island is the owner of three more. Here we saw no woods, except a few trees which were left round the island on the shore and formed as it were a tall, large hedge. The red maple *(Acer rubrum)* grows in abundance in several places. Its leaves are white or silvery on the under sides, and, when agitated by the wind, they make the tree appear as if it were full of white flowers. The water beech *(Plantanus occidentalis)* grows to a great height and is one of the best shade trees here. The water poplar is the most common tree hereabouts, grows exceedingly well on the shores of the river, and is as tall as the tallest of our aspens. In summer it affords the best shade for men and cattle against the scorching heat. On the banks of rivers and lakes it is one of the most useful trees, because it holds the soil by its extensively branched roots, and prevents the water from washing it away. The water beech and the elm tree *(Ulmus)* serve the same purpose. The wild plum trees are plentiful here and full of unripe fruit. Its wood is not made use of, but its fruit is eaten. Sumach *(Rhus glabra)* is plentiful here, as also the wild grapevines which climb up the trees and creep along the high shores of the river. I was told that the American elm tree *(Ulmus Americana)* forms several high hedges. The soil of this island is a rich mould, mixed with sand, which is chiefly employed in corn plantations. There are likewise large fields of potatoes. The whole island was leased for one hundred pounds of New York currency. The person who had taken the lease again let some greater and smaller lots of ground to the inhabitants of Albany for kitchen gardens, and by that means reimbursed himself. Portulaca *(Portulaca oleracea)* grows spontaneously here in great abundance and looks very well.

Peter Kalm's Travels in North America, ed. by Adolph B. Benson (New York: Wilson-Erickson Inc., 1937).

THE ASHOKAN RESERVOIR
IS BUILT

Alf Evers

A*LF EVERS (1905–   ) is the kind of historian who lives the history he writes. Any page of his lively, sprawling books* The Catskills *and* Woodstock *is a delight because it is likely to combine archival knowledge of the past with a present-day sense of time and place. Evers grew up on a farm in Ulster county, and now lives in Shady, so it is not surprising that his long memory is replenished by the contributions of friends and acquaintances who fill out his first-rate regional histories with linguistic idioms, and local customs, legends, and eccentric characters. That sense of inti-macy in the writing is what makes regional history so special a commentary on a place and a people. Of course, the leaders of politics, industry, and the arts are in the books, but the pecul-iar manners, dress, and speech of witch doctors, treasure hunters, tanners, traders, hermits, and plan old townsfolk find their way to add lots of color to the narrative. Town historian of Woodstock, the octogenarian Evers sits on the editorial board of the* New York Folklore Quarterly, *as well as finding time to write over fifty books for children.*

Here he tells the story of the Ashokan Reservoir, part of the Cats-kill system that also includes the Croton and Delaware. The three systems supply water to New York City from a nearly 2,000-square-mile watershed in the Catskill Mountains—18 reservoirs store more than 500 billion gallons of water. Consumer Reports *recently cited New York City for its "flawless or nearly flawless water," thanks to this engineering feat, which brings the cool, pris-*

*tine waters of the Catskill Mountains largely by gravity feed to
the great metropolis. As with many public works projects, the Ashokan
Reservoir met the demands of modern life for the urbanites while
transforming rural culture for those displaced by the 5½-mile-long
dam 90 miles from New York City. There are residents, particularly near the younger Delaware system, who still bear a grudge
against New York City for the loss of their communities to the
Pepacton Reservoir. In 1905, 2,000 people lived in the lower Esopus
Valley, which John Burroughs called the "Gateway to the Catskill Mountains." Eight villages were flooded to make way for the
Ashokan, among them Olive, Brown's Station, Marbletown, Bishop's Falls, Shokan—more than 500 houses, and hundreds more stores,
churches, mills, schools, and public buildings.*

*Today, climate changes, the threat of global warming, and
overpopulation of the cities frame the issue of water supply as
a strong environmental concern. Recent droughts in 1981 and 1985
have increased debate over possible use of the Hudson River to
meet the demands for more New York City water in decades to come,
a controversial plan that already has environmentalists and water
policy makers at odds.*

IN 1861 THE TRUSTEES of Kingston began looking toward the Catskills
in the hope of finding a good source of water for their growing village.
In that year a committee appointed by the trustees reported that
Kingston's water supply was far from adequate. The Committee
stated that once the village had been known for the large numbers of
its people who reached an advanced age, but this was no longer true.
A poor water supply was breeding disease and shortening lives. In
addition water was not available when fire broke out; a better supply
was urgently needed. The members of the committee did not
recommend the conveniently placed Esopus Creek as a source
because they found it to be badly contaminated by the tanneries
which were devouring the hemlock forests along the creek's upper
waters. Woodstock's Sawkill seemed more promising: its headwaters

were free from contamination. A quarter of a century after the committee made its report, the Esopus tanneries had disappeared with the hemlock forests. The stream's water had become less evil in smell and taste and Kingston considered building a reservoir at Bishop's Falls on the Esopus. There the bedrock was strong enough to support a big dam. For years a gristmill had stood beside the falls—it had been operated by a famous blind miller named Bishop. The miller was said to be able to do almost anything a sighted man could do. Local people, wondering at his remarkable adaptation to blindness, said that Jake Bishop could even tell the color of a horse by touching it. Bishop's Falls had long been a favorite goal for summer boarders who liked to watch the water tumbling down the walls of the rocky amphitheater beside the romantic-looking old mill where blind Jake Bishop had once gone about his work with confident steps. As the boarders exclaimed at the loveliness of the falls and as the trustees of Kingston dawdled over the project of damming the Esopus at that spot, engineers of a somewhat secretive corporation, the Ramapo Water Company, stepped in and seized the falls. Kingston had to be satisfied with a monopoly of the waters of Woodstock's Sawkill, Mink Hollow Brook, and Cooper's Lake.

The city of New York had grown in wealth and population during the last quarter of the nineteenth century. As the century approached its end, it became plain that what had once been suburbs of the city—places like Brooklyn, the Bronx, and Staten Island—had become for all practical purposes parts of one immense city, and in 1898 the boroughs officially did become parts of the city of New York. This made certain problems glaringly apparent. One was that the water supply of the consolidated city was a leaky patchwork of reservoirs, wells, and streams which could no longer be relied upon to take care of New York's needs. The men behind the Ramapo Water Company had been aware for some time that this moment of understanding would soon come and they had taken steps to profit by it. For years they had been assembling options on water rights. At first on New Jersey's Ramapo River. Later they fanned out into Connecticut, Rockland, Dutchess and Orange counties in New York. In 1899 they sent their men to invade the Catskills in search of all the water rights they could find, and soon they were buying options in Sullivan and Delaware counties. When New York City officials began considering planning a better supply of water they found themselves blocked wherever they looked by the Ramapo men. Ramapo made a proposition to the city: they would supply it with excellent water in virtually unlimited quantities—for a price.

As in the days of the fight to save the Adirondacks, New York business organizations took up the battle to save New York City from exploitation by men bent only upon private profit. A vast number of hearings, angry disputes, legal arguments and behind-the-scenes dealing followed before the battle was won and New York was free to have a publicly owned and operated water system using the Catskills' Esopus and Schoharie creeks and their tributaries. In the spring of 1905 the state legislature created state and municipal water commissions—over the vehement objections of Kingston's Judge A. T. Clearwater. On November 25 of that year the State Water Commission held the first of a series of public hearings at Kingston as a preliminary to buying land and rights and constructing two reservoirs with a combined watershed of 571 square miles, one on the Esopus and the other—to be built later—on the Schohariekill near Prattsville. This second reservoir would empty into the first by means of a tunnel bored through the underlying rocks of the Catskills. An aqueduct would convey the water ninety-two miles to the New York City line.

The hearing room was packed to capacity as Judge Clearwater took the lead in opposing construction of the Ashokan Reservoir. The legislative act under which the hearings were being held was unconstitutional, he argued. In addition the reservoir would constitute a perpetual menace to the towns and cities located downstream, for the Esopus creek in flood was a murderous tyrant which no amount of engineering skill could domesticate. The judge battled fiercely for he was representing not only his favorite client, the Ulster & Delaware Railroad, but also a troop of banks, business houses, large landowners, and business organizations. His client Samuel Coykendall spoke in person on behalf of his railroad which lay in the path of the proposed reservoir. By 1925 the reservoir would prove inadequate, he stated, so why not build a reservoir to take advantage of the far greater watersheds of the Adirondacks? Such a plan had been under discussion for more than a quarter of a century and corporations had been formed to promote it. The people of the Catskills did not want a New York City reservoir; their boardinghouse keepers would lose half a million a year in profits should the Ashokan Reservoir be built, Coykendall said—boarders would be frightened off by the thousands of rough men brought in to work with picks and shovels. The people of the Catskills would be saved from disaster only by the building of an Adirondack water supply for New York.

All arguments were in vain. The state Water Supply Commission decided in favor of the city of New York. The anger and resentment sputtering in and around the Catskills became a roar of protest. The city of New York now had the right under law to buy the land their ancestors had cleared from farmers and to force rural shopkeepers to find other employment. It was like the days of the Livingstons and the other old landlords all over again. "It is such acts as this that caused the Anti-rent War seventy years ago," the Kingston *Freeman* asserted. Unless New York City behaved with greater respect for the rights of mountain people, a "People's Rights War" might follow, so the Pine Hill *Sentinel* hinted on April 14, 1906.

The lawyers of Kingston reacted to the decision of the Water Commission with elation. To this day elderly Kingston people sometimes refer to the years of construction of the Ashokan Reservoir as "the time they shook the plum tree." They call the Esopus Valley "plum tree land." Never since the greatest days of the Hardenbergh Patent had such profits been squeezed out of the Catskills and into lawyers' pockets as during the years between 1906 and 1915 when the reservoir was completed and began sending water to the city of New York. But few citizens of the lands to be covered by the reservoir shared the lawyers' elation—not at first. When they protested against building the reservoir they saw themselves caricatured in New York newspapers as uncouth bumpkins. Later they were subject to the rudeness of surveyors who invaded their fields, cut down trees, and made gaps in their pasture fences as they prepared part of the Esopus Valley for conversion into a lake. Hidden hostility toward the New Yorkers who had been their summer boarders now came into the open. New York people, it was said, were arrogant Sabbath-breaking and ignorant barbarians who believed that the people north of their city line existed only for the convenience or profit of New York.

As the size and scope of the proposed reservoir and its watershed became known, apprehension increased. Two fleets of battleships could do battle on the reservoir. If all the water in the proposed reservoir should join that in all New York's other reservoirs and descend upon the city at once, New York would be flooded under two hundred and fifty feet of water and everyone there would be drowned—and a good thing too, thought many an upstater. Bishop's Falls would disappear behind the longest dam of its kind then existing anywhere in the world. The inhabitants not only of farms but also of seven hamlets would be forced to flee. They would be joined by the bodies of almost three thousand people who had been quietly awaiting the judgment day in thirty-two Esopus Valley cemeteries, for New York's almost twenty-four square miles of the Esopus Valley would be scraped clean of every vestige of its former inhabitants and their works before fastidious New Yorkers would drink the Ashokan Reservoir's water.

Resentment reached a peak early in 1906. And then it quickly faded. People who had taken out the Anti-rent War masks and gowns of their grandparents and were thoughtfully examining them for moth damage now put them away, got out pen and paper, and wrote to their lawyers requestioning appointments on urgent business. For the example set by lawyers and politicians was rousing hopeful interest in landowners, large and small. If the plum tree could be shaken for lawyers and politicians, why not—in a smaller way of course—for lesser folks? For a share of the proceeds, the mountain lawyers and those of the trading towns would be glad to help outsmart New York by assisting clients in getting more for their property than it was worth. And the local lawyers were shrewd enough in land matters—they had not been sharpening their teeth on the Hardenbergh Patent for more than five generations for nothing. Optimism soared. On June 9, 1906, the Pine Hill *Sentinel* quoted an editorial in the Kingston *Daily Freeman* predicting that "next New Year's Day will see every man in Ulster County free of debt and with money jingling in his pockets."

Until the last claims and lawsuits were settled a quarter of a century later, the bank accounts of local lawyers swelled into unbecoming corpulence. And lawyers' efforts had a pleasant side effect, which was to amuse newspaper readers clear across the country and even amid the frosts of Alaska. The case of scrappy seventy-year-old Mrs. Emma Cudney did much to cheer thousands of Americans. Mrs. Cudney had a "ginseng plantation" on her little farm and claimed that her ginseng was enormously valuable. Under the skillful direction of her lawyer, Judge Clearwater, the Cudney case went on appeal from court to court, piling up wagonloads of testimony as to the cash value of ginseng in "the China treaty ports" and to the Chinese faith in its value as an aphrodisiac and cure for almost any ailment. A claim of Saugerties manufacturers clustered on the banks of the Esopus had no sex interest, but it had what was almost as good; it involved millions. The manufacturers estimated the damage done to their prospects by the building of the reservoir at three million dollars and they threatened if their demands were not met to get an injunction just as the reservoir was about to begin sending water to New York. In this way they would dry up the city.

The owners of the farmlands bought for the reservoir and its surrounding protective border were well paid by the standards of the time—they received an average of $485 per acre. Claimants and litigants outside the reservoir proper did not do as well. Among the unfortunates for whom the plum tree did not shake were the Saugerties manufacturers and a very determined lady named Cecelia E. Wentworth. For years the doings of Mrs. Wentworth, her husband, and their onetime friend and neighbor, famous sculptor J. Q. A. Ward, had lightened many a dull day for the people of the Catskills and their summer boarders. Mrs. Wentworth was known locally as "one of the most noted artists of the world," her husband was a rich businessman; their fourteen-hundred-acre estate at the foot of Peekamoose Mountain served both as hunting and fishing preserve and an artist's retreat—as Mrs. Wentworth worked at her easel her husband doggedly pursued poachers. The Wentworths and the Wards were the chief movers in founding the Peekamoose Fishing Club located on lovely Peekamoose Lake. When Mrs. Wentworth discovered that a little spring on a cliff above the lake possessed what seemed to be miraculous curative powers, she built a chapel on the spot and invited kindly, scholarly Michael A. Corrigan, Archbishop of New York, to consecrate it. Protestant Mr. Ward was shocked at the prospect of seeing secluded Peekamoose Lake becoming "an American Lourdes" with daily deputations of hopeful pilgrims and with the steep mountainside which plunges so romantically down to Peekamoose Lake decorated with avalanches of discarded crutches. He called together his supporters at the club and had them elect him president of the organization. Wentworth assembled his forces and was also elected president. Sculptor Ward then appealed to the courts for relief. The case entertained readers of metropolitan newspapers for years. Local statisticians estimated that it required the abilities of thirty-two lawyers to keep the case alive for a combined fee in the vicinity of $100,000.

The Peekamoose Fishing Club case was hardly over with the club's dissolution by order of the court, when Mrs. Wentworth crashed through again as a public entertainer. J.Q.A. Ward at seventy-seven kept out of the act—he had just been married to a very young woman. The construction of the Ashokan Reservoir had lessened the value of the Wentworth estate by $20,000, Mrs. Wentworth claimed as she filed suit against the city of New York. The stores at which she bought her groceries were being demolished; the post office she used had disappeared; the church at which she worshiped and which had been built with her own money was being spirited away. Mountain people did not express much sympathy for the Wentworths and her suit faded from public attention.

From the time the first shovelful of earth was disturbed as construction began, believers in the tradition that the Catskills were a great storehouse of mineral wealth were on the alert. Many a rumor of rich strikes was solemnly repeated and then disproved. But at least one rumor lived long enough to result in the filing of a claim to mineral rights with the State government in Albany. Mr. William H. Burhans had observed with interest the building of a new railroad siding in Kingston for the Ulster & Delaware which was profiting enormously from Ashokan Reservoir business. The rock used for ballast caught Burhans' attention; he examined it and concluded that it contained gold, silver, lead, zinc, and copper. The rock had obviously migrated, but from where? Burhans traced it to a rock cut being made to accommodate the rerouted Ulster & Delaware tracks on the northern edge of the reservoir. He filed a claim which covered both the Kingston siding and the new cut. The claim was never worked. How could it be, old-timers asked, when working it met with a veto from both the rich city of New York and the rich Ulster & Delaware Railroad?

As lawyers, litigants, amateur prospectors, and construction workers kept busy, some people remained skeptical about the Ashokan project which they called the "Esopus Folly." It was being hinted that politicians had started the whole thing for unworthy motives of their own. It was predicted that even if the great hole in the ground should be completed it would be no more than a dry, weed-grown emptiness serving only as a monument in reverse to the human capacity for error and corruption.

But step by step the mountains of engineers' blueprints for the Esopus Folly were translated into such realities as vast excavations, footings for dams and dikes, demolished trees and buildings, blasted rocks, quarters for the workers who would man picks and shovels, horse-drawn wagons, earth scoops and steam shovels. A schoolhouse appeared for workers' children and was also used for evening classes in English for Italian, Polish and Lithuanian laborers who were taught American patriotic songs which they sang for visitors while slowly waving American flags in unison. A police station cared for weekend drunks and the fatalities that occurred in the course of arguments often arising in the taverns and whorehouses which appeared in response to the arrival of the construction workers but outside the bounds of their project. Reservoir officials liked to boast in their public relations releases that not only was their project one of the greatest engineering feats of all time but also that it had been carried out with a sympathetic understanding of the human beings involved, an attitude in keeping with the reforming spirit of the times. It was true that the quarters of many "better class" workers were not at all like the miserable shacks in which Italian laborers had lived while working on the railbeds of the Catskills during the 1870s and 1880s. They were neat and new and clean, if somewhat barracky; an infirmary with doctors and nurses stood ready and the wages paid were good. Never before had unskilled workers been so well treated in the Catskills.

But the unskilled foreign-born and native black men who did the rough and dirty work on the project fared less well. Although New York officials discouraged the padrone system which had been the cause of many evils, it was used by many contractors at Ashokan. Workers lived in slumlike conditions to which some responded with much publicized violence. Local citizens shuddered, double-locked their doors and spoke of a "reign of terror" as having come to the Catskills.

The Italians were joined by Irishmen from the dying bluestone settlements. Some cut stone for walls and for dam-facing in quarries soon to be buried under the waters of the reservoir. Other workers poured in from the mountains and the Hudson Valley as the plum tree spread its less juicy fruits far and wide. On September 9, 1913, the gates in the dams were closed so that water could begin to accumulate in the reservoir's two basins. The weather had been dry, springs and streams were low, and those who mocked the great plan as the Esopus Folly smiled smugly. They spread a rumor that the bottom of the reservoir had proved so porous that millions of dollars worth of a new and still secret compound would have to be used to calk the leaky basins. But as water rose behind the dam such rumors ceased.

On June 19, 1914, all the steam whistles used in the construction effort blew for a solid hour to proclaim that work on all the dams and dikes which were the reservoir's major engineering feats were completed except for the facing and finishing of the upper parts. By then Bishop's Falls were well under water, which stood ninety feet deep nearby, even though dry weather had continued.

Before the closing of the gates in 1913, the engineers had built a scow which they expected to float on the waters as they accumulated and which would be used in the job of facing the upper parts of the dams with stone. When the scow floated at last on the rising waters, the engineers paid their respects in song to believers in the Esopus Folly. Ever since their Ashokan job began, the engineers, in accordance with a custom of their profession, had run up new words to popular tunes to commemorate notable events. Now they sang:

Oh Noah built himself an ark, the dear old Christian soul,
Put all his family aboard and left, his neighbors in a hole.
As Noah pushed out in the stream, with all his kith and kin,
The neighbors stood up on the bank, and merrily said to him,

Chorus

Go to hell then, go to hell then and now
With your damned old scow
Cause it ain't gonna rain anyhow
It ain't gonna rain anyhow

Oh Noah got down on his knees and prayed that they would drown,
That the Lord in his almighty wrath would destroy the whole
        damned town
The animals kicked up a fuss, that would have raised your hair
And there was wafted on the breeze, this most ungodly air,

Chorus

For forty days and forty nights, the rain it did pour down,
The water stood 3000 feet o'er every hill and town
Old Noah walked around the ark, looked through a window pane,
Said now where are those poor damn fools who said it wouldn't
        rain? . . .

When water from the Esopus Valley began entering New York
in 1915, not even the most hardened skeptic could deny that the
Ashokan Reservoir was admirably accomplishing the end for which it
had been planned. Work on the Schoharie Reservoir and the Shandaken
Tunnel began at once. Later other Catskill streams were dammed and
sent gurgling to New York. The Rondout was dammed at Lackawack.
The Neversink and finally the East Branch of the Delaware were also
dammed. As each project reached its first stage, the same sequence
of events followed among mountain people. First the sense of shock
at the thought of having to leave their homes; then the merging of
the images of old-time landlords and New York City politicians; then
the invocation of the spirits of the Anti-rent warriors; then the

realization that, after all, there might be money in it; finally the retaining of lawyers to fight for every possible penny.

Once the Catskills had passed through their half century of pushing, gouging, blasting, and digging, for water-supply purposes, they had a different look. Gone were many of the old mill-centered valley hamlets with their verandahed inns and low open-fronted blacksmith shops; mill wheels vanished by the dozen; so too did time-stained covered bridges. The sites of Indian camps and of the orchard of Henry Hecken sank forever under water. Many families descended from Catskills' pioneers were dispersed by the thirst of the city of New York and their names are no longer heard among the Catskills. When the lakes that filled the valleys aged a little, they reflected the surrounding mountains with a charm that made some travelers think of England's Lake District. There the city of Manchester had annoyed tourists by putting to work and rudely enlarging an existing lake, Thirlmere, as a source of water. The absence of indications of longtime human activity on the shores of the Ashokan and other new lakes gave them a curiously aseptic and official character. After each reservoir was built, driving around it on the new roads provided by the bounty of the city of New York became a favorite Sunday treat. But before long this ceased to amuse or interest with its initial intensity. Only the great cluster of fountains which aerated the water before it left for New York continued to keep its appeal. Once tourists like Daniel Webster came to the Catskills to watch water tumbling down for a fee in a wilderness setting. Now tourists come to see water being thrown upward in a way that suggests, not the vanishing American wilderness, but the great fountains that once formed part of the settings of the palaces of European monarchs.

Alf Evers, *The Catskills: From Wilderness to Woodstock* (Woodstock, N.Y.: The Overlook Press, 1982).

GYPSY MOTHS AND MAN

Daniel Smiley

O*N THE OCCASION of his recent death, Daniel Smiley (1907–89) was eulogized in a* New York Times *obituary, which referred to him as an "old-fashioned naturalist in the spirit of Charles Darwin." Indeed Smiley, whose family founded the now 120-year-old Mohonk Mountain House at New Paltz in 1869, is highly esteemed for his contributions to the understanding of natural history in the Northern Shawangunks. Over the course of his long life Smiley wrote down his observations on just about everything— bird migration, flower blooming dates, local speech idioms, fleas, fish, wind, industry, trees, bees, salamanders. Because he was not a narrow specialist, he approached everyday life around him with the simple but steady tools of his own memory, general knowledge of the environment, and powers of observation, always open to the accidental or unusual turn of event.*

Every day for almost half a century Smiley took the air temperature at the cooperative weather station founded by his grandfather in 1896. From the 1930s until his death he measured the pH in lakes and streams, charting his findings, which decades later made him a pioneer in the analysis of data on acid rain. Much of what Smiley wrote down on his more than 14,000 note cards was compiled eventually into various papers on history and culture, natural science notes, and field and research reports, offering an invaluable research source on the region. Continuity is the hallmark of the Quaker Smiley family, which has run Mohonk continuously since its inception. So, it comes as no

*surprise to learn that Daniel Smiley himself had recorded forty-
six years of observations on mountain laurel blooming dates, and
thirty-eight on hepatica. He frequently used his grandfather's
hundred-year-old records to compare them with his own notes.*

*In many ways, Smiley followed in the tradition of eighteenth-
century self-trained naturalists, such as John Bartram and
Thomas Jefferson, and later Thoreau, who watched and recorded
natural life in one place, over a long period of time. The ultimate contribution of such men who knew the deep pleasure of a
solitary walk in the woods is as philosophic as it is scientific.
In their exemplary lives is an important lesson on the appreciation
of the natural history of each individual's unique world.
Fortunately, Smiley's world ranged over the 7,500 acres preserved
by his conservation-minded family at their mountaintop resort, 6,000
acres of which were set aside in 1963 as a forever wild sanctuary. The
selection which follows wonderfully illustrates Smiley's open approach
to all aspects of the ecosystem, with some surprising comparisons on
pesticides and natural predators in the life of the gypsy moth, an introduced species now resident in the Hudson Valley.*

Introduction

A SEVERE INFESTATION OF gypsy moth caterpillars can be a disturbing
experience for human observers. Thousands of acres of trees are
stripped of their leaves. The woods are as brown as in early spring.
The insects' droppings fall to the ground like an ominous rain, and
the large fuzzy caterpillars themselves may drop down on unwary
hikers and picnickers. No less fearsome is the frequent response to
this phenomenon: manpower is mobilized, trucks and airplanes are
deployed, and poisonous chemicals are sprayed over the land. Yet
the gypsy moth is not destroyed, and the unhappy spectacle may
soon be repeated.

This report is written in the conviction that fear is in part a
product of ignorance, and that understanding is prerequisite to a

durable accommodation between human interests and the natural environment.

The gypsy moth was introduced into this country in 1869 at Medford, Massachusetts, by an astronomer who had the fanciful idea that he could cross these insects with silkworms. He failed, but a windstorm is reputed to have broken his cages, allowing the insects to escape. Since then tens of millions of dollars have been spent in efforts to eradicate the gypsy moth. Today it continues to extend its range westward and southward. It is encouraging to note, however, that where it has been present longest the forests continue to grow and humans go about their lives with occasional temporary disturbance.

The life of the gypsy moth, like that of other insects, is divided into four stages. It starts as one egg in what is known as an egg mass. The egg mass looks like a piece of tan-colored suede and is likely to be found on a tree or building. In spring the egg hatches and produces a caterpillar which grows to be large, hairy, and hungry. It is the caterpillar, also called the larva, that defoliates trees by eating their leaves. The third stage of the lifecycle begins in early summer, when the caterpillar spins itself a brown cocoon and is transformed into a pupa. The pupa stage is brief—only ten to fourteen days—but it brings great changes. The pupa undergoes metamorphosis and emerges as the winged adult gypsy moth. The adult female cannot fly because of the weight of eggs she carries. Her scent, carried by the wind, attracts one or more males for mating. Her eggs are laid within crawling distance of where she emerged from the pupal stage. The following spring those eggs that survive the vicissitudes of winter will hatch into caterpillars.

Gypsy Moth Research at Mohonk

Since 1930 I have observed and recorded natural history at and around Mohonk Lake in the Shawangunk Mountains of Ulster County, New York. The adjustment of the ecosystem to the introduced gypsy moth is now part of that history.

The first defoliation of consequence in Ulster County occurred in 1957. Egg masses are said to have been blown across the Hudson River by the September, 1938, hurricane, and by inadvertent egg mass arrivals on construction equipment. Two decades passed before the gypsy moth showed itself in large numbers. In 1957 the U.S. Department of Agriculture undertook a vast program of aerial spraying with DDT, reportedly to "eradicate" the insect. Mohonk's forests were among the three million acres dosed. By the time of the next population increase, in the early sixties, the danger and undesirability of DDT had been recognized by some scientists. Those responsible for the Mohonk woodlands began to realize that a complex, *ecosystem* problem was at hand. Although there have been several more aerial spraying programs in Ulster County, each time we have requested the planes to turn off their nozzles while passing over Mohonk lands.

Because of this no-spray policy, Mohonk has been the site of several research projects that investigated the interaction of gypsy moths and the forest *without* human intervention with pesticides. In 1963 The Mohonk Trust (now Mohonk Preserve, Inc.) was formed as a charitable, scientific, and educational organization, and since then research has been conducted under its auspices.

In 1966 the New York State Museum and the Syracuse College of Forestry initiated a study of gypsy moth population dynamics. They investigated the cycles of population buildup and decline with particular attention to the number of eggs per egg mass and the viability of the individual eggs.

For three years in the 1970's the U. S. Department of Agriculture, Entomology Research Division, studied parasites of the gypsy moth. Five wasps and five flies have been identified; some parasitize the caterpillar, while others seek out eggs or pupae. These control organisms have "volunteered" at Mohonk; they were not introduced.

Dr. Gerd Heinrich, an authority on the subfamily of parasitic wasps, the *Ichneumoninae*, carried out baseline taxonomic studies at Mohonk, again because of the no-spray policy. It is probably that some of these insects use the gypsy moth as their host.

In 1973 The New York State Department of Environmental Conservation studied the predation role of small mammals, such as the deer mouse, in controlling the population of gypsy moths. The study was conducted on three kinds of terrain; in wild forest, in lawn areas interspersed with shade trees, and on the border "edge" between forest and lawn.

Since 1965 the Trust staff has recorded the location and degree of defoliation on the Mohonk woodlands, and from 1971 through 1981 an annual count of egg masses was made on a fifteen-acre-plot which includes shade trees on lawns, forest edge, and woodland. The count was discontinued because it became impractical to do it accurately.

Understanding the Problem

The public is gradually developing a deeper awareness of the interrelatedness of all things in nature. Below are some of the factors at work in the gypsy moth problem:

Forest Evolution. Before 1609, when Henry Hudson sailed up the great river bearing his name, the ecosystem of the region was in balance *but not static.* There were droughts, fires, hurricanes, and many plants and animals went through natural cycles of buildup and decline. Starting in the 17th century, the population of *Homo sapiens* began a buildup which continues to this day. Whereas the American Indian had been a modest force within the context of his environment, the civilization of the European immigrants became a noticeable and finally a major factor. Yet man continues to be a part of nature—the total ecosystem—dependent on it for shelter, nourishment, and breath itself.

All wooded areas of the Hudson Valley have been modified to some degree by human activities. Our present Shawangunk Mountain forests show the effects of past cutting for lumber, charcoal, and firewood. Forest fires were formerly allowed to spread uncontrolled, and for a time they were intentionally set by berry pickers (huckleberries and blueberries were thought to fruit more prolifically because of the pruning effect of the fire). Individual trees around buildings and in parks are adversely influenced by the removal of fertilizing litter, by soil compaction, by competition from grass, and by changed water tables in the ground. Trees, both in the wild forest and in cultivated areas, are living under stresses caused by human activities. With hindsight we might judge where human intervention was and is legitimate or ill-advised, but that would not change the facts of the altered ecosystem.

When a tree dies, we humans tend to notice the traumatic influence (fire, insects, storm, etc.) and overlook the long-term stresses that predisposed the tree to succumbing. At Mohonk our experimental management of oak woods on dry, poor soils has tended to show that the forest is ripe for change, perhaps by slow evolution but more often as a result of a traumatic event, such as insect defoliation. The future forest will be more diverse, both in the ages of the individual trees and in the number of different tree species present.

Weather. Weather is an essential part of an ecosystem. A change of one element will affect the balance of all. Deep snow in winter, for example, may make it possible for small mammals to eat gypsy moth eggs on the lower tree trunks. The snow protects the mammals from predators, but that in turn means that hawks and owls must find their meals elsewhere.

The amount of rainfall during the growing season may be critical in any large buildup of a gypsy moth population. Lower than average rainfall apparently is favorable for the gypsy moth while simultaneously subjecting the trees to unusual stress. The records of the Mohonk Lake Cooperative Weather Station show that from 1961 through 1970 the yearly precipitation was below normal, and in the severe drought years of 1962 through 1965 the growing season rainfall was only a fraction of normal. Wet weather appears to inhibit the gypsy moth, perhaps by fostering diseases.

Defoliation Damage. The damage done by defoliation is often misunderstood, in part because of the complexity of the subject and in part because of misrepresentation. In general, healthy deciduous trees can be completely defoliated for two or three years in succession without dying. Although the situation may appear to be catastrophic in June, later in the summer the trees leaf out again to make food. The loss of food-making time weakens them, but trees are large organisms and have reserves. The weather during and after defoliation is important.

Needle-bearing trees are not a preferred gypsy moth food, but the larger caterpillars will eat needles if deciduous leaves are not available. In 1966 I noted that only the outer ends of bundles of pine needles had been consumed. The remaining tufts allowed the tree to survive until it had put out new needles the following spring.

Woodlands completely defoliated in 1964 were not as hard hit the following year. This tends to confirm reports from Connecticut and it is unusual to have defoliation occur often enough in succession to kill many trees.

It sometimes appears that the gypsy moth seeks out weaker, more severely stressed trees. In 1965 I observed that on dry, thin-soiled rock ledges all deciduous trees of several species were defoliated. On the better soil of immediately adjoining stream valleys the same species were not noticeably defoliated.

Normal Losses. Mortality is normal in the forest. In a typical stand of trees of mixed species, it averages about 2% per year for trees over six inches in diameter. In times of unusual stress, such as drought or gypsy moth, losses of 6 to 10% may occur. Then the dead and dying trees become noticeable to human observers. But unless the adverse factors continue, the loss over the subsequent few years is less than 2%. The weak trees have already succumbed. Thus over a longer period of time the average loss remains about the same.

Dispersal. When the gypsy moth eggs hatch in spring, the tiny caterpillars crawl to a high point of the tree on which they were born. A silk thread is spun, and they hang from it. If a breeze of the right intensity comes, the caterpillars are being carried more than twenty miles. If they land in a favorable situation they have a chance to continue their lifecycle. Thus the absence of egg masses does not mean that certain trees will not be defoliated (the caterpillars may arrive by air), and the presence of egg masses does not mean that those trees will be affected (the caterpillars may float away before beginning to eat).

Population Dynamics of Introduced Species. Sometimes by design and sometimes by accident, humans have carried plants and animals to the far corners of the globe. It occasionally happens that when a species is introduced into a new environment, favorable to its growth and propagation and lacking in natural enemies, its population will "explode." This has been the case with the rabbit in Australia and the starling in North America. It was also the case with the gypsy moth in the Hudson Valley between 1957 and 1964. Two decades after it first gained a foothold, the gypsy moth population increased dramatically. The next step to be expected, based on the history of other introduced species, is a period of adjustment within the local ecosystem. The population fluctuates in obedience to controls that are not yet fully understood. Eventually we should see the population highs and lows even out as the gypsy moth finds its permanent place in the ecosystem.

Pesticides. Poisonous chemical sprays, applied from airplanes or ground equipment, have both obvious and subtle effects on the ecosystem. They are expensive—especially the ground spraying. I have found no evidence that the gypsy moth has ever been extirpated from any area by such sprays.

There has been a vast amount of research on the effectiveness of biological versus chemical control methods. The current recommendation by ecosystem ecologists is that the bacterial leaf spray (*Bacillus thuringiensis,* known as Bt) is as effective as the chemical spray known as Sevin. Bt is sold under several trade names. It is specific for lepidopterous insects and thus can kill any butterfly or moth larva exposed to it. Similarly, Sevin (a chemical spray), which has been widely used in the past for gypsy moth control, has undesirable ecosystem effects on other forms of life. It is especially lethal to bees, both domestic and wild.

Natural Enemies. One reason for the occasional, explosive, temporary increase of an introduced species is that the diseases and enemies that control it in its old home are not brought along. The gypsy moth is widespread in other parts of the world, but it is not a serious problem. For many years there have been experiments with introducing into this country the natural insect enemies of the gypsy moth. There has been some success with these introductions, and certain native insects have also become parasites and predators of the gypsy moth.

Benefits of Gypsy Moths. Change is constant in nature. An assessment of "good" and "bad" is closely linked to the viewpoint one assumes. It has been pointed out, for example, that frass (the caterpillars' droppings) is a fine fertilizer. The caterpillar is a productive recycling agent.

The defoliation of trees, and subsequent death of some, encourages shrubs and ground vegetation. More sunlight reaches the forest floor, and there is less competition for available soil moisture. On one rocky slope I have observed since 1964, nearly all the chestnut oaks died in the late sixties. This area is now covered with young trees and patches of blackberries, and it harbors a high population of cottontail rabbits. Deer, many species of birds, and other forms of animal life also prosper when the mature forest is replaced by more open growth.

One thoughtful ecologist has pointed out that if gypsy moth defoliation occurs at a time of drought, it may well benefit the trees since it reduces their water loss through the leaves. It would be the equivalent of pruning garden trees and shrubs when they are being transplanted.

Indications of Accommodation at Mohonk

Since the mid-1960's there has been a considerable loss of forest trees at Mohonk. I know of no way of determining scientifically how much of this was caused by the gypsy moth defoliations of 1965 and 1966, and how much by the five years of drought during the growing seasons.

In the spring of 1966 a significant observation was made. Among mountain laurel shrubs growing in defoliated chestnut oak woods, as many as half the laurels were killed back to ground level. Since the leaves were still on the bushes, the gypsy moth could not be blamed. I believe the laurel died from the drought. If so, might it not also kill the chestnut oaks overhead? One would expect the demise of the oaks to take longer, since as larger plants they would have greater reserves.

In 1967, 1968, and 1969 our unsprayed Mohonk forests suffered no defoliation. In June of 1969 a few individual caterpillars were found. Some were on the ground and seemed unable to crawl back up to a feeding area in the trees. I now believe that each one of them was harboring an internal parasite. If so, they would not have been able to transform into adults.

In 1970 there was a population buildup, but the degree of defoliation was mostly much less than 50%, so that it was not obvious to the average person. To the west of Mohonk, however, in the Catskill foothills, some areas were completely defoliated again, as they (and we) had been in the mid-60's. During that summer at

Mohonk, many caterpillars showed signs of wilt disease and never transformed into adult moths. Caterpillars and pupae were parasitized with considerable loss. Even so, a moderate number of adults were produced and egg masses were laid. As late as November the eggs were being parasitized by a small black wasp.

In 1971 there was noticeable defoliation, ranging from 25 to 75% of the leaves, but it was confined to a few preferred species (chestnut oak, white oak, red oak, gray birch) and then only in isolated areas.

Even during the resurgence of 1971, control factors must have been at work, for in 1972, 1973, and 1974 there was no obvious defoliation. Some individual trees showed a slight loss of leaf surface. I repeat that no spraying had been done. Natural controls effected the decrease. The research projects conducted at Mohonk suggest how some of these natural controls function in the population dynamics of the insect.

At low levels of population of density, animal predation is a major factor. The role played by our native deer mice is particularly interesting. During the resting stage in July the pupae are eaten by the mice, who even climb trees to get them. The preferred habitat of deer mice, because of food and protection, is woodland, although some can be found foraging along the edge of the forest. However, few mice are found around trees on neatly manicured lawns. Research at Mohonk has confirmed this inverse ratio—more gypsy moths survive where there are fewer deer mice living. By creating lawns with shade trees, especially oaks, and by providing buildings as welcome sites for laying eggs, humans have increased their gypsy moth problem.

Other predators contributing to gypsy moth population controls are birds, notably Catbirds and Blue Jays.

At the highest levels of population density the gypsy moths appear susceptible to a wilt disease that sweeps through their ranks. Also at this time, the number of eggs per egg mass decreases, as does the viability of individual eggs within the mass. This is significant because the number of egg masses per acre is often used to decide when to spray. The effort and money are wasted if the number of egg masses proves an unreliable indicator of the potential population of caterpillars, and if a population decline occurs anyway in the natural course of events.

Where drought and defoliation have killed significant numbers of trees, the replacement forest now growing up includes a greater diversity of species with a larger proportion of trees that are not preferred gypsy moth food. I expect fewer problems in this future forest.

The Philosophy of Accommodation

Our Mohonk ideas on how to meet the gypsy moth problem did not develop with a flash of insight. Nor are they the work of any one person. Members of the Research and Records Committee of the John Burroughs Natural History Society were particularly helpful, as we tried to understand some of the fascinating interactions within the web of nature. Our respect for ecosystem concepts has grown. Some decisions, such as not to spray, were first made on the basis of a hunch. Only later did justification for the decision appear. (Though money was not our motive, I believe that omitting the Mohonk forests from the areas sprayed has saved the taxpayers of New York about $30,000.)

We would not have chosen to have the gypsy moth added to our local ecosystem. It came uninvited. Its way was prepared by what humans had done to the forest flora and fauna in the past. This included some of my own ancestors, who were doing what seemed right in the light of their knowledge and values. No blame is intended here, just recognition of the fact.

If it were possible to eradicate the gypsy moth from North America, *and* if this could be done at reasonable cost and without injury to other living organisms, I would probably favor the effort. But there is no evidence that it could be done. Even the proponents of a vigorous spraying program no longer speak of eradication, they speak only of damage control. The gypsy moth is no longer an "invader," it has become a resident. Like the dandelion and many other introduced species, it is here to stay. We shall have to accommodate to one another.

We now have evidence that many organisms are responding to the challenge of the gypsy moth—from wilt disease and tiny wasps to birds and small mammals. Thus a new web of interrelationships is being formed within the ecosystem. Indiscriminate spraying will delay this process, for the simple reason that the spray is as lethal to many of the control organisms, such as parasitic insects, as it is to the gypsy moth. Spraying, whether bacterial or chemical, upsets the natural control process discussed above. There is no recourse but to spray again and again. It can become a vicious circle. And the gypsy moth, because of its unusual dispersal mechanism, can still blow in from a hatching site miles away.

Ecologists familiar with the gypsy moth history at Mohonk say that since we did not permit the forests to be sprayed in the 1960's, a small gypsy moth population has remained here, and it in turn has supported the control organisms during the low state of population. Today we are glad to see a *few* gypsy moths, for they assure us that the parasites and diseases are *also* present and available to work against a population buildup, such as developed in 1981.

Unlike some neighboring states, New York has allowed individual landowners to decide whether their forests would be included in the spraying program. At Mohonk we continue to request "no spraying." I am grateful for this option, for without it we never could have experimented with an alternate and scientifically sound approach to the gypsy moth problem.

One significant change at Mohonk is that in the 1970's the parasites and wilt disease began to take effect at a lower level of gypsy moth population density than in the 1960's. It remains to be seen whether these controls will in the future be so effective as to prevent noticeable defoliation if the gypsy moth is given a favorable combination of weather and other facts. I would not, however, view another population buildup as cause for alarm. On the human scale, twenty years is a long time to contend with a difficult insect, but it may be only a portion of the time required for natural accommodation.

Daniel Smiley, "Gypsy Moths and Man" (New Paltz, N.Y.: Mohonk Preserve, 1987).

SELECTED LETTERS

Cadwallader Colden

THERE WERE *few men in the colonies as learned as Cadwallader Colden (1688–1776), the Scotsman who pursued his interests in medicine, science, botany, physics, and philosophy from his manor house near Newburgh, which he called Coldengham. Even fewer of such intellectuals lived in New York which, in the middle of the eighteenth century, had no sophisticated culture, certainly not in comparison to Philadelphia. Colden, who settled upstate by 1730 on a 2,000-acre patent, became surveyorgeneral of the colony a decade earlier, and he served as Lieutenant-Governor from 1761–76. He also found time among his travels and public affairs to help found the American Philosophical Society, and to write a major study of the period,* The History of the Five Indian Nations, *having spent a great deal of time with the Mohawks especially.*

Colden was part of an international scientific circle of correspondents who included the Swede Linnaeus, who transformed the natural sciences; his student Peter Kalm; Gronovius, the Dutch botanist at Leyden; and the British merchant Peter Collinson. Collinson employed the self-taught Quaker botanist John Bartram of Philadelphia, where another member of the illustrious group, Benjamin Franklin, resided. Colden's letters reflect the widespread knowledge of these men who exchanged information on plants and animals, minerals, weather, diseases, and the revolutionary Newtonian physics. The Americans sent seeds from the New World—abroad they were particularly keen about the balm of Gilead in the Catskills—which Collinson eagerly planted and Linnaeus named, honoring Colden himself with the genus Coldenia. *Colden's daughter Jane was drawn into this privileged circle, becoming the first woman botanist in America and mastering the new Linnaean system. She helped her father identify and catalogue the plants of their surrounding area, supplying pen and ink drawings of them for correspondents here and in Europe.*

In addition to his volumes of political and personal correspondence, scientific papers on matter and the treatment of cancer, and observations on natural history, Colden left behind a farm journal, recently published in the Hudson Valley Regional Review, *that is considered the earliest extant record of its kind for the Hudson River Valley. It provides a fascinating look at the choice of crops, planting conditions, and grafting and fertilizing on his farm, while also revealing several kinds of apples planted there in the 1720s and 1730s—among them, Spitzenberghs, Newtown Pippins, and Golden Russets. The death of Colden, who was a Loyalist, on Long Island in 1776 coincided ironically with the Declaration of Independence.*

Colden was one of the relentlessly "curious" men of the eighteenth century who put all the knowledge that was available to them at this point in history to the task of understanding and naming the botanical and other pleasures of the New World. Long after the Mughal Gardens in India had been designed, and the exquisite perspectives of the Renaissance landscape painted, at the dawn of the Industrial Revolution Colden was gathering unknown wildflowers, in the wilderness that was his home in the American colonies.

From Peter Collinson to Cadwallader Colden

London, March 7, 1742

Dear Friend:

You have much obliged me with yours of the 22d June and I am glad to find my little offices were acceptable to you. . . .

Pray have you thought or can you give a conjecture how America was peopled, or was it a separate creation. Most of your vegetables and many of your animals are different from ours, and yet you have some exactly like ours of which I have specimens by me. For I have a large collection considering my years and station of natural rarities and some artificial, from most parts of the world, which I am obliged to my distant curious friend for sending me. They afford me great entertainment at my leisure hours and in the country. If I may boast my garden can show more of your vegetables than perhaps any in this island, which I have been collecting some years from seed, and growing plants sent me by my friends in your world. So that I am no stranger to America, being pretty well acquainted with most of its productions whether animal, vegetable, mineral, and fossil. Perhaps beyond which you can imagine the uses I make of them is to admire them for the sake of the great and all wise Creator of them to enlarge my ideas of his almighty power and goodness to mankind in making so many things for his profit and his pleasure.

I had a letter from John Bartram. He much laments the disappointment of not seeing you. I am persuaded you would have been pleased with him. You would have found a wonderful natural genius considering his education and that he was never out of America, but is an husbandman and lives on a little estate of his own at 5 or 6 miles from Philadelphia on the River Skulkill. He really surprised me with a beautiful draft on a sheet of paper of the falls of Mohocks River which he took when he was there, with a particular account of it, and also a map of his own making of Hudsons River, Delaware, Katskil and the bay.

My best wishes attend you. When leisure offers give a line to your sincere friend.

From John Bartram to Cadwallader Colden

January 16th, 1743

Respected Friend:

If I had not had some acquaintance with thy person and thy disposition, I should be apt to think thee could hardly believe the pleasure I received, in reading thy agreeable letter of December 22d, which I received yesterday. It put me in mind of what our friend Collinson wrote to me, last fall, and desired me to call and see, for that I should find thee a man after my own heart. I had before sent thee three letters, and had no answer, which almost discouraged me from writing, yet resolved to write once more.

I am now as well in health as I have been for several years; and since my recovery, have been along our sea-coast, as I gave thee an account of in my last letter, sent with the walnuts, which I am glad are under thy son's care; but am sorry that thee had not received them directly, soon after their arrival at York, for I had taken care to keep them in moderate moist vegetative condition until the day the sloop sailed with them; and if they dry or mould in the box, I doubt the vegetative life will be destroyed before they are planted, which I would have performed in this manner; after a spot of ground is dug, or ploughed, then hoe or plough a furrow two inches deep; then drop the nuts therein about six inches asunder, and cover them with earth. Next summer, they may grow six, eight, or ten inches high; then, the spring following they may be taken up, and planted in a row for a hedge, about five feet distance; and when they are grown as thick as one's arm, they may be plashed in the beginning of March, just before the sap interposes between the bark and the wood. Pray, is your river frozen so as to hinder boats to pass to and fro? Our rivers are very open this winter; and, in my garden, the Mezereon, Groundsel, Black Hellebore, Henbit, *Esula,* and *Veronica,* are in flower, and many others in bud; but we had a sharp time the beginning of November.

From Cadwallader Colden to John Bartram

Coldengham, November 7th, 1745

Dear Mr. Bartram:—

I am much obliged to you for the information in yours of the 4th of October, which did not come to my hands till the 3d of this month. Mr. Collinson wrote to me that he had forwarded my packet to Doctor Gronovius; and mentioned the curious instructions Doctor Gronovius had sent you, and wished I could see them. . . .

We have very few Mineral Springs in this Province.* All that I have heard of, is a stream on the south side of Anthony's Nose, a mountain in the Highlands, between my house and New York. It runs down a precipice into Hudson's River. Sloop men, who use the river, say that they have always found it purgative; and lately I heard that a sloop, being in want of water, took in some from that stream. They had many passengers, men and women. The water proved purgative to all of them. . . .

As there is no anchorage on that side of the river, near that stream, I never had any opportunity to observe it; and I doubted of the truth of the accounts I had casually received of it. But now, if I have any opportunity, I shall take some more notice of it.

There is a good deal of ore found in that hill—a mixture of iron and copper; and they being mixed, has made the ore of no use. I am not sufficiently acquainted with the methods of trying mineral waters. I have never thought on that subject; but I find that *Sal Ammoniac* will give a blue tincture to anything impregnated with copper, and galls give a black to the tinctures from iron. If my memory do not fail me, I shall try this with galls, and *Sal Ammoniac*. . . .

Mr. Collinson wrote to me, that he had directed my brother's letter to your care, and from thence I concluded that it was put up among your papers. I have received a letter from my brother since the date of that, which makes the loss of it of no consequence. I thank you for the piece of news, of the Russian Expedition to America, which is well worth the notice of Great Britain; as likewise for the seeds of *Saururus*, and Stargrass.

I inclose a few seeds of the *Arbor vitae*. When at my son's, in the end of September, I found the seed ripe, and gathered a little; but being obliged to return home speedily, I resolved to send my son John to gather more, who was then with me. Something made me delay it for five or six days; and when he came, the seed were everywhere fallen. I little suspected its being so soon gone, otherwise I should have taken care to have got you enough to send to your correspondents. . . .

---

*The waters of *Saratoga*, now so celebrated, and so much resorted to by the fashionable world, were then unknown.

From Cadwallader Colden to John Bartram

Coldengham, January 27th 1747

Dear M. Bartram:—

It is so long that I have lost the pleasure of my wonted correspondence with you, that I am afraid of my having fallen under your censure; and which would give me more concern, than the censure of some great men in the world. But if you knew the true reason of my discontinuing to write, as usual, you would be so far from blaming me, that you would pity me.

I was unexpectedly engaged in the public business, and when I entered upon it, I expected it would only have been for one single piece of service; but one drew on another, and I was kept more months from my family, than I expected to have been weeks from them.

But at last I have got to my country retirement, and to those amusements in which I place my delight; but not to enjoy them so fully as formerly, by reason of interruptions which unexpectedly break in upon me.

The distempers which you mention to have been epidemical with you, seem, by what you wrote to me, of the same nature with the malignant fever that was at Albany while I was there, and carried off many. It was of the remittent kind, accompanied with profuse sweating and prostration of appetite. Madeira wine proved the most effectual specific; which most people were surprised at, when I advised it; but I had so old an authority as Hippocrates for the use of wine in some kind of fevers. This was attended with so much success, that the use of it became common.

It gives me much pleasure to think that your name and mine may continue together, in remembrance of our friendship. I do not know the plant, of which you send me the description from Gronovius. It is none of them I described to him; and therefore I suppose you have sent it to him, and that he has borrowed it with your name.

It was not possible for me to comply with your desire, of sending you a plant of the *Arbor vitae*, for it was the 14th of December before I returned home from New York.

All my botanical pleasures have been stopped this summer, while I was at Albany. We durst not go without the fortifications without a guard, for fear of having our scalps taken; and while I was at New York, I was perpetually in company, or upon business, so that I shall be a very dull correspondent. However, I designed to have sent you something of our transactions, by Mr. Franklin, at his return from Boston; but he stayed so long, that I left New York before he returned; and I was at last exceedingly hurried, in leaving that place. If I had stayed one day longer, the river had become impassable.

Now, dear Mr. Bartram, take pity on me, and let me have some share of that pleasure which you receive from your correspondents. I have not a line from any, but a short one from Mr. Collinson, of the 3d of August. I expected to have heard from Gronovius, by a ship expected from Amsterdam, and by which I wrote to him; but I do not hear that she is arrived. I sowed some of the seed of the *Arbor vitae*, but it failed as yours did. Perhaps they may germinate next year.

Can you give me no hopes of seeing you, in your rambles next summer, in search of new knowledge of things? Pray, make my compliments to the good woman, your spouse, and be assured,

That I am your affectionate, humble servant

From Cadwallader Colden to Carolus Linnaeus

Coldengham, February 9th, 1749

Sir:

You have done me so much honor by your two letters, one of the 6th of August 1747, the other without date by Mr. Kalm, that I cannot otherwise account for it than by your willingness to encourage every attempt to promote knowledge. For I am so sensible of my want of skill in the botanical science that I can no way deserve the praises you are pleased to bestow on the little performances I have made. When I came into this part of the world nearly forty years since, I understood only the rudiments of botany and I found so much difficulty in applying it to the many unknown plants that I met with everywhere that I was quite discouraged and laid aside all attempts in that way nearly 30 years, til I casually met with your books which gave me such new lights that I resolved again to try what could be done with your assistance. If then I have been able to do any thing worth your notice, it is entirely owing to the excellency of your method. However, I still find myself at a loss in a fundamental point in botany. What is it that certainly distinguishes one genus from another of the same class, so as not to be in danger of confounding plants of different genera by reducing them into one, or by making different genera of such as are really one.

Give me leave on this occasion to make one observation, though it be a very obvious one. There are some plants and those the most necessary for human life which grow no where but when sown by men's hands and in cultivated lands, such as our Indian corn, or zea, wheat, barley, rice, etc. That they never were the spontaneous produce of the earth without the art and labor of man. Otherwise they must be somewhere found growing spontaneously. So likewise the household animals, dogs, cats, dunghill, fowls, etc., seem to have been concomitants to man from the beginning, and that they cannot live without him. For the species at least, I believe I may venture to say that the genera of household animals are no where wild but have from the beginning been dependents on man. Man therefore has a natural right over them whereas we seem to be in a state of war with the other animals. . . .

I have been obliged for near three years past to lay aside all my botanical amusements, the public affairs of this government having obliged me to be during the summer season on the frontiers of this government, where we could not go out of the fortified places during the cruel and barbarous war with the French Indians, without danger of being surprised by the sculking enemy Indians.

I hope now that we have peace it may be in my power to make some return to the obligations you have laid on me by sending some drid plants as you desire with such descriptions as I can make of them. I cannot hope for any great reputation from what I do of this kind, but if you think that my observations or descriptions can be of any use to the public you have my leave to make use of them in whatever manner you shall think proper. . . .

Mr. Kalm arrived so late last fall in Pennsylvania that the season of the year did not permit him to proceed in his intended voyage. He tells me that he designs for Canada next spring. I hope to see him at my house in his way thither, and to have the pleasure if I can be of use to him in making his voyage more convenient or safe for him. If you'll please to continue your favors of writing to me, Mr. Collinson of London with whom you correspond will take care of your letters to transmit them to me. Or if they be sent to Pennsylvania and directed to the care of Mr. Benjamin Franklin, Post Master in Philadelphia, they will come to my hands. God preserve you in health for the benefit of mankind. Before I conclude I must inform you that the title of Summus Perfectus no way belongs to me. I know not what has led you into this mistake. I am with great respect

Dear Sir,

Your most obedient humble servant

The Letters and Papers of Cadwallader Colden, Collections of the New-York Historical Society. New York: Printed for the New-York Historical Society, 1918, 1919, 1920); *Memorials of John Bartram and Humphry Marshall,* ed. by William Darlington (Philadelphia: Lindsay and Blakiston, 1849).

STORM KING SAVED!

Albert Butzel

I N 1963 Consolidated Edison applied to the Federal Pow-er Commission for a license to build a pumped storage hydro-electric plant at Storm King Mountain, in the Hudson Highlands. This proposal ignited one of the most protracted confrontations between energy and environmentalist interests in the history of U.S. conservation. Hudson Valley residents organized to fight the plant, strategically transforming a regional issue into a national one, even-tually influencing environmental law. Concerned citizens, who included among them Carl Carmer, formed the Scenic Hudson Pres-ervation Conference to fight Con Ed, and were soon joined by numerous other groups. These included organizations as diverse as The Cornwall Taxpayers Water Protection Association, The Town of Putnam Valley, The Sierra Club, The Nature Conservancy, The National Trust for Historic Preservation, and The National Parks Association. Everyone mobilized to protect Storm King and the Hudson from certain pollution, defilement, and depletion of natural resources.

The dedication of the Scenic Hudson coalition prevailed, when in 1965 a federal appeals court ruled for the first time that conservation groups have a legal right under the Federal Power Act to speak for the public interest. But the determined effort to preserve the landscape of the Hudson Highlands was to continue until 1980 before Con Ed surrendered its license, thus terminat-ing the project. So, for years organizations and residents, and dedicated lawyers, kept the pressure on with carefully planned

336

protests and legal actions. Robert H. Boyle and others formed the Hudson River Fishermen's Association as an opposition group, which was to supply essential information on the spawning grounds of fish in the river. To keep the controversy in the news, articles and editorials appeared over the years in local and national magazines and newspapers. The issues raised in the Storm King case generated interest in the magnificent natural beauty of the region, and alerted federal, state, and local agencies to their responsibilities for its management, fostering a growing awareness of environmental ethics. For the Hudson River, this was a turning point in its history. It is perhaps fitting that Albert Butzel (1938–), who worked on the Storm King case for seventeen years, should summarize its significant impact. As a young lawyer he was associated on the first successful appeal with Lloyd Garrison at Paul, Weiss, Rifkind, Wharton, and Garrison. In successive years he represented Scenic Hudson on the Federal Power Commission hearings and appeals, then in State court, and in Federal court, finally negotiating the terms of this landmark settlement in 1980. For the 1463-foot Storm King, which had been renamed more than a century earlier by Nathaniel P. Willis, who didn't think the original Butter Hill sufficiently described the mountain's grandeur, it signaled, in the end, the triumph of the rights of nature.

※

ON DECEMBER 19, 1980, Con Edison agreed to abandon the Storm King project that Scenic Hudson had so long fought, and to convey to the Palisades Interstate Park more than 400 acres of land where the plant was to have been built.

This is a victory shared with many others: the Hudson River Fishermen's Association and Natural Resources Defense Council, the Attorney General's Office and the City of New York, the U.S. Environmental Protection Agency and the N.Y. State Department of Environmental Conservation. But above all, it is a victory for Scenic Hudson and the Hudson Highlands.

Vincent Scully, in describing Storm King, said that rising like a great bear out of the River, it "embodies the most savage and untrammeled characteristics of the wild at the very threshold of New York. It can still make the city dweller emotionally aware of what he most needs to know: that nature still exists, with its own laws, rhythms and powers, separate from human desires."

This it is, above everything else, that Scenic Hudson has achieved: the protection of one of the most stunning natural regions in the country, and a reminder that nature does indeed exist separate from human desires. The plant that has been abandoned, carved 1,000 feet back into the mountain and 800 feet along the shore, would have subjugated Storm King: made it, as Dave Sive said, "Con Edison's mountain." Instead, it will remain free, one of the glories of the Highlands and a heritage for future generations as it has been for those past.

The Settlement: Another "First"

The abandonment of the Storm King plant is part of a comprehensive settlement of utility-related disputes on the Hudson—a settlement which itself has been properly described as "an historic achievement." The settlement was announced on December 19 by Russell Train, former EPA Administrator, who presided as mediator over 18 months of negotiations between Con Edison, the State Power Authority, Central Hudson Gas & Electric and Orange & Rockland Utilities on the one side, and Scenic Hudson, the Hudson River Fishermen, NRDC, The Environmental Protection Agency and the Department of Environmental Conservation on the other.

The negotiations focused on the impact of power plants on the Hudson River fisheries. If the Storm King case began as a struggle to protect the unique beauty of the Highlands, the issue of fisheries protection soon became an equal subject of concern when Bob Boyle and the Hudson River Fishermen discovered that Storm King lay at the center of the striped bass spawning grounds. Later, as new plants were built at Indian Point, Roseton and Bowline, concern for the survival of the fisheries grew, and EPA ultimately issued permits requiring cooling towers at these plants. The requirements had been stayed, however, pending evidentiary hearings on the seriousness of the impacts. In the meantime, the plants were operating without any mitigation at all.

The settlement imposes on the utilities a series of requirements designed to lessen the impacts of the existing plants. These include outages (i.e., the turning off of generating units) at Indian Point, Roseton and Bowline during the critical spawning season in order to reduce fish kills; the installation of new pumps and screens at Indian Point to lessen the number of fish drawn into that plant; the construction of a striped bass fish hatchery; continued monitoring of power plant impacts; and the establishment of a $12,000,000 fund for independent fisheries research on the River. In return, the utilities have been relieved of the requirement of building cooling towers (which would have ranged up to 560 feet in height and cost several hundred million dollars).

The New York Times described the settlement as a "peace treaty for the Hudson," and it is certainly that. But it is more. It constitutes one of the first *negotiated* settlements of environmental and energy conflicts in the country. It is an historic precedent—and not the first that has been established in the case. That had come 16 years earlier—on December 27, 1965—when the U.S. Court of Appeals handed down its landmark *Scenic Hudson* decision.

The 1965 Decision

The Court held at the outset that conservation groups had "standing" (the legal right) to challenge agency decisions that affected the environment, even though they would not suffer any economic damage themselves. This was the first decision to grant the right of judicial appeal based on non-economic interests and opened the door for environmental litigation.

The Court also concluded that the FPC could not stand by like an umpire blandly calling balls and strikes, but had an affirmative duty to seek out and present all relevant facts. This included the duty to investigate feasible alternatives that might avoid the damage—a requirement that shortly found its way into the National Environmental Policy Act.

But the real birth of modern environmentalism was in the Court's concern for the Hudson. The Storm King plant, it observed, was to be located "in an area of unique beauty and major historical significance," and Scenic Hudson was justified in its claim that these factors had to be taken into account. The court agreed that this had not been done, and in a ringing statement, it raised environment protection to a judicially-cognizable concern for the first time: "The FPC's renewed proceedings must include as a *basic* concern the preservation of natural beauty and national historic shrines, keeping in mind that in our affluent society, the cost of a project is only one of several factors to be considered."

Six months earlier, President Johnson had made a similar point: "The importance of natural beauty cannot be easily measured. It cannot be coded for computers or calculated by economists. But it is proved beyond doubt by the history of the race, and the experience of our own lives."

The Storm King decision rang in an era of such new occasions, and it stands today as a landmark precedent. It took another 15 years, however, before Storm King itself was safe.

Victories from the Jaws of Defeat

As important as the landmark events were, the most extraordinary part of the Storm King battle may well lie in the ability Scenic Hudson and its allies showed to survive defeat. In the first years, for example, when it was apparent that the FPC decision would be adverse, an alternate forum was created before Senator Pomeroy's Joint Committee on Natural Resources. These Bear Mountain hearings, organized by Jim Cope and Mike Kitzmiller, were the first to identify the gas turbine alternative that was to prove so important to the Court of Appeals: and here, too, Bob Boyle first drew attention to the dangers to striped bass. When the Pomeroy Report was issued, it urged re-evaluation of the project in light of this new evidence, to which was shortly added the concerns of the Interior Department, drawn out by a freshman representative named Ottinger in conveniently scheduled Congressional hearings.

A few months later, after the FPC had issued the Storm King license, Lloyd Garrison persuaded the Court of Appeals to set the license aside. No one had thought that possible—the FPC had never been reversed before.

In 1971, when the case finally returned to the Court, the outcome was different and the second license was this time upheld. But for two years, construction was held off with a new round of lawsuits in the state courts. When these were lost and the situation seemed hopeless, the Hudson River Fishermen came to the rescue. The fisheries analysis for Storm King had failed to recognize the tidal nature of the Hudson and had far understated the potential damage as a result. When this information was presented to the Court of Appeals, the case was ordered reopened. That marked the beginning of the end which came at last on December 19.

It was an end predicted by Ron Vandivert early in 1972—at our darkest hour—when he was asked what he saw in store. The Court of Appeals had recently upheld the FPC's second license, and while a petition seeking Supreme Court review was shortly to be filed, everyone knew that it had little chance. Nonetheless, looking to the future with his irrepressible cheer, Rod answered: "They'll get more electricity out of a hand crank than they'll get out of Storm King in the next 20 years."

The victory at Storm King is a tribute to the Rod Vandiverts and Frannie Reeses and Ander Saunders and all their fellow hand-crankers who, in their love for the Hudson, simply refused to give up.

It is a victory as well that all who have helped are entitled to celebrate.

Albert Butzel, *Scenic Hudson News* 1, no. 2 (Spring 1981), Poughkeepsie, N.Y.: Scenic Hudson.

OF THE SEASONS

Adriaen Van der Donck

W HEN HE ARRIVED in New Netherland in 1641, on board a ship that carried a few dozen other colonists, some cows, and grapevines, Adriaen Van der Donck (d. 1655) became its first lawyer, and certainly one of the most learned men of the Dutch colony. He was a graduate of the University of Leyden who had been hired as legal officer by the wealthy Amsterdam merchant Kiliaen van Rensselaer to enforce all financial, social, and religious regulations and contracts at his Rensselaerswyck patroonship. Farmers, shoemakers, servants, carpenters, millers, and tailors were already living there among the hundred or so immigrants. Van der Donck lived on a farm in the area, and spent a great deal of his time observing the customs of the Europeans and Indians, and the natural environment. A few years later he moved to his own 24,000-acre estate overlooking Spuyten Duyvil. He was a prominent, responsible official of the province, referred to by the Dutch term "Jonkheer" or squire that later was transformed into "Yonkers," the town that still bears his name.

In 1649, Van der Donck returned to the Netherlands as part of an official delegation of Nine Men to present the colonists' grievances against the mismanagement and abuse of Director-General Peter Stuyvesant to the States-General at The Hague. They called for a reduction in taxes, less restriction from the West India Company, more self-government, and free passage for settlers to the colony. Temporarily banished for his stance against Stuyvesant, Van der Donck, who was a great promoter of the opportunities in

342

*the Dutch colony, spent his time back home assembling one of its
earliest and most skillful portraits.* A Description of the New
Netherlands *offers a wealth of information on soil, forests, agriculture, minerals, animal life, and plant life, with an especially
sympathetic discussion of the Indians.*

*Van der Donck tells of the many fruit trees the Dutch brought
over, their roses, tulips, marigolds, and white lilies; the kitchen
gardens of lavender, tarragon, cucumbers, artichokes, asparagus,
and beans. It is a delight to follow Van der Donck's Renaissance
scholar's mind as he tries to understand the geography, ecology, natural history, and culture of New Netherland. "The superabun-
dance of this country is not equalled by any other in the world,"
he proclaimed. Washington Irving acknowledged that "Diedrich
Knickerbocker" relied on him for a* A History of New-York.

THE CHANGES OF the year, and the calculations of time, are observed as
in the Netherlands; and although these countries differ much in their
situations in south latitude, still they do not differ much in the
temperature of cold and heat. But to discriminate more accurately, it
should be remarked that the winters usually terminate with the
month of February, at New-Amsterdam, which is the chief place and
centre of the New-Netherlands. Then the spring or Lent-like weather
begins. Some persons calculate from the 21st of March, new style,
after which it seldom freezes, nor before this does it seldom
summer; but at this season a change evidently begins. The fishes
then leave the bottom ground, the buds begin to swell; the grass
sprouts, and in some places the cattle are put to grass in March; in
other situations they wait later, as the situations and soils vary.
The horses and working cattle are not turned out to grass until
May, when the grass is plenty everywhere. April is the proper
month for gardening. Later the farmers should not sow summer
grain, unless they are not ready; it may be done later, and still
ripen.

Easterly winds and stormy weather are common in the spring,

which then cause high tides; but they cannot produce high floods. The persons who desire to explore and view the country, have the best opportunity in April and May. The grass and herbage at this season causes no inconvenience in the woods, and still there is grass enough for horses. The cold has not overcome the heat produced by the wood burnings, and the ground which has been burnt over, is yet bare enough for inspection. The flowers are then in bloom, and the woods are fragrant with their perfume. In the middle of May, strawberries are always plenty in the fields, where they grow naturally; they are seldom planted in the gardens, but there, in warm situations, they are earlier. When the warm weather sets in, then vegetation springs rapidly. It is so rapid as to change the fields from nakedness to green in eight or ten days. There are no frosts in May, or they are very uncommon, as then it is summer. The winter grain is in full blossom. The summer may be said to begin in May, but it really is calculated from the first of June, and then the weather is frequently very warm, and there is seldom much rain. Still there are no extremes of wet and dry weather, and we may freely say, that the summers are always better in the New-Netherlands than in Holland. Rainy weather seldom lasts long. Showers and thunder-storms are frequent in summer, and will last an hour, an hour and a half, and sometimes half a day. It seldom rains three hours in succession, and the rains seldom do any injury, because the earth is open, and the water settles away, and on the high lands the rains are always desirable. A summer shower frequently will produce water sufficient to extend to the roots of the vegetation, and be immediately succeeded by a north-west wind, which will clear off the sky, as if no rain had fallen. Heavy dues are common, which in the dry seasons, are very quickening to the vegetation.

Now when the summer progresses finely, the land rewards the labor of the husbandman; the flowers smile on his countenance; the fishes sport in their element, and the herds play in the fields, as if no reverses were to return. But the tobacco, and the fruit of the vines, come in in September. There is plenty here for man and the animal creation.

The days are not so long in summer, nor so short in winter, as they are in Holland. Their length in summer, and their shortness in winter, differ about an hour and a half. It is found that this difference in the length of the days, causes no inconvenience; the days in summer are long and warm enough for those who are inclined to labour, and do it from necessity; and for those who seek diversion. The winters pass by without becoming tedious. The reasons for this, and the objections thereto, we leave to the learned, as we deem the subject not worthy of our inquiry. The received opinion on this subject is, that the difference in the length of the days and nights arises from the difference of latitude of the New-Netherlands and Holland. The former lies nearer the equinoctial line, and nearer the centre of the globe. As they differ in length, so also they differ in twilight. When it is midday in Holland, it is morning in the New-Netherlands. On this subject there are also different opinions. Most men say that the New-Netherlands lay so much farther to the west, that its situation causes this variation; others go further, and dispute the roundness of the globe. As the creation of the world is connected with this subject, which none will deny, and as the difference in the appearance of the eclipses supports the truth of the first position of the roundness of the globe, therefore the other position appears to be unsupported.

The autumns in the New-Netherlands are very fine, lovely and agreeable; more delightful cannot be found on the earth; not only because the summer productions are gathered, and the earth is then yielding its surplusage, but also because the season is so well tempered with heat and cold, as to appear like the month of May, except that on some mornings there will be frost, which, by ten o'clock will be removed by the ascending sun, leaving no stench or unwholesome air, and causing little inconvenience. On the other hand, the vegetation and grass produced in summer falls, and is trodden down, which is succeeded by a fall crop, growing as it does in Lent, bringing delight to man and pasturage for animals. There is not much rain in autumn except in showers, which do not last long; yet it sometimes rains two or three days. Otherwise there is day after day, fine weather and a clear sunshine, with agreeable weather. In short the autumns in the New-Netherlands are as fine as the summers of Holland, and continue very long; for below the highlands, towards the sea coast, the winter does not set in, or freeze much before Christmas, the waters remaining open, the weather fine, and in many places the cattle grazing in the fields. Above the highlands, advancing northerly, the weather is colder, the fresh waters freeze, the stock is sheltered, the kitchens are provided, and all things are put in order for the winter. The fat oxen and swine are slaughtered. The wild geese, turkeys and deer are at their best in this season, and easiest obtained, because of the cold, and because the woods are now burnt over, and the brushwood and herbage out of the way. This is also the Indian hunting season, wherein such great numbers of deer are killed, that a person who is uninformed of the vast extent of the country, would imagine that all these animals would be destroyed in a short time. But the country is so extensive, and their subsistence so abundant, and the hunting being confined mostly to certain districts, therefore no diminution of the deer is observable. The Indians also affirm, that before the arrival of the Christians, and before the small pox broke out amongst them, they were ten times as numerous as they now are, and that their population had been melted down by this disease, whereof nine-tenths of them have died. That then, before the arrival of the Christians, many more deer were killed than there now are, without any perceptible decrease of their numbers.

We will now notice the winters of the New-Netherlands, which are different at different places. Above the highlands, towards Rensselaerwyck, and in the interior places extending towards New-England, (which we still claim) there the winters are colder and last longer than at New-Amsterdam, and other places along the sea coast, or on Long Island, and on the South River, (Delaware). At the latter places, there seldom is any hard freezing weather before Christmas, and although there may be some cold nights, and trifling snows, still it does not amount to much, for during the day it is usually clear weather. But at Rensselaerwyck the winters begin earlier, as in 1645, when the North River closed on the 25th day of November, and remained frozen very late. Below the highlands and near the sea coast, as has been observed, it never begins to freeze so early, but the cold weather usually keeps off until about Christmas, and frequently later, before the rivers are closed; and then they frequently are so full of drifting ice during the north-west winds, as to obstruct the navigation; and whenever the wind shifts to the south or south-east, the ice decays, and the rivers are open and clear. This frequently happens two or three times in a winter, when the navigation will be free and unobstructed again. Much rainy weather, or strong winds which continue to blow from one quarter a long time, are not common, or to be expected in the country.

It is probably, (and many persons support the position with plausible reasoning) that the subtlety and purity of the atmosphere changes the water before it comes to the earth, or whilst it is still retained in the clouds, or in its descent to the earth, into hail or snow. The latter is sooner to be credited, for during the winter much snow falls, which frequently remains weeks and months on the earth, without thawing away entirely. But below the circle of the highlands, the southerly winds are powerful; there the snow cannot lay long, but is removed by the southerly weather.

It frequently happens once or twice in a winter, that the trees are silvered over with sleet, which produces a beautiful and speculative appearance when the sun shines on the same, particularly on the declivities of the hills and mountains. Many persons say that sleets and heavy hail are signs of good fruit seasons in the succeeding year.

It is strange and worthy of observation, and surpasses all reasoning, that in the New-Netherlands, without or with but little wind, (for when the weather is coldest, there seldom is much wind) although it lies in the altitude of Spain and Italy, and the summer heat is similar, that the winters should be so much colder, as to render useless all the plants and herbs which grow in those countries, which will not endure the cold weather. The winter weather is dry and cold, and we find that the peltries and feltings are prior and better than the furs of Muscovy. For this difference several reasons are assigned, which we will relate, without controverting any, except in remarking that in most cases wherein many different reasons are assigned to establish a subject, all are frequently discredited. Some say that the New-Netherlands lie so much further west on the globe, and that this causes the difference; others who compare the summer heat with Spain and Italy, deny this position; others declare that the globe is not round, and that the country lies in a declining position from the sun.

Others assert that the last discovered quarter of the world is larger than the other parts, and ask, if the world formerly was considered round, how that theory can be supported now, when about one-half is added to it?

Adriaen Van der Donck, "A Description of the New Netherlands," trans. by Jeremiah Johnson, Collections of the New-York Historical Society (New York: Printed for the New-York Historical Society, 1841).

VI

Regions of The Spirit

I LIVE IN
THE COUNTRY

Alan Devoe

F*ROM HIS HILLSDALE world of a hundred and twenty-five or so acres which he called Phudd Hill, Alan Devoe (1909–55) praised the simple pleasures of the* right here *of life. "Take a circumscribed piece of the world, any piece," he wrote, "and the whole world is to be discovered inside it." His writing reflects the timeless themes of country vs. city life, human artifice vs. nature that have folded themselves into the pages of nature writing since the time of the ancients. Devoe's "I Live in the Country" is his joyful, philosophical testament to a way of life that honors the measured rhythms of pure presence. But his lyrical tone goes beyond the merely personal to strike the universal attraction of the rural spirit.*

Devoe was a devoted animal lover who also followed with delight the lives of plants. He wrote about both kingdoms in regular contributions to Audubon *and* Reader's Digest, *and in books which include* Down to Earth *and* This Fascinating Animal World. *Devoe's field of view began right outside his own window. Here was the setting for the amusing narratives he devised about the curiosities of animal habits and habitats. Mostly, he watched, listened, recorded, with growing respect for his intelligent animal neighbors. After his death, friends founded the Alan Devoe Bird Club, which owns and operates Columbia county's 140-acre Wilson M. Powell Wildlife Sanctuary in Chatham. Set in a quiet woods, it is a fine memorial to a man who appreciated the subtle poetry of bird song.*

IT IS QUITE CLEAR that most of my friends feel very sorry for me. The reason for their condolence and commiseration is that I live in the country. A few of my more caustic acquaintances feel that this is cause of questioning the soundness of my reason, but most of them play the gentler role of pitying. While they pity they also wonder, and this manifests itself in certain perpetual questions. What on earth do I find to *do* in the country. What is there to *see*? How do I contrive to fill up my time? Yes, of course there is my writing, but what do I do when I want to *rest*? This last question is the most persistent of all, and when I furnish the brief but entirely adequate answer, "I rest," it seems merely to bewilder and infuriate them, and they suspect me of evasion and subterfuge.

It is true, of course, that there are certain kinds of mind so temperamentally opposite to my own that not the most artful exposition I might contrive could beguile them into agreement with me. And there are people who are so deep-rooted in metropolitan life, and so hardened by its hardness, that they have actually sloughed off every single vestige of that earth-affinity which ordinarily lurks, however deeply hidden, in all the descendants of Adam. For these wretches, narrow as the gorges between their office buildings, and impervious as the concrete beneath their feet, I can offer, obviously, no justification for my peasantry. It is useless for me to parade before them, however cunningly, all the sweet and subtle charms of my previous world of elemental sights and sounds and smells, for their natural receptivity to such awareness has long since atrophied. I have nothing to say to them, for they are no longer dwellers on this great grass-green and sea-wet planet.

My friends, of course, do not all belong to this category of hardened creatures. They are, for the most part, thoroughly amiable and amenable beings who have merely forgotten a little of their ancient earth lore, and, through long preoccupation with mastering the tricks and thought-habits of urbanity, have lost sight of the ageless and eternal simplicities. They condole with me because I have no radio, and imagine that I am anguished because eleven miles separate me from the post office. They speak with affecting sympathy of how very "dull" my life must be, and audibly marvel that I am content to "stagnate" here. And as you, my reader, have undoubtedly suspected, I receive these commiserations with profoundest scorn. For although there is small trace of the hermit in my make-up, I extract from this life of "isolation," as friends sympathetically term it, a deep and endless delight.

The house in which I live is very ancient and haphazard and somewhat askew; in some aspects I know that it impresses those whose homes are in the city or suburbs as even a little dilapidated. From this ancientness and crookedness, and even from these occasional evidences of actual decay, I derive a continuous solace and repose. Here in this tiny dining-room the china dogs on top of the old pine corner-cupboard have watched three generations at their feeding; in the great spool bed upstairs have occurred both births and deaths. There clings in these low-ceilinged rooms—with their faded flowered wall-paper, their horsehair sofas and wide-boarded uneven floors—an aura of the stalwart tranquility, the hard-toiling stoic patience, of that succession of homely Dutchmen who were our predecessors. Near the middle of the last century one of these Hollenbecks (for such was the name of the sturdy family of which this house was homestead) deserted the plow and the scythe for a life of seafaring. When he was an old man, and had voyaged in every quarter of the globe, he came back to this house to eke out a living in his retirement by mending stone walls, and by barbering the formidable beards of his farmer neighbors in what is now our kitchen. There still remains in one wall of that kitchen a considerable chink—which appalls my neat housekeeping friends from the city. It was made originally—this chink—in order that the wife of that tonsorial old seaman could peer through and learn how her husband was getting on with his work. And I shall leave it there. For it is—like that tattered sampler in the hayloft of our barn which reads, "Sweet Rest in Heaven," and like the crooked path that untold thousands of footsteps have worn through the clover field to our well—a link with the simple, earthy lives of those good souls who are vanished.

In every direction, as I look from the windows, are to be seen the green wooded summits of the rounded hills, untenanted by living man. They lie—these curved and molded masses of rugged earth—brooding in an ageless silence, baking their hummocked backs in the hot summer sun, shouldering the cold white weight of countless snows, existing immutable and eternal while the oaks and firs upon their slopes wither and die and are born again through the passage of myriad seasons. So green are these hills, and so round and so many, that they suggest the massive tumuli of some gigantic and immemorially ancient race of man. I have walked upon them and extracted from their timeless earthiness the profoundest peace which it is possible to know.

My friends who speak of "loneliness" and "isolation" must, I suppose, take no heed of the deep companionship of trees and rocks. Yet it requires no pantheist to discover, in lichen-covered boulders and in the cool smooth trunks of maples or the rough, pitch-fragment trunks of firs, an essence of being with which it is very easy for a man to commune. These high hemlocks are my fellows upon earth; together we face the elements, together struggle for sustenance, together are set upon by plagues and pestilences, together will return, when we die, to the dumb, eternal, embracing earth of this planet. And it is possible for me to walk upon the black leaf-mold in which these hemlocks have their roots, and to draw from that contact—to breathe, to inhale, to soak into myself—a profound inviolable tranquility of spirit. This relaxed contentment, which springs from simple oneness with the eternal and the inanimate, is a far more perfect purge for turmoil and vexation than my friends can possibly receive in the mere diversions afforded them by the movies, the theater or the radio of which they sympathetically deplore my lack.

The silence of the countryside is not, of course, usually silence at all, but a whole symposium of tiny shreds and tatters of sound. But occasionally—in very early morning or at the moment when twilight is just becoming night—there lies upon all this region a hush that is as tangible as fog. There was such a moment when I went out with my milk pail to-day. As I stood by the side of our dirt lane, in the pale light of early morning, I might have been—for all the sounds I could hear—the single living man in a vast and green inanimate universe.

Here by the roadside were rocks—cool and voiceless and immobile for all eternity; above me, the dew-wet green leaves of maples, shivering and rustling with a soft nonhuman sibilance; beneath my feet the huge eternal roundness of the silently brooding earth. At such a time it is very easy—standing for a moment motionless in the illimitable gulfs and chasms of noiselessness, and breathing deep the smell of the moist earth—it is very easy to drop the whole being and aura of one's personal self, and to become, for the briefest magic fraction of a second, a creature, a *thing*, as impersonal, as mindless, worryless, purposeless, as the wet lichen-covered rocks or the tall hemlocks. There are no agencies, I expect, but utter aloneness and utter silence that can work this particular miracle. It can surely be wrought nowhere but in the country.

This country life of mine, far from being barren of incident or of things to do and to see, is crowded from daybreak until nightfall. My personal routine of eating, working and sleeping and performing my various chores is sufficiently simple. But the details of the lives that surround mine and demand my attention—the lives of chipmunks and phoebes and woodchucks and of the very buttercups and yarrow that grow in our pasture—are so vastly absorbing as to require all my hours. It is inconceivable to me that I could possibly be "bored" even had I no more to occupy me than the contemplation of the meadow upon which I look out as I write this. It is a broad meadow, with an apple-orchard in one corner and a little brook, and just now the diffusely amber slanting sunlight of late afternoon lies across it, making brighter orange the blossoms of the devil's paintbrush and redder the knee-high flowers of the clover. It is never the same for two consecutive minutes, this meadow. Now there is a robin probing its spongy surface for earth worms; now there comes a little riffle of wind to sway the tall grass and the buttercups; now the high shoulder of one of the nearby hills eclipses the last ray of evening sun, and the green of the meadow grass deepens and grows cool.

I have a friend who, in times of worry or distress, follows an invariable ritual. He seeks some patch of earth and there he digs, with his hands, with his fingernails, a hole. He digs below the dry crust, below the grasses, below the terrain of earth worms, until he reaches that cool damp substratum that has the smell of roots and rain. And when he has dug this deep, he stretches himself on the ground and thrusts his head into this earthy cavity and speaks all his troubles into it, for he has a theory that all these worries and vexations are thus swallowed up by the great primordial earth and dissipated forever. To some this may seem a fantastic and senseless rigmarole; but to those who know the healing power of earth it will be seen to have at least a basis in reason. "One impulse from a vernal wood" may not teach you more of man than can the sages, but that "sense of something far more deeply interfused," which I have many a time drawn from communion with the leaves and roots and flowers and hearts of plants and of grasses in this meadow of mine, affords a remedy for neurotic frets and worries which no psychiatric method can match. And it is a remedy to be procured only in the country.

In such a rural district as that in which I live, introversion is impossible and a philosophically equable way of life is almost inevitable. That sickly "turning inward" which makes wretches of its victims has no opportunity to enter the mental habit here. Chattering chipmunks fend it off, and the passage of swallows across the evening sky, and the delivery of a new calf and a plague of botflies. All man's thought and energy and time are taken here, as they were in the beginning, in a constant coping with the problems presented by the earth and the elements, and in this whole-hearted preoccupation with soil and sky, with birds and beasts and growing things, there is no chance for the entrance of less enormous problems. Birth and death are on every hand, in withering sunburned crops, in the hen brooding on her eggs, in the crashing fall of timber on the mountainside. And living thus in daily contemplation of the vast swing and surge of the eternal cosmic machinery, man sees the minor woes of man assume a triviality and utter insignificance. Letters long unanswered—bills long overdue; these have, to be sure, their place in my mind. But they can assume no very formidable proportions, for I am looking out upon a broad and grassy meadow that is bright with buttercups and cinquefoil—a meadow where the buttercups and cinquefoil have bloomed each season down through the aeons of immeasurable antiquity and will bloom as long again— and whether my bills be paid or my letters answered, the red ants will yet march along the rough bark of that old apple tree, this year and the next and a million to come. In this fashion do the green long-lying hills and the deep snows of winter and the thunder storms of summer subdue to their proper stature the little worries and fribbling irritations that bulk so large in bedeviling my city-dwelling friends.

To those who inquire what I *do* in the country, it seems always to come as startling intelligence that I pass long hours of every day in walking. The country now is the only place in which it is still feasible to practice this venerable means of locomotion, and the walking which I do is solely for the joyousness of doing it—of placing one foot before the other upon the surface of the globe. Digging my heels into the mud or the loam or the moss, prodding at roots with my toe, jumping brooks, scrambling up hills—these, to me, are among the incomparable ecstasies of existence. On my walks I am able to meet and greet all my companions of this countryside—the trout and cabbage butterflies and tadpoles and hawks who are my fellow-dwellers in this section of the planet. With the aid of my two legs I can clamber up mountains and learn the feel of them, and I can scrabble in the beds of streams and look upon the moist infinitesimal particle of silt. And in this process of walking there is worked a certain magic not unlike that of my friend who speaks his troubles into a hole; out of the clasp of my fingers around the rough wood of my stick, out of the brushing of low leaves against my forehead as I pass, out of the warmth of the summer sun on my hair or the soft tenacious clinging of spider webs, there is woven a spell that banishes the whole horde of my small human worries and uncertainties and makes me companion to all the world of inanimate and speechless beings who accept their cosmic destinies in serene passivity.

Night has fallen on the writing of these lines. Where earlier was a broad meadow, glowing with the little flowers of devil's paint-brush and a-hum with furry bumblebees shouldering their way through the high grass, there is now only a void of warm and fragrant darkness, undisturbed by any sound save the sibilance of a tiny breeze and the clump-thump of two Jersey cows invisibly pasturing. From far away on the other side of the meadow, beyond the brook and beyond the line of ancient willows, I can hear the reedy trilling of the tree toads, presaging rain. And very close at hand—perhaps in the purple lilac which is just outside my window—a cricket chirps at intervals. There are no sounds but these in all this limitless ocean of the night. But in the warm darkness there lie, I know, long rounded ridges of motionless mountain, which have lain thus—with tall hemlocks upon their summits and gray lichen-covered rocks upon their sides—through epochs of incalculable number, and which will lie there still tomorrow. I am sure my city friends would think it very lonely here to-night.

Alan Devoe, *Phudd Hill* (New York: Julian Messner, 1937).

A PLACE FOR
REGIONALISM?

David C. Pierce and Richard C. Wiles

L ONGTIME RESIDENTS *of the Hudson Valley, David C. Pierce (1931–), Professor of Religion, and Richard C. Wiles (1934–), Professor of Economics, at Bard College, founded the* Hudson Valley Regional Review, *published there since 1984. Wiles, who continues to edit the journal, is also Director of the Hudson Valley Studies Program. In this joint essay, which inaugurated the review, the authors raise crucial issues in the construction of a regional perspective: what is the meaning of a sense of place? What is its relation to national culture? Region and nation, cosmopolitan and provincial, city and country—these are longstanding oppositions in the lives of nations, frequently used to wield political, cultural, and economic power. Once again they are relevant to contemplate, as the Hudson Valley confronts new environmental and economic challenges and evolving demographics.*

Pierce and Wiles present a dynamic view of societies in their belief that national cultural, social, and economic forces cannot be separated in any understanding of regional life. They rightly caution against nostalgia or isolation from larger world contexts. Recent global events have demonstrated the interconnection and mobility of peoples around the world, forcing new alliances in such diverse areas as the university, international finance, military strategy, and cultural exchange. Nonetheless, these political upheavals have equally proved how strong and deep is the need for local attachments rooted in the historical memory of a community over time. Attempts to define concepts such as identity and

*home, in a world of shifting populations and borders, have
grown more and more problematic.*

*As enormous transformations in world cultures are making Ameri-
cans see themselves in a global context, simultaneously there
is a growing interest nationwide in local history, historic restoration,
and conservation of local natural resources. For a region that
had been colonized as early as the seventeenth century, the Hudson
Valley is surprisingly underrepresented in American history books.
There are histories—of the arts, of social life, of industry, of horticulture—that have yet to be written. The current rediscovery
and reassessment of the Hudson River School of painting is perhaps
the first subject to reflect evolving contemporary attitudes
toward Hudson Valley culture and its relationship to the national
culture.*

THE DEBATE CONCERNING the meaning and usefulness of a "regional
approach" has been common in American intellectual life for well
over a century. The fields of history, literature, art and political and
social relations have, at one time or another, been invaded by such
discussions. Pros and cons of the desirability of a national culture,
literature or history fill the pages of American historical analysts and
literary historians. Much of the discussion stems from an attempt to
cope with the levelling tendencies of socio-economic phenomena in
the forms of growth of large scale industrialization and communication technologies. These themes rise and decline in cyclical pattern
over our national development. In recent years the discussion has
taken on new currency with the fear of the possible homogenization
of American culture and the consequent blurring of regional differences and characteristics.

Such debates, as current as they may be today, or as common as
they have been in the past, are most likely irresolvable. However, the
forums they have created and still create are the valuable elements in
such discussions. The fact that the topic recurs points to the fact
that regionalism has appeal and usefulness for the American public.

To begin this task it is worth asking once again: is there a place for regionalism? There is surely much that seems to necessitate a negative reply to this question. The long-term direction of our historical development has clearly been characterized by a shift away from the circumscribed social, political and economic horizons of village, town and province which defined much of the world over most of its history. Take, for example, E. J. Hobsbawm's description of Europe on the eve of the French Revolution. The world of 1789, he reminds us, was "at once much smaller and much larger than ours." It was smaller because population was a fraction of that of the contemporary world and the "area of effective human settlement" was less. But it was also smaller geographically because so little was known even by the best informed about much of that world. Yet if the world of 1789 was more limited in these respects, "the sheer difficulty or uncertainty of communications made it in practice much vaster than it is today."

Our world is less circumscribed than that of two centuries ago and less separated, less localized and more thoroughly centralized and integrated. In the political sphere, the nineteenth century witnessed the rise of the modern nation-state equipped with an effective bureaucracy capable of replacing the plurality of local and provincial powers with centralized and rationalized programs of political management. The United States moved somewhat more slowly in this direction. As late as the 1830's Tocqueville could note the astonishing absence of the signs of central government encountered in his travels, but the Civil War gave powerful impetus to the expansion of the instruments of centralized decision making, and the increasing demand for economic and industrial regulation by the end of the century prepared the way for the well-developed state and federal bureaucracies of twentieth-century America.

This shift in political power accompanied a corresponding movement in business and industry toward consolidation, a movement that was only beginning to get underway in 1789. The outcome was the dissolution of localized cottage industries, the breakdown of local systems of supply and consumption and the shift of population to industrial centers. Here again, the general movement is from smaller scale to large scale both in terms of enterprise and social organization. Moreover, economic horizons were not only being increasingly nationalized but internationalized as well. At mid-century Marx could declare: "In place of the old local, and national seclusion and self-sufficiency, we have intercourse in every direction, universal interdependence of nations."

Subsequent events have done nothing to diminish the significance of that claim. Our economy is truly global and the lines of our interdependence are only reinforced from day to day. The nails with which we build are from China or Yugoslavia, our clothing from Hong Kong, our electronic devices have been to Indonesia and back. American commerce spans the world in equal fashion as do Americans themselves. We are a mobile people and have been long on the move, as we are reminded by legend and story, as well as by our own passage from place to place, and the vast spread of our family connections about this continent and the world. We are "at home" in many areas. We may know Delhi as well as Detroit.

Our culture has in similar fashion been internationalized. Its ingredients are drawn from Africa and Asia, Latin America and the entire constellation of European peoples from Scandinavia to Spain and Ireland to Russia. Truly, that "Passage to India" which Whitman foretold with its global encirclement of cultural and material bonds has become reality. The spiritual traditions of India, the poetry of Japan are as much a part of our contemporary cultural inheritance as are the leisurely, expansive verses of Whitman himself.

Human society has, of course, rarely been *wholly* circumscribed by place or entirely isolated from outside influence. There were "international markets" in the second millennium B.C. and on the trading vessels and caravans of every epoch since have travelled ideas, stories and beliefs as well as cloth, pottery and spices. But until recently the distances were enormous, the time required formidable and the impact of these commodities and utterances counterbalanced by the weight of tradition and the durability of ties to family and soil. The horizon remained localized but it is no longer. The outcome is the blurring of that which is near at hand as we focus on more distant affairs and the erosion of the older ties to particular places and institutions as we find ourselves increasingly citizens of the nation and of the world. What point then in reopening the question of regionalism?

To begin with the essential: the local is the point of departure for all life. Even the most volatile mobility cannot wholly exempt us from the necessity of being *somewhere*, at some *time* and in some given set of conditions. For most of us, however long our lines of communication and cosmopolitan our knowledge and experience, we are more or less habitually inhabitants of a place. This conviction indeed constitutes a rich and continuing theme of American thought. Eudora Welty once argued with eloquence the importance of "place" for the novelist in a manner which applies as much to everyday life as it does to fiction. Such self-identity as we experience and much more of our experience is attained by participation in the near at hand. "Place," she said, "is the named, identified, concrete, exact and exacting . . . gathering-spot of all that has been felt, is about to be experienced. . . ." John Dewey, in his own extended reflections on the shape and dynamic of human experience insisted, in a similar way, upon the important depth and breadth of the immediate. Typically, when Dewey turned his attention to the problems of a fragmented society, he found an answer in the possibility of linking social inquiry to the art of communication and communication, he was convinced, rested upon "the vital, steady, and deep relationships which are present only within the immediate community." "The local," he said, "is the ultimate universal, and as near an absolute as exists." We must, said William Carlos Williams, "make a start, out of particulars. . . ."

But the local, for all this, is not enough. It is necessary but not sufficient for place comes to be what it is only in some larger pattern of matters and concerns. Let us return to the question of place. Place is, first of all, geo-physical. We find ourselves in some particular place on the earth. But that particular place, be it town, urban neighborhood or whatever else might be circumscribed by our habitual and familiar intimacy, is itself *placed* in a surrounding environment which contributes distinctiveness and definition to our particular locale. This is true whether that place is urban or rural. Manhattan is part of a geological configuration, including rock, river and sea, that extends in every direction and which not only defines that metropolis as an island with all the consequences for concentrated urban development but also as part of a larger system of geological formation, including mountains and rivers and climatic conditions bearing upon the possibility of life in that city. The local geo-physical circumstances lead out to wider contexts and are, in turn, situated in that context. We recognize this shared circumstance when we speak of "Sun-Belt" or "Mountain-States" or of the Mississippi or Hudson Valleys. These regions are, of course, bound up in larger geo-physical systems but this does not annul the durable characteristics of each particular environment. What must be observed is that "places" and "regions" will only rarely be well defined in terms of geographic boundaries. The edges overlap and become the matter of yet other places and regions and all will be part of yet larger systems of earth and climate. There will always be a vagueness at the periphery and there will always be particularity at the "center" of any regional perspective.

On this geo-physical base will be constructed the economic lives of the people. Out of the material resources of soil, vegetation and mineral deposits comes the means of livelihood, at least in the first instance, and upon such resources will be built the characteristic social and political possibilities of the local community. We are farmers, mechanics, shopkeepers, bankers as the place offers such possibilities to be realized in and through our labor. Here again the local is linked to a larger context. The economic life of the local area is bound up with that round about in profound mutual interdependence. The linkages between the earth and economic and social opportunities are not always obvious but they are rarely entirely absent. Services, labor supply, markets, natural resources, energy supply and even geographic ambience all unite local enterprise to wider circles of business and industry in the region.

Such interdependence is recognized by the presence of various agencies and programs which have for many decades directed their efforts to environmental, energy resource, recreational and health care planning on a regional basis. Not all such efforts have been wisely conceived and executed. "Regionalism," as Harvey Flad has observed, "has its limits." Too many examples of large-scale regional schemes remind us of their capacity to ride roughshod over local communities. Yet their very existence underlines the fact that we do live, for better or worse, as participants in regional systems, even as we live in the immediacies and contours of a particular place.

But a region is not only a thing of geographic, economic and political inter-relations, it is an embodiment of historical continuity as well. Thus Lewis Mumford:

> Local history implies the history of larger communities to a much greater extent than national history implies the local community. Every great event sweeps over the country like a wave; but it leaves its deposit behind in the life of the locality; and meanwhile that life goes on, with its own special history, its own special interests.

But such "deposits" of larger historical events as well as the "special history" of the locality represent choices made, causes pursued, courses followed. They possess for us a humanly recognizable shape insofar as earlier communities of men and women have shared in their making. Their historical labors will be reflected in the very reshaping of the topography and its record of economic activity but these labors will also be reflected in the literature, art and architecture of the region as well as its social institutions. The geographical world has been transformed, certain economic possibilities have been given priority, society has evolved in a given way, the imagination has taken certain distinctive shapes and forms. All this is part of the definition of a region as an historical and, therefore, a human achievement, a realization of values and worth.

"In the absence of perspective there is triviality," remarked Alfred North Whitehead. History helps to grant such perspective. It is a continual reminder that we are citizens of a larger community, that the shape we give to our world matters beyond the moment and to others beyond our generation, that as we live always out of the past so we live toward a future. Thus history points to our sense of relationship through time. The point of convergence between a region's history and the present occasion is the point at which a regional perspective commences for it is here that we begin to see ourselves and our community as genuine participants in a pattern of conditions, interests and events which are in some measure shared. It is this conscious grasp of the temporal context of the present moment as well as of the spatial spread of the particular place that constitutes the heart of a regional perspective.

Since this perspective is an evaluation, a personal appreciation, it cannot be taken to be an empirical entity. Is the Hudson Valley to be defined geographically as the River and the Mountains, i.e., the Catskills, the Highlands, and the Taconics? Do the economic and the commercial uses of this topography over the years give us a unified area of treatment? Or is a region defined as having had a common historical past—Dutch settlement, English development, political and ethnic heritage? Do architectural continuity and social patterns denote a region?

So-called regional writers abound in nineteenth and early twentieth-century American literature. But is the setting of a novel or series of paintings in the Hudson Valley enough to guarantee the regional sense we seek? One must distinguish between what used to be called "local color" and true regionalism. Is a liberal sprinkling of local scenes and place names in a novel enough to qualify a work as a regional one? Does a canvas that depicts a mountain that all can recognize and identify make the artist a regional one? These various attempts to provide a single definition are bound to fall short.

Here it is useful to speak of a "sense" of the region as something more than merely an inventory of its bounds, topography and socio-economic features. This "sense" cannot be imposed in any preordained manner. It is in many respects a personal response to the geographic presence of a place, its cumulative history and the pressure of present circumstances. In our opinion this "sense" is already present in a region's inhabitants—both natives and newcomers. Some have it to a greater or lesser extent. It must, in many cases, be elicited from them. What is elicited will no doubt be marked by infinite variety for there will of necessity be a multitude of perspectives upon the region as there are many places and persons. This is why diversity—one could say fragmented reponses—is of the substance of regionalism. If diversity is absent, then richness, complexity and variety are lost in nostalgia and parochialism. The region will not be a unified concept but a many-faceted way of interaction with place and circumstance.

* * *

Examples, perhaps, can bring us as close to this "feel" as is possible; the work of Mari Sandoz about her native Sand Hills area of Nebraska is a case in point. The sense of place in her *Love Song to the Plains* is perhaps a prime example of what we seek. This is no simple local color. It is instead a non-self conscious treatment of and feeling for a region. In our Hudson Valley, John Burroughs' writing of the irresistible pull of his boyhood hills in the western Catskills is a fine example. Sarah Orne Jewett's Maine comes alive for similar reasons.

But such a sense is not reserved for natives, life-long residents, or the expatriate returned. If this were the case, one would have a difficult time distinguishing such writings from that ever present danger to true regionalism—nostalgia. In many ways the region is in the individual author, artist, or historian. Effective regional writing often is an intensely personal response to a physical place—but not so personal that a reader or viewer cannot identify with it at least to a small extent. A work of Richard Jeffries, the English naturalist, called *Story of My Soul,* would seem at first glance to be an intense, almost solipsistic treatment of faith. Yet the work is permeated by a sense of his region, Sussex in England, that is presented in his other writings explicitly to his reader; yet never more powerfully than in his highly philosophical response. A look at writing of the Hudson Valley over the past may bring to light our own Jeffries.

While literature and art may be the most obvious place to seek this more qualitative response to regional settings, historical work can also provide it. Yet, it is rare. Regional historical work has often been too riveted to the locale and many times degenerates into a dry collection of facts. Regional history, if done well, transcends the local; it amalgamates and the whole is far greater than the sum of its parts. It also incorporates regional responses to national (or extra-regional) events. Perhaps New England historians and those from the South and West have done this most effectively in the past. In the opinion of David Maldwyn Ellis it remains to be accomplished for our region, a part of what he called in 1954 the "forgotten region." We are fortunate here because of the existence of one of the finest histories of a region in contemporary writing—Alf Evers' work on the Cats-kills. Few readers can come away from Evers' book without a recognition of the fact that Evers feels for the Catskills what Sandoz felt for the Sand Hills, or Jewett or Celia Thaxter felt for the coast of Maine. It is a seminal work—a model that can be carried, one hopes, to the broader reaches of the Hudson Valley.

The search for a regional "sense" or definition should not seek isolation, division nor a smug, self-conscious provincialism. "One place comprehended can make us understand other places better. Sense of place gives equilibrium: extended it is a sense of direction too," argued Eudora Welty. In one of the finest essays on the contrasts between regional awareness versus provincialism, Josiah Royce, the American philosopher, maintained that the former need not automatically lead to the latter, i.e., provincialism in the sense of exclusionism and elitism. Such a dichotomy has often been posed in terms of a conflict between the country and the city or metropole and province. These distinctions themselves are often the result of a "provincial" attitude. As Royce wrote: "In the sense of possessing local interests and customs, and of being limited to ideas of their own, many great cities are almost as distinctly provincial as are certain less populous regions." For Royce, regional identification need not be an exercise in parochialism, but an important identifying factor in a world that, in his mind, was tending toward the homogeneous. Royce boldly asserts his thesis: "In the present state of the world's civilization, and of the life of our own country, the time has come to emphasize, with a new meaning and intensity, the positive value, the absolute necessity for our welfare, of a wholesome provincialism, as a saving power to which the world in the near future will need more and more to appeal." And in a tone reminiscent of much of the writing of social critics in recent years, Royce continues: "The nation by itself, apart from the influence of the province, is in danger of becoming an incomprehensible monster, in whose presence the individual loses his right, his self-consciousness, and his dignity. The province must save the individual." This was written in 1902.

While we need not go so far in our claims, a sense of the region is attainable and desirable. But let each take what they will from the attempt at such a definition. We do seek an image drawn from the literature, art and history of the region; but an image that does not connote a conservatism in the worst sense of that term. A certain defensiveness must, by definition, be present; yet not the defensiveness in as strong a sense as that developed in the image of the South in American literature—*I'll Take My Stand,* published in 1930 by Donald Davidson, John Crowe Ransom, Robert Penn Warren, Alan Tate *et al.* In many ways, their "stand" involved an anti-industrial, pro-agrarian response to many of the same national tendencies that Royce feared. In the process of this the Southern past they constructed may not have existed at any time, a problem with many attempts at regionalism. As Davidson himself wrote some years after the statement of the "Twelve Southerners": "The writer of a given region cannot shut himself away under the name 'Regionalist'; but he must, from his region, confront the total and moving world."

David C. Pierce and Richard C. Wiles, *Hudson Valley Regional Review* 1, no. 1 (March 1984), Annandale-on-Hudson, N.Y.: Bard College Center.

ﾞﾉﾟｻｾﾞｻｾﾞｻｾﾞｻｾﾞｻｾﾞｻｾﾞｻｾﾞｻｾﾞｻｾﾞｻｾﾞｻ

HUDSON RIVER SIGHTS

Walt Whitman

I*F SOME MEN lamented the intrusion of Progress into
the natural world, Walt Whitman (1819–92) gloried in the
new technological achievements which outlined for him the democratic vistas of America's future. Here is the poet on a spring
day, celebrating the rhythms of the Hudson, in the long, lyrical line
of joy that has come to be called* Whitmanesque. *"I see, hear . . ."
Whitman had just spent a week with John Burroughs and his wife
at Riverby, which was to be the last of his trips there. Of that
visit with the man he so loved Burroughs wrote in his own journal, "April days with Homer and Socrates for company." In autobiographical jottings on excursions up the Hudson, published in
his fragmentary collection* Specimen Days, *Whitman exulted in
jaunts on the steamers, the fragrant air, bird song, a waterfall,
wildflowers, meetings with local characters, and picking rasp-
berries.*

*Burroughs was twenty-six when he met Whitman, nursing the
Civil War wounded, in Washington in 1863. Later, he wrote a
study of the author in which he announced, prophetically, "I pre-
dict a great future for Whitman, because the world is so unmis-
takably going his way." In the young country coming into its own
as a culture, Whitman was creating the idea of an American
literature, as Thomas Cole helped create an American painting.
Burroughs declared that the great currents of the century swept
through Whitman's work, namely, science, religion, democracy,
humanitarianism.*

There were other currents lighting up Whitman's body electric, those founded on the populist philosophies promoted by none other than Orson S. Fowler of octagon home renown. In his thirties Whitman fell under the spell of Fowler's homilies on personal magnetism, diet, sex, exercise, and, of course, phrenology. He was a frequent visitor to Fowler's "Phrenological Cabinet" in New York City, transferred some of the science's beliefs into his poetry, and published in the Fowler family newspaper, Life Illustrated. *Incidentally, the Fowlers were one of the distributors of the original edition of* Leaves of Grass, *in 1855.*

Whitman's search for his long song of the self took him in many directions, into the realms of both city and country life, but wherever he was he had that matchless gift of knowing how to breathe life into the description of an image. He left his spirit in the Hudson Valley at John Burroughs's Slabsides, which was eventually built after Whitman's death, near a forest of hemlock whose primeval solitude the poet had praised. Burroughs referred to the place as Whitman Land—*"elemental ruggedness, savageness, and grandeur, combined with wonderful tenderness, modernness, and geniality."*

✄

IT WAS A HAPPY thought to build the Hudson river railroad right along the shore. The grade is already made by nature; you are sure of ventilation one side—and you are in nobody's way. I see, hear, the locomotives and cars, rumbling, roaring, flaming, smoking, constantly, away off there, night and day—less than a mile distant, and in full view by day. I like both sight and sound. Express trains thunder and lighten along; of freight trains, most of them very long, there cannot be less than a hundred a day. At night far down you see the headlight approaching, coming steadily on like a meteor. The river at night has its special character-beauties. The shad fishermen go forth in their boats and pay out their nets—one sitting forward rowing, and one standing up aft dropping it properly—marking the line with little floats bearing candles, conveying, as they glide over the water, an indescribable sentiment and doubled brightness. I like to watch the tows at night, too, with their twinkling lamps, and hear the husky panting of the steamers; or catch the sloops' and schooners' shadowy forms, like phantoms, white, silent, indefinite, out there. Then the Hudson of a clear moonlight night.

But there is one sight the very grandest. Sometimes in the fiercest driving storm of wind, rain, hail or snow, a great eagle will appear over the river, now soaring with steady and now overhended wings—always confronting the gale, or perhaps cleaving into, or at times literally *sitting* upon it. It is like reading some first-class natural tragedy or epic, or hearing martial trumpets. The splendid bird enjoys the hubbub—is adjusted and equal to it—finishes it so artistically. His pinions just oscillating—the position of his head and neck—his resistless, occasionally varied flight—now a swirl, now an upward movement—the black clouds driving—the angry wash below—the hiss of rain, the wind's piping (perhaps the ice colliding, grunting) —he tacking or jibing—now, as it were, for a change, abandoning himself to the gale, moving with it with such velocity—and now, resuming control, he comes up against it, lord of the situation and the storm—lord, amid it of power and savage joy.

Sometimes (as at present writing,) middle of sunny afternoon, the old "Vanderbilt" steamer stalking ahead—I plainly hear her rhythmic, slushing paddles—drawing by long hawsers an immense and varied following string, ("an old sow and pigs," the river folks call it.) First comes a big barge, with a house built on it, and spars towering over the roof; then canal boats, a lengthen'd, clustering train, fasten'd and link'd together—the one in the middle, with high staff, flaunting a broad and gaudy flag—others with the almost invariable lines of new-wash'd clothes, drying; two sloops and a schooner aside the tow—little wind, and that adverse—with three long, dark empty barges bringing up the rear. People are on the boats: men lounging, women in sun-bonnets, children, stovepipes with streaming smoke.

Walt Whitman, *Specimen Days & Collect* (Philadelphia: David McKay, 1882–83).

AMERICAN SCENERY

Thomas Cole

T HOMAS COLE (1801–48), sketch book in hand, was
*frequently "in search of the picturesque" views admired in his
day for their aesthetic qualities. By the time he settled in the village
of Catskill in 1836, the British-born Cole had already painted
the spectacular wilderness around the Catskill Mountain House,
Kaaterskill Falls, and North Lake. Catskill itself welcomed many
travelers to its long dock where they would board a stagecoach for
the adventurous journey up the side of the mountain to the
hotel that virtually inhabited the sublime. Cole's landscape painting,
a highly successful alternative to portrait painting which dominated American art then, helped to create the taste for landscape
in the decades before mid-century. In this historical moment,
the beginnings of tourism coincided with American Romanticism.
It also marked the birth of the Hudson River School of painting, the most significant and long-lasting contribution of the Valley to the arts in America. The Hudson River School, as it came
to be called in the 1870s, did not simply define a style, its sprawling
landscapes embodied an entire ethos of a region, even more
so, a country.*

*Cole's paintings venerated the unspoiled landscape around him,
with its religious and moral overtones and primeval strength.
In a funeral oration for Cole, his great friend William Cullen Bryant—
the two are the subject of Asher B. Durand's well-known painting
Kindred Spirits—said of the painter's works, "It hardly transcends
the proper use of language to call them acts of religion." For
Cole, America was still the Garden of Eden, and everywhere he saw*

*God, the Creator. Though today the pleasures of mountain sce-
nery are described in somewhat more secular tones, nevertheless,
the Arcadian theme underlies contemporary descriptions of trips
to the mountains, as do their other profoundly spiritual, purifying
allusions which have historical links to Romanticism, and to
nature writing, in this country. The persistent theme, undeveloped
nature in contest with technological progress, was a subject that
inspired Cole throughout his life, and with special urgency in the
years before the Civil War, when the United States was expanding
so fiercely, economically and culturally. His remarkable* The Course
of Empire *series of paintings addressed this conflict in the historical, allegorical mode of the artist's heroic canvases.*

*But Cole was not entirely opposed to the inevitable process of
development in the America of his day. Like other writers and artists in this period, the architect Downing, for instance, he hoped
for the eventual cultivation of taste and refinement that comes with
age and experience, so that people could live in harmony with nature. Many of Cole's thoughts on art and nature are expressed in
the lecture offered here, which he delivered seven years before his
death at the Catskill Lyceum, not far from his home on Spring Street,
facing the soft blue outline of the mountains. A century and a half
ago he spoke of the careless destruction of local scenic spots on
the banks of the Hudson. But overall Cole celebrated American scenery in passionate comparisons with European scenery, quite a common subject at a time when the young country had constantly to
defend its wildness and lack of cultivation against the Old World's
picturesque elegance. The Hudson River itself was tirelessly compared
to the Rhine in the travel accounts of Americans and Europeans.
No less than James Fenimore Cooper had already conceded the
"noblest" scenery to Europe. Cole knew European scenery
first hand. He had traveled twice to Europe, and was deeply
moved by the styles of Claude Lorrain and Salvator Rosa.*

*Notwithstanding, his adopted country offered Cole singular pleas-
ures no longer possible on the continent. "The painter of American scenery has indeed privileges superior to any other; all nature
is new to Art," he exulted in his journal of 1835. For the Romantic Cole, that opportunity suggested the perfect perspective.*

⚜

IT IS GENERALLY admitted that the liberal arts tend to soften our manners; but they do more—they carry within them the power to mend our hearts. Poetry and painting sublime and purify thought, and rural nature is full of the same quickening spirit; it is in fact the exhaustless mine from which the poet and painter have brought such wondrous treasures—an unfailing fountain of intellectual enjoyment where all may drink and be awakened to a deeper feeling of the works of genius, a deeper perception of the beauty of our existence, and a more profound reverence for the Creator of all things.

> Heaven's roof to them
> Is but a painted ceiling hung with lamps;
> No more—that lights them to their purposes—
> They wander loose about; they nothing see,
> Themselves except, and creatures like themselves,
> Short lived, short sighted.

What to them is the page of the poet where he describes or personifies the skies, the mountains, or the streams, if those objects themselves have never awakened observation or excited pleasure? What to them is the wild Salvator Rosa or the aerial Claude Lorrain?

There is in the human mind an almost inseparable connexion between the beautiful and the good, so that if we contemplate the one, the other seems present; and an excellent author has said "it is difficult to look at any object with pleasure, unless where it arises from brutal and tumultuous emotions, without feeling that disposition of mind which tends towards kindness and benevolence; and surely, whatever creates such a disposition, by increasing our pleasures and enjoyments, cannot be too much cultivated."

It would seem unnecessary to those who can see and feel for me to expatiate on the loveliness of verdant fields, the sublimity of lofty mountains, or the varied magnificence of the sky; but that the number of those who *seek* enjoyment in such sources is comparatively small. From the indifference with which the multitude regard the beauties of nature, it might be inferred that she had been unnecessarily lavish in adorning this world for beings who take no pleasure in its adornment, who, in grovelling pursuits, forget their glorious heritage. Why was the earth made so beautiful, or the sun so clad in glory at his rising and setting, when *all* might be unrobed of beauty without affecting the insensate multitude, so they can be "lighted to their purposes."

It *has not* been in vain—the good, the enlightened in all ages and nations have found pleasure and consolation in the beauty of the rural earth. Prophets of old retired into the solitudes of nature to wait the inspiration of heaven. It was on Mount Horeb that Elijah witnessed the mighty wind, the earthquake and the fire and heard the "still small voice"; that voice is YET heard among the mountains! St. John preached in the desert; the wilderness is YET a fitting place to speak to God. The solitary anchorites of Syria and Egypt, though ignorant that the busy world is man's noblest sphere of usefulness, well knew how congenial to religious musings are the pathless solitudes.

He who looks on nature with a "loving eye" cannot move from his dwelling without the salutation of beauty; even in the city, the deep blue sky and drifting clouds appeal to him. And if to escape its turmoil; if only to obtain a free horizon, in the mere play of light and shadow over land and water, he finds delight; but let him be transported to those favored regions, where the features of the earth are more varied, or yet add the sunset, that wreath of glory bound around the world, and he indeed drinks pleasure from a purer cup than avarice or ambition have the power to give. The delight, such a man experiences, is not merely sensual, or selfish, that passes with the occasion and leaves no trace behind; but in gazing on the pure creations of the Almighty, he feels a calm religious tone steal through his mind, and when he has turned to mingle with his fellow-men, the chords which have been struck in that sweet communion cease not to vibrate.

In what has been said, I have in general alluded to wild and uncultivated scenery; but the cultivated must not be forgotten, for it is still more important to man in his social capacity; it encompasses our homes, and though devoid of the stern sublimity of the wild, its quieter spirit steals tenderly into our bosoms, mingled with a thousand domestic affections and heart-touching associations human hands have wrought and human deeds hallowed all around. And it is here that taste, which is the perception of the beautiful and the knowledge of the principles on which nature works, can be applied and our dwelling places made fitting for refined and intellectual beings.

If, then, it is indeed true that the contemplation of scenery can be so abundant a source of delight and improvement, a taste for it is certainly worthy of particular cultivation; for the capacity for enjoyment will assuredly increase with study and knowledge.

In this age, when a meagre utilitarianism seems ready to absorb every feeling and sentiment, and what is called improvement, in its march, makes us fear that the bright and tender flowers of the imagination will be crushed beneath its iron tramp, it would be well to cultivate the oasis that yet remains to us, and to cherish the impressions that nature is ever ready to give, as an antidote to the sordid tendencies of modern civilization. The spirit of our society is to contrive and not to enjoy—toiling in order to produce more toil—accumulating in order to aggrandize.

The pursuits and pleasures of taste, among which the love of scenery holds a conspicuous place, will serve to temper the harshness of such a state, and like the atmosphere that softens the most rugged forms of landscape, cast a veil of tender beauty over the asperities of life.

Did our limits permit, I would endeavor more fully to show how necessary to the complete appreciation of the fine arts is the study of scenery, and how conducive to our happiness and well being is that study and those arts.

There are those who, through ignorance or prejudice, strive to maintain that American scenery possesses little that is interesting or truly beautiful; that it is rude without picturesqueness, and monotonous without sublimity; that being destitute of the vestiges of antiquity, which so strongly affect the mind, it may not be compared with European scenery. But from whom do these opinions come? From those who have read of Grecian mountains and Italian skies, and never troubled themselves to look at their own? from those travelled ones whose eyes were never opened to the beauties of nature until they beheld foreign lands, and when those lands faded from the sight, were again closed forever? disdaining to destroy their transatlantic impressions by the observation of the unfamed and less fashionable American scenery? Let such persons shut themselves up in their narrow shell of prejudice. I hope they are few, and that the community, increasing in intelligence, will know better how to appreciate the treasures of their own country.

I am by no means desirous of lessening in your estimation the glorious scenes of the old world; that ground which has been the great theatre of human events; those mountains, woods and streams, made sacred in our minds by heroic deeds and immortal song; over which time and genius have suspended an imperishable halo. No! But I would have it remembered that nature has shed over *this* land beauty and magnificence, and although the character of its scenery may differ from the old world's, yet inferiority must not therefore be inferred; for though American scenery is destitute of many of those circumstances that give value to the European, still it has features, and noble ones, unknown to Europe. A very few generations have passed away since this vast tract of the American continent, now the United States, rested in the shadow of primeval forests, whose gloom was peopled by savage beasts and scarcely less savage men; or lay in those wide, grassy plains called the prairies—

> The gardens of the desert these
> The unshorn fields, boundless and beautiful.

And though an enlightened and increasing people have broken in upon the solitude, and with activity and power wrought changes that seem magical, yet the most distinctive, and perhaps, the most impressive, characteristic of American scenery, is its wilderness.

It is the most distinctive, because in Europe the primitive features of scenery have long since been destroyed or modified—the extensive forests that once overshadowed a great part of it have been felled; rugged mountains have been smoothed, and impetuous rivers turned from their course to accommodate the tastes and necessities of a dense population; the once tangled wood is now a grassy lawn; the turbulent brook a navigable stream; crags that could not be removed have been crowned with towers, and the rudest valleys tamed by the plough.

And to this cultivated state our western world is fast approaching; but nature is still predominant, and there are those who regret that with the improvements of cultivation the sublimity of the wilderness must pass away; for those scenes of solitude from which the hand of nature has never been lifted, affect the mind with more deep-toned emotion than aught which the hand of man has touched. Amid them the consequent associations are of God, the Creator; they are his undefiled works, and the mind is cast into the contemplation of eternal things. As mountains are the most conspicuous objects in landscape, they will take the precedence in which I may say on the elements of American scenery.

It is true that in the eastern part of this continent there are no mountains that vie in altitude with the snow-covered Alps; that the Alleghenies and the Catskills are not higher than four or five thousand feet; but this is no inconsiderable height. Ben Nevis in Scotland and Snowdon in Wales are not more lofty; and in New-Hampshire the White Mountains, in our own state the Adirondacks almost pierce the region of eternal snow. The Alleghenies are in general heavy in form: but the Catskills, though not broken and serrated like the most picturesque mountains of Italy, have varied, undulating and exceedingly beautiful outlines; they heave from the valley of the Hudson like the subsiding billows of the ocean after a storm.

American mountains are generally clothed to the summit by dense forests, while those of Europe are mostly bare, or merely tinted by grass and heath. It may be that the mountains of Europe are on this account more picturesque in form, and there is a grandeur in their nakedness; but in the gorgeous garb of the American mountains there is more than an equivalent; and when the woods "have put their glory on," as an American poet has beautifully said, the purple heath and yellow furze of Europe's mountains are in comparison but as the faint secondary rainbow to the primal one.

But in the Adirondacks of this state and the White Mountains of New-Hampshire, there is a union of the picturesque, the sublime, and the magnificent; there are the bare peaks of granite, broken and desolate, cradle the clouds; while the valleys and broad bases of the mountains rest under the shadow of noble and varied forests; and the traveller who passes the Sandwich range on his way to the White Mountains, of which it is a spur, cannot but acknowledge, that although in some regions of the world nature has wrought on a more stupendous scale, yet she has nowhere so completely married together gradeur and loveliness; there he sees the sublime melting into the beautiful, the savage tempered by the magnificent.

I will now speak of another component of scenery, without which every landscape is defective—it is water. Like the eye in the human countenance, it is a most expressive feature; in the unrippled lake, which mirrors all surrounding objects, we have the expression of tranquility and peace—in the rapid stream—the headlong cataract, that of turbulence and impetuosity. In this great element of scenery what land is so rich?. . . .

The river scenery of the United States is a rich and boundless theme. The Hudson, for natural magnificence, is unsurpassed. What can be more beautiful than the lake-like expanses of Tapaan and Haverstraw as seen from the rich orchards of the surrounding hills? What can be more imposing than the precipitous Highlands, whose dark foundations have been rent to make a passage for the might river? And ascending still, where can be found scenes more enchanting? The lofty Catskills stand afar off; the green hills gently rising from the flood, recede like steps, by which we may ascend to a great temple, whose pillars are those everlasting hills, and whose dome is the blue and boundless vault of heaven. The Rhine has its castled crags, its vine clad hills and ancient villages; the Hudson has its wooded mountains, its rugged precipices, its green undulating shores, and an unbounded capacity for improvement by art. Its shores are not besprinkled by venerable ruins, or the palaces of princes; but there are flourishing towns and neat villas, and the hand of taste has already been at work. Without any great stretch of the imagination, we may anticipate the time when the ample waters will reflect temple and town and dome in every variety of picturesqueness and magnificence. . . .

In the forest scenery of the United States we have that which occupies a vast space, and is not the least remarkable; being primitive, it differs widely from the European. In the American forest we find trees in every stage of growth and decay—the slender sapling rises in the shadow of the lofty tree, and the giant in his prime stands by the hoary patriarch of the wood—on the ground lie prostrate decaying ranks that once moved their verdant heads in the sun and wind. These are circumstances productive of great variety and picturesqueness. Green umbrageous masses; lofty and scathed trunks; contorted branches thrust athwart the sky; the mouldering dead below, shrouded in moss of every hue and texture, form richer combinations than can be found in the trimmed and planted wood. Trees are like men, differing widely in character; in sheltered sports, or under the influence of culture, they show few contrasting points; peculiarities are pruned and trained away until there is a general resemblance. But in exposed situations, wild and uncultivated, battling with the elements and with one another for the possession of a morsel of soil, or a favoring rock to which they may cling—they exhibit striking peculiarities, and sometimes original grandeur.

For variety, the American forest is unrivalled; in some districts are found oaks, elms, birches, beeches, planes, hemlocks, and many other kinds of trees commingled, clothing the hills with every tint of green, and every variety of light and shade. There is a peculiarity observable in some mountainous districts, where trees of a genus band together; there often may be seen a mountain whose foot is clothed with deciduous trees, while on its brow in a sable crown of pines; and sometimes dark belts of pine encircle a mountain horizontally; or are stretched in well defined lines from the summit to the base. The nature of the soil, or the courses of rivulets, are the causes of this variety, and it is a beautiful instance of the exhaustlessness of nature; often where we might expect unvarying monotony, we behold a charming diversity. Time will not permit me to speak of American trees individually; but I must notice the elm, that paragon of beauty and shade; the maple, with its rainbow hues; and the hemlock, the sublime of trees, which rises from the gloom of the forest like a dark and ivy-mantled tower.

There is one season when the American forest surpasses all the world in gorgeousness—that is the autumnal; then every hill and dale is riant in the luxury of color; every hue is there from the liveliest green to the deepest purple, from the most golden yellow to the intensest crimson. The artist looks despairingly on the glowing landscape, and in the old world his truest imitations of the American forest, at this season, are called falsely bright, and scenes in Fairy Land. The sky will next demand our attention. The soul of all scenery, in it are the fountains of light and shade and color. Whatever expression the sky takes, the features of the landscape are affected in unison, whether it be the serenity of the summer's blue, or the dark tumult of the storm. It is the sky that makes the earth so lovely at sunrise, and so splendid at sunset. In the one it breathes over the earth the crystal-like ether, in the other the liquid gold. The climate of a great part of the United States is subject to great vicissitudes, and we complain; but nature offers a compensation. These very vicissitudes are the abundant sources of beauty—as we have the temperature of every clime, so have we the skies; we have the blue unsearchable depths of the northern sky; we have the upheaped thunder-clouds of the torrid zone; we have the silver haze of England and the golden atmosphere of Italy. And if he who travelled and observed the skies of other climes, will spend a few months on the banks of the Hudson, he must be constrained to acknowledge that for variety and magnificence, American skies are unsurpassed. Italian skies have been lauded by every tongue and sung by every poet, and who will deny their wonderful beauty? At sunset the serene arch is filled with alchymy that transmutes mountains, and streams, and temples into living gold. But the American summer never passes without many sunsets that vie with the Italian, and many still more gorgeous, that seem peculiar to this clime. Look at the heavens when the thunder shower has passed, and the sun stoops below the western mountains—then the low purple clouds hang in festoons around the steeps—in the higher heaven are crimson bands interwoven with feathers of gold, fit for the wings of angels; and still above is spread that interminable field of ether, whose color is too beautiful to have a name.

It is not in summer only that American skies are beautiful, for the winter evening often comes robed in purple and gold, and in the westering sun the iced groves glitter as beneath a shower of diamonds—

and through the twilight heaven innumerable stars shine with a purer light than summer ever knows.

I will now venture a few remarks on what has been considered a grand defect in American scenery—the want of associations such as arise amid the scenes of the old world. We have many spots as umbrageous as Vallombrosa, and as picturesque as the solitudes of Vaucluse; but Milton and Petrarch have not hallowed them by their footsteps and immortal verse. He who stands on Mount Albano and looks down on ancient Rome has his mind peopled with the gigantic associations of the storied past; but he who stands on the mounds of the west, the most venerable remains of American antiquity, MAY experience the emotion of the sublime, but it is the sublimity of the shoreless ocean, unislanded by the recorded deeds of man.

Yet American scenes are not destitute of historical and legendary associations; the great struggle for freedom has sanctified many a spot, and many a mountain stream and rock has its legend, worthy of poet's pen or painter's pencil.

But American associations are not so much of the past as of the present and the future. Seated on a pleasant knoll, look down into the bosom of that secluded valley, begirt with wooded hills, through those enamelled meadows and wide waving fields of grain—a silver stream winds lingeringly along—here seeking the green shade of trees—there glancing in the sunshine; on its banks are rural dwellings shaded by elms and garlanded by flowers; from yonder dark mass of foliage the village spire beams like a star. You see no ruined tower to tell of outrage, no gorgeous temple to tell of ostentation; but freedom's offspring—peace and security dwell there, the spirits of the scene. On the margin of that gentle river the village girls may ramble unmolested, and the glad school-boy, with hook and line, pass his bright holiday; those neat dwellings, unpretending to magnificence, are the abodes of plenty. And in looking over the UNCULTIVATED scene, the mind may travel far into futurity. Where the wolf roams, the plough shall glisten; on the gray crag shall rise temple and tower; mighty deeds shall be done in the yet pathless wilderness; and poets yet unborn shall sanctify the soil.

It was my intention to attempt a description of several districts remarkable of their picturesqueness; but I fear to trespass much longer on your time and patience. Yet I cannot but express my sorrow that much of the beauty of our landscapes is quickly passing away; the ravages of the axe are daily increasing, and the most noble scenes are often laid desolate with a wantonness and barbarism scarcely credible in a people who call themselves civilized. The wayside is becoming shadeless, and another generation will behold spots now rife with beauty, bleak and bare. This is a *regret* rather than a complaint. I know, full well, that the forests must be felled for fuel and tillage, and that roads and canals must be constructed, but I contend that beauty should be of *some* value among us; that where it is not NECESSARY to destroy a tree or a grove, the hand of the woodman should be checked, and even the consideration, which alas, weighs too heavily with us, of a few paltry dollars, should be held as nought in comparison with the pure and lasting pleasure that we enjoy, or ought to enjoy, in the objects which are among the most beautiful creations of the Almighty. Among the inhabitants of this village, he must be dull indeed, who has not observed how, within the last ten years, the beauty of its environs has been shorn away; year by year the groves that adorned the banks of the Catskill wasted away; but in one year more fatal than the rest the whole of that noble grove by Van Vechten's mill, through which wound what is called the Snake Road, and at the same time the ancient grove of cedar, that shadowed the Indian burying-ground, were cut down. I speak of these in particular, because I know that many of you remember them well; they have contributed to your enjoyment as well as mine; their shades were long the favorite walk and ride. After my return from Europe, I was proud to speak of that delightful spot, to walk there with my friends, view it, and as we trod the velvet grass beneath those noble trees, and pointed out the distant mountains, and the quiet stream below, to say: This is a spot that in Europe would be considered as one of the gems of the earth; it would be sought for by the lovers of the beautiful, and protected by law from desecration. But its beauty is gone, and that which a century cannot restore is cut down; what remains? Steep, arid banks, incapable of cultivation, and seamed by unsightly gullies, formed by the waters which find no resistance in the loamy soil. Where once was beauty, there is now barrenness. But I will now conclude, and in the hope that, though feebly urged, the importance of cultivating a taste for scenery will not be forgotten. Nature has spread for us a rich and delightful banquet— shall we turn away from it? We are still in Eden; the wall that shuts us out of the garden is our own ignorance and folly.

Thomas Cole, *Northern Light* 1 (May 1841), Albany, N.Y.

THE HUDSON RIVER VALLEY: A BIOREGIONAL STORY

Thomas Berry

F ROM HIS *Center for Religious Research in Riverdale, the Catholic priest Thomas Berry (1914–) pursues his cosmic vision as a historian of cultures, with a special passion for their relationship to the natural world. Berry is one of a growing number of eco-theologians whose provocative reflections on nature are influencing what has been called the greening of religion. "Our human destiny is integral with the destiny of the earth," he writes in his latest book,* The Dream of the Earth. *In the coming ecological age he himself dreams of, Berry envisions an intimate earth community evolving from democracy to a higher level of consciousness called biocracy, which celebrates the presence of all life forms. For Berry, a Professor of Religion before his retirement from Fordham University, and author of works on Vico, and Eastern philosophy, nature itself is the primary text of divine revelation. Like other contemporary writers, Wendell Berry, for example, he questions the detachment of Judeo-Christian doctrine from the reality of the physical world inhabited by humankind. He is fond of reminding readers of their worldliness, and its accompanying "earth responsibilities."*

Berry also shares an affinity with the so-called "deep ecology" of philosophers on the cutting edge of rights of nature issues. Here anthropocentrism is superseded by the more radical biocentric perspective, which embraces the larger life-community in the conduct of world affairs. The large leap of the imagination in this world view is the recognition that natural history is part of the history of the world. Francis of Assisi, Pierre Teilhard de Chardin, Thomas Aquinas, Hinduism, and Buddhism are Berry's reference

*points, and closer to home, Aldo Leopold—one of the most eloquent
American voices to call for the linkage of philosophy and religion in a comprehensive environmental ethics.*

*Berry brings a global cultural perspective to his ecological posi-
tion, localized in this closing selection in the Hudson Valley.
He views it as a bioregion, broadly defined as a geographical area
of interacting life systems—geological, economic, cultural—that
is life-sustaining. His important spiritual contribution to the notion
of place is to encourage a reverence for habitat as sacred space,
and for the universe as an elaborate ongoing story of wonder. In
this sense, Berry lends mythic stature to the great narrative of
Creation, and a certain epic grandeur to the story of the Hudson
River Valley. His bioregionalism, a growing ecological concern
in America, outlines the shape of its emerging narrative. Prompted
by his desire to see a real spiritual bonding between people and
the land, Berry poses the kinds of questions that will increase in
significance in the coming decades as the region, even more
so the country itself, struggles with issues of cultural identity: what
does it mean to be a river people, a valley people?*

*This then, is the story of a people, and a place that is called the
Hudson River Valley.*

TELL ME A STORY. How often we said that as children. Tell me a story.
Story illumined the world for us in childhood. Even now we might
make the request: tell me a story. Tell me the story of the river and
the valley and the streams and woodlands and wetlands, of the
shellfish and finfish. Tell me a story. A story of where we are and how
we got here and the characters and roles that we play. Tell me a story,
a story that will be my story as well as the story of everyone and
everything about me, the story that brings us together in a valley
community, a story that brings together the human community with
every living being in the valley, a story that brings us together under
the arc of the great blue sky in the day and the starry heavens at night,
a story that will drench us with rain and dry us in the wind, a story

told by humans to one another that will also be the story that the wood thrush sings in the thicket, the story that the river recites in its downward journey, the story that Storm King Mountain images forth in the fullness of its grandeur.

It's a long story, a story that begins with the fracture across the eastern borders of the North American continent resulting from the clashing and rifting of tectonic plates, and it includes the molten intrusion whereby the Palisades emerged to terminate in those massive cracked columns to the west. The story of the great hydrological cycle that has drawn up from the Gulf and across from the Pacific and down from the Arctic and in from the Atlantic entire oceans of water and has poured them down in unending sequence over this region to give to the valley its shape, its fertility, and made of it a meeting place as the northern extreme of southern lifeforms and the southern extreme of northern lifeforms.

The story of the valley is the story of the glaciation that came down from the frigid north as recently as fifty thousand years ago to cover this area with ice more than a thousand feet in height, driving southward the multitude of living beings for some thousands of years and then returning northward some fifteen thousand years ago, leaving this region to take on its present shape and luxuriance of life, its trees and grasses and flowers, its singing birds and ambling bears, its red foxes, pheasants, wild turkeys, and bobolinks.

The story of the valley is also the story of the Indians who originally dwelled in this region. Even now, in the names of the area, we recognize the ghosts of the indigenous peoples: the Mahicans, the Wappinger, the Hackensack and the Raritan, the Kitawonks, the Tappans across the river, the Sinsinks of the Ossining area. These names of earlier tribes carry a mysterious abiding quality. As Chief Seattle once said of us and our cities: "When the last Red Man shall have perished, and the memory of the tribe shall have become a myth among the White Men, these shores will swarm with the invisible dead of my tribe, and when your children's children think themselves alone in the field, the store, the shop, upon the highway, or in the silence of the pathless woods, they will not be alone." Chief Seattle then continues with a profound insight into the enduring trauma being shaped in the psychic depths of the white man: "At night, when the streets of your cities and villages are silent and you think them deserted, they will throng with the returning hosts that once filled them and still love this beautiful land. The White Man will never be alone."

These voices are there in the wind, in the unconscious depths of our minds. These voices are there not primarily to indict us to our cruelties, but to identify the distortions in our relations with the land and its inhabitants, and also to guide us toward a mutually enhancing human-earth relationship in this beautiful valley.

The valley was at the height of its grandeur when one day the mainmast of a strange sailing vessel broke over the horizon. The sails unfurled to their full expanse as the *Half Moon* came into full view and sailed across the bar at Sandy Hook and on through the narrows into the channel and eventually up into the valley, past this region, to the shores of Albany.

Never was the region more brilliant in its color, in the exuberance of its life expression, in the grandeur of its tall white pines, in its beaver population, in the abundance of its oysters and clams, in its shad and tomcod and striped bass. Never were the woodlands more resonant with their songbirds, never were the skies more often witness to the peregrine falcon, the red-tailed hawks, and the bald eagles. Nor was the water ever more refreshing as it came down from the Adirondacks to meet the sea water around what later became Poughkeepsie.

We need to recall all this as we tell the story of the valley, for the valley required heavenly as well as earthly forces to bring it into being. It was a poignant moment then, when the sails from the east appeared over the horizon, for never again would the region have quite the mysterious brooding of the natural world in its pre-European phase, or that special mode of human presence to the natural world as was given by the indigenous peoples of this continent. When the sails appeared, the entire continent might have shuddered.

In 1907 there were numerous celebrations throughout the valley commemorating the arrival of our European ancestors in this region. Our settlements, our cultural and industrial achievements, were seen as high moments in the story of the valley. As we look back on these celebrations now, they appear to have had a certain naiveté, an exaggerated pride, even a certain arrogance, witnessing to our human tendencies toward self-glorification, oblivious of the larger consequences of our actions. These earlier celebrations honored the human at the expense of every other living being in the valley.

The distinguishing aspect of our more recent celebrations is that we now honor this region in and for itself, while trying to discover how our human presence to the region can be an enhancement rather than a diminishment. In this sense our celebrations are the opposite of those earlier celebrations. We have looked back over the centuries since the first European vessel sailed into the river and found that while they have been a period of glory and conquest for ourselves, what have they been from the standpoint of the valley in its natural forms.

What did it mean to the beaver that soon became extinct in much of the region? What did it mean to the millions of hemlock that were cut down simply for their bark for tanning hides? What did it mean for the great oyster beds and for the other shellfish that thrived so abundantly in the river? What did it mean to the organisms in the soil that later suffered from abusive agriculture? What did it forbode for the river that would receive the toxic runoff of chemical agriculture? What did it mean for the wetlands along the river that were filled in for trash heaps or to make way for railroads and highways? What did it mean for the river life when a nuclear generating station was set up at Indian Point? So we might ask ourselves those questions concerning the valley and the meaning of that moment when the mainmast of the *Half Moon* appeared above the Atlantic horizon.

As it came through the gap between Sandy Hook and the Rockaway Peninsula, through the Narrows into the upper bay, then into the river, the native peoples watching could have known nothing of their future or of the thoughts or intentions of the men in the great vessel. Nor could the men on the *Half Moon* have known fully their own minds nor the larger intentions of their political regimes or the cultural ideals or economic forces that had brought them. Obscure forces were at work, driving an awesome transformation of this planet, ambivalent forces capable of both benign and deleterious consequences, forces with demonic intensity, forces ready to tear the North American continent to pieces in a stupendous effort to transcend the human condition in some serene millennial fulfillment.

We have all experienced these forces. A kind of possession seized us, and every being on this planet has felt its impact on a scale somewhat like those great geological upheavals or like the descent of a glacier. The valley and ourselves are both somewhat shattered. And yet the enormous creative forces deep in the reality of things are asserting themselves. Gratefully the valley before us has not been ruined so extensively as those valleys where a long sequence of dams has been built or where toxic wastes have completely ruined the aquatic life or where the water has been drained off into the fields for irrigation projects. We think of Tennessee Valley, the Ohio, the Colorado, and the irreparable damage done to those and so many other regions over the years.

The Hudson River had not been dammed below the region of Troy. The abundant rainfall is sufficient for agricultural production. The river has, so far, been saved from exploitation of its fresh water because of the abundant water available from the Delaware Basin.

Even if the valley is more resilient than many other valleys of the North American continent and even if it has been saved from the devastation they have experienced, the river, the woodlands, and the soil have become seriously deteriorated over these past centuries, especially in this century, when the valley has been saturated with petrochemical residues in its air, its water and its soil. Every living species in the valley has experienced the deleterious influence of our human presence. Even now the increased occupation of the land for shopping malls, parking lots, roadways, corporate headquarters, industrial sites, and development projects is progressively eliminating habitat needed by various bird and animal as well as insect and plant species. Even now our chemical agriculture is damaging the soil and poisoning the streams; industrial waste products and city sewage are pouring through the valley. Realizing all this, we must ask what has happened?

It would appear that we could not possibly have done all this or presently be doing this, for we see now that it is all self-destructive. We must have been in a trance state—caught up in our illusory world of wires and wheels and concrete and steel and roadways—where we race back and forth in unending frenzy.

The world of life, of spontaneity, the world of dawn and sunset and starlight, the world of soil and sunshine, of meadow and woodland, of hickory and oak and maple and hemlock and pineland forests, of wildlife dwelling around us, of the river and its well-being— all of this some of us are discovering for the first time as the integral community in which we live. Here we experience the reality and the values that evoke in us our deepest moments of reflection, our revelatory experience of the ultimate mystery of things. Here, in this intimate presence to the valley in all its vitality, we receive those larger intuitions that lead us to dance and sing, intuitions that activate our imaginative powers in their most creative functions. This, too, is what inspires our weddings, our home life, and our joy in our children. Even our deepest human sensitivities emerge from our region, our place, our specific habitat, for the earth does not give itself to us in a global sameness. It gives itself to us in arctic and tropical regions, in seashore and desert, in prairielands and wood-lands, in mountains and valleys. Out of each a unique shaping of life takes place, a community, an integral community of all the geological as well as the biological and the human components. Each region is a single community so intimately related that any benefit or any injury is immediately experienced through the entire community.

So it is also with ourselves. We who live here in the Hudson River Valley constitute a single organic community with the river and the lowlands and the surrounding hills, with the sunlight and the rain, with the grasses and the trees and all the living creatures about us. We are all in some manner needed by one another. We may disdain the insects and the lowly plankton in the river, we may resent the heat of summer or the ice of winter, we may try to impose our mechanistic patterns on the biological rhythms of the region, but as soon as any one of these natural functions is disturbed in its proper expression, we are in trouble, and there is no further support to which we can appeal.

The natural world has produced its present variety, its abundance, and the creative interaction of all its components through billions of experiments. To shatter all this in the belief that we can gain by thwarting nature in its basic spontaneities is a brash and foolish thing, as is amply demonstrated by many of our past activities. If we do not alter our attitude and our activities, our children and grandchildren will live not only amid the ruins of the industrial world, but also amid the ruins of the natural world itself. That this will not happen, that the valley will be healed where it is damaged, preserved in its present integrity and renewed in its creative possibilities, is the hope that is before us.

Just now we are, as it were, returning to the valley, finding our place once again after a long period of alienation. At such a moment in our own history, as well as in the history of the region, we need first of all an extreme sensitivity to the needs of all the various components of the valley community—the needs of the river, the soil, the air; the needs of the various living forms that inhabit the valley; and the special needs of the human community dwelling here in the valley. We need to know how these relate to one another. Prior to our coming from abroad, all of these components of the region had worked out a mutually enhancing relationship. The valley was flourishing.

When we arrived we brought with us an attitude that the region was here for our exploitation. Even though we broke our treaties with the Indian tribes, we did recognize their rights and made treaties with them. It never entered our minds that we should also have made treaties with the river and with the land and with the region as a whole. In this we failed to do what even God did after the flood: "I set my rainbow in the cloud and it shall be a sign of the covenant between me and the earth. When I bring clouds over the earth and the rainbow is seen in the clouds, I will remember my covenant which is between me and you and every living creature of all flesh; and the water shall never again become a flood to destroy all flesh."

Such a treaty, or some such spiritual bond, between ourselves and the natural world, is needed, a bonding based on the principle of mutual enhancement. The river and its valley are neither our enemy to be conquered, nor our servant to be controlled, nor our mistress to be seduced. The river is a pervasive presence beyond all these. It is the ultimate psychic as well as the physical context out of which we emerge into being and by which we are nourished, guided, healed, and fulfilled. As the gulls soaring above the river in its estuary region, as the blossoms along its banks, the fish within its waters, so, too, the river is a celebration of existence, of life lived in intimate association with the sky, the winds from every direction, the sunlight. The river is the binding presence throughout the valley community. We do not live primarily in Poughkeepsie or Peekskill, Newburgh or Yonkers. We live primarily along the river or in the valley. We are river people and valley people. That fact determines more than anything else the way we live, the foods we eat, the clothes we wear, how we travel. It also provides the content and context for celebrating life in its most sublime meaning.

We celebrate the valley not in some generalized planetary context, but in the specific setting that we have indicated. It is a celebration of our place, but our place as story, for we need only look about us to appreciate the grandeur of these surroundings. The grandeur of the valley is expressed most fully in its story.

The story, as we have seen, is a poignant one, a story with its glory, but not without its tragedy. Now the story begins to express the greatest change in the valley since the modern story of the valley began in 1609. This is the moment of change from a sense of the valley as subservient to human exploitation to a sense of the valley as an integral natural community which is itself the basic reality and the basic value, and of the human as having its true glory as a functioning member, rather than as a conquering invader, of this community. Our role is to be the instrument whereby the valley celebrates itself. The valley is both the object and the subject of the celebration. It is our high privilege to articulate this celebration in the stories we tell and in the songs we sing.

Thomas Berry, *The Dream of the Earth* (San Francisco: Sierra Club Books, 1982).

BIBLIOGRAPHY

Berry, Thomas. *The Dream of the Earth*. San Francisco: Sierra Club Books, 1982.

Boyle, Robert H. *The Hudson River: A Natural and Unnatural History*. New York: W. W. Norton and Company, 1969; exp. ed., 1979.

Brandt, Clare. *An American Aristocracy: The Livingstons*. New York: Doubleday and Company, 1986.

Burroughs, John. *Birds and Poets, With Other Papers*. Boston and New York: Houghton and Mifflin Company, 1877.

Butler, Frederick. *Memoirs of the Marquis de Lafayette, Together with His Tour Through the United States*. Wethersfield, CT: Deming and Francis, 1825.

Butzel, Albert. "Storm King Saved!" *Scenic Hudson News* 1, no. 2 (Spring 1981). Poughkeepsie, N.Y.

Carmer, Carl. *The Hudson*. New York: Farrar & Rinehart, 1939; New York: Fordham University Press, 1989.

Church, Frederic E. Archives, Olana State Historic Site, New York State Office of Parks, Recreation and Historic Preservation, Taconic Region; (Palmer) McKinney Library, Albany Institute of History and Art, Albany; (Heade) Archives of American Art, New York.

Colden, Cadwallader. *The Letters and Papers of Cadwallader Colden*. Collections of the New-York Historical Society. Vols. 41, 42, 43. New York; Printed for the New-York Historical Society, 1918, 1919, 1920; *Memorials of John Bartram and Humphry Marshall. Edited by William Darlington. Philadelphia: Lindsay and Blakiston, 1849.*

Cole, Thomas. "Lecture on American Scenery." *Northern Light* 1(May 1841). Albany, NY. *The Collected Essays and Prose Sketches*. Edited by Marshall Tymm. St. Paul, MN: The John Colet Press, 1980.

Colonial Laws of New York. Vol. 1. Albany: James B. Lyon, 1894.

Crévecoeur, Hector St. John de. *Sketches of Eighteenth-Century America*. Edited by Henri L. Bourdin, Ralph H. Gabriel, and Stanley T. Williams. New Haven: Yale University Press, 1925.

Devoe, Alan. *Phudd Hill*. New York: Julian Messner, 1937.

Downing, Andrew Jackson. *Rural Essays*. Edited by George William Curtis. New York: George Putnam and Company, 1853.

Evers, Alf. *The Catskills: From Wilderness to Woodstock*. New York: Doubleday & Company, 1972; Woodstock, NY: The Overlook Press, 1982.

Fernow, B., trans. and ed. *Documents Relating to the Colonial History of the State of New York*. Vol. 13. Albany: Weed, Parsons and Company, 1881.

Fowler, Orson S. *A Home for All; or, The Gravel Wall and Octagon Mode of Building*. New York: Fowler and Wells, 1849; rev. ed., 1853.

Fulton, Robert. Livingston-Fulton Manuscript Collection. Research Library, Clermont State Historic Site, New York State Office of Parks, Recreation and Historic Preservation, Taconic Region.

Gordon, Theodore. "Fly-Fishing Near New York." *Forest and Stream* 62, no. 12 (March 19, 1904); *The Complete Fly Fisherman: The Notes and Letters of Theodore Gordon*, edited by John McDonald. New York: Charles Scribner's Sons, 1947.

Grant, Ms. Anne. *Memoirs of an American Lady*. Albany: Joel Munsell, 1876.

Hall, Captain Basil. *Travels in North America*. Vol. 2. New York: Harper & Brothers, 1863.

Hamilton, Alexander. *The Federalist*. Edited by Henry Cabot Lodge. New York: G. P. Putnam's Sons, 1888.

The Home Book of the Picturesque. New York: G. P. Putnam's Sons, 1851.

Irving, Washington. *The Sketch Book of Geoffrey Crayon, Gent*. Rev. ed., New York: George P. Putnam, 1850.

James, Henry. *The American Scene*. New York: Harper & Brothers Publishers, 1907.

Jameson, J. Franklin, ed. *Original Narratives of Early American History: Narratives of New Netherland 1609–1664*. New York: Charles Scribner's Sons, 1909.

Kalm, Peter. *Peter Kalm's Travels in North America*. Revised and edited by Adolph B. Benson. Vol. 1. New York: Wilson-Erickson Inc., 1937; New York: Dover Publications, 1987.

Libertymen's Declaration of Independence. Manuscripts and Special Collections. New York State Library, Albany, NY.

Lossing, Benson. *The Hudson, From the Wilderness to the Sea*. New York: Virtue & Yorston, 1866.

Martineau, Harriet. *Retrospect of Western Travel*. Vol. 1. New York: Harper & Brothers, 1838.

Mumford, Lewis. "The Value of Local History." *Dutchess County Historical Society Year Book*, Vol. 12. Poughkeepsie, NY: Dutchess County Historical Society, 1927.

O'Callaghan, E. B., ed. *The Documentary History of the State of New York*. Vol. 4 Albany: Charles Van Benthuysen, 1851.

Paulding, James Kirke. *The New Mirror for Travellers; and Guide to the Springs*. New York: G. & C. Carvill, 1828.

Pierce, David C., and Richard C. Wiles. *"A Place for Regionalism?" Hudson Valley Regional Review* 1, no. 1 (March 1984). Annandale-on-Hudson, NY: Bard College Center.

Roosevelt, Franklin D. President's Personal File 1820. Franklin D. Roosevelt Library, Hyde Park, N.Y.

Smiley, Daniel. "Gypsy Moths and Man: A Still Unfolding Story of Mutual Accommodation." New Paltz, NY: Mohonk Preserve, 1987.

Thacher, James. *Military Journal During the Revolution, From 1775 to 1783*. Boston: Richardson and Lord, 1823.

Tocqueville, Alexis de. *Selected Letters on Politics and Society*. Edited by Roger Boesche. Berkeley: University of California Press, 1985.

Trollope, Anthony. *North America*. New York: Harper & Brothers, 1863.

Van der Donck, Adriaen. *A Description of the New Netherlands,* Translated by Jeremiah Johnson, Collections of the New-York Historical Society. 2d ser., vol. 1. New York: Printed for the New-York Historical Society, 1841; Edited by Thomas F. O'Donnel. New York: Syracuse University Press, 1968.

Van Zandt, Roland. *The Catskill Mountain House*. New Brunswick, NJ: Rutgers University Press, 1966; Cornwallville, NY; Hope Farm Press, 1982; Hensonville, NY: Black Dome Press, 1991.

Vaux, Calvert. *Villas and Cottages*. New York: Harper & Brothers, 1857.

Wagan, Robert M. *Centennial Illustrated Catalogue and Price List of Shaker Chairs*. Albany: Weed, Parsons & Co., 1876.

Washington, George. *The Writings of George Washington*. Edited by John C. Fitzpatrick. Vols. 5, 25, 26. Washington, DC: U.S. Government Printing Office, 1938.

Whitman, Walt. *Specimen Days & Collect*. Philadelphia: David McKay, 1882–83.

INDEX